BENIN STUDIES

Benin Studies

R.E. BRADBURY

Edited,
with an Introduction, by
PETER MORTON-WILLIAMS

Foreword by DARYLL FORDE

Published for the
INTERNATIONAL AFRICAN INSTITUTE
by the
OXFORD UNIVERSITY PRESS
LONDON NEW YORK IBADAN
1973

Oxford University Press, Ely House, London, W.1.
Glasgow New York Toronto Melbourne Wellington
Cape Town Ibadan Nairobi Dar Es Salaam Addis Ababa
Delhi Bombay Calcutta Madras Karachi Lahore Dacca
Kuala Lumpur Singapore Hong Kong Tokyo

ISBN 0 19 724192 1

© International African Institute, 1973

Set by Gavin Martin Limited, London England.

*Printed in Great Britain by
The Camelot Press Ltd., London and Southampton*

Contents

Plates

Figures

Acknowledgements

The original sources of the papers reprinted in this book by kind permission of the editors and publishers concerned are as follows:

'The historical uses of comparative ethnography with special reference to Benin and the Yoruba', *in* J. Vansina, R. Mauny and L.V. Thomas (eds.) *The Historian in Tropical Africa*. London: Oxford University Press for the International African Institute. 1964, pp. 145-64.

'Chronological problems in the study of Benin history', *Journal of the Historical Society of Nigeria*, I, 4, 1959, pp. 263-87.

'Continuities and discontinuities in pre-colonial and colonial Benin politics (1897-1951)', *in* I.M. Lewis (ed.) *History and Social Anthropology*. London: Tavistock Publications, 1968, pp. 193-252.

'Patrimonialism and gerontocracy in Benin political culture', *in* M. Douglas and P.M. Kaberry (eds.) *Man in Africa*. London: Tavistock Publications, 1969, pp. 17-36.

'The kingdom of Benin', *in* D. Forde and P.M. Kaberry (eds.) *West African Kingdoms in the Nineteenth Century*. London: Oxford University Press for the International African Institute, 1967, pp. 1-35.

'Father and senior son in Edo mortuary ritual', *in* M. Fortes and G. Dieterlen (eds.) *African Systems of Thought*. London: Oxford University Press for the International African Institute, 1965, pp. 96-121.

'Fathers, elders, and ghosts in Edo religion', *in* M. Banton (ed.) *Anthropological Approaches to the Study of Religion*. London: Tavistock Publications, 1966, pp. 127-53.

'Ezomo's *ikegobo* and the Benin cult of the hand', *Man*, LXI, 165, 1961, pp. 129-38.

'Ehi: three stories from Benin', *Odù*, No. 8, October 1960, pp. 40-48.

Our thanks are due to the Association of Social Anthropologists for a grant from the Radcliffe-Brown Memorial Fund towards the printing costs of the plates and the re-drawing of some of the figures. We are also grateful to Mr. W.B. Fagg of the British Museum for supplying prints of the photographs taken by himself and Dr. Bradbury.

Foreword

When R.E. Bradbury came up to University College London in 1947, he developed so strong an interest in Anthropology, initially his subsidiary field of study, that he transferred to Honours in the subject, joining a group of very able students in the recently established department, among whom there was lively debate and no little emulation. 'Brad's' thoughtful and lucid seminar papers and his quiet but always cogent comments in discussion commanded everyone's respect. He took a First Class Degree and was able to embark on his first research with the award of a Horniman field studentship in 1951-2.

Bradbury greatly welcomed the suggestion that he should undertake a study of the Kingdom of Benin among the Edo-speaking peoples of southern Nigeria on which little had been written of ethnographic value since the studies of Ling Roth and Northcote Thomas early in the century after the bronzes and ivories of Benin art first became widely known in Europe following the military expedition. Jacob Egharevba had published the first of his valuable accounts of Benin oral traditions and there were some general indications and challenging clues in unpublished government reports, but the complex political and ritual organization of the Benin Kingdom had not been studied. There were only fragmentary indications of the roles of offices and associations in the life of the palace and the capital and even less was known about social organization and cults of the villages or their modes of economic and political integration in the kingdom.

Bradbury was fortunate in being able to explore this rich field in a series of further field studies in 1952-4 as a Research Fellow of the International African Institute and later as a member of the Benin History Project and a Research Fellow of the University College of Ibadan from 1956-60.

When I visited him during his first spell of field work some 30 miles from Benin City, he had begun to work out the complexities of the age-grade organization and was excited by the system of land rights controlled by the senior age grade in which there was no place for large corporate lineages. Later I was able to see him at work on his studies of the palace and the town organisations in Benin City when he was

engaged on the political organization and history of the kingdom and
making an intensive study of the symbolism and the cultural and social
contexts of the cycle of ceremonies which linked the Oba and the
palace to the city and the kingdom. Speaking fluent Edo and being a
familiar figure in Benin, where as a research student of slender means he
was affectionately known as 'the white man on the bicycle' (cars were
not *sine qua non* for field work in the fifties), Bradbury came to know
the culture, traditions and social life of Benin over a range which few
Edo themselves could claim. Equally at home with palace officials and
other state chiefs as well as with untitled men and women of the capital
and the villages, counting both priests and traders among his close
friends, knowing the techniques of the brass workers as well as those of
political rivals in the changing political context of the fifties, his range
of experience and understanding was quite exceptional. Indeed, it even
became an *embarras de richesse*. When, after writing his doctoral thesis,
he was pressed to contribute a section of the Ethnographic Survey to
fill the gap of ignorance concerning the Edo-speaking peoples, he wrote
with reluctance, feeling that anything he said was likely to need revision
when many unanswered questions had been gone into.

In the event, that section of the Survey: *The Kingdom of Benin and
the Edo-speaking peoples of Southern Nigeria,* has proved to be an
excellently balanced outline, still indispensable as a background to his
detailed and special studies on the political system at the end of the
nineteenth century. Already he was able with new evidence from
documents and oral tradition to present firm outlines of the
development of the Benin kingdom and to characterize the ritual
symbolism of kingship; the economic relations of the kingdom to its
capital and the special features of central control of external trade.

He returned from Nigeria in 1961 to take up a lectureship in
Anthropology at University College London and in 1963 moved to
Bitmingham to take a leading part in the establishment of its Centre of
West African Studies. During the few years before his untimely death at
the age of forty in 1969, although he gave generously of his time and
energy to his teaching, reflection on his Benin field researches and the
clarification of theoretical problems as well as those of presentation to
which they gave rise were always uppermost in his mind.

He had a temperamental reluctance to committing himself to
publication when he felt that on any topic on which he was writing
there was more to know and that a further search in the wide range of

his documentation might turn up something which would require qualification of any general statement or inference. This could sometimes be the despair of his friends and colleagues since they well knew that even the first drafts of his papers were marked by an originality, richness of documentation and clarity of expression that few could match.

The early loss of one who commanded such a rich store of rare knowledge and so strong an integrity in presenting and analysing the results of more than six years of life and intensive study among the Edo, deprived many in African studies and social anthorpology not only of a much loved colleague but of the further harvest, which in his good time he would have gathered in. But the papers he wrote—eight detailed studies and as many shorter contributions as well as his doctoral thesis — are all of them subtly linked to one another through the continuity and development of concepts he formulated in his first Survey.

There must be many in Benin, from the Oba and the chiefs of the palace and the town to the villagers with whom he lived, who learned with sadness of the loss of an old friend and who will treasure his writings as part of the knowledge he shared with them, and from which their successors too will benefit.

With the help of Mrs. Bradbury, who became his partner in much of his research, all Bradbury's fieldwork records and the detailed diaries he kept over those years of research have been calendared by Mrs. Merran Fraenkel and the safe keeping of his documentation has been arranged for the benefit of other scholars who will surely come forward, probably from among the Edo themselves, to contribute further to the study of the life and history of one of the most remarkable peoples of West Africa.

The importance of making Bradbury's writings on Benin more accessible in a collection of studies was appreciated by his colleagues, and in view of his close connection with it in his earlier work, the International African Institute has been happy to provide for this in this book. It is greatly indebted to Dr. Peter Morton-Williams, who had been closely associated with much of Bradbury's work, not only for his careful editing of the papers and the sections of the doctoral thesis that have been brought together in this volume, but also for his Introduction which gives so clear a view of the range and development of Bradbury's thought, both on the social life, culture and history of the Edo-speaking

peoples and on the problems of method and theory which engaged him
so deeply.

DARYLL FORDE
April 1972

Introduction

Most of R. E. Bradbury's published work is reprinted here and it will be seen to form patterns of two kinds. Their grouping in this book shows the different themes in anthropology that attracted his attention; but the writings considered as a series develop in intellectual power as investigations of the society and culture of Benin. In editing his work, I have removed some summaries in later papers of topics developed in more detail in earlier ones. The other task has been the selection of material from his unpublished doctoral thesis on 'The Social Structure of Benin: The Village Community'. Only parts of the sections on domestic and family groupings, unilineal descent, and village community cults are included here, and it is to be hoped that the whole of his study of domestic organization in a Benin village will eventually be published. The sections selected or summarized here supplement rather than duplicate the brief but comprehensive outline of the social organization in his admirable volume on Benin in the *Ethnographic Survey of Africa*, Western Africa, Part xiii (Bradbury, 1957); for example, the section on age organization has been omitted. I have preferred to use the space available for the interpretive description of the rites of the cult of *Ɔvia,* as it is an especially detailed and vivid account among the rather few that we have of such integrative and purifying rites among the peoples of West Africa.

This study of the Benin village of Ekho was undertaken (in 1951-52) to acquire both a thorough acquaintance with a small community and also to develop skill in field work before Bradbury attempted the far more difficult study of the city of Benin. While in Ekho he lived in a room in the Enogie's house, in this he was a pioneer of this intensity of ethnographic experience; and so he not only became aware of all that was going on in the village, he could also see and hear his host's reactions and comments; and of course it made it easier for him to gain his magnificent command of the Edo tongue. He was helped by a youth who was to become his field assistant through all his years in Benin, Samuel Atalobor. Samuel was at first employed to help with the language. He would repeat in clear Edo whatever Bradbury was trying to say to an informant, and then judge the translation of the reply into English (a method I also found effective when struggling to learn Yoruba); Samuel could also repeat such speech as prayers or invocations observed in different activities for the ethnographer to write down. Later he learned how to give other assistance in the sometimes hectic conditions of observation and note-taking in crowded and many-sided ceremonies in the capital.

When Bradbury moved to Benin city he began a study of a kind for which the methods and even the aims of the social anthropology of the time were hardly adequate, and which set him problems in analysis and exposition that occupied him for all his short life. He had had the good fortune to read for his B.A. and − between field trips − for his Ph.D. at University College London while Daryll Forde, who was the Professor of Anthropology and head of the Department, was still working over his material on the Yakö and publishing the long series of essays, begun in 1936, exploring Yakö society and culture. In that series, he attempted to resolve the problems set him, on the one hand, by a large, densely populated and complexly structured community (very different from those studied by most contemporaries in African anthropology) and, on the other, by his concern to relate social organization to technological culture, habitat, and to Yakö ideas and beliefs − to place social structure in its ecological and cultural contexts, and avoid its reification. Daryll Forde's studies of the Yakö and his university teaching directed many of us who in those days were preparing for field research in Africa always to look at social institutions in the setting of culture and ecology, and consequently to think of the idea of 'function' as more than an understanding of the self-maintenance of social structures. At the same time his trenchant, sometimes even wounding, criticism of his students' shortcomings in accuracy, completeness of analysis, logic, or clarity of writing, taught us all to be dissatisfied with anything but our best.

Benin added to the problems of social anthropological study not simply a greater institutional complexity and a populace so large that techniques developed for the study of small, face-to-face, communities were insufficient. There were the challenges of extending the research to an understanding of a world-famous art of an evidently iconic and narrative sort; and of a profusion of historical evidence (both archival and traditional) to be discovered and used for diachronic analysis. These were not challenges to be postponed until a synchronic, structural functional analysis framed in an ethnographic present had been completed; there were insistent demands for immediate attention to them from colleagues and sponsors and editors. After a first spell of field work in Benin City as holder of a field research fellowship of the International African Institute — and including a brief survey of other Edo-speaking peoples in northern and eastern Benin Province — Bradbury continued his research as a Research Fellow of the Scheme for the Study of Benin History and Culture under the direction of the historian K. Onwuka Dike, with two colleagues in the scheme, Alan Ryder working on Benin History, and Philip Dark making a survey of the material culture and assembling a corpus for a systematic stylistic analysis of the famous bronzes.

The essays collected in this book were written as contributions both to ethnography and also to the extension of social anthropological method to meet these challenges. Most of them are occasional pieces too, written for conferences or symposia on specific themes. Nevertheless they form a sequence of great value to social anthropology.

Following upon his doctoral thesis, which was argued in the terms of contemporary structural-functional analysis and presented in 1956, and the contribution of the sections on Benin and other Edo-speaking peoples for the International African Institute's Ethnographic Survey of Africa (1957), where the conventional divisions in that series into the several modes of organization and the main cultural features are followed, he turned to review, in a paper for the Historical Society of Nigeria, one of the difficulties of trying to link historical and anthropological methods in African studies, that of combining the archival and traditional sources to arrive at a dated sequence (Bradbury, 1959a). This is not simply a problem of waiting for 'the historian' to get the record straight, for the anthropologist has usually to provide the techniques for collecting and using traditional sources of various kinds: king lists, genealogies, drum histories, traditions of ceremonial or institutional innovation, and the identifying of possibly historical evidence in myth, while learning how to extract the most information from patchy archival records of different sorts and reliability.

While still in the field, he also contributed a descriptive article 'Divine kingship in Benin' for a local periodical, *Nigeria, a quarterly magazine of general interest* (1959). Although not technical, it is of real interest, pointing up as it does the dramatizing, in state ceremonies, of the divine attributes of the kingship in Benin; but the account depends on its splendid accompanying illustrations and it has not been possible to reproduce it here. He also collaborated with Francis Speed in making a remarkable film of these ceremonies and recorded the sound-track for it. Copies of this are fortunately still available from the film library of the Royal Anthropological Institute.

Shortly afterwards, he returned to London, to a lectureship at his old College. While settling in, he was stimulated by the interest of William Fagg of the British Museum, who had visited him in Benin, to write the paper 'Ezomo's *ikegobo* and the Benin cult of the hand', published in *Man* (1961) under Mr. Fagg's editorship and illustrated with his photographs of the *ikegobo*. This sensitive iconological analysis of a piece of narrative sculpture shows what a talented contribution he might have made to the understanding of Benin and other Edo art. But at University College he began the series of important essays in the fields of social anthropology and history that are his mature work. In 1964 he moved to Birmingham University to join the newly established Centre of West African Studies, teaching there and also in the Faculty of Commerce and Social Science until his death on 23 December 1969.

The first paper in this illuminating series is the most general one, continuing his attempt to solve in theoretical terms the technical problem of imagining the form of a historically informed social anthropology. It was his contribution to the International African Institute's seminar on 'The Historian in Tropical Africa', the essay 'The uses of comparative ethnography, with special reference to Benin and the Yoruba'. The picture is a rather Durkheimian or Radcliffe-Brownian one, of 'a structure' undergoing elaboration or change due to internal developments or external contacts. The ethnographer, he argues, can only make use of oral traditions after he has grasped the social and cultural motivation for their existence and the contexts of situation in which they are used. From his observations not only can he demonstrate the existing social structure and its cultural setting, but also he can try to recapture the structural form before it changed under colonial administration. Then only can he see what the historical problems are. Benin offers the two-fold cluster of interdependent problems concerning internal change and external relations; and Bradbury argued that they could yield to a socio-cultural approach based on the analysis of Edo institutions and comparisons of them with those of neighbouring peoples. He planned a culture history rather like the developmental history of some prehistorians; and he perhaps remembered here the special flavour of V. Gordon Childe's course in prehistory he had followed as an undergraduate. 'This culture-history approach ... concerns itself with configurations of culture-traits and social forms rather than with unique events and individuals' (1964:148) he writes, and suggests there may then be opportunities to relate phases of culture history to datable evidence so 'that history proper, as we are accustomed to think of it, begins to emerge'.

Where, in the rest of the paper, he goes on to illustrate how he planned to write that culture history with a brief account of the political institutions of Benin and to compare them with those of the two Yoruba kingdoms of Ife and Oyo (and assuming a common origin for the three polities) he does not simply describe and compare structural forms; he carries the analysis further to show the principles organizing the structures. He tells us, for example, not only the rules governing succession to office in Edo and Yoruba institutions of government but also the respective concepts of succession, the principles they rest on, and the consequences flowing from them. He infers that, some centuries ago, there was a 'replacement of the principle of descent by that of association for the distribution of power' even at the level of village organization (1964:164). He concludes that the comparison of Benin, Ife, and Oyo shows that the unique features of the Benin polity are for the most part to be explained in terms of Edo social and cultural patterns. The rules of succession, the absence of large lineages to support office holders, and a system of palace associations, gave the Benin kings more freedom to command policy than the Yoruba kings ever enjoyed.

The concern to elucidate principles of organization as well as structural forms is explicit in the two substantial papers he published next, where he makes detailed analyses of features of Benin social, structure. At this time he was, as he acknowledges, enjoying stimulation and encouragement from a growing friendship with Meyer Fortes, who had recently been considering the same kind of problems as those he was facing. 'Father and senior son in Edo mortuary ritual' (1965) and 'Fathers, elders, and ghosts in Edo religion, (1966) both explore the connection between belief, rites, and authority. In the first, Edo interment and funeral rites are the contexts of discussions of how these are expressed through ritual; first, the sets of social relations between father and heir, and lineage and family groups, and the redefinition of statuses after a death; and, secondly, the values linking Edo dogmas about death to more general ideas. The paper shows how the Father-Son relationship and age-seniority function as organizing principles within the field of kinship relations. The second paper widens the discussion to the relationships between living and dead within the Benin village. Besides carrying forward the earlier analysis of the ritual expression of two types of authority, the father's and the elders', within the lineage, Bradbury shows how the authority of the village elders and their responsibility for the ordered life of the village find their expression in rituals directed towards their predecessors as the incorporated dead of the community and contrasts this with responses to the fear of the unincorporated dead. He characteristically ends with an attempt to put these ideas into the pattern of general ideas he was forming about Edo society: the 'ritual episodes ... constitute, for the Edo themselves, explanatory models for their own society ... These models ... are extended to embrace other sets of social relations in other fields of authority ... and link them together in a meaningful synthesis.' The classes of the dead and the rites are a model at a low level of abstraction of status categories and social relations; at a higher level, the imagery of their beliefs and rites orders ideas into sets of alternatives (day and night, bush and village, growth and control, etc.) that give form and limitations to Edo thought about their social experience.

He turned from the study of ritual to write his contribution to that useful symposium edited by Daryll Forde and Phyllis Kaberry, *West African kingdoms in the nineteenth century.* This is a masterly essay, condensing into a short paper the fruits of years of field work and hard thinking about a very complex polity. It is a firmly drawn outline of the structure of authority throughout the kingdom and of the pattern of politics, especially of succession to office, in the capital, set in the historical context of the nineteenth century. At the end comes the usual modest disclaimer of finality and the pointing forward to new problems arising from this particular formulation of the structure of government. We are told that the essay has been confined to the political kingship, and that although attention has been drawn to its mystical aspects, we must wait for a fuller study of 'the key problem of the Benin polity – the relationship between the political kingship and the divine kingship'. That was a problem made more difficult, as the essay shows, by the interregnum, 1897-1914, following the British conquest and the exile of the king; and by the redefinition of the Oba's role later during the colonial administration.

He continued to deepen his analysis of the polity in the last two papers he wrote. The first of these was the long paper 'Continuities and discontinuities in pre-colonial and colonial Benin politics (1897-1951)', written for discussion by the Association of Social Anthropologists at its 1966 meeting. Here, the political competition and conflicts in the half-century following the conquest of Benin are traced, showing how members of the Benin political class planned their actions.

The form of the essay is narrative history and the actors the most conventional in such histories: members of the political class appearing in different guises: sometimes as grouped into associations of hereditary nobles, or town chiefs, or one of the palace associations, jointly pursuing their interests; or as the individual incumbents of offices — the Oba, the Iyase, the Edaiken, the English Resident, trying to manipulate groups and other men holding offices or hoping for them, in the furtherance of their ambitions or commitments; or aggregating into sets of different degrees of formal organization — the paramount chiefs, the district heads, the 'old guard', the 'new men', the ruling clique, the 'radical modernist element', and various short-lived factions and coalitions; or as prominent men enjoying or struggling for power. The generality of the rural populace suffers passively the extortions of those in power and is politically effective only occasionally and briefly, as a mob aroused by some set of the political class and lured by its empty promises, or simply as an inarticulate social order whose discontents can be used as a threat by the principals.

Periods, too, are sharply defined. The reader may first feel simply admiration at the clarity of the story, the firmness with which the emergence and fortunes of the various interests are depicted, and the speed with which this skill in the writing of history has been acquired by a social anthropologist bred in the structural-functional school at the height of its achievement. But the whole essay is informed by anthropological analysis, not merely in the confident handling of the structures of groups and the interrelations between actors; but in the perception of the stereotypes of organization (sometimes contradictory ones) that conditioned the views and moves of the actors, whether Bini or English; and behind these 'conscious models' of political society, in the elucidation of the habits of thought of the Bini, their 'unconscious model', with its categories, usually dyadic, and their roots in the polity and divine kingship of pre-colonial Benin. The essay could not have been written without the analyses in the previous two papers; and it pointed forward to the anthropological topic discussed in the next, his last, paper.

In 'Patrimonialism and gerontocracy in Benin political culture', Bradbury returns to the problem of defining more sharply the structural principles of Benin political organization, and also of expressing them in a conceptual language that facilitates comparative study. However immersed he was in his Benin researches, he felt that he was writing for an audience of other anthropologists, who were likely to be interested in Benin mainly for comparative purposes and to the extent that its study contributed to growth of theory and technique. At this stage in his work, the 'principles' current in ordinary, ahistorical, social anthropology had little scope for further application. He could have illustrated with more ethnographic detail patterns of kinship, descent, marriage and affinity, and association; or the interpretations, in the resolution of disputes by chiefs or in the Native Courts, of the rules governing these patterns of behaviour and structural form. But he was still grappling with the analysis of a polity both sociologically and historically. He was, as well, by temperament almost incapable of such labour and felt tortured when required to array ethnographic observations in an existing scheme. His bent was to follow the facts to see where they led him, and they always led him to general theoretical ideas. As early as the mid-1950's, while still in the field, I recall short discussions with him of the possibility of introducing some of Max Weber's ideas into anthropological research. The difficulty was more than the contrast between the synchronic approach of social anthropology and the historical one of Weber's sociology; it was to avoid the arbitrary and eclectic use of concepts devised in the course of a completely different kind of analytic method from the positivism and realism of contemporary social anthropology. It was only after he had broken out of the synchronic frame of his earlier analysis to deal with social process in its historical setting that he was able to make use of Weber's ideal types of authority and legitimacy as conceptualizing general principles of organization, to be studied in their application from the aspects of social structure and as part of the unconscious culture of the Bini; and not simply as the direct bases for action that Weber's insistence upon abstracting ideal types from the actor's conscious, subjective appreciation of his situation would otherwise make of them. The yeast of Weber's ideas leavened this study of Benin politics. This final paper not only interprets some of the ceremonial of Benin kingship as dramatizing political structure; it also shows that the structural opposition between king and chiefs can be understood in terms of two of Weber's principles of legitimate authority. The first is that of gerontocracy in the statuses and roles of the hereditary chiefs and the town chiefs as the elders of Benin, and the second is patrimonialism in the kingship and its supporting palace organization. The rites centring on the divinity of the king and the parts played by the chiefs in them, especially in rites of succession, assert the principles in the idiom and presuppositions of Benin culture.

The group of papers beginning with 'Father and senior son' can now be seen to display both intellectual unity and a progressive gain of power in the depth and scope of analysis. The interplay between anthropological and historical research put forward in the essay 'The historical uses of comparative ethnography' directed Bradbury's thinking towards a kind of culture-history, as he had anticipated. But the internal dialogue between the ethnographer and the historian he had also to educate himself to become was a more subtle and a more continuous one than he had foreseen. In the end he achieved a unity of method that is neither conventional social anthropology nor conventional history and places him in the intellectual company of the great historical sociologists.

We are grateful to the International African Institute and to its Director, Professor Daryll Forde, for arranging the publication of this collection. It has demanded much patient editorial work from Professor Forde and Miss Barbara Pym.

Bradbury's original fieldnotes have been listed and indexed by Mrs. Merran Fraenkel, at the request of the Association of Social Anthropologists of the United Kingdom, and are in the custody of the Library of the University of Birmingham. A duplicate of the lists and index is with the Department of History at the University of Ibadan.

P.M. W.

1
Historical Studies
of the Kingdom of Benin

The historical uses of comparative ethnography with special references to Benin and the Yoruba

The Scheme for the Study of Benin History and Culture, under the direction of Dr. K. O. Dike, in which I have been engaged during the last few years, was set up as experimental inter-disciplinary study in response to the growing and deeply felt need among African intellectuals, and scholars throughout the world, for a reconsideration of African history as something more than the history of European interaction with, and influence upon, African peoples. The Benin Kingdom was chosen for several reasons. It was known to be one of the oldest and most stable of the larger political entities in the forest zone of West Africa and a well-established king-list of some thirty-seven rulers provided at least the framework of a tentative chronology, against which historical and traditional events could be plotted. Secondly, its four and a half centuries of contact with European nations held out hopes of a considerable body of archival material waiting to be brought to light. Another important source of evidence lay in one of the most extensive bodies of African art in existence; an art which, moreover, is usually narrative in character and thanks to the imperishable nature of the media, covers, for Africa, a very long time-span. Finally, within Southern Nigeria, Benin occupies a geographical position between the non-centralized, though structurally complex, Ibo-type societies to the east and the urbanized, centralized, Yoruba kingdoms to the west, which is clearly reflected in its own social and cultural forms, and in the influence which, through its military, political, and cultural dominance, it has itself exerted on its Ibo, Yoruba, and other neighbours.

The Scheme has comprised three main branches of activity: (*a*) research into bibliographic and archival souces, (*b*) the study of Benin art and material culture, and (*c*) ethnographic field work in and around Benin itself. It is with this last aspect that I have myself been mainly concerned.

THE ANTHROPOLOGIST'S ROLE IN AFRICAN HISTORICAL STUDIES

Where indigenous written records do not exist for the precolonial period and the testimony of European visitors is scanty, lacks continuity, and is for the most part superficial and biased in content towards the interests of traders, missionaries, and government officials, unorthodox approaches are necessary for getting at evidence of the past. Material remains are valuable sources of information, but their value increases in proportion to the degree to which they can be related to a living culture and society. It is necessary, then, not only to record what people say about their past, but also to make a thorough study of the end-products of the historical processes it is desired to uncover, that is, of present-day cultural, political, and social configurations. There is no reason why historians should not themselves collect, as well as make use of, oral traditions, but until recently academic attitudes have inhibited all but a very few from doing so. The anthropologist, on the other hand, is committed to the ethnographic study of living communities. It is not, however, merely his willingness to go into the field that is at issue. One of the great difficulties facing the historian of African peoples is that, even if he himself has it, he cannot assume that his readers have access to the necessary background knowledge of the social and cultural atmosphere in which the historical processes he is describing have taken place. One can go further and say that very often historical problems cannot be defined until some knowledge of the societies with which we are concerned is available. The provision of socio-cultural models is a basic requirement and, until the training of African historians is radically altered, it is the ethnographer who is in a position to supply them. Moreover, the evaluation of oral traditions itself demands a grasp of the social and cultural motivations which produce, perpetuate, and modify them. They cannot be isolated from the contexts in which they are used in the society itself if African history is ever to be more than the rationalization of myth.

METHODS AND PROCEDURES

A first aim of this study was, therefore, to acquire the data for an understanding of present-day Benin society and culture. Then, since the rate of historical change has been greatly accelerated and its agents immensely diversified in the colonial and post-colonial periods, it has been necessary to reconstruct a socio-cultural model for the years immediately before the British conquest of 1897. Only with these models in view can reasonable inferences be made from the various kinds of evidence of the past available. Given this socio-cultural orientation the problems presented by the Benin past seemed to be twofold:

(a) Those involved in charting developments in Benin society itself, and
(b) Those relating to the historical interactions of the Benin polity with its neighbours.

Yet the dichotomy between internal change and external relations is artificial in the sense that these two aspects of history are closely inter-dependent. It is, indeed, very difficult to draw the line between internal affairs and external relations in a political system characterized by a complex interlocking of fields of power, and of spheres of interest and sentiment, rather than by well-defined frontiers between sovereign states. Nevertheless, for the ethnographer this division is a very real one, for he is faced with political, economic, and cultural interaction across cultural and linguistic boundaries which are more sharply defined than are, say, those between many neighbouring European states.

In theory the extreme linguistic, social, and cultural diversity of the area I am dealing with should, I believe, present certain advantages for historical research, for once a thorough understanding of one culture is acquired it is often not very difficult to pick out cultural and institutional elements deriving from outside. Insofar as these alien traits, absorbed and adjusted to varying degrees, are evidence of culture contact bringing about social change, they are the stuff of history, and the concern of the historian as much as of the ethnographer. There is, on the other hand, the very practical disadvantage that it is rare for a single scholar to have an equally penetrating knowledge of two or more neighbouring societies and cultures. It is often difficult to judge whether institutions and culture patterns common to two societies are evidence of borrowing or migration, or of the political or cultural dominance of one over the other, or whether they derive from a basic cultural substratum having its roots deep in pre-history. Yet to be able to make such distinctions, that is, to establish what we may call 'phases of identity and contact' between the cultures of neighbouring societies, is, I believe, a fundamental step in our understanding of the dynamics of African history. This culture-history approach is closer to that of the pre-historian, armed with archaeological data, than to that of the modern historian, furnished with an embarrassment of written records, since it concerns itself with configurations of culture tráits and social forms rather than with unique events and individuals. Whereas, however, the archaeologist's data consist of artefacts and geological structures, the ethnographer is concerned with people who are able to talk about their behaviour and institutions. But, while the former has at his disposal stratigraphical sequences, chemical tests, &c. which provide direct chronological evidence, the latter's data are social and cultural observations disposed on the plane of the ethnographic present and they must somehow be projected on to a time-scale. It is only when phases of culture history, posited on the basis of such data, can be related, with some degree of plausibility, to other sources of evidence — such as traditions and contemporary records — that history proper, as we are accustomed to think of it, begins to emerge.

Ideally, we should compare neighbouring cultures in all their aspects, but neither our present information nor the space at our disposal permit this. I shall confine myself, therefore, to suggesting some of the historical problems that emerge when contrasting features of Benin and Yoruba political organization are set against the historical traditions linking the dynasties of Benin, Ife, and Oyo.

THE CONVERGENCE OF BENIN AND OYO TRADITIONS

Benin City (Edo) has been the focus of a large, powerful, and structurally complex political entity since long before the Portuguese first visited it in 1485. Tradition, backed up by some cultural and institutional evidence, attributes the earliest phases of Portuguese activity there to the reigns of Obas Ozulua and Esigie, fifteenth and sixteenth in the list of kings which now numbers thirty-seven. Traditions relating to the pre-Portuguese period are unsupported by written records, but their internal logic leads to the supposition that the dynasty may have been founded early in the fourteenth century.[1] The dynastic list thus provided a tentative chronological framework covering some six and a half centuries, more precise dates being assignable to reigns from the first half of the eighteenth century onwards. The Benin people order their past in terms of 'dynastic time', relating significant events to the reigns of particular Obas. This has its drawbacks in that the better-remembered Obas tend to attract

[1] See Bradbury, 1959, for a discussion of the problems of constructing a dynastic chronology.

attributions to themselves; and, insofar as they become type-figures, particular *kinds* of events become associated with them. We must nevertheless allow some validity to this view of the past if we are to proceed at all.

The dynasty to which I have referred was preceded, we are told, by a succession of kings known as 'Ogiso', and there may have been others before them. It is impossible at present to set a date to the beginning of kingship at Benin or to know how it came there; the creation myth makes the first king contemporaneous with the peopling of the world. But the story of the coming of the last or 'Oranmiyan' dynasty marks a threshold between traditions of a quasi-historical character and the 'earlier' ones which are more uncompromisingly mythological.

The Benin capital is situated in the forest zone some eighty miles west of the Niger, round about the geographical centre of a linguistically defined bloc known as the Edo-speaking peoples who, despite a wide range of variation in the scale and forms of social and political organization, share a distinctive substratum of cultural identity.[2] They are bounded to the north by the Igbirra, on the east by the Igala and Ibo, on the south by the Itsekiri and Ijaw, and on the west by the Yoruba peoples. The Edo languages, and those of all their neighbours except the Ijaw, belong to the Kwa branch of the Niger-Congo family. Rough basic vocabulary counts suggest that Yoruba, Edo, and Ibo may have started to diverge not much less than 4,000 years ago, Edo being insignificantly closer to Ibo than to Yoruba.[3] While this figure need not be taken too seriously, it does give a sense of proportion to our discussion of oral traditions which have generally been assumed not to go back more than say 1,500 years. There is no reason to suppose that the divergence of these languages from a parent stock has not taken place side by side more or less *in situ*. Any theory which would derive the carriers of one of them, *en masse*, from far afield, when the others were already established in the area, would raise historico-linguistic difficulties of great magnitude. This is not to deny that these groups may have been affected to varying degrees by external stimuli or incursions of a warlike or peaceful nature, or that such external influences may not have had a profound

2 See Bradbury, 1957, pp. 13-17 and *passim*.
3 Cf. Professor Armstrong's conclusions regarding the relationship of Yoruba. Igala, Idoma, (Armstrong, 1964). While the assumptions made, and the methods used, are too crude to admit any claim to accuracy, they do suggest the need to preserve an open mind regarding the antiquity of the separate linguistic and cultural traditions involved.

effect on social and cultural forms. But it seems reasonable to assume that any immigrants were linguistically absorbed and that such innovations as they brought were reinterpreted in the climate of the aboriginal cultures. Benin, Ibo, and Yoruba culture, as we know them today, are certainly the product of a long process of development within what is today Nigeria. Moreover they must already have been clearly differentiated from each other at the earliest period to which oral traditions can be assumed to refer.

The last thirty-seven remembered kings of Benin belong to a dynasty which is supposed to have its origin in Uhe (the Edo name for Ile Ife), the spiritual and cultural metropolis of the Yoruba. The Ogiso dynasty having come to an end, the 'elders' of Benin are said to have asked the Oluhe (king of Ife), for a prince to rule over them. He sent his son Oranmiyan, who, we are told, soon realized that a foreigner, unconversant with the Edo language and customs, could not hope to rule there. He therefore returned to Ife, having first impregnated the daughter of a village chief who, he said, would bear a son that would become king. The son was duly born and, fostered and instructed by the followers his father left behind for the purpose, eventually became the Oba Eweka I. Other traditions suggest a less peaceful establishment of the dynasty, for Oranmiyan was preceded by other princes who were never allowed to reach Benin; and the dynasty was not firmly seated until the fourth Oba, Ewedo, occupied the present site of the royal palace in a battle which is re-enacted at the commencement of each new reign.

That this dynasty was derived from Ife is beyond reasonable doubt. Certainly in the sixteenth century the death of the Oba was reported to Ife and his heir received a brass cross, cap and staff from the Awgenni (i.e. Oghene=Oluhe), approving his succession;[4] and right up to the British conquest the remains of the Obas were sent to Ife for burial. Yet the essential point of this foundation legend is that, while the kingship was from Ife, its first incumbent was a native-born Edo. This assertion is made in other forms, in legend and ritual. When he occupied the palace site Ewedo, it is said, was given the throne of the Ogiso kings; and Ewuare, the twelfth Oba, whose mother was descended from the Ogiso, united in himself the two dynasties. Up to recent times, in an annual rite, the Oba's cheeks were imprinted, in chalk, with Yoruba tribal marks, which were then erased, at the sacrifice of a cow. All these

4 de Barros, Dec. I, Bk. 3, Fol. 3-4.

symbolize the acceptance of an alien form of kingship and its moulding to the forms of an already existing culture. This Edo attitude to Ife origins as in contrast with that found in the great Yoruba kingdoms where pride in the Ife derivation of the kingship is not, so far as I know, tempered by the desire to assert a separate and more fundamental cultural self-sufficiency.

The same Oranmiyan (Oranyan) who begat the first Oba of Benin himself became according to Yoruba tradition, the founder and first king of Oyo. Thus the two great dynasties which between them, at various periods in the last five centuries dominated most of what is now Nigeria to the south and west of the Niger trace their origins to a common ancestor. Whatever the historical status of Oranmiyan he must be taken to represent an epoch of far-reaching developments which led to the rise of two expansionist empires and dominant cultures. If we could further assume that these innovations occurred among two as yet socio-culturally undifferentiated groups our historical task would be greatly simplified, but, as we have seen, this is unlikely to be so. For Benin there is evidence of a previously existing centralized political system whose surviving cultural associations (in the form of names, titles, religious cults) show few similarities with the Yoruba; and while Oranmiyan is said to have founded a new capital at Oyo, this represented, according to the Oyo story, a transfer of the effective political power from Ife, where he had already become king.[5] Evidence is accumulating of a fundamental discontinuity in the political and cultural development of the Yoruba-speaking peoples and it seems to be associated with an Ife-Oyo polarity (e.g. in title systems and in the dichotomy between two distinct groups of deities associated respectively with these two centres). Whether 'Oranmiyan' has a specific connexion with this discontinuity is a big problem, but it is unlikely that it antedates 'him', though it may flow from later influences on Oyo which lay on the northern fringe of Yorubaland. Yet both Benin and Oyo agree on the Ife origins of Oranmiyan and I think we must assume that the innovations he represents were set in motion there. What does seem probable is that the rise of Benin and Oyo coincided with the decline of Ife as an effective political empire, though it has retained its primacy as a religious metropolis and the source of true divine kings up to the present.

Let us assume, therefore, that round about 1400 (about forty-two

5 Johnson, 1921, pp. 8-12.

reigns ago at Oyo, thirty-seven at Benin) important political developments at Ife led to the founding of dynasties at Benin and Oyo and, ignoring for present purposes the likelihood of subsequent profound external influences on any of these groups, that the latter-day political systems of the three kingdoms are the eventual outcome. The next step is clearly to make a thorough comparison of the relevant features of these polities. We cannot measure the changes they have undergone against any assumed undifferentiated state, nor can we hold one of them to have retained its archaic form and thus provide a model against which changes in the others can be measured. We must, therefore seek more roundabout means.

BENIN, OYO, AND IFE – SOCIAL AND CULTURAL COMPARISONS

Despite profound dissimilarities Ife and Oyo belong to the same linguistic and cultural bloc. The Benin Kingdom is part of an entirely different one. On the other hand the dynasties of these three kingdoms, together with those of other Yoruba, Edo, and Western Ibo chiefdoms, are linked by traditions of origin, sentiment, and ritual practice, in what we may call the 'Ife dynastic field', since Ife is, at present, the ultimate traceable source of common elements in the institution of kingship and its associated institutions. The different ways in which these institutions have developed in different socio-cultural climates is, I believe, of fundamental historical interest.

Kingship apart, the state title systems of Oyo and Ife show marked differences in content (in the actual designations), in the principles on which they are organized, and in the distribution of power. They are nevertheless more alike than either is like Benin, whose title system shows virtually no correspondences in content with either and few in modes of recruitment, organization and operation.[6] Moreover, in many aspects, both constitutional and ritual, the Benin kingship is a very different institution from its Yoruba counterpart. What do the specifically Benin features in these institutions owe to the Edo social and cultural background against which they have developed?

The Yoruba king is chosen from candidates presented by different

---

6 It should be stated that the title systems of some southern Yoruba chiefdoms, such as Ondo and Ijebu, show closer similarities in structure and operation to that of Benin. See Lloyd 1962, pp. 41-3, 105-9, and 146-50. These groups also differ markedly from the northern Yoruba in regard to the structure of descent groups (ibid., pp. 33-5).

branches of the royal lineage (usually in rotation), the final choice resting with a non-royal group of 'kingmaker' chiefs. In Benin the rule is that, subject to legitimacy rules, the king is followed by his senior surviving son; here the corresponding chiefs are kingmakers only in the sense that they receive fees from and install the heir. In both societies succession conflicts are frequent, but they are couched in different terms. Among the Yoruba the dispute centres on whether it is the turn of a particular lineage segment to provide the next king or on the qualities of the various candidates. In Benin the dispute is always between the two oldest sons of the late Oba, each claimed by his faction to be the true legitimate first son. In restrospect the successful claimant is always said to have been the rightful one, a view which follows from the dictum that 'kings are made in heaven'. The custom in some Yoruba states whereby the new king ate the heart of his predecessor is felt by the Edo to be unnecessary.

From these different concepts of succession many consequences flow, especially as regards the distribution of power and authority. The Oyo Misi are not only kingmakers but, if the king does not fulfil expectations, king-despatchers. Morton-Williams writes: "The ultimate power of the Oyo Misi over the Alafin appears to have been complete ... the Basorun (leader of the Oyo Misi) can declare, after divination, that the king's fortune ... would be bad and that his *orun* — spirit double in the sky — no longer supports his stay on earth. Found unfit to rule, he must poison himself.'[7] In Benin, by contrast, there is no legitimate procedure for getting rid of the Oba. Some kings (far back) are said to have committed suicide, but this is interpreted in terms of infirmity rather than misrule. The only deposition of a well-established king is expressly said to have been achieved by trickery.

Consistent with this difference in the conception of the kingship is that between the degree of power enjoyed by the Oyo Misi and the Uzama, the group at Benin who most closely resemble them, in that they constitute the highest-ranking and most ancient order of chieftaincy.[8] The Uzama are identified with the 'elders' who sent to Ife for Oranmiyan, though whether the titles themselves already existed or were created by Eweka I is disputed. Now it seems likely that the Oyo Misi and Uzama derive from an ultimate common political conception,[9]

7 1960, p.364.
8 See Bradbury, 1957, pp. 35-6, 43-4.
9 There are seven Uzama titles. The first five — Oliha, Edohen, Ezomo, Ero,

but whereas the former have retained a great deal of power the latter seem to have lost theirs at an early date.

What are the historical implications of all this? Is there any evidence of the process by which the form of succession at Benin and Oyo came to differ so markedly? How did the Uzama, while retaining their rank, lose their effective power? With regard to the first question we have the amusing paradox that while Johnson considers the Yoruba form of succession to be a deviation from original primogeniture, Egharevba has it that primogeniture was established at Benin only by the late seventeenth century Oba, Ewuakpe. Johnson's detailed chronicles do little to support him, though the fact that the Alafin's first son had to die when he died suggests that the notion of primogeniture was not entirely absent. The retention or establishment (whichever it might be) of the primogeniture rule at Benin is explicable in terms of Edo culture generally, for primogeniture is one of its distinctive features.[10] Ewuakpe was preceded by six or seven Obas whose genealogical relationships are not recorded, while for still earlier times genealogies indicate a collateral form of succession, but no division of the royal lineage into segments each claiming the right to provide candidates. While it is possible that the rule was not properly established till the late seventeenth century, 250 to 300 years would seem a very long period for the adjustment to an aboriginal form.

---

and Eholo — are found in variant forms in chiefdoms ranging from Onitsha on the Niger, right through the southern part of Western Nigeria at least as far as Abeokuta. Among the Onitsha and Western Ibo they are demonstrably, and among some eastern Yoruba groups just conceivably, Benin-derived. But they also occur in parts of the former Oyo empire (e.g. the Ede-Oshogbo area — see Johnson, p.77) where Benin influence is presumably ruled out. Yet they are missing from Oyo itself and (with one exception) Ife. Nearly everywhere these titles correspond in status to the Oyo Misi. Do they represent a pre-Oranmiyan phase of political development affecting both the Yoruba and the Edo of Benin?

10 The argument here rests on some fundamental differences in Edo and Yoruba practices regarding inheritance and succession. Space prevents their being detailed here (see Lloyd, 1962, Ch. 9, and Bradbury, 1957, pp. 46-7), but note that: (a) whereas among the Yoruba property is 'divided rigidly into as many equal parts as the man had wives bearing children' (Lloyd, p.37), in Benin it is divided unequally between the eldest of each set of full brothers, the oldest son of all taking by far the largest share; (b) whereas among the Edo brothers have no inheritance rights so long as there are sons, junior brothers among the Yoruba have certain rights in respect of land and houses.

It should also be noted that among the Yoruba land is held and transmitted within descent groups, whereas Benin lineages do not hold joint rights in land.

The political insignificance of the rather shallow Benin lineages as compared with their politically important, widely based Yoruba counterparts seems to me to be correlated with these differences in inheritance and land-holding, as does the contrast between Edo primogeniture and Yoruba collaterality in succession to office.

Moreover Ishan dynasties of Benin royal origin which claim to have been founded long before Ewuakpe's time have no traditions of a period when succession was other than by primogeniture.

The failure of the Uzama nobles to retain their political dominance is probably related in two ways to this principle of succession. First, tradition indicates a long struggle between the Oba and Uzama, lasting from the founding of the dynasty up to the reign of the sixteenth Oba, Esigie (early sixteenth century). From then on they appear to have had little power *as a group*. The fact that they had no right to unseat the Oba must be regarded as a factor in their decline. Secondly, the Uzama titles themselves pass to the first son and the effect of this (together with the fact that lineages do not hold land) is to deprive their holders of the support of a wide effective lineage, since only the oldest sons have the possibility of succeeding to the title and the wealth and privileges that go with it.

If any reliance is to be placed on tradition the period during which the Uzama were fighting a losing struggle for supremacy also saw the emergence of two other major orders of title holders, the Eghaevbo n'Ore and the Eghaevbo n'Ogbe, or Town and Palace Chiefs. With one or two exceptions these titles are exclusively Edo and wherever they are found outside Benin they can be explained as deriving from Benin influence. I do not suggest that the palace-town dichotomy is a specifically Benin conception, but only that the particular form it takes is understandable in the light of certain Edo social principles.

First it is significant that these titles are non-hereditary. They do not belong to particular lineages, but are in theory open to competition among all freemen. The creation of new titles and the re-awarding of vacant ones rests with the Oba, who also makes promotions to higher titles, both within and across the groups. Apart from the Oba himself it is with the holders of the highest-ranking town and palace titles that the greatest power and influence lies. The two groups represent different kinds of interests. While the palace chiefs are generally men who have come up through the elaborate palace organization, the town chiefs tend to be those who have made their own way in life, achieving wealth, prestige, and following through warfare, farming, trade, etc. They, too, must pass through the grades of the palace associations (see below), but they may do this very rapidly if necessary. They are brought into positions of official responsibility because they would be dangerous outside them, but they tend to remain in opposition to the palace group. The title of their leader, 'Iyase', is said to mean 'I make you to surpass them' and to have been created by the fourth Oba, Ewedo, seeking support in his struggle against the Uzama. But the Iyase, in turn, became the focus of opposition to the Oba and even up to recent years the major conflicts have tended to crystallize around these two offices.

The palace titles are divided into three sections, whose members can be characterized as Chamberlains (Iwebo), Household Officers (Iweguae), and Harem-keepers (Ibiwe-Eruerie). The normal progress to a palace title was by initiation into and promotion through the grades of one of three palace associations, Iwebo, Iweguae, and Ibiwe, each of which has its exclusive apartments in the palace. Having achieved the rank of *uko* (messenger) or its equivalent in one of these, the member becomes eligible for an individual title in any of them (or indeed among the Town Chiefs). Taking a title is a very expensive procedure, for it involves paying fees to the title holders of all orders except the Uzama. Traditions attribute the foundation of each association and title, and of various reorganizations and re-orderings of precedence, to the reigns of particular Obas, and these attributions are associated with ritual obligations. It is thus possible to get some picture of the progressive elaboration and specialization of the palace organization.

What we are concerned with here, however, are the general historical implications of the different principles according to which political power is distributed as between Benin and Oyo-Ife. One very striking difference lies in the fact that, while among the Yoruba the titles conferring most political authority are generally the property of particular lineages, in Benin this is never so. Benin titles either go from father to senior son or are open to competition among free-born men. Thus while the widely based lineage is an effective unit in Yoruba political organization, it is not so at Benin. At the latter place associational qualifications take the place of descent-group qualifications for the achievement of many of the highest positions of authority. This applies especially to the palace titles, but also to the town titles. The importance of this associational principle in the Benin structure derives, I suggest, from another characteristic principle of organization among the Edo-speaking peoples – and one which they share with some Ibo. For among most Edo-speaking groups outside the Benin kingdom political authority at the village and village-group levels is acquired through membership of title associations.[11]

11 Title associations are an important feature of political organization among

Superficially the Benin palace and town chiefs bear a resemblance to the Inner and Outer chiefs of Ife. On closer examination, however, the Outer chiefs of Ife prove not only to be representatives of particular lineages but also the heads of territorial sections of the capital. Here again there is a fundamental difference, for the ward organization of Benin is completely independent of the state title system. The city is divided up into forty or fifty wards each characterized as having a special craft or duty which it performs primarily or exclusively for the Oba. Each has its own age-grades and its *odionwere* or oldest man, though his political authority may be qualified by the presence of a titled hereditary or non-hereditary ward headman. The wards are, in fact, a special development of the typical Edo village pattern. If we were to follow up this comparison it would lead to a discussion of the historical significance of Yoruba urbanism versus the characteristic Edo village community.

The general hypothesis that I put forward is that the particular forms taken by Benin kingship and its attendant centralized institutions, insofar as they differ from their Yoruba counterparts (with which a common origin is assumed), are in some degree explicable in terms of a process of adjustment to basic Edo social and cultural patterns; and that a detailed understanding of these patterns is necessary for historical reconstruction. I have singled out for attention such factors as primogeniture, the absence of widely based lineages as effective political units, the importance of the associational principle as a mechanism for distributing authority, and the typical village pattern of society. I believe it might be argued that these factors have led the Benin political system in the direction of a greater potential for monarchical autocracy than is found among the Yoruba. The rule of succession, the absence of large lineages with continuing rights in offices, and the open character of the palace association system, have given the Oba of Benin greater security of tenure and a greater freedom to manipulate political mechanisms than were available to his Yoruba counterparts. The absence of a powerful royal lineage giving backing to

the uncentralized Edo communities to the north (Northern Edo) and south (Urhobo-Isoko) of Benin, where they occur in very similar forms (Bradbury, 1957, pp.16-17, 90-3, 103-5, 114-19, 139-46). Their diminished importance in the small Ishan chiefdoms and their absence from the larger Benin kingdom are probably to be explained in terms of a simplification of political institutions of the village and village-group level in accordance with a concentration of authority and political activity at the centre. The Northern Edo and Urhobo share other cultural features missing from Benin, though there can be no doubt as to the strong basic cultural identity of the whole area.

the Oba, on the other hand, might be thought to work in the opposite direction. As it stands this argument is impressionistic and open to many objections, but it is by raising and attacking such problems as these that, I suggest, the social anthropologist can make a contribution towards the unfolding of African history.

Chronological problems
in the study of Benin history 1

The Scheme for the Study of Benin History and Culture is an experiment in inter-disciplinary cooperation. Its main aim is to discover how much can be learnt of the history of Benin through whatever sources and methods are available and practical, and so to lay a foundation for further historical studies in the central area of Southern Nigeria. This problem is being approached from three angles: that of the historian, who depends largely on archival and bibliographic sources; that of the student of art and material culture who is concerned with the material legacy of the past; and that of the anthropologist employing ethnographic methods of enquiry and observation among the living population of the area. A fully rounded study would demand the participation of at least two other disciplines − archaeology and linguistics − but it has not been found possible to fit them into the present Scheme.

Each discipline has its own problems, methods and standards of validity and much of the Scheme's work will have to be written up within the framework of the separate disciplines. The special character of the Scheme, however, lies in its attempt to synthesize some of the findings of each discipline in order to throw light on historical processes in a limited geographical area whose internal history is, as yet, largely a matter of speculation. The necessity for inter-disciplinary cooperation derives, of course, from the inadequacy of written sources concerning a people who, till the present century, had no system of writing of their own. The only contemporary written records before 1897 are those of European visitiors to Benin who never stayed long enough to acquire a thorough knowledge of the area, the people or the language and who, in

1 As this paper has been written at Benin, away from documentary and bibliographic sources, it has not always been possible to give precise references. I am most grateful to Dr. A. F. C. Ryder, the historian of the Benin Scheme, for providing me with certain information from documentary sources and his notes on the original Dutch version of Dapper. Any errors in the use thereof are, of course, my own responsibility.

any case, were not primarily interested in giving an account of the country. Their accounts are, therefore, for the most part, superficial, of doubtful accuracy and severely limited in scope and detail. While, as the only contemporary accounts, they are of great importance (particularly for the history of contacts with Europe) they are, by themselves, quite inadequate for the reconstruction of Benin history.

The only other direct accounts of the past are those of oral tradition. Traditions are, of course, subject to very severe limitations as sources of historical fact and, in themselves, are at least as inadequate as the written sources. Their interpretation can only be attempted on the basis of a very full knowledge of the culture and society and of the motives which lead to their being recounted and refashioned through successive generations. Hence the need for a thorough ethnographic study.

To the collection of direct accounts of the past, contemporary and traditional, must be added enquiries and observations among the Edo peoples and their neighbours about the forms and distribution of social intitutions and cultural pattern from which it may be possible to make inferences about historical processes in the area. The material culture, too, is of great importance. The history of Benin art is itself an important aspect of Benin history and it is of further significance in that bronzes, ivories and wood carvings often purport to depict historical personages and events.

In this paper I am not concerned to show how these various approaches may be combined and their results synthesized to enable us to form a coherent picture of the past. While much material is already available its analysis is a long-term problem. It is, however, necessary to indicate that what we are likely to achieve will in many ways be more akin to pre-history than to history proper. The period up to the late fifteenth century is likely to remain the field of pre-history. From about 1470 onwards a few ascertainable dates and a few contemporary accounts will lend a greater degree of exactness to our findings. Even for this period, however, while it will be possible to distinguish broad phases of development in a number of aspects of Benin culture and society, and in its external political, economic and cultural relations, our history will be wanting in the detailed evidence of successive incidents, of individual and group character and motives, and of background circumstances which only adequate contemporary records can supply. Tradition may record major events but it rarely, if ever, explains their background or their effects convincingly.

The primary requisite for a historical study is some kind of time-scale, however tentative or relative. The problem of setting up a chronology for Benin history involves all the disciplines and methods at our disposal and at this point it is impossible to assemble and analyse all the evidence. Two chronologies have previously been published and both of them are based on correlations between traditional and contemporary sources. Before making a fresh attempt with a more varied and systematic approach it is perhaps worthwhile to review the work that has already been done in its own terms. That is what is proposed in the present paper.

The obvious foundations for a Benin chronology are, on the one hand, contemporary written accounts and on the other, the traditional list of kings of the present dynasty[2]. The Benin people see the past in terms of what may be called 'dynastic time'. In so far as they find it desirable to place an actual or postulated event on a linear time scale they link it with the reign of a particular Oba[3]. Basically this conception of the passage of time is not very far removed from that afforded for, say, the English people by their own king-list but it differs from it in that there is no independent calendar against which the reigns of successive kings of Benin can be measured. Talbot[4] and Egharevba[5] have tried to rectify this by supplying Obas with approximate A.D. dates.

Needless to say many Benin people are as hazy as many English people as to the chronological order and genealogical relationships of their kings, and few have any conception of the absolute time-scale involved. Most people know the names and some of the deeds attributed to the more prominent Obas and many have views about genealogical succession over certain sections of the king-list. Some Obas are credited with very long reigns, others very short ones, but few informants are prepared to estimate the number of years involved.

2 The present dynasty is said to have been founded when the Benin people, having rid themselves of their former kings, sent to the Oni of Ife for an Oba. He sent his son, Oramiyan, but the latter returned to Ife after begetting a son, Eweka, who became the first Oba of the dynasty. This is of course, not so simple as it sounds.

3 There are traditions in Benin of kings before Oramiyan but at this point the dynastic conception of time breaks down. The pre-Oramiyan kings live in a timeless semi-mythical world and it is impossible to construct any kind of linear time-scale, however relative, from the traditions about them. We shall therefore confine ourselves to the Obas of the present dynasty.

4 Talbot, 1926, Vol. 1, Ch. IV.

5 Egharevba, 1953, pp. 85-85 and passim.

Where they do so the figures are usually conventional. Other informants, particularly those whose lives have been bound up with the royal court, have a fuller knowledge of the order of succession and genealogical relationships, while a few, especially the priests of the royal ancestors, can (or could) recite the whole list. Comparing information from the best informants there is little disagreement. This is not surprising and is itself neither encouraging nor discouraging.

Three king-lists have already been published and these are given below together with a list collected recently from Esekhurhe, the priest of the royal ancestors. In the case of Talbot's and Egharevba's lists their own approximate dates are shown.

Roupell[6]	Talbot		Egharevba[7]		Esekhurhe
	Orhamiyan	1300	Oranmiyan	1170	
Eweka	Eweka		Eweka 1	1200	Eweka
Omobesa	Omovberha	1340	Uwakhuahen		Ihenmwihen
	Egbeka		Ehenmihen		Uwakhuaemwe
Ewedon	Ewedo	1370	Ewedo	1255	Ewedo
Oguola	Ogwola	1400	Oguola	1280	Oguola
			Edoni	1295	Edali
			Udagbedo	1299	Dagbedo
Ouhe	Awhen	1430	Ohen	1334 (1330)*	Eronbiru
	Ezuara	1450	Egbeka	1370	Egbeka
Ezoti			Orobiru		Ohen
Olua	Uwafe-Ekun		Uwaifiokun		Uwaifiokun
Ebowani	Ewuare		Ewuare	1440	Ewuare
	Ezoti	1475	Ezoti	1473	Ezoti
	Oluwa		Olua	1473	Olua
Ojolua	Ozolua	1480	Ozolua	1481	Ozolua
Esige	Esigie	1520	Esigie	1504	Esigie
Osogboa	Awrhogba		Orhogbua	1550	Orhogba
Ehenbuda	Ehengbuda	1570	Ehengbuda	1578	Ehengbuda
Ohuon	Ohuan	1610	Ohuan	1608	Ohuan
Ahejai	Ehenzai	1630	Ahenzae	1641	Akenzae
	Akengbayi	1650	Akenzae	1661	Akenzae

6 This list was collected in Benin in 1898 by Captain Roupell and published in Read and Dalton (1899) and in Ling Roth (1903) pp. 6-7.

7 In two instances the dates in the list given in pp.85-86 of Egharevba's *Short History* differ slightly from those in the text.

		1670 Akengboi	1669	Akengboi
	Akenzama (Akenzayi)			
		Akenkpaye	1675	Akengbedo
Akenbedo		Akengbedo	1684	Ore-Oghene
		Ore-Oghene	1689	Ahenkpaye
Nakpe	Ewakpe	1685 Ewuakpe	1700	Ewuakpe
	Obiozuere	1715 Ozuere	1712	
Akedzua	Akenzua	Akenzua 1	1713	Akenzua
Erizoyne	Eresoyen	1740 Eresoyen	1735 (1733)*	Eresoyen
Okenbuda	Ahengbuda	1760 Akengbuda	1750	Akengbuda
Osifu	Loisa	1803 Obanosa	1804	Obanosa
		Ogbebo	1816	
Esemede	Osemede	1815 Osemwede	1816	Osemwede
Adolo	Adolor	1852 Adolo	1848	Adolo
Overami	Overami	1888 Ovonramwen	1888	Ovoramwe
		Eweka II	1914	Eweka II
		Akenzua II	1933	Akenzua II

In terms of simple chronological order the three published lists are in general agreement. The differences between them may be summarized as follows:-

1. From Ewuakpe onwards the only disagreement is in the omission of Ogbebo by Talbot and of Oghbeo and Ozuere by Roupell. Both are frequently left out by informants as temporary usurpers. Usurpation is a matter of opinion and definition. Ewuakpe is said to have decreed that succession should henceforth be by primogeniture but, while this principle has been theoretically adhered to, it has not prevented succession disputes between several pairs of brothers. I have found no disagreement among good informants as to the order in which Ewuakpe's descendants reigned.

2. There is concordance between all three authorities in respect of Obas Ozolua to Ahenzae and between Talbot and Egharevba (and informants) from Uwaifiokun to Ahenzae.

3. The differences between the lists from Egharevba's Akenzae to Ore-Oghene correspond to a strange lack of tradition about this period. Talbot's Akengbayi is probably Egharevba's Akengboi and his Akenzama (Akenzayi) may correspond to Akenzae, though Egharevba gives the name Akenzama to Ewuakpe's father who never became Oba.

Egharevba, who gives genealogical relationships between all the remaining Obas, before and after, cannot do so for this period. From Ahenzae to Ewuakpe, according to him, succession was neither from father to son not brother to brother though it remained within the same royal clan. He further claims that most of these Obas reigned in old age but this may be simply an explanation of the short reigns attributed to them. The names of all these Obas are known to informants but the order of succession from Akengboi to Ore-Oghene is uncertain.

4. Of the Obas before Uwaifiokun there is general agreement between the published lists and informants concerning the order of those who are best known — Eweka, Ewedo, Oguola and Ohen. Oranmiyan is not usually considered to have been an Oba in Benin and the founding of the dynasty is normally attributed to his son Eweka. Omovberha (Roupell's Omobesa) seems to mean simply 'child and father' and may have been the informants' way of indicating a succession of Obas whose names were not recalled. Uwakhuahen, Ehenmihen, Edoni, Udagbedo, and Orobiru are little known, and Egharevba himself has nothing specific to say about them. Informants sometimes agree with Talbot in replacing Egbeka with Ezuara (or Ozuare).

It would be unwise to consider these three lists as being independent of each other. Roupell's was available to Talbot and both Roupell's and Talbot's to Egharevba. Chief Egharevba has informed me that his own list was compiled with the help of the late Esekhurhe, priest of the royal ancestors, whose duties included memorizing the dynastic list and sacrificing to each Oba in turn at the annual Ugigun rites, (though it is doubtful whether some of the less-known Obas were included in these rites). Clearly he was dealing with what should have been the best possible informant, though it is not always easy to tell where the Benin historian has reinterpreted his basic information. Many attempts have been made to check the list with other informants. A list recited by the present Esekhurhe (the son of Egharevba's informant) is given above and will be seen to differ from Egharevba in a few early placings only. Again, however, this cannot be treated as entirely independent evidence for Esekhurhe has himself consulted Egharevba on occasions and still tends to call for the latter's works when in doubt. It is in fact extremely difficult to be certain of getting independent accounts at this stage. Egharevba's books have been avidly read in Benin and even where an informant has not himself read the book he may have had it read to him or least have been influenced by it, perhaps unconsciously, in conversation. It is unlikely then that Egharevba's king-list can be *proved* to be seriously incorrect from oral tradition though for the earlier reigns it is equally difficult to prove him right. This applied with even greater force to the problem of genealogical succession.

From Ozolua to Ohuan, it is universally agreed, each Oba was succeeded by his son, though not necessarily the eldest son. Tradition does not define the genealogical connections between Obas Ahenzae to Ewuakpe. From Ewuakpe onwards, omitting Ozuere and Ogbebo, there is no suggestion that any Oba was not the son of the previous one. From Eweka to Ozolua, according to both Egharevba and my informants, succession was from father to son or brother to brother but agreement on how this worked out in detail is by no means complete. I have the strongest doubts as to whether the genealogy of the early Obas can be accepted with any degree of certainty. We shall return to the genealogical problem later.

For two periods the dates given by Talbot and Egharevba are in fairly close agreement, namely from the last quarter of the fifteenth century to the first decade of the seventeenth; and from the second decade of the eighteenth up to the present century. In regard to the earlier of these periods both authorities lean heavily on the firm tradition in Benin that Ozolua was reigning when the first European visited the city. This is presumed to have been d'Aveiro who reached there in 1485 or 1486 and this date provides a fulcrum for both chronologies. Talbot gives little indication of how he arrived at his dates for the earlier centuries. A glance at them reveals that up to the beginning of the nineteenth century they are expressed in very round figures. With few exceptions the Obas are spaced out in multiples of ten years and his attribution of either twenty or forty years reign to each of the five Obas Ozolua and Ehengbuda to Akengbayi is clearly arbitrary, though it may be based on the Benin practice of reckoning in multiples of twenty.

Chief Egharevba has told me that his time scale is based on information given to him by the late Esekhurhe and another informant as to the number of years each Oba reigned, though he is prepared to admit that his dates before the reign of Ozolua are very approximate. I do not wish to dispute the fact that such figures were given to Chief Egharevba, whose industry and integrity deserve the praise and gratitude of all who are interested in Benin; his informants at the time he worked were in all probability better informed than any available today. But my enquiries concerning the years each Oba ruled have met with nothing like the precision which Egharevba's dating implies. Nor have I found evidence for a mechanical method of recording lengths of reign such as is described for some other West African kingdoms. As indicated above some Obas are credited with very long reigns (such as Esigie, Ehengbuda, Akengbuda and Adolo) and others with very short ones. Two of the senior priests of the royal ancestors were willing to say that Olua reigned for 6 years and Ezoti for 14 days. They were very uncertain about Adolo whom they gave 60 years and repeated the well-known saying that Ehengbuda lived for 200 years as a prince, 200 as Edaiken (heir-apparent) and 200 as Oba. When I put this to one whom I consider the best of informants he laughed unbelievingly and said 'How could any man live for so long? The truth is he lived for 60 years as a child, 60 years as Edaiken and 60 years as Oba'. It is not therefore very easy to place much reliance in Egharevba's statement. 'It is said that Ehengbuda lived thirty years as (prince), thirty years as Edaiken of Uselu and thirty years on the throne'.

If we are to evaluate Egharevba's chronology it seems wise to work backward from the nineteenth century, that is from the known to the less known. It is extremely frustrating to find that of the many European visitors to Benin between 1485 and 1897 very few indeed have left us the name of the Oba reigning at the time or, indeed, of any other Oba. Even where names are given the transliteration sometimes creates ambiguities and in one case the name is not identifiable at all. The earliest mention of an Oba's name is by Dapper whose book was first published in 1668. The Portuguese records have revealed no names, not even baptismal ones. Nor with very few exceptions do we get the names or titles of other Benin chiefs.

The period 1715 to 1897

When Ovoramwe's reign was brought to an end by the Benin Expedition of 1897 he had been Oba for about nine years. Punch, who was first in Benin City in 1889, says that at that time 'It was more than a year after Adola's death and Adubowa (Idugbowa, the personal name of Ovoramwe) was full king.' (Ling Roth p.102). Adolo is said to have had a long reign, usually described as 'forty years' though this is probably a round figure, multiples of twenty being a feature of Benin counting. Burton, who was in Benin in 1862, wrote:-
'Jambra is the second son of Oddi, or Odalla, the king of Benin in

Belzoni's time (1823) who was described by Messrs Moffat and Smith (who were in Benin in 1838) as a robust old man . . . His elder brother is Bawaku, whose birth not having been reported in due time by his mother, the cadet became, according to the law of the land, the senior. When the old king died there was of course a fight. The chiefs and ministers preferred the milder and more easily managed man. Jambra therefore changed his name to Atolo, seized his father's property, and became Oba. Bawaku, whose temper is despotic, resisted for a time, but was presently expelled the country. He then fled towards the Niger and settled at Isan, a city said to be seven days march from Benin and three from Igarra. Since 1854 the brothers have been constantly at war.'

'Jambra' is Burton's version of 'Odin-ovba', the personal name of Adolo. His struggle with Ogbewenkon (Bawaku) is vividly recalled in Benin. Burton describes Adolo, at the time of his visit as 'a strong young man of about 35'. Baikie, quoting a Mr. Snape, reported in 1854 that 'the present King is a young man and succeeded to the throne about 1850'.

The name Oddi or Odalla must refer to Osemwede though it is not obviously identifiable with his private name Erediae-uwa. There is no other contemporary reference to his name. In tradition he is chiefly remembered for his initial struggle for the throne with his brother Ogbebo who eventually burnt down the palace and committed suicide; and for the reconquest of Akure and much of Ekiti which is said to have taken place in the early years of his reign. These events are referred to in several contemporary accounts. Lieut. King, who was in Benin in 1820, says: 'During the last insurrection the King was killed and a large portion of the palace was burnt down, but enough remains to bear witness to its former splendour'. Fawckner who was there in 1825 describes the Oba as 'a fine stout handsome man'. He also visited the Ezomo who he tells us was a 'youth of about 16 . . . . I afterwards found that his father, who held the situation, had recently been sent to conduct the war in the interior and had fallen in battle'. (Fawckner, 1837,p.81) Benin tradition has it that Ezomo Erebo, who was in command of the Akure campaign, died before he could return to Benin after extending his conquests beyond Akure into the Ekiti country. A most interesting unsigned communication to the Royal Gold Coast Gazette of 25 March 1823 confirms that the war referred to by Fawckner was the one with Akure. The anonymous writer, whose account appears to have been hitherto unnoticed, tells us that 'the whole place was destroyed by civil wars only a few years since, in consequence of a dispute as to the sovereignty; and the junior brother who was the favourite of the inhabitants of Benin, was deposed after a sanguinary conflict'. He goes on to say that 'the inhabitants of Eccoorah have been in a state of revolt for five years and the Captain General of the Benin Army (i.e. the Ezomo) has been in camp during that period.' From all this it appears likely that Talbot's and Egharevba's dates for the commencement of Osemwede's reign are not far out.

There are no contemporary accounts of the reign of Obanosa whom informants credit with a reign of about twelve years. His father is said to have lived to a great old age, so much so that Obanosa used to pluck the grey hairs from his own head and send them to him as a hint of his impatience. It is necessary to go back to the eighth and ninth decades of the eighteenth century before we get any further contemporary records. Referring to his first visit to Benin City in the year 1778 Landolphe speaks of the Oba as being 'about sixty-five years of age' but 'without a single wrinkle on his face' (Landolphe Vol. I p.108). He also says (ibid. Vol.2 p.56) that no Oba died while he was visiting Benin, that is from 1778 (or possibly 1769 when he was first at Ughoton) to 1799 when he made his last visit. All this accords with Egharevba's dates and the tradition that Akengbuda was one of the longest-lived of Obas. If Landolphe's estimate of his age in 1778 is correct he would have been about ninety in 1804 when, according to Egharevba, he was succeeded by Obanosa.

There is, however, one account which is probably contemporary with Landolphe that does not seem to fit in. Capt. John Adams, whose book was not published till 1823, was apparently in Benin before the end of the eighteenth century, probably in its last decade. He describes the Oba as about 45 years old and gives him the name Bowarre which is not identifiable.[8] Both his account and Landolphe's share the doubtful quality of having been published long after the events they describe took place but the latter's is both fuller and more circumstantial.

In one of his most interesting passages Landolphe (Vol. II pp.58-9) describes a meeting between the Oba and his recognized heir, 'Chiffau'. Chiffau is clearly Osifo, the personal name of Obanosa. Landolphe calls him 'le jeune roi' but makes no estimate of his age. The meeting almost certainly took place in 1787 or earlier and it is clear from the description that Osifo had already been recognised as Edaiken (i.e. the

8 It is possible that Adams had picked up the name of the much earlier Oba Ewuare.

Oba's heir) at the time and was living at the Edaiken's court at Uselu. The practice was for the Oba to recognize one of his sons (in principle the eldest legitimate son) as Edaiken, while two or three of his other older sons would be given petty chiefdoms to rule over. This process was called *y'omo y'isi*. If the Oba failed to do it before his death the heir would be made Edaiken soon afterwards and would himself award chiefdoms to his junior brothers. Akengbuda is said to have been the last Oba to *y'omo y'isi* during his lifetime and this is regarded in Benin as an additional proof of his longevity. It is also said that he became too old to rule actively himself and that before he died his son used to sit with chiefs in the palace to judge disputes. The length of Akengbuda's reign is important for the evaluation of some information about the earlier part of the eighteenth century that has recently come to light, and which will be considered below.

Osifo is the last absolutely identifiable name of an Oba left to us by the chroniclers. A most useful date has, however, recently been established by Dr. A. F. C. Ryder from the newly discovered papers of the Dutch West India Company which had an establishment at the Benin port of Ughoton from 1715 to 1738. These records have not yet been fully translated and studied but they do reveal that an Oba died in 1734 or 1735 and Dr. Ryder informs me that this was probably the same Oba who signed an agreement with the Company in 1715. While the absence of a name makes final proof impossible it is nevertheless remarkable that Egharevba dates the accession of Eresoyen to 1735. The exactness of this correspondence may be coincidental but in the absence of evidence to the contrary it now seems very likely that Egharevba's dates over the last 250 years or so are substantially correct.

It is to be presumed then that the Oba with whom the Dutch company dealt in 1715 was Akenzua I, about whom there is a considerable body of tradition. His reign is linked with a revival of the fortunes of the kingdom. He is remembered as one of the wealthiest of Obas and this prosperity is said to have continued into the reign of his son Eresoyen who is also associated with a resurgence of the art of bronze-casting. Informants say that more brass was available at this time than ever before and a legend has grown up that in Eresoyen's time brass fell from the sky. Perhaps it is not too fanciful to link this tradition of prosperity and plentiful brass with the renewal at this period of intensive trade with the Dutch. The Dutch Company's records, indeed, make it clear that a considerable amount of brass was imported.

The early part of Akenzua's reign, however, is said to have been difficult. Before he could be installed he had to oust his brother Ozuere who had had himself made Oba. Ozuere was supported by the Iyase[9] of the day, Iyase n'Ode, who after Ozuere's defeat is said to have settled at a village some twenty miles to the north of Benin where he continued to maintain a hostile attitude. He was eventually defeated by Ehenua the first of the present hereditary line of Ezomo, or war-captains. According to the Ezomo family Ehenua was, in fact, an illegitimate older brother of Akenzua who had lived as a youth in Ishan and later moved to the Isi district in the north-east corner of the present Benin Division. When grown up he came to Benin, entered the service of Akenzua and for his success in establishing the Oba's position was made Ezomo. The royal parenthood of Ehenua is not always accepted by other informants but the rest of the story is generally agreed both in Benin and in south-east Ishan and the Isi District. In Ewohimi, Ishan, I was recently shown an old carved wooden head which was said to represent 'Ahenua'. Up to 1897 the Ezomo remained responsible to the Oba for Isi and part of Ishan.

Now it is of some interest to compare this tradition with a passage in Nyendael whose account was published in 1704[10] and who was himself in Benin in 1699 and 1701. Nyendael writes:-

'The ruin of this town and the surrounding land was occasioned by the King causing two kings of the street to be killed, under pretence that they had attempted his life, though all the world was satisfied to the contrary, and thoroughly convinced that their overgrown riches were the true cause of their death, so that the King might enrich himself with their effects, as he did indeed. After this barbarity, the King found also a third man that stood in his way, who being universally beloved, was timely warned of that prince's intention, and accordingly took to flight, accompanied by three-fourths of the inhabitants of the town; which the King observing, immediately assembled a number of men from the bordering country, and caused the fugitives to be pursued, in order to oblige them to return; but they were so warmly received by this king of the street and his followers,

---

9 The Iyase is the head of the non-hereditary group of chiefs known as Eghaevbo n'Ore. Though appointed by the Oba, the Iyase often seems to have become the leader of a wealthy independent faction in opposition to the Oba and palace chiefs.

10 Nyendael in Bosman, 1705. The original Dutch edition was published in Utrecht, 1704.

that they forced them to return with bloody noses and give their master an account of their misadventure. But he resolving not to rest there, made a fresh attempt, which succeeded no better than the former; but this was not all; for the fugitive, thoroughly incensed and flushed, came directly to the city, which he plundered and pillaged, sparing no place but the King's court, after which he retired, but continued incessantly for the period of ten years to rob the inhabitants of Great Benin, till at last, by the mediation of the Portuguese, a peace was concluded between him and the King, by which he was entirely pardoned all that was past, and earnestly requested by the King to return to his former habitation; however, he would not trust himself there, but lives two or three days journey from Benin where he keeps as great a court and state as the King '.

These two accounts, the traditional and the contemporary, have certain features in common. 'King of the Street' probably refers to the chiefs known as Eghaevbo n'Ore of whom the Iyase is the head. The retirement of the rebellious 'street-king' to some distance from Benin is consistent with the Benin tradition. The men from the borders who were assembled to support the Oba could be Ehenua and his followers. Thus Nyendael may have been in Benin, if the traditional account is correct, shortly before the defeat of Iyase n'Ode. But this is mere speculation and it illustrates the difficulty of attempting to match contemporary accounts with oral traditions. One can only hope that the newly-found Dutch records will throw further light on this period – and it is already known that they make some reference to the Ezomo.[11] This should be Ehenua himself for according to tradition he lived on into the reign of Eresoyen.

In his pamphlet *The City of Benin*, (pp.10-11) Egharevba quotes Nyendael's account with reference to the reign of Ewuare, which on his own dating is impossible for Nyendael makes it clear that he is describing contemporary events. If it should prove that the traditional and contemporary accounts above do refer to the same series of events Egharevba's chronology would be seriously upset at this point. According to him Nyendael would have been there in the latter part of Ore-Oghene's reign (1699) and the early years of Ewuakpe's (1702). Of the former the Benin historian tells us only that 'there was a general peace and concord in the land during his reign'.

Tradition shows the authority of the king in the early years of

11 Personal communication from Dr. Ryder.

Ewuakpe as being at its lowest ebb. He is said to have been ostracized after causing many people to be killed but there is no suggestion of prolonged hostility with a rebellious 'street-king'. Egharevba does say however that Iyase n'Ode retired to the village of Ugha before Ewuakpe's death,[12] and it seems possible that the traditions of these two reigns may have become confused. If Ewuakpe became Oba in 1700 the situation Nyendael describes would not have had time to develop by the time of his last visit in 1702. Again if Nyendael's two visits were separated by the death of one Oba and the installation of his successor it is strange that he does not mention the fact. Nyendael's account, thus, throws doubt on the correctness of Egharevba's accession dates for Ewuakpe or Akenzua I and it is possible that the commencement of Ewuakpe's, if not Akenzua's, reign should be put back to about 1690. It is not impossible that Akenzua's reign should have begun as early as this. Nyendael describes the Oba he met as being about 40 which would have made him about 30 in 1690 and 75 at his death in 1735.

Ehengbuda to Ore-Oghene

Dapper, whose book was published in 1668, refers to an Oba Kambadje or Kombadje. Dapper was never at Benin himself and got his information partly from a Pieter de Mareez but mostly from a Samuel Blomert whom he says lived in Africa for several years. Unfortunately it is not clear if or when either of these persons were at Benin though the fact that Dapper's account is one of the best we have suggests that the information had not passed through many hands. Ling Roth traced the name of a Samuel Blomert (who had 'distinguished himself in Java and then seems to have been lost sight of') in a work published in 1853. Whether or not this was the same man it gives us little clue as to the date at which he might have been in Benin.

Dapper makes two references to Kambadje. One tells of a Benin victory over a people known as Isago who bordered Benin on the west. The Isago are said to have attacked Benin with 1,000 horses but they were defeated and since that time had not attempted anything against the Oba Kambadje. The other speaks of the inheritance of Kambadje's wives by his son, the reigning Oba, and thus implies that at the time the information was collected Kambadje was already dead. The names in

12 Egharevba, 1947, p.21.

the traditional king-list which are most readily identifiable with Kambadje are those of Akengboi, Akenkpaye and Akengbedo but on Egharevba's dating all these would have reigned too late to be mentioned in a work published in 1668. Moreover, while Dapper implies that Kambadje was succeeded by his son, Egharevba states that none of these Obas was the son of his predecessor. This may not seem a serious discrepancy for the European visitor to Benin may have assumed that the reigning Oba was the son of the previous one. On the other hand Dapper goes into the question of succession in some detail, asserting that the crown passes from father to son or, in the absence of sons to brothers, but that the multiplicity of wives usually ensured a son. It is one of the sad defects of the early accounts that they almost invariably deal in generalities rather than specific instances. In Dapper's case it is rather difficult to tell where he passes from the general to the specific but he does state that a few years before the reigning Oba had had his brother and the latter's followers killed for trying to poison him, which suggests, (though it does not prove) that at the time the information was gathered a son had succeeded his father.

It seems just possible that Dapper's information derived from a somewhat earlier period than that of the three shadowy Obas named above and that Kambadje should be identified with Ehengbuda. The son referred to would then be Ohuan. If so the 1,000 wives with which Dapper credits him do not seem to have done him much good for according to the tradition he died childless.[13]

The description of the war with Isago is intriguing but the name Isago is not easily identifiable. No major wars are associated in tradition with the reigns of Akengboi, Akenkpaye and Akengbedo. Ehengbuda, on the other hand, was one of the greater warrior Obas. In his reign is said to have occurred a war with Oyo in which the Benin armies were led by the Iyase Ekpenede. Dapper refers to the Iyase (Owe-Asserry or Siasseere) as the commander of the army but, of course, gives no name. The fact that the enemy fought on horseback and came from the west is consistent with it being Oyo (though directions in the early chronicles seem often to be suspect). On the other hand Dapper also mentions the kingdom of Ulkami which one more readily associates

13 There is something very odd about Ohuan. Tradition says that he was born a girl and that his father had him treated with medicine and made into a man. Then he sent him out naked into the streets to convince the people of his fitness to rule. The more sophisticated version of this story says that Ohuan was simply of effeminate appearance.

with Oyo. Whether he derives the two names from the same authority is
not clear. The only possible link between Oyo and Isago — and it is a
very tenuous one — is through the name Shango, one of the early
legendary deified Alafin whom the Edo call Esago. In Pereira's
Esmeralda (c.1506. See Mauny, 1956, pp.134-5) we read 'To the East
of this kingdom of Beny, a hundred leagues into the interior, they
know of a country which today has a king called Licosaguou. He is said
to be the lord of many and possessed of great power. Quite near there is
another great lord who is called Hooguanee. He is considered among the
Negroes like the Pope among ourselves'. Despite the direction given
Hooguanee is almost certainly the Oni of Ife whom the Edo call
Oghene, and it seems probable, therefore that Licosaguou is Oyo.
Talbot (Vol.I pp.281-282) assumes that this is so and associates the
name Licosaguou with Shango. Here we are in the swamps of
speculation but it is at least possible that Isago and Licosaguou both
refer to Oyo. Ther is therefore a very slight justification for identifying
Kambadje with Ehengbuda. Dapper's authorities would seem to have
been in Benin at a time when its fortunes were good and the kingship
strong and if any weight is to be placed on tradition this would apply
more to the reigns of Ehengbuda and Ohuan than to those of the later
candidates.[14] This does not put us much further forward with our
dating problems unless it should prove possible to identify the period at
which Dapper's authorities were in Benin.

Though various groups of missionaries reached Benin during the
seventeenth century none of them is known to have left any
information that would help to date the successive Obas.

Ewuare to Orhogba

The late fifteenth and the sixteenth centuries are perhaps the most
interesting and, at the same time, the most tantalising period in Benin
history. There is little doubt that the first Portuguese arrived at Benin
when its political and military fortunes and its cultural and social

14 The only Benin bronze plaques which depict actual warfare show bearded
Benin warriors dragging enemy horsemen with prominent facial markings from
their saddles and despatching them. Are these the Isago? Mr. William Fagg would
date these plaques to the sixteenth or seventeenth century. Dapper himself,
describing the palace, refers to 'wooden pillars, from top to bottom covered with
cast copper, on which are engraved the pictures of their war exploits and battles,
and are kept very clean'. Of the bronze plaques still extant only those mentioned
above fit this description. But this does nothing to solve our dating problems.

development were on the upsurge and this tendency was no doubt given additional impetus by the slave trade and the position which Benin soon came to occupy as the entry-point of European arms and trade goods for a wide hinterland. The Benin people attribute to Ewuare, Ozolua and Esigie the introduction of most of the political institutions and much of the economic, craft and ritual specialization that continued to characterize Benin up to the end of the nineteenth century. There are more traditions and legends concerning these Obas than any other; indeed their fame is such that there is a tendency to attribute events to their reigns whenever there is a doubt about them — and this is, of course, one of the dangers of relying too heavily on oral tradition.

It is with these Obas that early contacts with Europeans are most closely associated in Benin tradition but the Portuguese records for this early period are unfortunately scanty and not easily evaluated. The information in them relevant to the dating of Ewuare, Ozolua and Esigie may be summarized as follows:-

1.   About 1472 Ruy de Sequeira explored the coast to the south of Benin and according to Galvano it is possible that he visited Benin City.

2.   d'Aveiro's visit to Benin in 1486, first mentioned by de Pina, has generally been assumed to be the first by a European. d'Aveiro possibly made a second visit to Benin and apparently he died in the area, though the date of his death is not known. According to de Barros and de Pina an ambassador from the Oba visited Portugal in the reign of Dom Joao II (1481-1495).

3.   Missionaries were in Benin by 1515, if not before, for in October 1516 Duarte Pires wrote to the King of Portugal: 'It is true I am a friend of the King of Benin... We eat with his son... When the Missionaries arrived the King of Benin was very delighted, the Missionaries went with the King to the war and remained a whole year. At the end of the year, in the month of August, the King ordered his son and those of his greatest noblemen to become Christians, and he ordered a church to be built in Benin, and they learnt how to read and did it very well.'

4.   In August 1517 a Portuguese official in the island of Principe reported that a priest was going to Benin to convert the Oba 'although he is not ruling, except through two of his captains, because he is a youth and under their control'.[15]

15 Personal communication from Dr A. F. C. Ryder.

In Egharevba's interpretation of this period two dates, 1486 and 1515, are of crucial importance. Given the tradition that Ozolua was Oba when the first Portuguese arrived, and that this was d'Aveiro, the argument is that Ozolua must have been Oba in 1486. The importance of the second date lies in the fact that Egharevba assumes that the war referred to by Pires, which was going on in 1515/1516, was the war with Idah, which plays such a big part in Benin tradition and marks the last occasion before 1897 when Benin City itself was seriously threatened by an external enemy.

Bearing in mind Egharevba's dates for the Obas Ewuare to Esigie, let us examine tradition a little more closely. There is no suggestion whatsoever that Europeans visited Benin in the time of Ewuare. On the other hand he is said to have introduced coral beads and red flannel cloth (ododo) to Benin for the first time, and these could only have come from European sources. One of the best-known legends of Ewuare tells how he went to the palace of Olokun, the god of the sea, and stole some coral beads. Ewuare is also credited with founding the Iwebo palace association which since his time has been in charge of all the royal regalia. Iwebo is divided into a number of 'apartments' each created by a different Oba and controlled by a group of chiefs. Ewuare is said to have created the first of these apartments for the specific purpose of looking after the newly acquired coral and red cloth. The working, stringing and control of valuable red beads, both of coral and stone, has remained in the hands of Iwebo up to the present day. The word Iwebo itself is often construed as meaning 'the apartment of the Europeans' but it is by no means certain that this was its original meaning.

It is tempting to suggest that the legend of Ewuare and Olokun's beads may refer to an early direct or indirect contact with the Portuguese. Ewuare's route to Olokun's palace is said to have been through Ughoton, the port of Benin to which the Portuguese first came. Ughoton was also the main centre of the Olokun cult and while it seems almost certain that Olokun was worshipped there before the Portuguese arrived, there are reasons for supposing that the emphasis on Olokun as the god of wealth may have been encouraged by the coming of new forms of wealth from overseas. It would be unwise to place too much reliance on speculation of this kind but Egharevba's date for Ewuare fits in fairly well with the first exploration of the coast south of Benin by the Portuguese and it is likely that European goods arrived in Benin before the Europeans themselves.

Equally intriguing and equally unsatisfactory are the stories which connect Ewuare with the cult of the supreme deity, Osanobua. The legend has it that Ewuare sent some of his close followers to visit Osanobua and that Osanobua himself came down to Benin three times. The three spots where he alighted are the sites of shrines up to the present day. Now the story has grown up — though I doubt whether it is a very old one — that these shrines are on the site of former Portuguese churches. I do not believe that there is much evidence to support this except in one case. That the one exception had some connection with early Christianity in Benin is made likely by the fact that its priest, up to the present century, wore a brass cross round his neck. The problem of the Portuguese church, or churches, is, perhaps, susceptible only to an archaelogical solution and it is to be hoped that this will be attempted before too long. It is, of course, very likely that. the Benin people worshipped a supreme deity before the Portuguese came and that the name Osanobua was taken over by the Portuguese, as it has been by missionaries of more recent times.

In the traditions concerning Ewuare, then, possible links with early European activity in the Benin area are of the vaguest and most indirect kind. The tradition that the first European visited Benin City in Ozolua's time, on the other hand, is a very firm one — though Roupell was told in 1897 that this happened in the time of Esigie. There is, however, little else to connect Ozolua with the Portuguese. The only other story that I have heard is that Ozolua was suspicious of the Europeans whom he believed to be intriguing with his son Esigie, and that Esigie advised them to go away and return after he himself had become Oba. Esigie is said to have allowed the missionaries to build a church and to have learnt to speak Portuguese. It is also said that he had his son Orhogba educated by them. There are, too, various indirect suggestions that Esigie had a great deal to do with the early Portuguese. At Ughoton, the port, one is still shown the site of *Ugha-Esigie* (Esigie's Hall) where up to the nineteenth century European traders were received and had their feet washed. The attendants of this building were known as *ibierugha-Esigie* — 'servants of Esigie's Hall'. Again, there is at Benin City a ward known as Iwoki whose members had, among other functions, that of looking after the Oba's guns and cannon. The Iwoki date their foundation to Esigie's reign and some claim to be descended from Europeans called Ava and Uti. Ava and Uti are said, on one occasion, to have protected the Oba by standing with guns, one on each side of him and up to the present day, on ceremonial occasions, the

Oba is flanked by two Iwoki with guns. The shrine of the god of iron at which the Iwoki worship is called Ogun-Esigie. It seems likely then that the Iwoki was founded to look after guns when they were first introduced, according to the pattern by which Benin City was divided into wards, each of which had special duties to perform for the Oba. Another tradition connects Esigie with developments of the art of bronze-casting and some informants have it that the organization of the bronze-casters into a ward-guild dates from his reign. It is probable that at this period brass became available in greater quantities than ever before, as a result of European importations.

This and other evidence make the attribution of the early intense activity of the Portuguese at Benin to Esigie's reign fairly convincing and it is, therefore, probable that Obas Ewuare to Esigie did, in fact, span the late fifteenth and early sixteenth centuries. When, however, we examine Egharevba's dates for Esigie, in the light of points three and four above, we find ourselves in difficulty for if both of these contain accurate information it is virtually certain that an Oba died in late 1516 or early 1517. The war with Idah is one of the outstanding traditional events of Esigie's reign. The Attah of Idah's forces are said to have reached the gates of Benin City before being driven back across the Niger. Tradition is very clear on this matter and the course of the war can be traced through the traditions of many villages between Benin and Idah. Duarte Pires writing in 1516 states that missionaries went to the war with the Oba and Egharevba has assumed that this must have been the Idah war, though I have found no independent tradition in Benin that Europeans were present on this campaign. Another Portuguese at this time reported that to visit the Oba in his war-camp he had to travel eighty leagues[16] and, while he gives no direction, this is not an outrageous estimate of the distance from Benin or Ughoton to Idah – though it is exaggerated.

Assuming that the official on Principe had the right information (this is by no means certain) and that our general assumptions about this period are correct, the Oba who died in 1516 or 1517 could only have been Ozolua or Esigie. Benin traditions of Esigie's reign lend no support to the idea that he died immediately after the Idah war. On the contrary they suggest that this war occurred relatively early in what was to be a long reign. Ozolua, on the other hand, is said to have been killed at Uzea in north-east Ishan (which is on the way between Benin and

Idah) while fighting a campaign against Uromi. On the face of it, it seems more likely that this, rather than the Idah war, is the one referred to in the Portuguese accounts, and that, therefore, Esigie became Oba in about 1517. Without further evidence, however, this remains a very speculative conclusion.

Despite the fact that European missionaries and traders continued to visit Benin throughout the sixteenth and seventeenth centuries nothing has come to my notice which provides any clear evidence for the dating of any Oba. No deaths or accessions are reported and no name is given until that of the Kambadje mentioned in Dapper. According to Talbot (Vol. I p. 158) there is a Portuguese record to the effect that an Oba of Benin visited Portugal in 1544 but the source of his quotation has not come to light. This alleged visit is not confirmed by tradition, though some informants believe Orhogba went away with the Portuguese for some years, and it is universally agreed that he lived on Lagos Island for some time and founded a dynasty there. Research into early Lagos history and tradition may possibly throw further light on this period. It has been assumed that Orhogba was the Oba whom Windham's party met in 1553 and who could speak Portuguese but there is no written evidence to confirm this.

The period up to 1485

For the period from the beginning of the dynasty up to 1472 there are no opportunities whatsoever for cross-checking between traditional and contemporary sources. Tradition presents a mixture of myth and apparent reality with a few major landmarks such as the founding of the dynasty by Oramiyan of Ife through his son Eweka; the establishment of the palace on its present site by Ewedo; the building of the town walls by Oguola and Ewuare; and the founding of the Itsekiri kingdom by the son of Olua. Some of Egharevba's early Obas are, at best, mere names to most informants and some informants would differ from him in matters of order and genealogy. All agree that Ewedo was the father of Oguola who was the father of Ohen, that Uwaifiokun and Ewuare were the sons of Ohen, and Ezoti, Olua and Ozolua the sons of Ewuare, though Egharevba's order of seniority between brothers is not always accepted. Where there are differences there is no reason for preferring one version to another. Let us, therefore, examine Egharevba's chronology on his own evidence. The genealogy represents Egharevba's own conception of the way in which

BENIN STUDIES

the title of Oba descended from father to son and brother to brother. Brothers names are shown in order of seniority and the numbers refer to the order in which the Obas are said to have ruled.

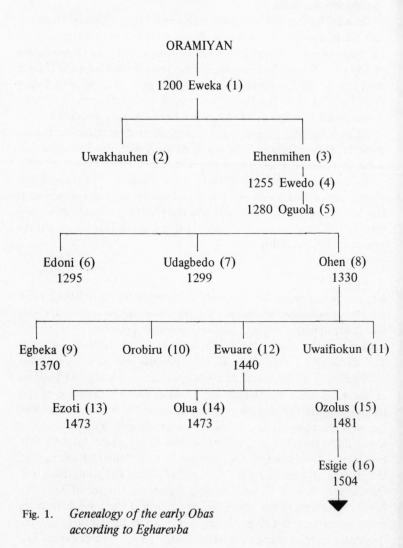

Fig. 1. *Genealogy of the early Obas according to Egharevba*

The reigns of Egharevba's first fourteen Obas occupy about 280 years giving the not unreasonable average of twenty years each. If Eresoyen did succeed about 1735 the five Obas (excluding Ogbebo) who ruled between that date and 1888 reigned for an average of about 30 years each. Assuming that Egharevba and other informants are correct, different modes of succession obtained at these two periods. If Ogbebo is left out, succession in the later period was from father to son, and it seems likely that this pattern would make for longer average reigns than brother-to-brother succession.[17] Even so Egharevba's average of 20 years for the earlier period is not outrageous, though some of his Obas, such as Ezoti and Uwaifiokun, apparently reigned for very short periods.

Where brother-to-brother succession obtains, however, the length of a generation of rulers must be taken into account. From Eweka to

17 In the later period succession went theoretically from father to eldest son. In fact this principle rarely worked smoothly. In successive reigns Ogbebo and Osemwede, Adolo and Ogbewenkon and Ovoramwe and Orokhorho contested with each other and each was able to claim some justification for the view that he was the rightful heir. The ambiguities that this implies derive from the ill-defined concept of legitimacy in this context and from the apparent unwillingness on the part of Obas to recognize their successors. According to the most prevalent theory an eligible heir must have been the first son born after his father had been recognized by the reigning Oba as his heir or at least after he had been accorded adult status. Children born to him before that time were to be regarded as 'children the leopard begets and throws away'. The latter were not always willing to accept this status however and when the time came they could usually find a faction to support them. Thus Ovoramwe's birth is said to have been concealed by Adolo from the Oba Osemwede. When Adolo died there was a brief struggle between Ovoramwe and his brother Orokhorho who had been born about the time of Adolo's succession. Ovoramwe who had built up formidable support won easily though his opponents claimed that he was ineligible on the grounds quoted above. On the other hand Ehigie, the eldest son of Ovoramwe, was apparently never considered as a candidate, on the same grounds.

It is doubtful whether any Oba after Obanosa received official recognition by his father as Edaiken, though some of them occupied the Edaiken's village of Uselu. The latent hostility which is likely to be present in some degree between a man and the son who will succeed him is probably intensified where an important title and a position of great power is at stake. This is evident not only in the institution of kingship but also in regard to other hereditary chiefs who sometimes seem to have delayed recognition of their eldest son's marriage as long as possible. This hostility is recognized by the Edo both directly and indirectly. A good example is the former rule forbidding the Edaiken to see his father or live in the same palace. Another interesting expression of this hostility is to be found in statements by informants that chiefs delayed their sons' marriages because they were afraid that the first son of the marriage might be a reincarnation of themselves, the implication of this being obvious.

The general effect of delaying recognition of a son's right to produce an heir would be to reduce the age of accession and increase the length of reign. Thirty years is in fact a very high average compared with many recorded dynasties. It is worth noting, too, that the Ezomo title appears to have been held for an average of about 30 years over the last eight generations.

Ozolua inclusive there were, according to Egharevba, 7 generations in 304 years, or 43 years per generation. For the four generations including Oguola to Ozolua the average is 56 years; and for the three generations Edoni to Ozolua 70 years. A figure of 43 years per generation is not entirely without the bounds of possibility if we assume that Obas went on having children in their old age. There is a certain internal logic in Egharevba's genealogies and dates in that the Obas of one generation are shown as the children of the last Oba of the previous one (though Ewuare, the last Oba of his generation is said not to have been the youngest). Nevertheless 43 years seem an unlikely average to be kept up over seven generations. Credibility breaks down when one is faced with 3 sets of brothers (from Edoni to Ozolua) occupying the throne for 209 years.

If we inspect the figures and genealogy more closely we see that the four brothers Egbeka, Orobiru, Uwaifiokun and Ewuare occupied the throne between them for 103 years. Of the first three, who held it between them for seventy years, we are told little. Egbeka 'had very little, if any, idea of government'; Orobiru's reign 'was full of peace and prosperity'. Ewuare, the most famous of all the Obas, who is said to have governed with such vigour, conquered so widely, and introduced so many lasting innovations had apparently to wait for 70 years after his father's death before he could become Oba. Small wonder he was constrained to murder his younger brother Uwaifiokun who had, even then, got in before him! Ewuare, after waiting 70 years then proceeded to rule for another 33. How old he was at the time of his father's death we are not told.

Chief Egharevba willingly admits that his dates for the early Obas are very approximate and it is doubtful whether he could ever have been given figures for the length of reign of such shadowy rulers as Egbeka, Orobiru, Edoni, Udagbedo, Uwakhuahen and Ehenmihen. In fact he gives no length of reign or date of installation for Orobiru and Uwaifiokun and Uwakhuahen and Ehenmihen and no length of reign for Egbeka or Eweka I. It is obviously impossible that anyone could have remembered how long groups of three Obas reigned and not the length of each reign separately.

One must conclude, then, that Chief Egharevba, in his admirable attempt to record his country's history, has, for the earlier period at least, gone much farther than his information warrants. On the evidence he gives his chronology is not tenable, and my own opinion is that oral tradition cannot provide, for the period up to 1485 a detailed chronology of the kind that Egharevba aims at. In the first place we have no means of knowing how accurate is the king-list or the genealogy posited. It is in the nature of tradition that its carriers should seek to impose a degree of order on the amorphous and unrecorded past which it does not necessarily possess. Although it is strongly held that Ewuakpe introduced the principle of primogeniture it is evident that both Egharevba and my informants tend to look at the earliest period of history with this conception at the back of their minds. With few exceptions he makes the eldest son succeed his father and with the exception of Ewuare/Uwaifiokun the latter's brothers follow him in order of seniority. Ezoti would have been succeeded by his eldest son if Ozolua had not killed the latter, we are told. A mode of succession in which the Obas of one generation are the sons of the *last* Oba of the previous one strikes the anthropologist as unlikely. It does not conform to the custom in Yoruba country whence the dynasty presumably came, and it has no justification in Edo social organisation. [18]

Conclusions

In this paper we have pursued the limited aim of evaluating the chronologies of Talbot and Egharevba in the terms in which they were arrived at. This is not the only approach and we have by no means exhausted the evidence that can be brought to bear upon this problem. We have been led to some useful if tentative conclusions:

(1) For the period from 1715 onwards we can be fairly certain that both Talbot and Egharevba are approximately correct in their dates. From Eresoyen onwards the accession of each Oba, except for Akengbuda, can be dated fairly precisely. It is no small achievement on the part of Egharevba to have achieved such accuracy over a period of some 250 years and if it was indeed Akenzua who died in 1734 or 1735 his accuracy at this point is almost bewildering.

(2) There is sufficient evidence from traditional sources to assume

18 Primogeniture appears to be a long-established feature of Edo social organization. If Ewuakpe did in fact introduce it as a principle of succession to the kingship he was probably only adjusting that institution to the general pattern of Edo society, though 1700 seems a very late date for this adjustment to have been made. There is some support for this view, however, in Dapper (1668) who implies that for commoners the eldest son is the sole heir while the Oba chooses his heir from among his sons. On the other hand as late as the seventeen-eighties, according to Landolphe, this was still the case and, he says, the choice rarely fell on the eldest son. It must be borne in mind, however, that Landolphe may have read Dapper and that his statement should in any case be evaluated in terms of what has been said about legitimacy (see footnote above).

that Obas Ewuare to Orhogba covered the late fifteenth and most of the sixteenth century though it is not possible to date any of them very certainly. Much depends on whether the suggestion that a new Oba. succeeded in 1517 is correct.

(3) The spacing of Obas Ehengbuda to Ore-Oghene remains very uncertain and neither Talbot's nor Egharevba's dates for this period are completely convincing.

(4) For the period from the founding of the dynasty up to Ewuare there is no satisfactory basis for absolute dating and in the absence of any possibility of contemporary records this period will probably remain pre-historic. If Ozolua was reigning in 1485 and was the fifteenth Oba it appears likely that the dynasty began not later than about 1300. On the basis of our review of Egharevba's own evidence his date of about 1200 must be regarded as too early. But for this period nothing is certain.

It may seem a little unfair to examine Egharevba's work so rigorously. In its time and place his *Short History* has been of inestimable value and its charm and character will continue to give it an important place in Benin studies. All who are interested in Benin will remain in his debt. His accuracy for the last two centuries of Benin's independent history is a tribute to his industry and integrity. The character of his book is so compelling, indeed, that his chronological conclusions have been accepted too uncritically, especially for the period up to the first European contacts. His date of 1200 for the founding of the Benin dynasty has often been quoted as established fact. The date he gives for Oguola's accession, 1280, has been taken as marking the introduction of the bronze-casting technique to Benin. William Fagg, for example, writes 'About 1280 Oba Oguola asked the Oni to send a master-founder to teach bronze-casting to Bini apprentices'.[19] It is true that the traditions of the bronze-casters trace their origin from Ife in the reign of Oguola, though it is generally said that they came against the Oni's wishes, but from our analysis above the date is clearly not so well-established as Fagg's statement suggests. On the available evidence Oguola may well have reigned a hundred years later.

19 W.B. Fagg, 1958 p.64. I should say that in a discussion after the publication of his essay Mr Fagg and I found that we had by then come to similar conclusions about the incorrectness of Egharevba's dating. It was partly as a result of this valuable discussion that I made a further scrutiny of Egharevba's evidence and this led to the conclusions given above concerning the period up to 1485.

When the limitations of the hitherto accepted chronologies have been pointed out we are still left with a useful tentative time-scale for our historical studies. A deeper analysis of Benin traditions, the checking of these against the traditions of neighbouring peoples and the possibility of further information from contemporary sources should help us to arrive at more precise conclusions, at least from the end of the fifteenth century onwards. The Benin people relate such events as wars and conquests, the founding of social and political institutions, the creation of titles and title-groups, the planning of Benin City, the progress of ritual and occupational specialization, developments in bronze-casting, and the introduction of new cults to the reigns of specific Obas. By setting these events against our dynastic chronology it should be possible to obtain a fairly coherent picture of at least the broad phases of Benin history. More than this cannot be expected. Comparing the social institutions and culture patterns of Benin and neighbouring areas can help us to formulate more precise theories about the political and cultural currents that have influenced the internal history of the central area of Southern Nigeria.

The Kingdom of Benin

The Dynastic Myth

In March 1897 a British military expedition took possession of
Benin City *(Ɛdo)*; in the following September Ovonramwen, the
thirty-fifth Ɔba (king) of Benin, was deported to Calabar. Thus ended
the independence of what had been one of the largest and longest lived
of the West African forest states. It was not the end of the kingship,
however, for when Ovonramwen died in 1914 his son Aiguobasimwin
was made Oba. Conscious that his accession marked the beginning of a
new era, Aiguobasimwin styled himself Eweka II after the first king of
the dynasty. According to tradition, it was in the reign of the fifteenth
Oba, Ozolua, that European visitors had first set foot in Benin City. As
this event probably took place in 1485, it is unlikely that the dynasty
was founded later than the early fourteenth century. The Edo believe
that it was preceded by other dynasties. We are told that when the last
of these came to an end the country fell into chaos, so the elders of
Benin – today identified with the *Uzama* nobles (see p.57) –
dispatched messengers to the *Ɔghɛnɛ n'Uhɛ*, asking him to send them a
prince. The *Ɔghɛnɛ* (*Ɔɔni*, to give him his Yoruba title) was the ruler
of Ile Ife, the cosmic metropolis of the Yoruba people to the west and,
for most of the states of the Bight of Benin, the cradle of divine
kingship. He sent his son Oranmiyan, who, however, found Benin
uncongenial, so after a short stay he departed for home, but not before
he had impregnated the daughter of an Edo village chief. She bore a
son, who in the course of time was enthroned under the name Eweka.

It is impossible to say, with assurance, what historical reality
underlies this myth, but its symbolic meaning is plain. It states that the
kingship is of alien provenance but that it came into being by the will
of the Edo and was nurtured in Edo culture. The same assertions are
expressed in other myths, and they are recurrent motifs in state ritual.
At various points in the annual cycle of kingship rites, the Oba receives
fictitious gifts from his 'father', the *Ɔghɛnɛ*. Before 1897 part of the
remains of a dead king were sent 'back' to Ife by his son, who sought

the Ɔghɛnɛ's formal approval of his own accession. These and other symbolic acts,

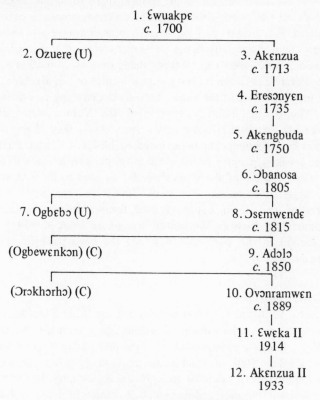

1. Ɛwuakpɛ
c. 1700

2. Ozuere (U)

3. Akɛnzua
c. 1713

4. Eresɔnyɛn
c. 1735

5. Akɛngbuda
c. 1750

6. Ɔbanosa
c. 1805

7. Ogbɛbɔ (U)

8. Ɔsɛmwɛndɛ
c. 1815

(Ogbewɛnkɔn) (C)

9. Adɔlɔ
c. 1850

(Ɔrɔkhɔrhɔ) (C)

10. Ovɔnramwɛn
c. 1889

11. Ɛwɛka II
1914

12. Akɛnzua II
1933

U = Brief reign. Considered usurper.
C = Unsuccessful Contestant.

Fig 2. *The Benin dynasty (from 1700)*

and the myths with which they are associated, establish the roots of the royal line outside Edo society and link it up, through Ife, with the dynasties of other kingdoms. Thus, they make explicit the Oba's apartness and his right to rule. In many contexts 'Oba' and 'Edo' are opposed concepts. Yet in another sense the Oba *is* Edo, for while Oranmiyan was an alien, his son Eweka was Edo-born and the latter's successors were bound to rule through Edo institutions and according to Edo customs.

The dynastic myth links up the Benin kingship with the dynasties of most Yoruba states, especially with that of the great Oyo empire, for Oyo, too, claims Oranmiyan as the founder of its royal line. Thus, the traditions of the two great empires, which for several centuries dominated the greater part of what is now south-western Nigeria, converge in a single hero-figure. It seems certain that the political innovations which gave rise to these states were set in motion at Ife. Yet however similar the central political institutions of Ife, Oyo, and Benin may have been at the outset, they developed along very different lines. Though the political systems of the Yoruba states differ considerably in detail (Lloyd, 1954 and 1962), they share many common basic features. The Benin kingdom, however, is located among the Edo-speaking peoples, whose social institutions are in many respects more akin to those of the small-scale Ibo societies to the east. It has been suggested elsewhere (Bradbury, 1964) that the characteristic features of the Benin polity resulted from a lengthy process of accommodation between the central notions of divine kingship, that were current in this part of Africa, and the basic patterns of Edo culture and society.

The Benin Kingdom

It is useful to distinguish what we may call the Benin Kingdom from the outlying territories which at various times accepted the Oba's suzerainty. Roughly coterminous with the present-day Benin Division of the Mid-West State of Nigeria, the Benin kingdom was the area in which the Oba's writ ran most strongly and consistently. It was not a single administrative unit, and its boundaries cannot be precisely drawn. The great majority of its inhabitants spoke Edo, the language of Benin City, with negligible dialect variations, but there were Ibo settlements on the eastern borders, Itsekiri and Ijaw lining the rivers in the south-west, and Yoruba villages on the north-west whose relations with the Oba were, in most respects, similar to those of the Edo themselves. Generally speaking, the Benin kingdom may be defined as the area within which the Oba was recognized as the sole human arbiter of life and death. Within it no one could be put to death without his consent, and any person accused of a capital offence had to be brought before his court. In accordance with this principle, he retained control over the administration of sasswood to suspected witches. Outside the Benin kingdom authority to inflict capital punishment, make human sacrifices

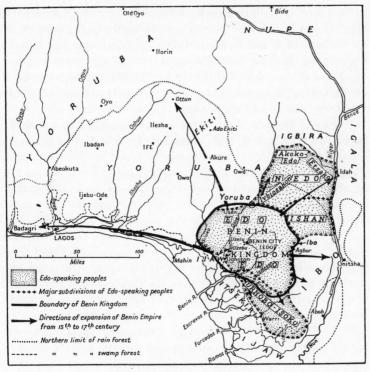

THE KINGDOM OF BENIN

or order the sasswood ordeal was delegated to, or retained by, local
rulers.

The inhabitants of the Benin kingdom considered themselves to be
the true *eviɛn-Ɔba*, 'slaves' of the Oba, that is free subjects of the
throne. They wore the same body markings, and they regarded
themselves as superior to all their neighbours. All male commoners in
the Benin kingdom were the Oba's retainers in that they were nominal,
if not initiated, members of the associations that administered his
palace. Finally, throughout the Benin kingdom virtually every
community or domestic ritual of a confirmatory or periodic nature
made reference to the worshippers' allegiance to the Oba.

The Extent and Decline of the Benin Empire

In its heyday the boundaries of the Benin state stretched far beyond its solid core, taking little account of linguistic and cultural divides. The kingdom was bounded by Yoruba speakers on the west and north, Ibo on the east, Ishan and Northern Edo on the north-east, and Urhobo, Itsekiri, and Ijaw on the south. The Edo of the Benin kingdom, together with the Ishan, Northern Edo, Urhobo, and Isoko, make up the Edo-speaking peoples, and they share a basic cultural substratum (Bradbury, 1957: 13-17 and *passim*).

In the late fifteenth century Benin was a well-established state with a large army conducting long campaigns far afield. It was already approaching the peak of its power and prosperity. By the late sixteenth century its frontiers had reached out westwards along the coast to beyond Lagos, north-west through the country of the Ekiti Yoruba to Ottun, where there was a boundary with Oyo, and eastwards to the Niger. Thus, it embraced considerable populations of eastern Yoruba and western Ibo. The former largely retained their characteristically Yoruba political systems. Their titles, regalia, and ceremonial forms were influenced by Benin, but these were matters of style rather than structure. Within a limited framework of controls exercised by the Oba – tribute, assistance in war, facilities for Edo traders – they enjoyed internal autonomy. Many western Ibo groups developed into small centralized states in which Benin-type institutions, copied with varying degrees of similitude, were superimposed on and accommodated to local social forms. Most of their chiefs *(obi)* accepted the Oba's suzerainty, but others, some of them founded by dissident groups from Benin itself, lay beyond his control.

While the Benin empire embraced non-Edo peoples, it is improbable that firm control was ever established over the whole Edo-speaking area. To the immediate north-east of the Benin kingdom were the Ishan chiefdoms (Bradbury, 1957: 61-80), whose chiefs (*enigie, enije*) paid tribute to the Oba, provided contingents for his armies, and required his consent for their accession. To the west of Ishan the non-centralized Ivbiosakon (Bradbury, 1957: 84-99) had a similar allegiance, as did some of the nearer Urhobo chiefdoms and village groups to the south. But, to the north, the open rocky hill country of Etsako (ibid., 100-9) and North-West Edo (Akoko-Edo) (ibid., 110-26) and, to the south, the swamp-encompassed lands occupied by the remoter Urhobo and Isoko (ibid., 127-64), were resistant to enduring Benin control.

The last three centuries of Benin's independence saw a gradual shrinking of the area from which its government could enforce delivery of tribute and military service and secure safe passage for Benin traders, though this decline was by no means uninterrupted. During the eighteenth century there were many campaigns aimed at maintaining control over the western Ibo area. In Osemwende's reign, in the early nineteenth century, control over the Ekiti Yoruba to the north was reconsolidated. Throughout the nineteenth century this latter area was the most important, though not the only, hinterland for Benin traders. Overseas goods, such as guns, powder, salt, and cloth, were obtained at the river 'beaches' on the south-west fringes of the kingdom from European merchants and Itsekiri middlemen, who, in return, bought Benin palm-oil, kernels, ivory, vegetable gums, and, in earlier times, slaves. The European goods were head-loaded to inland markets along well defined routes, the return traffic being in slaves, livestock, stone beads (from Ilorin), leather, and other commodities. This long distance trade was controlled by various trading associations, each operating in a different direction. The most important of these associations was called *Ekhɛngbo* (*ekhɛn*, traders; *ɛgbo*, forest). It monopolized the route from Benin to Akure, which was the main base for trade in the north-east Yoruba country. *Ekhɛngbo*, and similar associations operating towards the east and north-east, were controlled by title-holders and other prominent men from Benin City. The Oba of Benin is said to have been a member of all of them. It was in the interests of the traders to uphold the integrity of the Benin polity in order to ensure a state of security in which trade could flourish. Competition for power and prestige in the state itself provided a major incentive to engage in this trade. On the other hand, the interests of free trade were in potential conflict with the interests of the Oba, and the ruling policy had always been highly protectionist. No 'foreign' traders from the interior were permitted to operate in the Benin kingdom itself, and stringent controls were exercised over the waterside commerce with European and Itsekiri merchants. Heavy dues were demanded from visiting ships, the Oba's monopolies in certain exports were strictly enforced, and general trading was allowed only when he and his chiefs had completed their business. Disagreements between the palace officials, who supervised this commerce, and the European and Itsekiri merchants often led to the latters' withdrawal or to the Oba's placing an embargo on all trade with them. State control aimed at maintaining the economic power of the ruling élite and, by limiting the distribution of firearms and powder, at preserving the integrity of the kingdom. These aims were largely achieved, but at the expense of economic vitality. It was no accident that the immediate cause of the expedition which led to Ovonramwen's deposition was the massacre of a British mission which sought to persuade him to facilitate free commerce.

In the period leading up to the expedition Benin fortunes were at a low ebb. Protected by its forest environment, the kingdom itself had remained secure from Fulani attacks and infiltrations such as had helped to break up the Oyo empire. Indeed, the Benin kingdom had apparently suffered no serious external attack since the legendary war with Idah in the sixteenth century. But in the second half of the nineteenth century the Nupe-Fulani swept down to the northern borders of Ishan and Ivbiosakon, forcing most of the Northern Edo groups to pay regular tribute to the Emir of Bida. Meanwhile, the penetration of European commerce through Lagos on the west, and up the Niger on the east was slowly whittling away the Benin trading hinterland and loosening the Oba's hold over his subject populations. When the Ekiti states were beset by Fulani raiders from Ilorin and by the growing military forces of Ibadan, the Oba was able to afford them little protection. Benin warriors played some part in the Ekiti wars, but on a freelance basis: they took advantage of the confused situation to raid for slaves and loot. They sent gifts to the Oba, for they were dependent on the Benin route for their supplies. In return he occasionally despatched reinforcements to help them, but his control over them was minimal. In the 1880s the official Benin army, under the *Ezɔmɔ*, was occupied subduing rebellious villages on the very north-west borders of the kingdom itself, no more than fifty miles from the capital. Some Ishan and Western Ibo chiefdoms continued to pay tribute, but payment was becoming more difficult to enforce and revolts more difficult to put down. By the 1890s the Oba and his chiefs were becoming increasingly apprehensive of the intentions of the British, who by this time were firmly established in the rivers to the south.

In these circumstances it is indeed remarkable that the Benin kingdom suffered no serious internal collapse. The capacity for survival shown by the Benin polity can be put down partly to the immense value attached to the kingship, which, over the centuries, had accumulated a great aura of mystery, fear, and respect. These attitudes were deliberately fostered by the Oba's retainers and priests and, though there is a hint of desperation in the apparently great increase in human sacrifice during this period, they were largely successful. But the strength of the state lay also in the structure of its central institutions and in the balance between competing power groups. The

nature of these institutions and key role of the kingship form the main
subject of this essay.

Territorial Administration

The population of Benin Division, which we equate with the Benin
kingdom, was reckoned at about 292,000 in the 1952 census. Some
54,000 of these lived in the capital, Benin City, and the rest in several
hundred compact villages, ranging in size from less than 20 to (in one
case only) more than 6,000 souls. The great majority of villages had
populations of less than 1,000; 400 or 500 may be taken as typical.
Before 1897 Benin City probably had less than half its 1952
population. Even so, its urban, metropolitan character contrasted
sharply with the small scale of village society.

The village was made up of a number of households containing
simple, compound, and patrilineally extended families. Households
were grouped into wards on a territorial basis, though a small ward
might correspond to a descent group. Villages were not associated with
kin groups, and all but the smallest of them contained members of
many different clans. The kinship system had a marked agnatic bias, but
the effective lineages (Bradbury, 1957: 30–31) were small, and neither
at the village nor the state level was the balance of power conceived of
in terms of lineage representation.

The narrow range of Benin lineages can be partly explained in terms
of a high incidence of population movements between village and
village, village and capital, and between the Benin kingdom and
neighbouring areas. The primary factor, however, was the unusual
pattern of land rights, which itself may have been related to population
movements. Outside the capital population density was low, land was
abundant, and rights in its exploitation were vested in the village
community rather than in its component descent groups. Along with
this lack of lineage control of land went primogenitary succession.
Those offices that were hereditary passed, in principle, from father to
eldest surviving son. Lloyd has shown that common interests in land
and political offices were the basis of lineage solidarity among the
northern Yoruba. The absence of such common interests in Benin had
far-reaching implications for the political as well as the land-holding
system.

In the village the predominance of community over kin-group
interests was maintained through a three-tier age-grade organization

(Bradbury, 1957: 32). The oldest man, subject to 'citizenship' qualifications, was in most villages the sole village head (*ɔdiɔnwere*). He and his fellow elders (*ediɔn*) made policy, controlled access to village resources, kept order, settled disputes, and mediated with the central authority. The elders directed the warrior and executive grade of adult men (*ighele*) and the grade of youths (*iroghae*) which performed 'public works'. Supernatural sanction for their authority came from their access to the spirits of past elders of the village (*ediɔn-ɛbho*) and from their collective superiority in magic.

In many villages, however, the *ɔdiɔnwere's* authority was shared with and limited by that of a chief (*onogie*) whose office descended by primogenitary succession. Most *enigie* were descended from the immediately junior brothers of past kings, but some claimed lines going back beyond the incorporation of their chiefdoms into the state; and a few were descended from non-royal appointees of the Oba. The chiefdom might consist of one or several villages. In the central area round the capital and in the territory to the west of it there were few *enigie*, and here each village dealt directly with the central authority through its *ɔdiɔnwere*, though it might combine with neighbouring villages for certain purposes. To the north and east a much larger proportion of the population was included in chiefdoms. The more remote they were from Benin, the larger the chiefdoms tended to be and the greater their internal autonomy. The more distant *enigie* might control up to a dozen or more villages, some of which themselves had hereditary *enigie*. The more important *enigie* conferred titles on their 'palace' officials and on their agents in the subordinate villages. They had rights to game and tribute and they held courts for the settlement of disputes between their subjects. Having some of the attributes of kingship, they were the focus of rituals patterned on, though less elaborate than, those which took place at the Oba's palace.

The *onogie's* authority was checked both from above and below. Each of his villages had its own council of elders headed by the *ɔdiɔnwere*, and he could do little against their combined will. If his rule was oppressive they could appeal to the Oba to restrain him. To the Oba the *onogie* had such obligations as to collect and despatch tribute, to supply labour and military recruits, and to refrain from and prevent hostile acts against the king's subjects in other chiefdoms and villages. Some *enigie* held official positions in the state military organization. Unlike the Oba's Ishan, Yoruba, or Ibo vassals, the *enigie* of the Benin kingdom lacked the authority to put their subjects to death; all capital offences committed in their chiefdoms had to be referred to the Oba's court. Finally they held their offices at the Oba's will. It was he who settled cases of disputed succession, and the *onogie's* heir could not be installed until the Oba had given him permission to carry out his father's mortuary rites. Generally, the heir spent a period of instruction at the Oba's palace before he was escorted home and presented to his people by palace officials. In the last resort the Oba could depose him.

Twice yearly, every village in the Benin kingdom was required to send tribute to the Oba in the form of yams, palm-oil, and other foodstuffs.[1] The more remote vassal chiefs sent slaves and livestock. Refusal to contribute, on the part of a village or chiefdom, was construed as revolt (*isɔtɛ*) and its headman or chief was designated 'the Oba's enemy' (*oghian-ɔba*). Such revolts were put down by force. Apart from regular tribute, *ad hoc* levies were raised for particular purposes. Thus, if the Oba needed palm kernels for export (one of his monopolies) he could send out his palace officials to organize their collection.

For administrative purposes the Oba's domains were divided not into major provinces but into a large number of tribute units — single villages, village groups, and chiefdoms. Most of these 'fiefs' (as for convenience sake we may call them) served the Oba through the agency of one of his appointed counsellors of the Palace or Town orders, but other fief-holders included the hereditary *Uzama* nobles, the *Iyɔba* (Oba's mother), *Edaikɛn* (Oba's heir), non-titled palace retainers, and, it is said, some of the Oba's wives.

The fief-holders' main reward lay in their right to receive tribute, usually reckoned as half the amount passed on to the Oba. They could also demand labour services and received gifts from those who sought their aid and protection, but they had no direct control over land or resources. A fief-holder could arrange with the *onogie* or elders of his villages to settle his dependents or slaves there to farm for him, but this was not an exclusive right, for the village authorities could make similar arrangements with other residents of the capital. His chief functions were to see that tribute was paid and to conduct its carriers to the

1. The yam was the basis of the subsistence economy, and its cultivation was mainly men's work, each man with a yam farm being expected to contribute to the village tribute. Subsidiary crops, such as corn, groundnuts, peppers, melons, and beans, were planted and tended by women. Kola and coconut trees were individually owned, but oil palms belonged to the village collectively, any member being free to use them at will, except where they were growing on current farms. See Bradbury, 1957: 23-26, for a brief account of the economy.

palace; to recruit labour for such works as the rebuilding of the Oba's palace; and to assemble men for service in the state armies. Fief-holders were required to live at Benin City. They used their own servants and kin to carry instructions to the *enigie* and *ediɔnwere*. From the point of view of his 'subjects' the fief-holder was their official sponsor through whom they could communicate requests, complaints, and disputes to the Oba. Benin villagers strongly maintain that their sponsors had no judicial authority over them, but, while they had no official courts, it is clear that they did often settle disputes without bringing them to the Oba's notice.

Though each of the higher-ranking counsellors controlled many fiefs, these were dispersed throughout the Oba's territories. If this arrangement had administrative drawbacks, it also had the advantage of preventing any one chief from building up too much personal power in a large consolidated area. Since most fiefs were in the hands of non-hereditary officials, they did not become permanently controlled by particular aristocratic lines. Nor were fiefs and titles indissolubly linked. When a man was awarded a title he expected to be given the fiefs that his predecessor had controlled, but the Oba had the right to redistribute them and used with circumspection, this right could be a powerful political weapon.

It must be stressed that the fief-holders were not the sole channel of communication between the Oba and his subjects. Some *enigie* had the right of direct access to the king. In the more distant vassal chiefdoms the Oba stationed his own agents to watch over his interests and convey intelligence to him. Within the Benin kingdom his palace officials were constantly going out to the villages on a variety of secular and ritual missions.

II. THE CENTRAL POLITICAL INSTITUTIONS

The Capital

The Benin capital was encircled by a massive earth wall and ditch some six miles in circumference. Within the wall the town was divided into two unequal parts by a long, broad avenue running approximately north-west to south-east. This spatial division corresponded to a Palace/Town dichotomy of great political significance. Ogbe, the smaller area to the south-west, contained the Oba's palace (*Ɛguae-Ɔba*) and the houses of most of his Palace Chiefs (*Eghaɛbho n'Ogbe*). In Orenokhua, to the north-east, lived the Town Chiefs (*Eghaɛbho n'Ore*) and here, too, were located most of the wards of occupational specialists. There were forty or fifty of these wards, occupied by groups having special skills or duties which they performed, full or part time, primarily for the Oba. Each ward had its internal political organization, based on the grading of its male members, and headed by an *ɔdiɔnwere*, an hereditary chief, or an appointed leader.

On the western and southern sides of the town were a number of settlements that lay outside the main wall but within a second wall, standing a mile or so farther out. Some of these were inhabited by groups of ritual specialists and must be considered wards of the capital. Idunbhun-Ihogbe, for example, contained one section of the *Ihogbe*, priests of the past kings and of the living Oba's Head. In the same area were located the villages of six of the Seven *Uzama (Uzama n'Ihinrɔn)*, hereditary nobles and 'kingmakers'. The seventh *Uzama* was the Oba's eldest son and heir, the *Edaikɛn*, whose court was at Uselu, just outside the second wall to the north-west. In fact, as we shall see, no *Edaikɛn* was installed during the nineteenth century. Uselu also housed the court of the Oba's mother, who ranked with the Town Chiefs rather than the *Uzama*.

The hereditary *Uzama* and the two groups of *Eghaɛbho*, whose titles were non-hereditary, constituted three great orders of chieftaincy which, between them, were responsible for the continuity and government of the state. In order to understand the administrative system and the nature of political competition at Benin, it will be necessary to describe the manner of recruitment to these orders, their respective competences, and their relationship to each other and to the king.

The Uzama n'Ihinrɔn

Tradition identifies the *Uzama* with the 'elders' whose request resulted in Oranmiyan being sent from Ife to found a dynasty at Benin.[2] This is consistent with their role as 'kingmakers' (the *Edaikɛn* being excluded from this role) and with their position as the highest-ranking order of chieftaincy. As the elders of the state they take up the position of greatest honour at palace rituals, directly facing the Oba. In the ceremonial 'salutations', through which all the chiefs reaffirm their royalty, the *Uzama* are the last to make obeisance and the first to

2. Strictly speaking, this applies only to the first five titles, *Oliha, Edohen, Ezɔmɔ, Ero,* and *Eholɔ n'Ere*. The first *Ɔlɔtɔn* was a follower of Oranmiyan, and the *Edaikɛn* was added to the order by Oba Ewuare.

The Palace Associations

	Iwebo	Iweguae	Ibiwe-Eruɛrɛ	
Eghaebho n'Ogbe (Senior Palace Chiefs)	1. Unwaguɛ 2. Eribo 3. Osaguɛ 4. Ayɔbahan 5. Ɔlaye 6. Ɔbaraduagbon 7. Esasɔyɛn 8. Ɔbamarhiayeɫ†	1. Esere 2. Ɔʔazelu 3. Ɔbasɛkiɫ† 4. Ɔbadagbonyi 5. Akɛnuwa	1. Inɛ 2. Ɔbazuaye 3. Ɔbahiagbon 4. Ɔbabhɔnyi† 5. Ɔbayuwana†	1. Osodin 2. Uso 3. Ezuakɔ 4. Ɔbazɔwa
Ekhaɛnbhɛn (Junior Palace Chiefs)	Many titles†	Many titles†	Many titles†	
Grades of Un-titled Officials (Simplified)	Ukɔ n'Iwebo Ɔdafen Ibierugha	Ukɔ n'Iweguae Ɔdafen Ibieruga Emada	Ukɔ n'Urhoɛrie Ɔdiɔn Eruɛrie n'Ibie	

* Titles hereditary by primogeniture.
† New titles created by Ovonramwen.

Uzama (Hereditary nobles)
1. Oliha*
2. Edohen*
3. Ezɔmɔ*
4. Ero*
5. Ehɔlɔ n'Ire*
6. Ɔlɔtɔn*
7. Edaiken* (Oba's heir)

h'Enɛ Eghaebho

Eghaebho n'Ore (Town chiefs)
1. Iyasɛ
2. Esogban
3. Esɔn
4. Osuma
5. Esama
6. Ologbosɛ*
7. Osula
8. Ighama (Ima)
9. Ɔbarisiagbon
10. Ɔbasuyi
11. Ɔbaraye
12. Ɔbayagbonaɫ†
13. Aiwerioghɛnɛ†

Ibiwe Nekhua (Junior Town Chiefs)
1. Edogun*
2. Ɔza
3. Eso
4. Ezɔmurogho, etc., etc.

Fig 3. The principal orders of chieftaincy in Ovonramwen's reign

receive the Oba's kola nuts and palm wine. *Oliha* alone does not kneel before the king, for it is he who speaks the words that inaugurate a new reign. When *Oliha* himself dies his heir is installed by the Oba in person, whereas all other state chiefs are inducted by the *Iyasɛ* as senior Town Chief, on the Oba's instructions.

In the last centuries of independence the *Uzama's* power, as a group, was not commensurate with their exalted rank. Some of them, especially *Ezɔmɔ* and *Ɛro* had important executive functions, but collectively they played a smaller part in the day-to-day direction of the state than did either of the *Eghaɛbho* orders. They had few administrative duties, controlled relatively few fiefs, and attended policy-making and judicial councils at the palace only on the most critical occasions. Nevertheless, as guardians of custom and of the kingship, they retained considerable prestige and moral authority. An Oba could not be lawfully installed, nor could he properly worship his predecessors, without their participation and new laws and major policy decisions required their formal consent. Ritual sanction for their authority lay in the cult of their collective predecessors, the *Ediɔn-Uzama*, whose worship, at a shrine in *Oliha's* custody, was essential for the nation's well-being.

The authority of the *Uzama* was probably most effective in times of serious disagreement between the Town Chiefs and the Palace. Their ability to act as a 'third-force' — sometimes allying themselves with the Town group against the Palace, sometimes identifying themselves with the Oba's interests *vis-à-vis* his appointed counsellors — derived not only from their status as 'elders' but also from the considererable autonomy that they retained in their own settlements. They were not the Oba's equals; they could not sit in his presence nor put anyone to death without his consent. Yet in another sense they were his peers. Like the Oba, and unlike the *Eghaɛbho*, they were hereditary territorial rulers in their own right. Their territories consisted only of the villages or hamlets in which they lived with, in some cases, one or more villages farther afield; but in the internal affairs of these territories the Oba ought not to interfere. Their inhabitants were subjects of the *Uzama* rather than of the Oba. Freemen of Uzebu, for example, were *eviɛn-Ezɔmɔ* rather than *eviɛn-Ɔba*. *Ezɔmɔ* could make direct demands on their services and confer titles on them; the Oba could not. The *Uzama* themselves had some of the attributes of kingship. They had their own priests to bless their Heads, whereas the *Eghaɛbho's* Heads were blessed by the Oba's priests, *Ihogbe*. They lived in 'palaces' which, in principle at least, were organized along the same lines as the Oba's palace, with associations of retainers bearing titles similar to those conferred by the Oba on his own courtiers. In the nineteenth century most of the *Uzama's* courts were more nominal than effective, but some of them especially *Ezɔmɔ* were able to keep up impressive establishments.

The *Uzama* had not always been set apart from the management of the state, if reliance can be placed on traditions of a prolonged struggle waged by the early kings to assert their supremacy over them. Up to the reign of the sixteenth Oba, Esigie, *Oliha* is portrayed as the Oba's main antagonist, but as time goes by this role passes to the *Iyasҽ*, the leader of the Town Chiefs. Ritual expression is still given to the ancient opposition between the Oba and *Uzama* in the *irɔn* rite, which forms part of the annual Festival of the Oba's Father (*Ugie-Erha-Ɔba*). *Irɔn* takes the form of a pantomimic battle in which the *Uzama* after challenging the Oba by showing him their archaic 'crowns', are defeated by loyal warriors. Then they accept the Oba's kola nuts and palm wine in token of their submission. This rite, and myths relating how various kings got the better of the *Uzama*, have a continuing social meaning in that they reassert the Obạ's unchallengeable supremacy over those who are closest in rank to him. But it is likely that they refer, also, to an historical decline in the power of the *Uzama* correlated, the evidence suggests, with the rise of the *Eghaҽbho* orders; and with a shift towards a doctrine of automatic primogenitary succession to the kingship. The successful assertion, by the kings of Benin, of the right to assign major administrative and judicial functions to counsellors appointed by themselves gave them considerable power *vis-à-vis* the *Uzama*. The rule of primogeniture, though ineffective in eliminating succession strife, *made the Uzama's* role as kingmakers more ceremonial than political. They continued to receive the new king's installation fees and to inaugurate his reign, but they had no more effective voice in determining his identity than did the *Eghaҽbho*.

It is instructive to compare the nineteenth-century position of the *Uzama* with that of their analogues at Oyo (Morton-Williams, 1960: 362-7).[3] The *Ɔyɔ Misi* formed the central policy-making council, played a major administrative role in capital and state, and had a

---

3 These comparisons were made before I had read the study on Oyo by Morton-Williams which appears in this volume *[i.e. West African Kingdoms in the Nineteenth Century.]*

decisive voice in selecting the *Alafin* (king) from candidates put before them by the royal lineage. Moreover, their ultimate authority over the king was complete for, if his rule proved unsatisfactory, their leader, the *Bashɔrun*, could order him to commit suicide. At Benin no one could claim the right to bring a reign to an end.

Whereas the *Ɔyɔ Misi* titles were vested in powerful landholding lineages, the *Uzama* titles descended by primogeniture through narrow lines of descent. Though it did not always prevent succession conflict, the rule of primogeniture at least set narrow limits on the range of possible aspirants, for, unless a *Uzama* died without sons, his brothers and the latters' descendants were automatically excluded from a direct interest in the title. Nor, since land was not lineage-held at Benin, were they dependent upon him, nor he upon them, for access to resources. Thus, two strong motives for lineage solidarity present among the Yoruba were absent from Benin. Wealthy *Uzama* could extend patronage to their kinsmen but, on the other hand, succession disputes were destructive of lineage unity. Many *Uzama* collaterals evaded the authority of their noble kinsmen by, for example, moving into the capital and seeking the Oba's preferment. Those *Uzama* who had many subjects seem to have recruited them mainly from slaves and clients rather than on a descent basis. A further difference between the two groups lay in the fact that, unlike the *Ɔyɔ Misi*, the *Uzama* did not have administrative and judicial authority over major sections of the capital.

Thus, the *Uzama* depended for their influence on personal wealth and following and, in this respect, their hereditary status gave them (with the *Ezɔmɔ* a conspicuous exception) no special advantages over the Oba's appointed counsellors. In Benin great wealth was attained through fief-holding, control of political patronage, long-distance trade, and participation in war and slave raiding. Wealth was invested mainly in buying slaves, who were set down in villages to farm for their masters. Except for the *Ezɔmɔ*, the *Uzama* controlled relatively few fiefs — the result, probably, of deliberate policy on the part of the kings. Since they exercised few administrative functions, they had little patronage to offer. Successful traders needed to move about freely, making new contacts and closely supervising their agents. In this respect the *Uzama* were hampered by the dignity of their quasi-kingly offices, which demanded that they remain in their palaces rather than wander· about in search of wealth. Nor, except for the *Ezɔmɔ*, did they have any special role in the state's military organization.

The *Ezɔmɔ*'s position was unique. Though third in rank in its order, this was one of the great offices of state, and its holder most nearly approached kingly status. The wealth and prestige of successive *Ezɔmɔ* remarked by many European visitors in the eighteenth and nineteenth centuries, was derived from their function as war captains, in which respect only the *Iyasɛ* equalled them. It was the *Ezɔmɔ* who took charge of most national campaigns, and their military activities enabled them to accumulate many slaves, subjects, and fiefs. However, this role had little to do with their *Uzama* status. They were directly responsible to the Oba, and there is no evidence that they regularly used the power in the interests of their order. The specific character of the *Ezɔmɔ's* military functions meant that his relationship to the king was sharply defined and lacked the element of polar opposition which bedevilled the king's relations with the *Iyasɛ* or, in earlier times, the *Oliha*. The *Ezɔmɔ*'s military power could be an important factor in succession disputes, but he had no monopoly of physical force, for there was no standing army at his command; when warriors were needed they were recruited by the Oba through his fief-holders, most of whom were *Eghaɛbho*. In at least one nineteenth-century succession dispute the *Ezɔmɔ*'s support for one of the candidates appears to have been crucial, but he was not automatically in a position to dictate the succession. In the dispute which occurred when Adolo died, *Ezɔmɔ* Osarogiagbon seems not to have taken an overt stand.

The Palace Organization

The palace was the religious and administrative centre of the nation. The Oba's living quarters were incapsulated in a vast assemblage of council halls, shrines, storehouses, and workshops surrounded by a high compound wall. Immediately behind this wall, where it bounded the avenue separating Ogbe from Orenokhua, stood rows of huge walled quadrangles containing the altars of past kings. Beyond these was the main palace block, where the Oba lived and conducted his government; and, behind it, the *Ɛrie*, where his wives (*iloi*) lived in strict seclusion.

The main palace buildings comprised three major divisions – *Iwebo, Iwɛguae*, and *Ibiwe*. These were the names of three associations (*otu*) of freeborn retainers that administered the royal court and participated in the government. Access to the apartments of each *otu* was confined to its initiated members, except that a court in *Iwebo* served as a common forum for the chiefs of all three associations. The Oba could move freely through the palace. In one of the courts in each division there was a dais on which he sat when he met privately with its chiefs to discuss palace affairs or public policy. Other courts lay outside the jurisdiction of any *otu*, and in these the Palace Chiefs joined with the Oba, the Town Chiefs, and, on occasions, the *Uzama*, in a general council of state assembled for decision-making and judicial purposes.

The three associations were characterized by their primary duties at court. First in rank were the *Iwebo*, who had charge of the Oba's state regalia, including his throne and his ceremonial wardrobe and accountrements. *Unwaguɛ*, as head of *Iwebo*, was head of the palace organization. This was one of the key offices of state, conferring great prestige and patronage on its holder.

The *Iwɛguae* division contained the Oba's private apartments. Its chiefs were his household officers, and his cooks and domestics were chosen from its lower ranks. It also included his pages (*emada*, lit. 'swordbearers'), boys and young men who had been given to the Oba by their fathers and who were bound in absolute service to him until, well into manhood, he saw fit to give them wives and send them into the world as free men. They provided him with a small personal reserve of force and, as they moved about the palace on their errands, they used their eyes and ears to furnish him with intelligence about the intrigues of his courtiers. They also helped him to maintain direct contact with his subjects by arranging private audiences for people who wanted to see him, thus by-passing the official channels of communication through the fief-holders.

Also associated with *Iwɛguae* were the *Ewaisɛ*, the Oba's doctors and diviners, though in some contexts these were regarded as a separate *otu*. They lived in Orenokhua under their own chiefs, but had apartments in the palace, where they prepared and stored the medicines and magical paraphernalia used to protect the king and foster his vitality.

The *Ibiwe* were the keepers of the Oba's wives and children. Their chiefs were divided into two hierarchical series, *Ibiwe* and *Eruɛriɛ Inɛ n'Ibiwe* was the senior chief, but *Osodin*, as head of *Eruɛriɛ*, had direct charge of the *ɛriɛ*. He and his subordinates maintained discipline there, settled disputes between the wives, and reported to the Oba on their conduct and condition. The *Ibiwe* chiefs cared for them in their own homes when they were sick or pregnant and acted as guardians for the Oba's sons, who left the palace in early childhood. *Ibiwe*, as a whole, were responsible for provisioning the *ɛriɛ* — a major task, for, including the servants of the Oba's wives, it housed several hundred women.

Apart from these retainer duties the palace associations performed important political functions, which may be summarized as follows:

(1) They were institutions for recruiting and training personnel for specific administrative, judicial, and ceremonial tasks and for the general exercise of royal authority.

(2) They were organized into an elaborate system of grades and hierarchies which served to channel competition for power.

(3) They were a powerful instrument of centralization and a force for stability in the state.

Every freeborn man in the Benin kingdom considered himself a member of one of the palace *otu*. In nearly every village there were a few men who had actually 'entered the palace', that is had been initiated into an association, but the majority had only a nominal affiliation inherited from their fathers. Nominal membership gave no access to the *otu*'s apartments, no voice in its affairs or share in its revenue. Nor, so far as one can tell, did differential palace affiliations give rise to regularly opposed groups within the village community. What they did was to afford each individual a sense of personal identification with the central institutions of the state, and thus they helped to maintain popular support for a highly exploitative political system. In its relation to the capital, the village had the quality of a peasant culture. Except for the heirs to *enigie* and hereditary priests of community cults, the ultimate pinnacles of ambition lay outside the village. Relatively few managed to transpose themselves from the age-ascriptive hierarchy of the village to the achievement hierarchy of the state, yet virtually everyone had a kinsman or neighbour who had succeeded in doing so. When a man was made an elder *(ɔdiɔn, ɔdafɛn)* of his palace *otu* he automatically became an elder of his village and, to this extent, there was a measure of integration of village and palace hierarchies. Such men gained prestige and influence if they returned to their villages, for they had consorted with the great and might still be used to carry favour with them. The odd villager, even achieved a state title. By doing, so he was lost to the village as a resident, but could use his influence at the centre on behalf of his kith and kin.

To 'enter the palace' was the first step towards a state title in either the Palace or(but see above, p. 56) the Town order. Apart from the heirs to some hereditary offices and subjects of the *Uzama*, any freeborn commoner (but no close agnates of the Oba)[4] could enter the palace, provided he could meet the expense of initiation. Many young men from all over the kingdom were initiated as *ibierugha* ('children' or 'servants' of the apartments). The candidate spent an initial period of seven days in the apartments of his *otu*, during which he paid fees to its chiefs, swore oaths of loyalty and secrecy, and received instructions in his duties. He was then liable to be called upon to perform the more menial tasks that fell to his *otu*, to act as a servant to its chiefs, and to accompany the Oba's emissaries on their missions. By paying additional fees, providing more feasts, and undergoing further rites of passage, the retainer could then seek promotion to the *ɔdiɔn* or *ɔdafɛn* grade and, subsequently, to the highest untitled grade of *ukɔ* (messenger, emissary). To the *ediɔn*, *edafɛn*, and *ikɔ* fell more responsible tasks inside and outside the palace. With increasing responsibility went emancipation from menial tasks, more perquisites, and a greater voice in the association's affairs. Some, like the bead-workers of *Iwebo*, were craftsmen; others had organizational, ritual or ceremonial duties or undertook missions to the villages on the instructions of the Oba and the chiefs.

Once a man became *ukɔ* he was eligible to apply for a title. All non-hereditary titles were at the Oba's disposal when they fell vacant through the death or promotion of the previous holder. There was no constitutional means of preventing him awarding a title to whomsoever pleased him, simply by sending his messenger to inform the successful applicant. Nevertheless, the chiefs of the relevant order or association expected to be consulted, and any aspirant was well advised to seek their advocacy, for they exercised great influence with the Oba. Moreover, if they could not stop the Oba from awarding a title they could prevent its recipient from enjoying its privileges, for the latter

4. It was a feature of the Benin political system that the Oba's close male patrikin were excluded from political office at the centre and from membership of the palace organization. In theory, the Oba's oldest legitimate son succeeded him, the next two or three sons being appointed *enigie* of villages outside the capital, where they were supposed to remain, taking no part in the central direction of state affairs. Younger sons were supposed to reside, after childhood, in a ward of the capital set aside for them under the supervision of a non-royal headman. Though membership of the royal clan conferred a measure of prestige, it afforded little material benefit. The lack of lineage-held land, the exclusion of royals from office, and the rule of primogenitary succession to the kingship meant that neither a single royal lineage nor a series of lineage segments existed as corporate power-seeking groups. The king's daughters and sisters, who were married to senior chiefs, often enjoyed his favour and became rich and powerful. Their descendants were powerfully represented in the *Ibiwe Nekhua* and *EghaƐbho n'Ore* orders (see p. 100).

had to pay fees to the king and both orders of *Eghaɛbho*, after which, at a public ceremony held in the Oba's presence, he was formally inducted by the *Iyasɛ*. Until this was done he could not begin to exercise the prerogatives of his office. Clearly the mechanism for awarding titles afforded much scope for the political arts of compromise and patronage.

In each *otu* there were two main grades of titles — *ekhaɛnbhɛn* and *eghaɛbho*. The latter had precedence over the former, and in each grade of each association all the titles were arranged in a single hierarchical series. In a normal career a retainer would take one or more of the lesser titles before achieving *eghaɛbho* rank, and the senior *erghaɛbho* titles — *Unwaguɛ Ɛribo, Esere, Ɔbazelu, Inɛ, Ɔbazuaye, Osodin* — normally went to men who were already *eghaɛbho*. However, promotion was not automatic. The death of a senior chief did not mean that all those below him moved up one step. All titles were open to competition each time they fell vacant. Moreover, each time a man gave up one title for a more exalted one he had to pay increasingly higher fees and be installed afresh. On the other hand, a title was an investment, for it afforded its holder new opportunities for acquiring wealth.

A high proportion of initiates were sons of retainers and Town Chiefs, and this proportion was undoubtedly higher in the senior grades. This was partly because courtiers' sons were in a better position than most men to afford admission and promotion, but it was also because families resident around the palace maintained a continuing tradition of retainer service. Thus, wealth and family tradition combined to produce something in the nature of an hereditary aristocracy of retainers, through the generations of which administrative and political skills were passed down. Yet, at any one time, all ranks of the palace associations included a leavening of 'new men' who had risen from lowly origins. The strength of the palace organization as an instrument of centralization and stability lay, in part at least, in the way it thus combined a solid core of continuity with an open system of recruitment.

The sons of a senior palace official or Town Chief were distributed between the various *otu*. The manner of their distribution was not rigidly fixed, though the first son and one or more others always joined the father's association. What is significant is that brothers were assigned different palace affiliations. Particular associations did not become identified with particular descent groups, and the non-hereditary, competitive nature of palace titles was strongly maintained. The fact that a man entered his father's *otu* did not imply that he would necessarily remain in it, for it was possible to transfer from one *otu* to another in pursuit of advancement. Once a man became *ukɔ n'iwebo* or *ukɔ n'urhoɛriɛ (Ibiwe)* he was eligible for either a Palace or Town title. Initiates of *Iwɛguae* did not transfer to *Iwebo* or *Ibiwe* because, it is explained, they were too closely acquainted with the mysteries of the Oba's personal life, but they could take certain Town titles. Though most retainers probably remained in the same *otu* throughout their careers, many men held titles consecutively in different associations or orders.

Thus, while most retainers were drawn from a limited section of the population of Benin City, the mechanism of transfer and the non-hereditary status of palace offices ensured that neither the *otu* as groups, nor particular offices within them, were directly representative of descent group interests. The unity of an *otu* was based on the common interests of its members in preserving their prerogatives, but unity was not always easy to maintain in the face of the obligations of individuals to their kinsmen and fellow members of other groups, such as trading associations. Competition between the *otu* existed, but it was limited partly by the need for the palace to present a common front to the Town Chiefs and *Uzama*, and also by a fairly strict segregation of administrative competences.

All three associations were concerned with palace revenues and stores. The *Iwebo* had charge of the Oba's reserves of cowrie shells, beads, cloth, and other trade goods. Tribute in yams, etc., was stored partly by the *Iwɛguae,* who catered for the Oba's personal household and for the feasts he gave his chiefs; and partly by the *Ibiwe,* who were responsible for the provisioning of the wives' quarters. Certain commodities, such as fish, palm wine, and wooden utensils, were supplied to the palace by particular village communities, and certain *ekhaɛnb hɛn* were responsible for seeing that they met their commitments. *Unwaguɛ* and *Ɛribo,* the two senior *Eghaɛbho* of *Iwebo,* had the important and lucrative task of supervising trade with European merchants at the river port of Ughoton, and some of the *eɛhaɛnbhɛn* performed similar functions at the river beaches where the Itsekiri came to trade. Among the *Ibiwe* were a group of 'buyers' *(idenbhin)* who purchased goats, fowls, and other materials for sacrifice at palace rituals. *Ibiwe* were also ultimately responsible for the Oba's own livestock, but most of their missions were concerned with girls betrothed to the Oba, some of whom became his wives, while others were bestowed on men whom the Oba wished to favour. *Osodin* controlled the *igban* oath. This was a custom whereby any subject could declare his own wife or any other woman to be 'the Oba's wife'. He might do this out of anger at the woman's conduct, or as a means of bringing a personal dispute to the Oba's notice. Once the matter had been settled, *Osodin* was called upon to revoke the oath, a service for which he expected remuneration from those concerned.

Apart from these and other regular tasks, officials of all three *otu* were sent to the villages to organize levies, gather information, investigate complaints, represent the Oba at village rituals, and present *enigie* to their people. Assignment to these missions was keenly sought after, for they could be very rewarding. The emissaries not only received customary gifts from the recipients of palace favours but often lived for extended periods at the villagers' expense, and they are said to have been adept at extracting presents from men who wanted to make use of their influence, or fines from those whom they held to have broken taboos and regulations. They could also use their missions to establish trading contacts, negotiate marriages, and make arrangements for loaning out animals, or for settling their dependents in villages to farm for them.

The Palace Chiefs were also responsible for the special occupation groups in Benin City. Each 'guild' was affiliated to one of the palace associations, The craft guilds (such as the bronze-casters, smiths, carvers, leather-workers) were linked with *Iwebo*, the keepers of the royal regalia, as were most of the bands of musicians who performed at palace ceremonies. To the *Iwɛguae*, the keepers of the Oba's person, were allied various groups of ritual specialists, while the *Ibiwe*, who looked after his wives and children, also controlled his sheep - and cattle-keepers. The Palace Chiefs mediated between the Oba and the guilds and received fees from the successors to hereditary guild heads in validation of their titles. The Chiefs were able to draw on the services of the guilds, and they also, no doubt, received their share of the gifts that the Oba bestowed on specialists who pleased him.

Thus, there were many ways in which palace retainers could enrich themselves, and there was a constant flow of wealth from the lower ranks towards the chiefs who distributed tasks. However, the Palace Chiefs were not wholly dependent on these perquisites, for they, and many of the *ekhaɛnbhɛn*, were assigned fiefs from which they drew tribute and labour, and gifts for acting as sponsors and settling disputes.

The number of fiefs held by a chief was broadly proportionate to his rank, and the senior *Eghaɛbho* each controlled many villages. They invested their wealth in trade and the purchase of slaves whom they set down in camps, or attached to existing villages, to farm for them under the surveillance of their own kinsmen.

Finally, the Palace Chiefs were not mere executives carrying out the Oba's instructions. They were his inner circle of advisers and had much influence over him, for he was largely dependent upon them for the exercise of his authority. This was especially the case in the early years of his reign, when the governmental and political experience of the palace staff who had served his father greatly exceeded his own. Together with the Town Chiefs, they formed a council of state which met frequently with the Oba himself to take decisions, try capital charges, and hear appealed disputes. Indeed, the only political sphere from which they were excluded was the military one.

The Town Chiefs

There were two main orders of chiefs associated with Orenokhua, the *Eghaɛbho n'Ore* and the *Ibiwe Nekhua*. According to tradition, the former order was constituted by the twelfth Oba Ewuare, who included in it two already existing titles, *Iyasɛ* and *Esɔgban*, and two others, *Esɔn* and *Osuma*, of his own creation. By the 1890 s there were thirteen titles, of which eight had been added by eighteenth - and nineteenth-century kings.

Apart from *Ologbosɛ*, which was hereditary, all the titles were in the Oba's gift, and any of his freeborn subjects (except the heirs to certain hereditary offices, subjects of the *Uzama*, and the Oba's close agnates) could aspire to them. They were arranged in a single hierarchical sequence, the first four title-holders making up a senior grade. Variously known as *Eghaɛbho n'Ene* (the Four *Eghaɛbho*) or *Ikadal'Ene* (the Four Pillars), the latter were associated with the four days of the Edo week. On his own day each one performed, in his home, the rite of *zematɔn,* which corresponded to a similarly named rite that took place daily at the palace when, as the Edo say, 'the king who is like the day gives food to the day'. It was an act of purification and a renewal and release of the Oba's mystical power. That it had to be performed by the Four *Eghaɛbho* is one manifestation of a constant motif in Benin ritual, namely that the Oba and the Edo are in a relationship of mystical interdependence. In many contexts, this mutual dependence is expressed through acts of ritual communion

between the Oba and his predecessors, on the one hand, and the people
and their dead, on the other; but the notion underlying *zematɔn* is that
the mystical power of the living king has its complement in the living
community.

As we have suggested, the conceptual opposition of 'Oba' and 'Edo'
was linked up with the alien origins of the royal clan. It also had
continuing political connotations. The Oba/*Uzama* opposition, as we
have seen (p.58), was expressed in a mock battle. The potential
hostility between the Oba and Town Chiefs was also played out in
ritual. For example, when the Town Chiefs, swords in hand, danced
homage to the king they were shadowed by his palace retainers, swords
upraised as if to strike them down should they attack him. Unlike the
Uzama, who were hereditary nobles, the Town Chiefs were commoners
who, by their enterprise and the Oba's favour, had risen to positions of
power. In many contexts it was they who were 'the Edo', in opposition
to the Oba and the Palace, for they were held to embody the will and
power of all the people. As the fingers are to the thumb, say the Edo,
so are the Four *Eghaɛbho* to the Oba.

In one context, the Oba's authority, derived from his descent from
Oranmiyan, was opposed to that of the *Uzama,* derived from their
predecessor, the *ediɔn-Uzama*, originators of the state. In another, it
was the *ediɔn-Ɛdo*, the collective dead elders of the whole people, that
stood opposed to the line of dead kings. Every descent group, village
and association had its cult of the *ediɔn*, the past elders who laid down
its customs and continued to uphold its values. Just as the *ɔdiɔnwere*,
the oldest man, was the village head and priest of the dead *ediɔn* of the
village, so the *Esɔgban* was *Ɔdiɔnwere- Ɛdo*. In his official house, which
directly faced the palace across the open space between Ogbe and
Orenokhua, he kept a staff symbolizing the *ediɔn-Ɛdo* whom, with his
fellow *Eghaɛbho*, he served on behalf of the Oba and the people. Why,
one may ask, was *Esɔgban* and not *Iyasɛ* the *Ɔdiɔnwere- Ɛdo?* The Edo
explanation is that the *Iyasɛ* was a war captain who was sent on long
campaigns while *Esɔgban*, his deputy, remained behind to look after
the town. Another explanation, perhaps, is that the *Iyasɛ* was seen as
the chief protagonist of the people against the power of the Palace, a
role hardly consistent with that of a priestly guardian of national peace
and harmony.

A Benin writer has described the *Iyasɛ*, with some truth, as 'the
prime minister and the leader of the opposition'. When the Oba wished
to propose a new law, prosecute a war, or take important administrative

action he was bound to seek the advice and approval of the *Uzama* and his Town and Palace Chiefs. After meeting separately to formulate their views, the three orders assembled with the Oba in a full council of state. The sole right to argue with or censure the Oba in public was held to lie with Town Chiefs and, more especially, with the *Iyasɛ*. When one of them died, the Oba sent his men to claim his lower jaw, 'the jaw he had used to dispute with the Oba'. This act symbolized the ultimate supremacy of the king over the Edo.

Except in this last symbolic act, it was difficult for the Oba to impose his will on the Town Chiefs. They controlled many fiefs, and he was dependent on them for tribute, labour, and troops. Many of them had great personal followings, since the people saw them as their main protection against the demands of palace officials. Apart from *Iyasɛ*, they included two other senior war chiefs, *Ologbosɛ* and *Imaran*, on whom the king regularly depended for the prosecution of his campaigns against rebel vassals. Since no state chiefs could be installed without their acquiescence, the Town Chiefs could render the Oba's appointments ineffective. Finally, the king himself often needed their support lest he became too dependent on his Palace Chiefs.

The best interests of the common people lay in the maintenance of a balance of power between the Town Chiefs and the Palace. Even in the present century, political factions have tended to gather round the Oba and the *Iyasɛ*, and popular support has swung from one side to the other. In tradition, the *Iyasɛ* is regularly portrayed as the focus of opposition to the Oba's power. However, we must beware of over-simplifying. We cannot assume that the interests of the Oba and the Palace Chiefs always coincided, or that the orders themselves always presented unanimous fronts towards each other or towards the Oba. Kin and other loyalties cut across obligations to fellow chiefs. Moreover, it was in the Oba's interests, as in his subjects', to keep a balance between different power groups and to advance his own interests by dividing theirs.

We have already seen that any man who had reached *ukɔ* rank in the palace was qualified for a Town Chief title. An alternative avenue of advancement lay through the *Ekaiwe* association composed mainly of descendants of the Oba's daughters. From *Ekaiwe* the Oba appointed men to titles in the *Ibiwe Nekhua* order, which had mainly military and ceremonial functions. These titles were regarded as a step towards Town Chief rank. Since it was customary for the Oba to marry his daughters to the Town Chiefs, many of the latters' children became

Ekaiwe and *Ibiwe Nekhua*. Thus there was a degree of descent continuity within the Town order. However since *Ekaiwe* status was not the only qualification for Town titles, the Oba was able to inject men of his own choosing into the order. Frequently he filled these titles from the palace ranks, but others were given to men who had made their way in life independently, acquiring wealth through trade, farming, or the pursuit of crafts or war. It was in the Oba's interests to bring such men into positions of authority and to bind them in oath and obligation to him. By allying himself with them he could strengthen his position *vis-à-vis* the palace establishment. Moreover, since there was always a danger that the Town Chiefs would grow too powerful and come into conflict with the king, it was useful to introduce among them men who were as yet little involved in political intrigue. It is worth noting that the *Iyasε* title was often given to men who, though Edo-born, had made their fortunes by trading or slave raiding on the fringes, or beyond the bounds, of the Benin state.

The Oba

It should already be clear that the Oba of Benin was neither a mere ritual figurehead nor a constitutional monarch, but a political king, actively engaged in competition for power. His main political weapon lay in his ability to manipulate the system of Palace and Town offices. By making appointments to vacant titles, creating new ones, transferring individuals from one order to another, introducing new men of wealth and influence into positions of power, and redistributing administrative competences, the kings tried to maintain a balance between competing groups and individuals.

The distribution of authority was such as to prevent any one group from obtaining too much power in a particular administrative sphere. While the Oba depended on his fief-holders for the administration of his territories and the collection of revenue, these were not drawn from a single order, and the holdings of any one of them were fragmented. Moreover, the fact that a village or chiefdom 'belonged to' a chief did not prevent the palace staff entering it on specific royal assignments. The same principle of overlapping authority operated in other contexts. In Benin City the Town Chiefs were associated with and lived in Orenokhua, but they had no *ex-officio* authority in the ward-guilds that made up Orenokhua; the guilds served the Oba through the Palace Chiefs. Nor was there any concentration of military offices in one order. There were two alternative commands, one led by *Ezɔmɔ (Uzama)* assisted by *Ologbose*; the other by *Iyasε* with *Edogun (Ibiwe Nekhua)* as his second-in-command. Their warriors were recruited by the fief-holders on the Oba's instructions. To take a last example, while *Unwague* and *Eribo* were in charge of overseas trade, the Oba appointed their assistants from all three palace *otu*.

Though the Oba had considerable room for manoeuvre in exercising his prerogatives, he was not free to act entirely according to the expediency of the moment. He had to operate within the framework of conventions sanctioned by tradition and sanctified by ritual. To a certain extent, he could rearrange the hierarchical orders, but the uppermost titles in each series remain fixed. Their holders had indispensable ritual functions, and any attempt to displace them met with general opposition. Nor, once he had appointed a man to a title, could he lawfully remove him, except by ordering him to commit suicide, if a treasonable charge was made out against him. Moreover, though in principle the Oba was free to reallocate duties and privileges, if he did so too often, or too arbitrarily, he risked consolidating the chiefs against him. To prevent this he had to play them off against each other, and this could be done only by a judicious devolution of power.

His interests lay in fostering competition for his favours, both within and between chiefly orders and palace associations, and competition for titles was worth while only so long as the relationship between rank, perogatives, and privileges remained fairly constant. When a man applied for a title he did so in the expectation that he would succeed to the fiefs and perquisites that his predecessor had enjoyed. If these expectations had not been regularly fulfilled competition would have broken down.

All monarchies have to face the problem of the succession, and their success in solving it has an important bearing on their continuity and integrity. The succession at Benin had a complicated history, but by the nineteenth century the principle of primogeniture was firmly established. According to tradition, it had been introduced in Ewuakpe's reign, in the early eighteenth century, with the purpose of avoiding succession conflict (Egharevba, 1960: 40). This aim was not achieved, for two of the last three successions before 1897 involved civil war, and in the third it was avoided only because one candidate had secured overwhelming support. In theory there should have been no dispute, for it was the Oba's right to make his heir apparent by installing him as *Edaiken* of Uselu. In fact, none of the nineteenth century kings did this, because, it is said, they were afraid that their heirs, once officially recognized, would begin to accumulate too much power. The result was that, in each case, factions formed round two of the Oba's oldest sons. The rewards of success lay in the patronage that the new Oba could dispense, and in the influence that his backers hoped to exert through him. In the last resort force was the decisive factor, but each faction was concerned to validate its candidate's right to succeed. The dispute was conducted in terms of the relative age and legitimacy of the rival brothers, the arguments employed being too complicated to detail here. What is significant is that the factions that emerged seem to have cross-cut rather than followed cleavages between the main power groups described above. Competition for the kingship was not, as in Fulani Bida (Nadel, 1942) or Zaria (Smith, 1960), between dynastic segments, but between two brothers. The royal clan had no corporate existence as a power segment and no say in the choice of a successor. The rival candidates had to assemble support piecemeal from each of the main chiefly orders and from influential men outside them. When the Oba died it was the senior Palace Chief, *Unwaguε*, who formally named his successor, in a public gathering of chiefs — the convention being maintained that the late king had disclosed the identity of the legitimate heir to him. But he did so in response to the *Iyasε's* inquiry, and it was the latter who installed the heir as *Edaikεn,* after he had paid fees to the Town and Palace orders. Before he could be enthroned he had to pay further fees to the *Uzama*, and it was they who inaugurated his reign. Only then could he enter his palace, which, in the meantime, remained in *Unwaguε's* custody. Thus, if civil war was to be avoided one of the candidates had to secure overwhelming backing in all three orders.

The new Oba had no right to dismiss the chiefs appointed by his father, and since at the beginning of his reign they were more experienced in the direction of state affairs than he was, he was highly dependent on them, especially the Palace Chiefs. At the same time he had to satisfy his personal supporters, many of whom, up to the time of his enthronement, had lacked official positions. It was customary for a new king to create two new titles in the Town order and in each palace association, so he could give immediate rewards to his closest and most ambitious henchmen. It was difficult, however, for him to place these new titles anywhere but at the bottom of the various hierarchical series. In the early years of Ovonramwen's reign there was a bitter contest between 'those who came with the Oba' *(iguɔmɔre)* and the old palace guard. Between 1889 and 1897, as a result of this struggle, and through dissension within the palace *otu*, a number of chiefs were murdered and others put to death or ordered to commit suicide by the Oba.

Ovonramwen was able to use the vacancies caused by these killings and by natural deaths to introduce and promote his favourites into positions of power. Traditions suggest that this may have been the normal pattern of events in the early part of a reign and that, as time went by, the Oba was in a position gradually to increase his personal power.

The kings of Benin seem to have had more security of tenure than many of their African counterparts. It is true that two kings of the eighteenth and nineteenth centuries were removed by force, shortly after they had occupied the palace, and replaced by their brothers, but once the Oba had survived the initial succession crisis it became progressively difficult to remove him. It is conceivable that some kings may have been despatched by secret regicide, but there was no instance of constitutional dethronement after the introduction of primogenitary succession. The explanation lies partly in the mode of succession itself, in the doctrine that succession can be validated only by the proper performance, by the senior son, of his father's funeral rites. The dogma was that kings were chosen in 'heaven' not by men. This did not prevent violent conflicts for the throne, but it did ensure that the ideological issue in such contests lay in the age and legitimacy of the rival aspirants, not in their personal qualities. As the Oba was not, in theory, chosen on the basis of his fitness to rule – whatever happened in practice – he could not, in theory, be removed if his conduct did not live up to expectations. But the explanation lies, too, in the balance of right and power between the main orders of chieftancy. We have seen that no single order could, by itself, determine the identity of the legitimate heir. Nor could any of them claim undisputed right to bring his reign to an end. While the *Uzama* 'owned' the kingship, the Town Chiefs represented the people's will, and the Palace Chiefs were both the king's servants and the custodians of his person. Nor was there, in Benin, any institution corresponding to the *Ogboni* of Oyo (Morton-Williams, 1960: 364-6) which could co-ordinate public opinion and bind the chiefs to common action. The Oba may have feared that he would be secretly disposed of, yet his best chance of survival lay not in accepting the role of a passive constitutional monarch, but in using his power to maintain competition and dissension between his chiefs.

In emphasizing the more obviously political aspects of the Benin kingship, as we have done in this essay, we inevitably distort that institution. For the Oba was, of course, no ordinary political leader. In succeeding his father he gained access to powerful instruments of political control and manoeuvre. But by that same act of succession he ceased to be a mere man. Once installed, dogma had it, the king needed neither food nor sleep, nor would he ever die. In short, he was a divine king, the living vehicle for those mystical forces by which his predecessors, from the inception of the dynasty, had ensured the vitality and continuity of the nation. His principal sacred functions were: first, to maintain the bonds of ritual communion between himself and his predecessors, on the one hand, and his people and their dead, on the other; and, secondly, to foster his own magical powers and to deploy them for the good of his people. The sanctity of his authority lay in the indispensability of these functions, which only a legitimately enthroned king could perform.

In an essay of this length it has been impossible to do more than hint, from time to time, at the extent to which the political and mystical aspects of kingship interpenetrated. The key problem of the Benin polity − the relationship between political kingship and divine kingship − is left unresolved. Here we can only suggest some of the lines along which it might be approached. Firstly, we would need to consider how, in both organizational and ideological terms, divine kingship performed its general unifying functions; to show, for example, how the worship of past kings was interwoven, in contrapuntal fashion, with the worship of various categories of the dead, at all levels of the social system; and to consider the links between ideas and practices relating to the person of the living Oba, and the general Edo dogma of personality and its expression in ritual. We would have to explore the role of the kingship in Edo notions about the interaction of the natural with the social world; and to show how local cults of nature deities were incorporated, by organizational and mythological techniques, into a state pantheon in which the Oba, as 'king of the dry land', was identified with *Olokun*, 'king of the waters'.

More specifically, it would be necessary to demonstrate how mutual ritual obligations, sanctioned by the general world-view, served to counter disruptive tendencies in the pursuit of conflicting political interests. Every political role, we would find, implied ritual roles. The distribution of rights, duties, and privileges among the complex hierarchies of officialdom received constant expression in an endless series of palace rituals. The continuity of the state and the sanctity of its institutions were reiterated in ritual by linking each significant office and institution with the king who had created it or shown it special favour, and by giving it a part to play in the rites addressed to him. The loyalty of the chiefs to the king was constantly reaffirmed. One may mention here the Festival of the Beads, in which the regalia of the king and his chiefs, symbols of their authority, were brought together and re-dedicated, by human sacrifice, to the common purpose. At *Igue*, the central rite of divine kingship, the royal priests blessed not only the king's Head but those of his *Eghaɛbho* too.

Finally, it would be necessary to consider how the whole ideational complex centred on the king's divinity interacted with individual and group interests in the day-to-day political life of the kingdom. This would be the most difficult of our tasks. For it would be necessary to balance those factors which contributed to the strength of the Oba's position against those factors which placed restraint on his freedom of action. On the one hand, we should have to try to assess the force of the universal belief in his supernatural powers, a belief sustained and fostered by the king himself, by the multitudinous ritual functionaries who were directly beholden to him, and by the chiefs themselves, whose authority, in the eyes of the people, derived from him. Attitudes towards the kingship were a complex of affection and awe, pride, and fear, but the overriding notion, I believe, was one of fearfulness. He was the giver of life but also the giver of death. 'Death, Great One', 'Child of the Sky whom we pray not to fall and cover us, Child of the Earth whom we implore not to swallow us up' − these are the kinds of epithets most frequently used of him. One of the most important meanings of the human sacrifice, for which Benin became notorious, lay in its capacity to demonstrate the sole right of the Oba to take human life. He was addressed as *Omo* 'Child' to distinguish him from all other men, who, in relation to him, were *eviɛn*, 'slaves'. On the other hand, we would have to take account of the fact that the Oba was unable to fulfil his ritual and mystical functions without the active participation, in their sanctified roles, of the representatives of the people. Refusal, on the part of the chiefs, to perform their ritual obligations was one of the most powerful weapons that they could use against monarchical tyranny, for, as we have suggested, the sanctity of the king's authority lay in acceptance of his ability to control those mysterious forces on which the vitality of human society depended. [5]

5. The data used in this essay were gathered during field researches supported by the Royal Anthropological Institute (Horniman Studentship) and the International African Institute (Research Fellowship), and during the period 1956-61 when I was attached to the Benin Historical Research Scheme (Director, Dr K. O. Dike), University of Ibadan. To all these bodies and to their relevant financial sponsors, my grateful thanks are due.

Continuities and Discontinuities in Pre-colonial and Colonial Benin Politics (1897-1951)

This paper sketches the broad outlines of Benin political history between the years immediately before 1897, when the independence of this ancient West African kingdom was abruptly terminated, and 1951, when Nigerian regional and national politics had begun to make a direct impact on its internal affairs. Despite their subjection to alien rule and the destruction of their traditional framework of government, the Benin (Edo) people — especially the residents of the capital — displayed an unflagging appetite for the game of politics. Their exuberant and fluid factionalism and their tendency to internal, unstable dichotomization constantly taxed the wits of their colonial over-rulers, whose ability to understand and control these processes was limited by their lack of adequate information about Edo political culture. On several occasions the British officers on the spot found that the 'native authority' recognized by the government as the instrument for the implementation of its objectives, had become transformed into an unpopular 'ruling' clique, to which they themselves were assimilated; and from which, in order to avoid a complete breakdown of order, they had, sooner or later, to withdraw their support.

One approach to ·the explanation of these insurrectionary crises would be to regard them simply as responses to alien rule. Certainly, determined resistance to regulations and measures imposed from outside Benin society is a component of all of them. But to adopt this starting-point is, I believe, to take too negative a view of the political skills and propensities of the Benin people themselves. In this paper I try to account for the pattern of political conflict and the course of political change by looking at them from the 'inside', that is in terms of the pursuit, by the Edo themselves, of individual and group interests, in an environment of changing structures, goals, and opportunities. I also attempt to explore the ways in which the effects of external impulses to change (political, economic, educational, ideological, etc.), are shaped and modified by concepts, norms, and strategies derived from the pre-colonial polity and from successive phases of interaction and accommodation between indigenous and exotic structures.

GOVERNMENT AND POLITICS IN NINETEENTH-CENTURY BENIN

The late nineteenth-century Benin polity has been briefly described elsewhere (Bradbury, 1967). Here we can do no more than point up some of its salient characteristics. From its apogee in the sixteenth and seventeenth centuries, the Benin state had suffered a prolonged decline, interrupted by periods of resurgence. Immediately before the British conquest the king's writ still ran, however uncertainly and intermittently, over an area considerably wider than that of the Benin Division, which the British were eventually to demarcate as his successors' sphere of competence; and which roughly corresponded to what I have called the Benin Kingdom proper, that is, the core area of the Benin empire (Bradbury, 1967, pp.3-4). We need be no more precise than this because the politics with which this paper is concerned are essentially politics of the capital. Though some village chiefs may be regarded as having been marginal to it, the pre-colonial political class was, to all intents and purposes, wholly resident in Benin City (Edo), which contained perhaps an eighth of the kingdom's quarter of a million or so inhabitants. The rest of the population was distributed through several hundred villages with populations ranging from a dozen or two to as many as four thousand souls; a typical village might have four or five hundred people. Between the political life of the village (Bradbury, 1957, 1967) and the capital there were marked discontinuities. A villager who wished to participate in the direction of the nation's affairs had to leave home and seek advancement through one of the various hierarchies located in the capital. It was by no means impossible for an able and enterprising man to do this, but villagers started at a considerable disadvantage compared with the sons of the king's chiefs and retainers, in terms both of family wealth and influence and of opportunities to acquire political and administrative expertise in the normal course of growing up. Thus the political class, and *a fortiori* the political elite within it,[1] were in large measure self-perpetuating.

1. I use the term 'political class', following Bottomore (1964, p.8) 'to refer to all those groups which exercise political power or influence, and are directly engaged in struggles for political leadership'. 'Political elite' refers in this paper to those who actually hold offices and especially, so far as the traditional polity is concerned, to titled chiefs.

Family continuity must be clearly distinguished from descent-group eligibility for office. As compared with most African states (even nineteenth-century Buganda or Dahomey) corporate descent groups played a negligible role in Benin political organization. Inheritance and succession were patrilineal, but lineages were shallow and weakly corporate. Land — the basic resource — was vested not in kin groups but in kin heterogeneous ward and village communities. In the absence of corporate rights to resources, a marked primogenitary emphasis in the rules of inheritance and succession — including succession to the minority of political offices that were hereditary — served to weaken rather than to strengthen kin-group solidarity. Neither at the village nor at the state level were political roles conceived in terms of the representation of descent groups.

The conduct of public affairs was vested in the *oba* (king) and the titled members of a number of tiered and opposed chiefly orders. Three orders — the *uzama*, the *eghaebho n'ore*, and the *eghaebho n'ogbe* — stood out in prestige and authority above the rest.

The *uzama* comprised six hereditary nobles and (in principle) the *oba*'s heir-apparent (*edaiken*). The hereditary character of their offices, transmitted by primogeniture, set them apart from the other orders, whose ranks were filled by royal appointment. Originators and custodians of the kingship, guardians of sacrosanct custom, the six nobles were looked upon as the 'elders' of the state. We may describe them as the king's peers. In their own villages, just outside the inner walls of the capital, they enjoyed relative immunity from interference by the *oba*. On the other hand, they participated less in the day-to-day conduct of public affairs and were less powerful as a group than either *eghaebho* order. Nevertheless, their prestige and moral authority carried considerable weight, especially in times of national crisis. Individually, one or two of them had important executive functions — especially the *ezomo* who, as one of the two regular commanders of state armies, was always a force to be reckoned with.

For commoners the *eghaebho* titles constituted the pinnacles of political ambition. They were the object of intense competition which all freeborn men (except the *oba*'s agnates, heirs to hereditary offices, and subjects of the *uzama*) were, in principle, free to enter. Formal qualifications for a title had normally to be acquired by initiation into and promotion through the grades of one of the associations of palace retainers. Once a man reached the senior untitled grade (*uko*), he was eligible to apply to the *oba* for a title, either in his own or another palace associations, or in the *eghaebho n'ore* order. Within each association, individual titles were grouped into two tiers (*eghaebho n'ogbe* and *ekhaenbhent*); and each tier titles were arranged in a single hierarchical series. Promotions from one title to another could be sought either within or across the boundaries of orders and associations. Few men reached the highest ranks without first having held one or more lesser titles. An alternative route to *eghaebho n'ore* titles lay through the *ekaiwe* association and the *ibiwe nekhua* order, membership of which was reserved for descendants of the *oba's* daughters (Bradbury, 1967, p.27). While it was not impossible for rich men whom the *oba* wished to favour to acquire the essential formal qualifications summarily, progress to the top was normally long and arduous. It was also expensive, for each advancement required the payment of substantial fees to the *oba* and members of all the non-hereditary orders, and the provision of costly entertainments. On the other hand, a title brought its holder influence and prestige, the ability to dispense patronage, a range of secular and ritual competences, rights to tribute and labour, a share in the revenue of the holder's order, and other perquisites.

Each retainer association had a range of functions within the *oba*'s palace – the care of royal regalia, the commissariat of the king's household, the care of his wives and children, etc. As well as administrating these functions, the palace chiefs, especially the *eghaebho n'ogbe*, played a major role in the day-to-day conduct of public affairs. In the king's name they despatched retainers to the villages on a variety of fiscal, political, and ritual missions; regulated the conduct of overseas trade; managed state revenue; organized the services of special occupation groups, and so forth. The senior *eghaebho n'ogbe*– *unwague, eribo, ine n'ibiwe, osodin, esere* – were in a position to wield great personal power and patronage and to exert influence on the *oba* himself. Together with the king, the *eghaebho n'ore* and, on occasions, the *uzama*, they constituted a state council which met frequently to take major policy decisions, try capital cases, and hear appealed disputes.

Formally senior, as an order, to the *eghaebho n'ogbe* – the prestige ranking of titles across order boundaries was a different matter – the *eghaebho n'ore* had fewer routine administrative roles. Although they were appointed by the king and exercised authority in his name, they were looked upon as the defenders of the commonalty against the threat of palace autocracy. Their leader, the *ivase*, was 'the *oba*'s first subject'. It was he who inducted all new title-holders in the king's

name. As a military commander, his rank was at least equal to that of
the *ezomo*. On the other hand, he was regarded as the champion of the
Edo and he had a unique right to challenge the king's actions in public.
In the 'conscious model' of the Benin polity it was the *iyase* who waş
most likely to emerge as the leader of any anti-*oba* or anti-palace
faction. In dynastic traditions major political crises are repeatedly
expressed in terms of personal confrontations between *oba* and *iyase*.
The continuing effectiveness of the *eghaebho n'ore* as a constitutional
check on the power of the *oba* and the palace was, in part, a function
of their ritual roles. The mystical compact between the *oba* and his
subjects, on which the legitimacy of the political order depended, could
not be maintained without their cooperation (Bradbury, 1967, pp 25-26).

This elaborate configuration of unitary and segmented orders,
graded associations, and tiered and opposed hierarchies, with the
politico-divine kingship at its centre, constituted both the enduring
framework of government and the arena in which the political game
was played. As an overall pattern of government, evolved over several
centuries, sanctified by tradition, and constantly reaffirmed in ritual, it
was, as far as we can tell, never seriously challenged. Its structural
details and operational rules were, of course, subject to revision through
the interplay of conflicting interests and environmental factors; but
both oral traditions and the accounts of visiting Europeans suggest that
its main outlines had remained remarkably stable. As a political arena it
offered wide scope for intrigue and competition, and all the available
evidence suggests that factional alignments were extremely fluid. Each
corporate segment of the political elite was jealous of its collective
interests and strove to defend and expand them *vis-à-vis* other segments
and the king himself. On the other hand, segmental solidarities were
subject to the weakening influences of intensive internal rivalry (see
below) and of cross-cutting interests and obligations. The character of
the non-hereditary title system was itself such as to promote
individualistic opportunism. The fact that the great majority of these
appointive titles constituted a single promotional system made loyalty
to a particular segment contingent upon personal ambitions and
opportunities. The *oba*, the 'establishment' within the various
hierarchies, and individuals looking for advancement all sought to
manipulate the system to their own advantage. It was necessary for the
ambitious young politician to enter into alliances in many directions.
Bonds of kinship, affinity, and friendship cut across the boundaries of
chiefly orders and served as a basis for political cooperation and

intrigue. There were, too, certain corporate interest groups which, though marginal to the political order itself, had important implications for it. The most significant of these were a number of trading associations, each of which controlled one of the routes along which European goods, obtained at riverside beaches in exchange for palm-oil and other local products, were transported to inland markets; the return traffic being in beads, slaves, and other commodities for internal consumption. Participation in this trade, open only to initiated members of the associations, constituted one of the principle sources of economic support for the Benin political elite. Chiefs invested their spoils of office in slaves purchased at the hinterland markets, whom they placed in villages and forest camps to farm for them. Detailed accounts of the operation of these associations are difficult to recover but it is clear that they cross-cut the chiefly orders and that their interests were potentially in conflict with those of the *oba* and the chiefs of the *iwebo* association who were responsible to him for the regulation of the riverside trade.

Furthermore, while many governmental functions were segregated as between orders and associations, some of the most important ones were distributed among chiefs of several or all the orders. There were for example, two alternative military commands. The *ezomo (uzama)* had as his deputy the *ologbose (eghaebho n'ore)*; while the *iyase (eghaebho n'ore)* was seconded by the *edogun* head of the *ibiwe nekhua* order. Again the *unwague* and *eribo*, as heads of the *iwebo* association, regulated overseas trade, but their assistants were recruited from other palace associations. The functions of territorial administration were much more widely dispersed. Title-holders of all orders were each assigned one or a number of scattered villages for which they were responsible to the *oba* for the levying of tribute and labour and for military recruitment; and from which they drew labour and tribute for their own support. But the power of 'benefice-holders' over their villages was limited by the fact that the *oba,* through his Palace Chiefs, could send his retainers into their villages on a wide variety of missions. This dispersal of functions was clearly designed to prevent concentration of particular kinds of power in particular segments, but it also implied a complex ramification and interlocking of interests. One should not, therefore, expect to find that the pattern of political conflict directly mirrored the formal group structure of the political elite. Documentary and oral sources both present evidence of a fluid factionalism, in which political alignments were as likely to cross-cut as to coincide with formal cleavages.

In its mystical aspect the kingship supplied the ideological keystone of the political system. The continuity and integrity of the polity depended upon (a) the commitment of all sectors of the population to the belief that their well-being depended on the proper deployment of the *oba*'s own divine energy, and of his ritual authority as the intermediary with his predecessors; and upon (b) their acceptance of the need for the king, chiefs, and people to cooperate in ensuring that these functions were fruitfully deployed. Every title had its ritual roles and the higher a chief's rank the more indispensable his ritual functions. The economic support afforded by the people to the political elite was given in token of their performance of these functions. Villagers strove to defend themselves against the exploitative proclivities of chiefs and retainers by playing them off against each other; they did not challenge the legitimate basis of their authority.

The condition of the polity at any particular time was a function of the interaction of these ideological factors with the pursuit of group and individual interests. In the political process the king himself played a crucial role. According to his skills and opportunities (which were variable at different stages of his career as well as contingent on environmental factors), he could be a near autocrat, the instrument of a palace oligarchy, or a judicious statesman maintaining an equable balance of power. For brief periods effective power might lie with a faction setting itself up in opposition to the palace, but this was a situation conducive to violent conflict. Unless it succeeded either in bringing the *oba* over to its side or in placing its own candidate on the throne, such a faction would have difficulty in retaining popular support for very long.

The *oba*'s capacity to exercise personal power depended on his ability to maintain a balance between competing groups and individuals within the political elite; and (the two factors were closely related) his success in keeping open multiple channels of communication with other sectors of the population. The flexibility of the appointive system and the subtle distribution of segregated and dispersed competences bear witness to the relative success of kings, over the centuries, in preserving their freedom of manoeuvre. In their struggles with the chiefs they were hampered by the fact that their mystical roles confined them within the palace. On the other hand, the *dignitas* and mystical authority of the kingship, and the existence in Benin City of numerous groups of ritual functionaries and craft specialists whose interests were closely bound

up with those of the *oba*, constituted built-in advantages. The king's
power was constrained by the interplay of immutable 'constitutional'
conventions with political and environmental factors. There is no room
to catalogue these constraints here; a few examples must suffice. Thus,
while the king alone could confer vacant titles and create new titles, a
title, once conferred, whether by the reigning king or his predecessor,
could not be taken away. Again, by such techniques as refusing to
accept title fees or simply by refusing to collaborate with the new
title-holder, the chiefs had the collective power to render his
appointments ineffective. Within limits the *oba* could confer favours on
his supporters by altering the ranking of titles within hierarchies but the
uppermost titles in each order remained sacrosanct, by virtue of age-old
tradition and their indispensable ritual functions. He could seek to alter
the distribution of power by re-allocating administrative competences,
but the limits of expediency in this respect were set by the need to
maintain a viable balance between the expected and actual rewards of
political competition. An *oba* who transgressed such basic rules of the
political game as these risked consolidating the chiefs against him. By
boycotting his councils and his rituals they could render him politically
ineffective.

Major political crises occurred when the 'normal' scatter of
counterbalancing sectional and personal interests gave way to a radical
dichotomization of the political class around particular crucial issues.
From oral tradition, European chronicles, and the testimony of old
informants, three recurrent types of crisis can be discerned. In two
cases the nature of the polarization is clear. The first of these was
succession conflict. In nineteenth-century Benin the rule of legitimate
primogenitary succession was universally acknowledged. In theory the
reigning king made his rightful heir apparent by conferring on him the
title *edaiken* and establishing him in his own court at the village of
Uselu. In practice — either because they feared that a designated
successor might constitute a threat to their own tenure, or because they
found some other political advantage in leaving the issue in doubt —
king after king failed to do so. The result, in each case, was a struggle
for the throne between two sons of the king, who sought to justify
their respective claims in terms of conflicting criteria of legitimacy.
Each candidate proceeded to build up a faction by seeking two kinds of
support: (*a*) by assembling a personal following of 'strong', ambitious
younger men, recruited on the basis of friendship, clientage,
matrilateral kinship, affinal ties, etc.; and (*b*) by seeking the patronage

of influential chiefs in each sector of the political elite. It was necessary to do this because the wide dispersal of power (particularly in respect of military and territorial-administrative functions) made it impossible for any single order to determine the succession. This dispersal of power and authority was reflected in the ceremonial procedures by which the kingship was transmitted, the head of each major order having an indispensable function to perform (Bradbury, 1967, p.30). In practice the succession was determined by the relative strength of the factions mobilized by the rival brothers, tested, if necessary, by armed conflict. Two of the last three successions of the pre-colonial era were settled by civil war.

The second type of major crisis, which we can characterize as a struggle between the *old guard* and the *new men*, was a direct consequence of the first. As we shall describe a particular struggle of this type below (p.206) we need say no more about it here.

It is much more difficult to determine the nature of the polarization process in the third type of major conflict that we wish to distinguish. Oral traditions, and the one contemporary account of a crisis of this type (Nyendael, in Bosman, 1967, p. 466, and the present writer's note, p. 574), invariably describe a contest for power between the *oba* and one chief or a group of chiefs, leading to the formation of dichotomous factions and often to civil war. Some of these confrontations are explained, in very general terms, as being due to the *oba*'s disregard for his chief's prerogatives, or vice versa; others as resulting from a particular tyrannous or outrageous act on the king's part; still others as issuing from a personal quarrel between the *oba* and one of his chiefs. No major confrontations of this sort appear to have occurred in the late nineteenth century and folk memories of earlier crises are too vague to allow us to determine the detailed composition of the opposed factions. In some cases the evidence appears to point to a contest between the *eghaebho n'ore* and a palace clique; in others it seems more likely that the factions cut across the chieftaincy orders. In all these crises, however, one must infer the presence of issues of sufficiently wide concern to provide common ground between groups and individuals whose interests were 'normally' divergent. We are not concerned, in this paper, to speculate about what these issues might have been. However, broadly analogous confrontations, consciously assimilated by the Edo themselves to the major conflicts recounted in dynastic traditions, recur during the colonial period. In the following pages one of our aims is to analyse the process of dichotomization as it appears in these conflicts and to identify the issues involved.

BENIN POLITICAL HISTORY, 1897-1951[2]

The interregnum, 1897-1914

Benin City (Edo) fell to a British military force on 17 February 1897. Leaving aside the complex antecedents of this débâcle, we need only note that the immediately precipitating event was an attack, some six weeks earlier, on a British delegation *en route* to seek negotiations with the *oba*; its main declared purpose being to persuade him to remove embargoes which he had placed on external trade. *Oba* Ovonramwen fled from his palace as the troops approached and remained in hiding in the bush until the following August, when some of his chiefs, who had made their peace with the British, persuaded him to submit. At his 'trial', which began on 1 September, no evidence was forthcoming to indicate that the *oba* had been personally responsible for the massacre; indeed witnesses unanimously asserted that he had tried to restrain his chiefs from attacking the white men. After the trial the stated intention of the Consul-General, Sir Ralph Moor, was to make use of the *oba*'s authority. He told him that 'he could no longer order the people about as before, but that proper villages would be apportioned to him, with servants, food and all other necessaries as for a big chief, for he would probably still be the biggest chief, that position depending on his ability to govern. At the same time the Consul-General proposed to take the king and two or three other chiefs with their wives and servants on a tour for a year or so to Calabar, Lagos and the Yoruba country to see how other lands were governed' (Ling Roth, 1903, App.III). These proposals aroused the *oba*'s deep mistrust and on 9 September, the day appointed for their further discussion, he failed to appear. When a party was sent out to apprehend him he tried unsuccessfully to escape, whereupon Moor not only ordered his banishment to Calabar but announced that he would never again be allowed to return to Benin.

Ovonramwen's banishment removed any possibility that the old political order might be reconstituted as an instrument of British rule. The various hierarchies and structural oppositions of the traditional polity had all been defined with reference to the kingship, and with its elimination they collapsed. The charred ruins of the royal palace were left deserted, and the palace associations, which had been the chief mechanism for recruiting, training, and allocating administrative

2. Much of the material relating to the colonial period was obtained from the Benin Provincial and Divisional Offices in the early 1950s. At that time I did not envisage writing a historical narrative and my ignorance of historiographic techniques was even greater than it is now. Consequently my notes are very inconsistent in respect of the identification of sources. Where possible I quote file numbers or indicate the nature of the source document in the notes below

personnel, as well as for chanelling competition for power, ceased to have any meaningful existence. Since most important titles had been in the king's gift they could no longer be filled when their incumbents died. Even the heirs to hereditary offices required the *oba*'s approval before they could rightfully assume their fathers' titles. The kingship rituals, one of whose principal functions had been to reaffirm, and maintain support for, the distribution of authority and precedence, were abandoned.

In these circumstances, we should not expect to find anything like the degree of continuity between the pre-colonial and colonial political systems that has been described for such kingdoms as Zaria (Smith, 1960) where the colonial rulers were able to carry out their policies through going concerns. The first British administrators at Benin had to construct an administrative *bricolage* (Lévi-Strauss, 1962, p.26 ff.) out of their own meagre resources of personnel and the fragments of a shattered indigenous polity. At the outset they had very little information about the interior of the kingdom or its outlying territories to the north and east. The establishment of effective authority over these areas was a lengthy process, involving the constant threat and frequent use of force, but it could not have been accomplished at all without the more or less willing cooperation of many of the Benin City chiefs who had exercised authority under Ovonramwen. The need to maintain the authority of these chiefs was a constant theme of early policy statements.

On taking office, the first Resident was instructed to ascertain who were the 'reliable' chiefs and to enrol them in a central Native Council which would advise him on custom, sit with him in judicial hearings, and help to set the government's economic, educational, and other policies in motion.[3] From the British point of view, the chiefs constituted an unstructured aggregate whose status as a ruling class was evident from their possession of titles, wealth, and influence. Most of the early council chiefs were, in fact, of *uzama* or *eghaebho* rank, but they were not chosen, or accorded authority, with reference to their specific placement in the traditional orders of chieftaincy. It was, indeed, to be many years before the British began to obtain even an approximate understanding of the structure of the traditional polity; and even if they had understood it they could not have operated it in the absence of a king. The basis on which the council chiefs were selected, therefore, was simply the Resident's assessment of the

3. P.2/97. C. & C.C. to Res. Benin 25-3-97.

capacity of individual chiefs (and some non-titled men) to command obedience and respect, and of their willingness and ability to carry out his orders. Some of the older chiefs who failed to win the confidence of the new rulers, or declined to adjust themselves to the new order, faded into obscurity. It was those who most rapidly perceived the personal advantages to be gained from cooperation that emerged as the new elite, and prominent among them were some of the ambitious younger politicians of Ovonramwen's reign, men whose fortunes were rising before the débâcle, and who had avoided becoming too deeply implicated in the massacre of the British officials.

Outstanding among these latter was a man called Agho.[4] He had been intimately associated with Ovonramwen from childhood, for the latter, as Prince Idugbowa, had been placed in the care of Agho's father, Ogbeide Oyo whom *Oba* Adolo had made *ine n'ibiwe*. In the early 1880s Idugbowa, tired of waiting for his father to designate him as the official heir *(edaiken)*, had defiantly established himself in a house at Uselu, close to the Edaiken's palace, a gesture which affirmed his determination not to be deprived of the throne which, as the oldest son, he regarded as his birthright. From Uselu he proceeded not only to curry favour with the senior chiefs who would have a major voice in the determination of the succession, but also to build up a strong personal following of young ambitious men who would fight for him if the need should arise. For it was clear that he would be opposed for the throne by his younger brother, Orhokhorho, whose claim rested on the fact that, unlike Idugbowa, he had been born after his father's accession. In the ensuing struggle which reached its climax after Adolo's death in 1889, Agho's role might perhaps best be described as that of a manager of Idugbowa's faction. In the event civil war was averted. After his father's death Idugbowa made his determination plain by repeatedly marching through the capital at the head of a large, vociferous force – a gesture which probably helped to speed agreement among the most influential senior chiefs that he was the rightful heir.

One of a newly enthroned *oba*'s prerogatives was to create one or two new titles in each order of chieftaincy, which he could use to reward his most active personal supporters. For Agho, Ovonramwen coined the title *obaseki*, placing it third among the *eghaebho* of the *iweguae* association. This was easily the highest rank accorded any of

4. This brief account of the political conflicts of Ovonramwen's reign and of Agho's role in them is constructed from oral testimony, and in particular that of the late Chief Eghobamien, who was Agho's paternal nephew and a young servant to Idugbowa both at Uselu and, after his accession, in the palace.

the new titles. Agho's assignment to *iweguae* was an important strategic manoeuvre. It was in the *iweguae* section of the palace that the *oba* had his living quarters and his personal commissariat. Thus his security depended to a considerable extent on the loyalty of the *iweguae* chiefs. That Ovonramwen mistrusted them is evident from the fact that for some two years after his accession he is said to have refused to live in *iweguae*. It was only when the ranks of that association had been thinned out by a series of ruthlessly executed manoeuvres, that he consented to do so.

The sequence of violent episodes that marked the early years of Ovonramwen's reign, and which resulted in the deaths of a considerable number of chiefs and palace retainers, partly reflected the *oba's* determination to root out any lingering loyalty to his brother. An overlapping, and longer-term source of conflict was the struggle for ascendancy between the 'old guard' of senior chiefs surviving in office from the previous reign and the 'new men', Ovonramwen's personal clients (known as *iguomore*, lit. 'I come with the child' − i.e. the new *oba*), who were now impatient to reap the highest rewards. The *oba's* position between these two factions was a difficult one. He was strongly obligated to the senior chiefs who had ensured his peaceful accession, and highly dependent upon their political and administrative experience. On the other hand he could not afford to ignore the importunities of his personal followers, whose support he needed if he were to obtain any freedom of action in the face of the power of the entrenched old guard. The dominant political personality at the beginning of his reign was Egiebo, the *unwague*, head of the *iwebo* association and the most senior palace chief, a man of formidable character and influence whose backing had been eagerly sought by both rivals for the throne. While lending support to the *iguomore* in their efforts to dislodge other established chiefs, Ovonramwen was at pains to remain on good terms with the *unwague*. By 1895, however, the latter had so overplayed his hand in seeking to make the *oba* the instrument of his own power as to incur the hostility of his own *iwebo* chiefs. Accusing him, among other misdeeds, of plotting with the British, and possibly assuming that the *oba* would be glad to be rid of him, they eventually waylaid and assassinated him. Ovonramwen demanded immediate vengeance and, when four of the *eghaebho* of *iwebo* had been killed or had committed suicide, it was to *Obaseki* Agho's influence that the remaining conspirator turned in seeking reconciliation with the *oba*. The effect of this insurrection within the *iwebo* association had been to create five vacancies among the senior palace positions. These afforded the *oba* new opportunities to exercise his patronage and opened up possibilities of promotion to the *iguomore*. Agho, as the recognized leader of the new men, was now in an enviable position, and by the time of the débâcle, though by no means first informal rank, he was certainly one of the most powerful palace chiefs.

Obaseki fled with the *oba* before the British advance on the capital, but he soon returned to Benin and made his submission. Some accounts say it that was the *oba* who sent him back to try to negotiate a settlement. However this may be, it is clear that by the time the *oba* gave himself up the old patron-client relationship between them had been substantially reversed, for by then Agho was already beginning to impress the British by his influence and ability and he was soon to become a key member of the Native Council. It was in *obaseki's* house that Ovonramwen spent his last few weeks before his banishment and during that period Agho seems to have behaved quite correctly towards him. Once he had gone, however, *obaseki* wasted no time regretting the past but devoted his energies to securing the leadership of the new order. So adroit was he at handling the new regime that the other chiefs soon requested that he should be treated as their intermediary with the Resident. By March 1899, the latter was writing in his Quarterly Report that the Native Council worked well and regularly.[5] Chief *Obaseki* took the lead in everything and was a most intelligent man with influence among the other chiefs. Though allegations of extortion and oppression were frequently made against him in subsequent years, and in October 1899 there was even a suggestion that he might have to be exiled, this favourable view of him is repeatedly echoed in the judgements of successive administrators.[6] And he continued to be an indispensable instrument of British rule almost up to his death in 1920.

Before 1897, the *oba's* domains had been divided, for limited administrative purposes, into many units — villages, village groups, sub-chiefdoms — responsibility for which the *oba* assigned to a wide range of chiefs and non-titled retainers. During the interregnum the British authorities adapted this system of territorial administration to their own requirements. The degree of continuity that was maintained is a matter for further investigation but it would appear that while,

5. P.15a/99.
6. In 1914 Resident James Watt described him as 'by far the ablest native chief whom I have ever met'. BP. 16/14, 5-10-14.

initially, some of the chiefs who had controlled particular areas for the *oba* managed to secure recognition as 'paramount chiefs' over those same areas, in other cases those warranted as paramount chiefs had had no previous authority over the areas assigned to them. As chiefs died, or were replaced on grounds of incompetence or tyranny, more and more administrative units came to be concentrated in the hands of a relatively small number of chiefs and non-titled men who enjoyed the patronage of *obaseki* and the confidence of the British officers. Thus, throughout the interregnum, there was a tendency for administrative areas within the Benin kingdom to become consolidated into larger units. The acquisition of paramount chieftaincies was to be a major object of political competition throughout this period, for they afforded their holders unprecedented opportunities for personal aggrandizement.

Though it bore a superficial resemblance to the pre-colonial pattern, the interregnal system of territorial administration operated in an entirely different context of structures and values. Before 1897, a chief's rights and obligations as a territorial administrator constituted only one of a configuration of roles conferred on him with his title. Fulfilment of his other roles, both ritual and secular, took up a great deal of his time and interest, and involved him in a network of structural loyalties and oppositions that placed restraints on his dealings with the villages entrusted to him. As I have noted above (and see Bradbury, 1967) alternative channels of communication between the *oba* and his subjects could be utilized from both ends to check the power of the territorial chiefs. Again, while the interests of the *oba*, his chiefs, and his people were often in conflict, they shared a common set of beliefs and values and subscribed to a single political ideology (see above p.82). The authority of the territorial chiefs, though often abused, was legitimate because it derived from the king and was designed to fulfil the purposes of the kingship. The rules of the political game and the limits of expediency were widely understood and ultimately sanctioned by the forces of political competition operating within a framework of common value orientations.

In the interregnal situation these rules and limits were no longer effective; the guidelines of political behaviour had to be drawn afresh. For an evolved polity, with built-in checks and balances, the British substituted a monolithic administrative pyramid in which the paramount chiefs occupied the middle ground. As the agents of alien conquerors, motivated by unfamiliar goals and values, they lacked the legitimacy accorded by the ordinary Edo to their pre-colonial counterparts. On the other hand they enjoyed the determined support of their new masters who, while holding a monopoly of effective force, were greatly dependent on them for the implementation of their policies. 'It is imperative that you uphold the power of the Benin Chiefs and force obedience of their orders and of those of the Native Council . . .' wrote the Counsul General to the Resident at Benin in 1899.[7] The Resident passed on the message to his officers: 'The most important point to bear in mind is that the power of the Benin City chiefs must be upheld and the territories worked through them and officers should always be accompanied by one one of the chiefs when visiting the country'.[8]

At this time, internal security was still a problem. *Ologbose*, the chief who had led the attack on the massacred British officials, was conducting a guerilla campaign only forty miles away, and in many parts of the *oba's* territories British rule was still being met with spirited resistance. The Consul General was hardly less exercised by fears of the encroachment of the Lagos Government on the one hand and the Royal Niger Company, on the other, on his own sphere of authority. But the long-run consideration underlying the government's determination to bolster up the chiefs' power was an economic one. Long before the massacre had provided a justification for 'punitive' action, commercial interests in the Delta had been urging the British Government to open up the hinterland to them by taking over Benin, and the government was increasingly inclined to heed their representations. Certainly the Benin chiefs were expecting a British attack long before the massacre, which was itself the outcome of their anxieties. In the excitement of military action the primacy of commercial interests was never lost sight of. Moor's first instructions when Benin City had fallen defined the objects of the administration as pacification, winning the confidence of the natives, and the opening-up of trade.[9] From a perusal of the records of the early years of British rule, it is clear that the first two objectives were regarded primarily as a means to the third.

Attempts to promote economic development were soon under way. Metal currency was introduced; languishing markets were revived; the Edo were encouraged to tap wild rubber and collect other natural products; collective village rubber plantations were established;

7. P.7/99, 7-3-99.
8. P.24/99.
9. P.1/97, Moor to Res. & officers, Benin, 14-3-97.

everybody was encouraged to trade freely in palm kernels which had formerly been a royal monopoly; and timber concessions were allocated. The paramount chiefs and council chiefs (frequently the same men) were assigned a vital role in making these policies known and promoting their implementation; as well as enforcing new regulations such as those devised to control the working of wild rubber. Generous inducements were held out to the chiefs for their active cooperation. They were permitted to collect tribute at an official rate (in 1902) of 5 yams per household and a goat for every 10 households.[10] They were assigned a generous proportion of profits accruing to village communities from a variety of sources. In the early stages these consisted mainly of rents imposed upon Urhobo immigrants who, from 1897, began to enter the Benin kingdom in large numbers to exploit its oil-palm resources; and on 'native aliens' and European firms who set up trading establishments. To rents were subsequently added timber royalties and the profits of village rubber plantations.

Another source of income derived from the chief's duty to recruit carriers and labourers for road-building and other purposes required by the government. Of the money allocated to the chiefs to meet the costs of these services, one-third was paid to the labourers, another third used to provide food for them, while the chief himself retained the remaining third. These, at any rate, were the official proportions. It is unlikely that they were often adhered to. The chiefs were also encouraged to set an example in taking up new productive enterprises. Seedlings were supplied to them for the establishment of private rubber plantations and their servants received training in the working of both wild and domesticated rubber. The estates which many of them laid down have continued to furnish their heirs with a regular income up to the present day. The chiefs were important to the administration then, not only because they already possessed authority, but because it was considered that their enrichment was the most direct path to economic diversification, and the expansion of trade. By tying part of their income to the profits accruing to villages under their control, it was thought that they would actively stimulate palm oil and rubber production. Another example of this policy is the attempt in 1898 to promote intensive cotton growing. American seed was distributed to many of the chiefs, who were to supervise its cultivation, either directly or through the agency of headmen of their subject villages; but this scheme proved unsuccessful.

10. BP. 16/14

While many of them cooperated wholeheartedly in these schemes and derived great benefit from them, the paramount chiefs did not confine their activities to the promotion of economic development. Freed from the manifold traditional obligations associated with their titles, they devoted their close and continuous attention to the management of their benefices, in which they were allowed great latitude. They did not, of course enjoy complete security of tenure. Chiefs were occasionally removed from office for misappropriation of funds, general incompetence, or excessive exploitation. Villages taken away from one chief were assigned to another, usually one of those who had proved most capable and competent according to the government's standards. Political action took the form, in these circumstances, of competition between the chiefs for government favours; and conflict between the chiefs and their subjects.

Administration officers spent a lot of time assessing the validity of complaints made by villagers against the paramount chiefs. The truth was often difficult to establish. Residents were naturally reluctant to dismiss chiefs who had proved their usefulness; and competence in terms of the government's objectives was not necessarily incompatible with self-aggrandizement at the expense of the unfortunate villagers. Edo informants confirm that personal relations between government officers and a few trusted chiefs were more intimate at this period than in any subsequent phase of colonial rule. The great strength of the paramount chiefs lay in the breadth of their administrative roles which gave them a high degree of control over the flow of communication between the villages and the government.

Provided he did not directly defraud the government (or was not found out defrauding it), a paramount chief's capacity for survival depended largely on his ability to judge (a) how far he could carry his exploitation without provoking a general revolt in his benefice; and (b) where his over-rulers would draw the line between the necessity of maintaining the chiefs' authority and their responsibility for protecting his subjects from oppression. The second condition was closely dependent upon the first. That is, the test for determining when a strong chief had become an intolerable tyrant was the degree of unrest that his *ultra vires* actions provoked. The most 'reliable' chiefs were those whose exploitative activities were sufficiently selective for them to retain a reasonable amount of support among their subjects. It was when complaints became too general, when a chief exercised too little discipline over his agents, and particularly when a stong local leader emerged who was prepared to challenge the chief's authority, that the government was forced to conclude that a change was due.

We may take as an example the disturbances at Urhonigbe, a large village in the south-east corner of the Benin Kingdom, between 1909 and 1914. In 1909 the Urhonigbe people were in general revolt against their paramount chief (*P.C.I*) whom they accused of extortion, slave-dealing, and general oppression. The government's decision to remove him was no doubt influenced by the fact that he had failed to obtain either carriers or government tribute from Urhonigbe for some years; that is, the authorities were as much concerned with his administrative incompetence as with his alleged tyranny. The revolt was led by the priestly headman (*A*) of Urhonigbe whose aim was to get it declared a separate administrative unit with himself as paramount chief. However, the government preferred to appoint *P.C.II*, a non-titled paramount chief, who already held other benefices. Unrest soon broke out again and *A* was, with government approval, carried off to *P.C.II*'s house at the capital. After six months he escaped and resumed his activities. By 1913 *obaseki* was warning the District Commissioner that serious trouble was threatening in Urhonigbe. The people were said to be 'swearing juju' against both the paramount chief and the D.C. himself. Complaints poured in and they are worth quoting in summary form:

The chief was said to have bought three slaves and placed them in the house of one of his agents at Urhonigbe. He had taken 30 women from the town and married them by force. He was always ordering the people to go and haul logs without payment. One day when they heard the D.C. was visiting the town they collected three cows to present to him but the chief objected to this and took them away. He asked the people to bring out their idols and make juju for ·him against anyone who tried to take the town away from him. He left his brother *E* in charge of the town. Every nine days they gave him 600 yams. The women were called upon to carry these to Abraka where they were taken in canoes to the coast for sale. *E* collected fines and sent them to the chief. 264 people were fined amounts of £2 to £10 to have their cases settled by the chief. They did not receive their share of timber royalties. A town on Urhonigbe land had paid £100 rent but the chief had kept it all. They did not want him but wanted their own court in Urhonigbe.

The truth or falsity of any one of these charges is now beyond verification, but it cannot be doubted that exploitation of this kind was common in interregnal Benin. The reactions of the government are interesting. Following an investigation by the D.C. in March 1913, 'grave charges' were made against *P.C.II* in the Supreme Court and his deposition was recommended. Subsequently, however, the charges were withdrawn 'for political reasons' and the Lagos authorities refused to approve his deposition. *A* was removed from Urhonigbe. Otherwise nothing further was done and the matter remained in abeyance until it was overtaken by the extensive administrative changes which accompanied the restoration of the kingship in 1914. In the meantime *P.C.II* kept away from Urhonigbe, his personal agents left the town, and it remained in the hands of the local elders. On the other hand he was allowed to retain his benefices in other parts of the kingdom.

The pattern of conflict between villages and their paramount chiefs is clearly illustrated by the Urhonigbe affair. The outlines of political competition and conflict among the Benin City chiefs are, however, much more difficult to discern. At one stage in the Urhonigbe investigations the D.C. had recommended that *P.C.II* should be replaced by another increasingly trusted chief, *B*. However, this recommendation was withdrawn when suspicion arose that *B* had himself been intriguing with the dissident elements in Urhonigbe against *P.C.II*. The wealth and power to be gained from benefice-holding and the highly unequal and arbitrary distribution of these advantages inevitably created resentment and intrigue within the indigenous elite of Benin City, but it does not appear to have resulted in the emergence of factions, or of a radical polarization.

It will be recalled that in 1897 the first Resident had initiated a Native Council of chiefs. The first proposal had been that it should consist of only five members so as 'to give the chiefs some incentive to become members'. In the event a dozen or more were appointed by the end of 1897, most of them *uzama* or *eghaebho*, but including one or two lesser title-holders; and to these the *oba*'s two eldest sons were added. In 1900 a second rank of 'minor chiefs' had been created. There were about fifty of these who formed a roster from which court members were chosen. At this time there were sixteen 'head chiefs' (the number was later to be increased to a limit of thirty) who sat in turn as court Vice-President for a month each. From time to time promotions were made from second to first rank. However, after the earliest years, when it was called upon to advise on such questions as to what to do with Ovonramwen's wives and slaves, there is no evidence that the

Council ever acted as an effective advisory or policy-making body. The impression that emerges from administrative records and oral traditions is that the administrative officers came to rely more and more heavily for their information and for the implementation of their decisions on a very few chiefs, among whom *obaseki* was by far the most prominent. This interpretation is confirmed by various brief surveys of Benin administrative history prepared by administrative officers during later periods of reorganization. Thus the Acting Lieutenant-Governor reported to the Governor in 1920: 'At the outset the original seniority of the chiefs was to a great extent maintained but gradually *obaseki*, owing to his capacity and ability, took senior place, was recognized as the senior Paramount Chief and practically all Government orders were issued through him. Rule was direct and he was regarded as the mouthpiece of Government . . . . .'[11] My own oral inquiries largely confirm this view, though it is clear that some administrative officers established close personal relations with chiefs other than *obaseki* and used them as a check on his advice and activities.

The absence of overt factional politics is attributable to the fact that in the post-conquest situation, the main concern of the British was to establish the habit of obedience to their orders. The *oba* had striven to rule by manipulating competition between individuals and groups arranged in a complex configuration of opposed hierarchies and cross-cutting interests and obligations. The Resident, having direct access to overwhelming force, had no need of such subtleties; his interests were best served by the suppression rather than the encouragement of competition for power. *Obaseki* was able to dominate the centre of the stage for so long because the monolithic administrative structure made no provision for the emergence of a focus of opposition to him. However, the old political norms and habits were not dead, only dormant. Waiting in the wings was the uneasy figure of Aiguobasimwin, Ovonramwen's eldest son, always regarded as an object of some suspicion if never a serious threat.[12] The government's decision in 1914, to try him out in a leading role, enables us to present the next stage of Benin history as an unfolding drama, rather than as a series of mechanically repetitive episodes.

11. CC.2884/12; BP.1/1914; BP.842/14; Rpt. by E.D. Simpson, D.C.25-3-13.
12. On several occasions Aiguobasimwin had been rumoured to be plotting for the return of Ovonramwen, especially in 1906 when fears of widespread insurrection led to troops being brought in. On the other hand, both Aiguobasimwin and his brother Osuanlele were accorded chiefly status and competences during the interregnum.

The restoration and the reign of Eweka II, 1914-1933

Ovonramwen's death, at Calabar in January 1914, conveniently coincided with the amalgamation of the Northern and Southern Provinces into the Colony and Protectorate of Nigeria. Lugard was Governor in Lagos, indirect rule was in fashion, and 'the opportunity was taken to inaugurate (at Benin) a native administration on the lines of those which had proved successful in the Northern Provinces' (Burns, 1929, p.217). Indirect rule demanded that there should be a 'native authority' and, to this end, the government was prepared to restore the kingship, at least for a trial period.

Aiguobasimwin's right to the throne was never strongly challenged by his nearest brother, Osuanlele, as it would probably have been in pre-colonial times. His only serious rival was the *obaseki* who would not have turned down the opportunity of founding a new dynasty. James Watt, then Resident at Benin, would certainly have welcomed the accession of the government's most trusted agent had there been any chance of legitimizing it. However, it was soon made clear to him that any such move would be strongly resisted by the chiefs and the. people.[13] Dynastic continuity was the first axiom of Edo political values, and there was almost universal agreement that Aiguobasimwin was the only acceptable candidate.

The British aim was not simply to rehabilitate the pre-colonial Benin polity. In fact they made very little effort at this point to discover how it had worked. The organizational model they had in mind was derived from the developments which had taken place in the Northern Nigerian emirates where Lugard had worked out his concept of indirect rule. Those responsible for setting up the native administration recognized that this model would require adaptation to local conditions, but their reference was as much to the interregnal administrative structure as to the traditional political system. They made it clear to Aiguobasimwin that they had no intention of transferring to him the power which had been acquired by *obaseki* and the other elite chiefs of the interregnum On the contrary they would continue to rely upon – and expect him to rely upon – the experience and advice of these chiefs.

The restoration made it possible to begin making new appointments to the titles that had fallen vacant on the deaths of those who had held them in 1897, and thus to bring about a somewhat closer correspondence between traditional precedence and *de facto* influence and prestige. The senior titles naturally went to the elite chiefs and

13. See Talbot's brief survey of Benin political history under British rule dated 7-9-20.

inevitably, Agho became *iyase*, 'the *oba*'s first subject', the previous *iyase*, Okizi, having died in 1901. The *oba* later told Talbot that it was he who had suggested to Resident Watt that Agho should be made *iyase*,[14] but it is unlikely that he did so unprompted or without misgivings. Agho himself had a decisive voice in the first allocations of other senior titles and *iyase* is certainly the one he would have chosen for himself. The 'prime-ministerial' aspect of the *iyase's* traditional role made Agho's accession to the title very appropriate in British eyes, but this appointment meant a great deal more to the Benin people than it did to the government. The officials at Benin certainly foresaw the danger of a personal struggle for power between Agho and Aiguobasmwin but it is unlikely that they were aware that, in the 'conscious model' (Lévi-Strauss, 1963, p.281) of the traditional policy, *oba* and *iyase* occupied polar positions around which political factions were, sooner or later, bound to coalesce. Reaffirmed by the particular circumstances and consequences of the restoration, this conceptual polarity was to remain a significant factor in Benin politics over the next forty years.

In July 1914 the government presented its proposals for a Native Administration to the *oba*-designate and principal chiefs. There would be a small council of chiefs to advise on the formulation and implementation of policy, and suitable chiefs would be selected to staff judicial courts. The *iyase* would be president of the Native Court and the *oba*'s chief advisor. In place of the still fairly numerous districts administered by paramount chiefs, Benin Division would be divided into four large consolidated Districts, each under a District Chief (later called District Head) who would also be president of the courts in his district. Benin City would be divided into Quarters, each under a Quarter Chief who would take charge of sanitation, the maintenance of order, and the collection of rates. The system of remuneration was to be rationalized. Fees, fines, market dues, timber royalties, rubber receipts, rents, and the proceeds of a direct tax on all able-bodied men would form the revenue of a Native Treasury from which the salaries of the *oba*, the *iyase*, and council, court, district, and quarter chiefs and other administrative expenses would be met.[15]

This programme was substantially put into effect over the next few years, though not without strong opposition to some of its features. In particular, the chiefs firmly resisted the principle of direct taxation for they saw that it would not be to their advantage to have the tax

14. Ibid.
15. BP.16/14, 8-7-14; and other papers dated 1916.

obligations of individuals too rigorously defined. Only in 1920 was direct taxation to become an established fact; in the meantime a system was devised whereby villages were assessed to pay fixed annual sums. The other major proposals were in operation by 1916. However, I am not so much concerned here with the detailed, time-table of administrative reorganization as with the unplanned currents and rhythms of political behaviour that were unleashed by the restoration.

Aiguobasimwin was installed on 24 July 1914, styling himself Eweka II, after the founder of the dynasty. His accession met with popular acclaim. Gifts poured in from the Benin villages, and from some outside what the government now regarded as his domain. The palace was rebuilt with voluntary labour and resumed its place, in the popular mind, at the centre of the kingdom's affairs. The chiefly orders and palace associations were reconstituted and a body of retainers assembled; wives were recruited for the *oba*'s harem and women to be their servants. The elaborate network of ritual relations between the *oba* and his chiefs and subjects was reactivated and some of the rituals of divine kingship began to be performed again, if in attenuated form. The *oba* himself was embarrassed by some of the spontaneous responses to his accession and had constantly to consult the administrative officers as to what customary practices were still permissible.[16] The British welcomed (with reservations) the enthusiasm with which people renewed their services to the *oba*. It was recognized that Eweka needed to acquire popular respect and prestige if he was to be a useful symbol of the authority of the Native Administration. However, they could neither foresee nor fully control the degree to which the dormant behaviour patterns of the old political culture would be reawakened.

At Eweka's accession the government reserved all rights in regard to policy-making and the allocation of administrative responsibilities. The *oba* was permitted to make the first formal nominations for positions on the councils and for the district and quarter headships, but it is clear that allocations were worked out in consultation with the administrative officers and the elite chiefs of the interregnum. The district chiefships were, in the government's view, the key to efficient administration; and, from the chiefs' standpoint, the most desirable prizes. Inevitably they were assigned to the *iyase* and three other chiefs, now all of senior *eghaebho* rank, who had proved themselves most 'useful' during the interregnum. These four, together with three other *eghaebho* and an *uzama*, were also appointed to the *oba*'s council. The

16. BP.679, August 1914.

nine Quarter Chiefs included three or four of sub-*eghaebho* rank but few, if any, were the *oba*'s personal clients.

The *oba* was conscious, from the outset, of the obstacles to the establishment of his personal authority presented by the continuing dominance of the interregnal oligarchy. In this respect his position was broadly analogous to that in which Ovonramwen had found himself at the commencement of his reign, when confronted with the power of the chiefs appointed by his father, Adolo. Eweka's capacity to manipulate the situation was, however, much less promising than Ovonramwen's had been. The accession of the 'reliable' chiefs of the interregnum to the district and quarter headships, and the presence of an overriding authority determined to make full use of their experience, were bound to strengthen and perpetuate their hold over him. Before his installation the *oba* had privately urged the Resident that two men should be appointed to look after each district so that they would check each other's activities. The chiefs, he suggested, would not tell the truth because of the bribes they would be offered in the villages. He begged the government to support him lest the chiefs should overthrow him as they had (in his view) overthrown his father.[17] Some heed was taken of the Edaiken's representations. In 1915, it was decided that tax should be collected by village heads and handed over to the District Chief in the presence of the *oba*'s representative. The headman and District Chief would each receive a percentage and the latter would hand the balance to the *oba* to be paid into the Treasury. Nevertheless, given the compactness and size of their new domains and the fact that they were now supposed to reside in their districts and to be presidents of district courts — all radical departures from precolonial practice — the district heads were in an even stronger position than they had been as paramount chiefs. Though their roles were now officially defined in more bureaucratic terms there was, in fact, little to stop them treating their districts as personal fiefs.

The *oba* naturally responded to the weakness of his position by trying to build up a personal clientele. There were, in Benin, men who had achieved wealth and influence in various ways without securing administrative competences and some of these were prepared to ally themselves with the *oba*. They included, for example, some who had been resident in the Benin trading post at the Yoruba town of Akure at the time of the British take-over, and who had since returned to Benin but continued their commercial relations with the hinterland. Another

17. BP.16/14, Edaiken to Governor's Deputy, 19-7-14.

potential source of support for a 'king's party' lay in the fact that there were now a number of ex-paramount chiefs whom reorganization had robbed of income and prestige. By restoring the kingship but denying the king effective authority, the British created a nucleus of great symbolic potency, around which the grievances of the dispossessed chiefs and other traditional title-holders lacking government appointments could crystallize. The *oba* could and did hand out titles to men whose support he wished to acquire. Soon after his accession he submitted a list of 'household chiefs' which the government approved, though no provision had been made for integrating them into the new administrative order. Titles without official competences were, however, of little value. The *oba* might, perhaps, make recommendations for court membership and minor posts in the Native Administration but his powers of patronage compared unfavourably with those of the chiefs who, during the interregnum, had gained the government's confidence.

As the situation develops, in the early years of Eweka's reign, it is possible to identify five main sets of political interests, those of:

1. the administrative officers, concerned with maintaining order and with the development of an administrative organization which would be effective in implementing its policies;
2. the district chiefs and their clients and agents;
3. the *oba*, his palace staff, and others, such as ritual specialists, men (and women) of a traditionalist outlook, whose standing in the community was closely bound up with the *oba*'s authority and prestige; and the *oba*'s personal friends and clients, bound to him by various social ties and common interests and by their opposition to the elite chiefs whose power constituted an obstacle to their own commercial and political ambitions;
4. the ex-paramount chiefs, intent on recovering their former sources of income and prestige;
5. the general populace in the capital and the villages, seeking to defend itself against exploitation and the demands of the government.

The story of the years 1914-1929 is one of a constant struggle between the *oba* and the district chiefs, with the remaining chiefs and the people being drawn by structural and personal loyalties and interests into partisanship of one side or the other. The position of the British representatives on the spot is complicated. The new policy measures which they sought (or were required) to introduce provided fuel for factional dispute. On the one hand, they were bound to give their support to the indigenous ruling clique whose interests favoured 'acquiescence in these measures; on the other, to act as mediators in the conflicts that resulted. They have to be seen not merely as external manipulators but also as participants in internal political processes over which they had only limited control.

In July 1915 the Resident, Benin, felt able to recommend confirmation of the *oba*'s and the *iyase*'s appointments. In his view, Eweka had done his utmost to rule his people wisely and follow the advice given to him. Confirmation would add to his prestige. The *iyase*, for his part, had served the *oba* as loyally as he had served the government, although he was now second man instead of first.[18] By December of the same year this sunny picture was beginning to be clouded. The reduction in the number of administrative officers caused by the outbreak of war in Europe had led to a widespread rumour that the white men were leaving Benin. After some carriers had been taken to Duala it became very difficult to recruit any more. The *iyase* assured the government that everything was all right, but also advised that it would be prudent for the administrative officers to take chiefs on tour with them. The Resident reported: 'The *oba* has been loyal and useful but has not exercised enough control over his household and messengers and unauthorized persons claiming to be his messengers who have been claiming things from the villagers. People under the impression that they are serving the *oba* do not see why they should also serve the chiefs' The Resident felt that the trouble was partly due to the fact that the chiefs had important duties to perform, opportunities for extortion and no recognized income[19] – the district head system was not yet operative.

Evidently the villagers were beginning to resume their customary method of self-defence, that is, by playing off one set of officials against the other. In their eyes the palace emissaries were to be set off against the territorial administrators as they had been before the British arrived; and, in this matter, the *oba*'s interests tended to coincide with those of the villagers. His predecessors had striven to retain their freedom of action by keeping open alternative channels of communication between themselves and their subjects. By 1916, when the district head system had become operational, it was obvious to Eweka that he was not going to find it easy to emulate their example.

18. Watt to S.S.P., 22-7-15.
19. Watt to S.S.P., 10-12-15.

The government's organizational model made no provision for overlapping spheres of competence. It accepted the desirability, if the *oba*'s prestige was to be maintained, of his retaining some direct links with his people and receiving some customary services from them; but these activities could not be allowed to interfere with the operation of the monolithic administrative structure which the British saw as best suited to the attainment of their objectives. The chiefs, for their part, regarded themselves as responsible directly to the administrative officers, a view which fitted in well with the latter's own wish to exercise as much personal supervision over them as possible.

This issue, in various guises, is a constant theme throughout the era of the district headships. The chiefs regularly complain that the *oba*'s emissaries tell the villages not to serve them. The *oba*, in return, accuses the chiefs of keeping his messengers out and of preventing villagers from making appeals to the *oba*'s court. Definition of the competences of palace staff took a long time to achieve. Along with the introduction of district headships went the first official recognition of village headships, both hereditary and non-hereditary. Legitimation of the succession to these headships was recognized to be the *oba*'s prerogative and this involved such matters as the presentation of village chiefs to the people by the officials of the palace associations. The *oba*'s right to send his representatives to village rituals could hardly be gainsaid. Indeed, as we shall see, the *oba's failure* to fulfil his ritual obligations was later to be interpreted as an anti-government plot. It was also accepted that the *oba* had the right to expect his people to contribute to the cost of state rituals, by providing animals for sacrifice. These contributions had always been paid for (with nominal sums) and, in time, the role of the *oba*'s itinerant 'buyers' was to be regularized and the 'price' of particular animals fixed. On the other hand, if palace officials were to visit the villages for these purposes, how could they be prevented from intriguing against the district heads?

Given the European value-orientations of the administrative officers, the royal harem provided the *oba*'s enemies with plenty of ammunition. In the old days one of the tasks of the *ibiwe* association had been to recruit large numbers of wives for the *oba*. By no means all of these entered into actual marital relations with him; many of them were given to loyal subjects as a reward for their services. When Eweka became *oba* the *ibiwe* chiefs resumed their traditional functions of arranging marriages and seeing to the upkeep of, and maintenance of discipline in, the harem. As a result, there were endless allegations of women being kept there, or married off, against their will. The *oba* in return, complained to the government that chiefs took away his wives and encouraged their followers to seduce them.

Certain actions by administrative officers did nothing to ease Eweka's position. In 1917 Resident Watt, angry about delays in the construction of a bridge, instructed the *oba* to order members of his palace associations to carry cement. The *oba* according to his own explanation, pointed out that such work would be contrary to the customary dignity of his retainers. Nevertheless he was obliged to carry out the Resident's commands. The consequence was that his retainers, accusing him of weakness in not protecting them from humiliation, ceased to attend the *oba*; the audiences which he had given in the palace each evening to hear complaints no longer took place.[20] The novelty of having an *oba* again was beginning, by this time, to wear thin. The dispossessed paramount chiefs became increasingly aware of the *oba*'s impotence to right their grievances. According to Eweka's own version, they blamed him not only for the fact that their benefices had been taken away from them but even for the loss of their slaves — though this was due to the general abolition of slavery by the government in 1915. Other chiefs, including those entitled by Eweka himself, found that their expectations of administrative competences and perquisites remained unfulfilled.

The *oba*'s increasing isolation and frustration are reflected in an anonymous letter received by the Governor in July 1918.[21] The writer — whom the Resident divined (probably correctly) to be a palace servant — complained of the ill-treatment of the *oba* by the 'whitemen and native chiefs' and requested His Excellency to come to Benin to set matters right. When the *oba* talks, the letter goes on, the white men and chiefs always disobey him. Young men always try their very best to obey him. Since he became *oba* he has not done any wrong or abused the law. Yet the chiefs have told the white men that they do not want the villages to serve the *oba* again, that he should not be allowed to send messages to the villages. The writer begs His Excellency to raise the *oba* above all kings in Nigeria.

It was inevitable that the general malaise should manifest itself in a form familiar in Benin dynastic traditions, a direct confrontation between the *oba* and the *iyase*. The conflict took on traditional forms of expression. In August 1918 allegations were made that the *oba* had

20. *Oba* to Res., 28-11-18.
21. BP.13/1918.

sent to the Yoruba town of Ondo for a 'native doctor' to 'make medicine' to protect him against the *iyase*. The native doctor alleged that the *oba* had told him that the *iyase* was taking his wives away, combining with the white men and all Benin to accuse him of taking their slaves and property, and taking half of all the presents sent to him. According to the doctor's own version, he had remained at Benin four months making medicines — but had drawn the line when the *oba* asked him to use his arts to kill the *iyase*. The Resident refused to credit the last part of the story, preferring to believe that the doctor had, in fact, tried to blackmail the *oba*.[22] However, there is evidence that the *oba* felt obliged to conciliate the *iyase* at about the time when these events were alleged to have taken place. Eweka himself was later to refer to an occasion when he had gone to the *iyase*'s house and knelt at his feet to beg forgiveness[23]; and the Resident reported that, about the same time, the *oba* had asked the *iyase* to assure him that all was well between the two of them.[24]

Despite an interregnum of 17 years, the ideology of divine kingship retained enough force for it to be a factor in political conflict. In November 1918 the administrative officers were perturbed by the general disquiet generated by the *oba*'s failure to perform *ugie-erha-oba*, the annual festival in honour of his father's spirit. Deaths and disasters were being blamed on the omission of these rites and the government's anxieties were increased by the approach of an influenza epidemic. When asked to explain why he had not performed the rite, the *oba* blamed it on the *iyase*'s refusal to take part — on the grounds of his having become a Christian. The Resident regarded the whole affair as a plot to arouse resentment against the *iyase* and the government. There may well have been some truth in this view but the political motivations were probably not all on one side; to boycott the palace rituals had always been one of the sanctions that disaffected chiefs could employ against the *oba*. The exasperated Resident was moved to suggest that Agho should give up the *iyase* title and take the style Chief Counsellor, while retaining his offices of District Head and President of the Native Court. Another, purely ritual *iyase* might then be appointed, so that the festivals could go on.[25] This suggestion was hardly likely to appeal to either Eweka or Agho, but it is indicative of the government's tendency at this time to think of the kingship as having purely symbolic utility.

22. R.1/18(c), Res. to Lt. Gv., 17-8-18.
23. Ibid. *Oba* to Res., 24-11-18.
24. Ibid.
25. Ibid. Res. to S.S.P., 11-10-18.

The *oba's* feeling that the *iyase* and the administrative officers were in league against him is readily understandable. The latter tended to regard the *oba-iyase*-conflict as being a mere clash of personalities. Commenting on the affair of the native doctor, the Resident gave it as his opinion that: 'the political situation in Benin is that the *oba* is a weak man and, being in a position of hereditary authority, jealous of anyone under him whom he recognized as being stronger, wiser and better than himself'. He lent himself 'to the counsel of flatterers' and resented any restriction on his power by the government. That he was required to deal with the villagers through the District Heads was resented by the *oba* and his followers. The *iyase*, on the other hand, was loyal to the *oba* because (said the Resident) he believed in that way he was being loyal to the government. It was he who was making the administration a success.

In fact the *oba* was privately warned, about this time, that if he did not mend his ways he would follow in his father's footsteps. With the scales so heavily weighted against him it is not surprising that Eweka seems to have decided that it would be safer to join the *iyase* than to go on fighting him. He requested the Resident to mediate between them and, seven months after the *ugie-erha-oba* affair, their reapprochment had so far progressed that, as we may read in the 1919 annual Report: 'In mid-June Benin City went en fête when two of the *oba's* daughters were married — Iyashere (*iyase*) married the second, Edogun the third'. Fulfilment of the custom whereby the *oba* was bound to give a daughter (ideally his first daughter) in marriage to the *iyase* helped to cement a mutually profitable partnership between Agho and Eweka. The *oba's* position was much ameliorated and Agho, with the Resident in one pocket [26] and the *oba* in the other, had reached the crowning point of a remarkable political career. However, as we shall see, by 'capturing' Eweke he had both overreached the tolerable limits of his personal power and undermined the king's own legitimate authority.

Believing the clash between Agho and Eweka to be mainly a question of personalities, the Resident was delighted to see them reconciled. The festive atmosphere created by the royal weddings added to the government's optimism and it was now felt safe to press on with the plans to introduce direct taxation. This, however, was the spark that was needed to set fire to the smouldering resentment of the dispossessed and deprived sectors of the political class. Furthermore, it was an issue on which the latter could be assured of popular support.

26. In his Annual Report for 1919 the Resident referred to the *iyase* as the only District Head who required no supervision.

In July 1920, Chiefs Esogban and Oloton sent a petition to the Governor on behalf of the titled chiefs of Benin City.[27]. Their opinion was that the native administration since 1914 had been wholly bad. The Government had obtained their consent to (what the chiefs were now calling) the joint rule of the *oba* and the *iyase* by promises of power and emoluments. Since then 81 principal houses had been abandoned and were in ruins. The chiefs condemned the behaviour of the *oba* and the *iyase* in similar terms. Both had used their power to exact private tribute and free services from all the villages. The *oba* had taken the chiefs' former household slaves and set up new villages with them to work plantations for him. Others he had given to his daughters on their marriages to the *iyase* and *edogun*, and still others to the *iyase* himself. The chiefs demanded the abolition of the district head system; the restoration of their villages to the paramount chiefs; the removal of the *iyase* from the permanent vice-presidency of the Native Court, and the rotation of all court vice-presidencies among the chiefs, and the abandonment of the new 'head taxes'. Perhaps most significantly of all, they demanded that all administrative matters should be publicly discussed at *Ugha-Ozolua* (the great courtyard which housed the shrine of the fifteenth-century *oba*, Ozolua). They objected strongly to the *oba* and *iyase* (as they put it) arranging things privately with Resident Watt at his bungalow. Later on a supplement to this petition was presented,[28] giving lurid details of the misdeeds alleged to have been perpetrated by the *oba*, and especially by the *iyase* against the inhabitants of a number of villages; and demanding that the *iyase* be suspended pending negotiation.

The government was greatly perturbed. Having helped to paper over the cracks between the *oba* and the *iyase* only a year or so before, it now found itself faced with a concerted revolt by the other chiefs and the villagers against the combined power of the *iyase*, the *oba*, and the Resident. About this time P. Amaury Talbot replaced James Watt as Resident. With characteristic industry and curiosity, he set out to make himself familiar with the whole history of the Benin administration. One detects at this point an entirely new spirit of inquiry, a genuine desire to come to grips with the realities of the political situation.

In the new crisis the fragility of the *oba*'s compact with the *iyase* was soon revealed. In a letter to the District Officer dated 30 August 1920, Eweka, recalling the glory of his predecessors, gave vent to his feelings of humiliation and resentment:

27. BP.462/20, 28-7-20.
28. Ibid., 12-8-20.

The *iyase* is ordering me at which I am not pleased because I do not want anyone but the British Government to command me. A servant cannot command his master . . . [The *iyase*] has many times come to the *oba's* house and boasted that his orders surpass the *oba's* . . . I am deprived of my boys by the *iyase* and have to attend farm myself to keep my wives and children'.

In the light of the chiefs' complaints against the *oba* himself, this last lament must be regarded as an exaggeration. The *oba* also had his own proposals for the future. He asked that the warrent chiefs should be made presidents of the district courts, and the *oba* himself President of the Benin Native Court. He also wanted to take over the *iyase's* district and to have all communications to the government passed through himself. For Agho he prescribed a pension. Meanwhile, he recommended that he should be suspended, a proposal which the District Officer found 'preposterous' − it would throw the whole N.A. into chaos.[29] Talbot, however, was less committed to the long-standing dogma of Agho's indispensability.

Agho's downfall came with dramatic suddenness. In a report dated 6 September, Talbot described a meeting which he had had with the *oba* and all the Benin chiefs except the *iyase*.[30] Every one of them, District Heads included, supported the *iyase's* suspension. Since there was no one to speak for him, Talbot inferred, he must have abused his power. Though very capable, he was dictatorial and arrogant. His power rested entirely on his favour with the European.

Indeed, it might seem that his life depended on it, for, on 9 September, the day Talbot's report left Benin, Agho died. Yet, Talbot's last remark fails to do justice to the political acumen and nerve that Agho had already demonstrated before 1897, and proved through more than twenty years of colonial rule. His loss of favour with 'the European' was a concomitant, not the cause, of his downfall, which, as we have seen, was the outcome of factional conflict generated in the intercourse of different political cultures. However, Talbot did see more clearly than his colleagues that the symbiotic relationship between Agho and successive Residents, which had been effective before 1914, was incompatible with post-restoration political realities. In retrospect, we recognize that *obaseki's* supremacy during the interregnum had seemed unchallengeable not only because he enjoyed overwhelming external support, but also because his role and its structural context

29. BP.462/20, D.O. to Res.
30. Talbot to S.S.P., 6-9-20.

were alien to Edo political experience. The British were no less determined to uphold his authority after 1914, but the confrontation between *oba* and *iyase*, and the opposition between district chiefs and palace retainers which the restoration engendered, could be more readily assimilated to the traditional political culture. Hence, pre-colonial political norms and tactics, suppressed during the interregnum, re-emerged with Eweka's accession. The environment in which they operated was, however, very different.

The most salient difference lay in the drastic curtailment of the functions of the indigenous political elite — particularly in respect to policy-making and the control of effective force. The Benin chiefs found that, by political action, they could influence the details and timing of administrative structures and measures, but the taking of major policy decisions was out of their hands. In this situation, ambitions and interests were narrowly focused on intense competition for administrative competences which, though in some respects more differentiated, were much less widely dispersed than they had been before 1897. The stability of the pre-colonial polity had depended, to a considerable degree, on the maintenance of an elaborate structure of competition for titles which carried well-defined expectations of competences and rewards (Bradbury, 1967). After 1914 the traditional chiefly orders were reconstituted, but they had lost their corporate governmental functions, and placement in their hierarchies was no longer consonant with the distribution of administrative roles and perquisites. Whereas, in the nineteenth century, there had been a single organizational model and a common normative framework, in terms of which individuals and groups could formulate their interests, alternative and contradictory models were now available. To the 'traditional' model there had been added the 'interregnal' and the 'Northern' models, and these were differentially valued by various interest groups. Each group, while selecting favourable elements from all three models, tended to formulate its major objectives in terms of one or another of them. In crude terms, the *oba*, his palace staff and ritual functionaries, and the villagers, were wedded to pre-colonial norms and structures; dispossessed paramount chiefs conceived their interests to lie in a return to the interregnal pattern of administration; while the District Heads and their clients had nothing to lose by acquiescing in the modified Northern model favoured by the government as an instrument of rationalization. In the absence of an underlying consensual framework, the contradictions inherent in this plurality of conceptual means to the attainment of opposed interests led, through a series of factional realignments, to a 'revolutionary' confrontation. Reduced essentially to the *iyase*, the Resident, and the *oba*, the ruling oligarchy found itself implacably opposed by a coalition of dispossessed and deprived interest groups able to mobilize mass support. The government, forced to withdraw into its mediatory role, at this point perceived the need for a new structural synthesis.

In the continuation of his report on the meeting described above, Talbot went on to suggest what changes needed to be made in order to give the Native Authority a chance of success. The government, he said, ought to take full advantage of the Benin people's respect for the kingship and the traditional hierarchies. He described the *oba* as 'shy, loyal and above average ability and intelligence'; he had had a lot of responsibility and too little power and his position needed to be strengthened in every way. Talbot also envisaged a more active role for the *oba*'s Council which ought, in his view, to be composed of 'the most important of the capable chiefs' — a reversal of earlier formulations. The District Heads had had too much power and required closer supervision. By hiving off their judicial competences it would be possible to provide posts for more of the discontented chiefs.

Talbot's report led to further inquiries by the Lieutenant-Governor of the Southern Provinces. To a meeting of the *oba*, the Benin chiefs, and some of the more important village heads, Lieutenant-Governor Moorhouse presented the alternatives of 'making indirect rule along the lines of the Northern Emirates work, or reverting to direct rule'. The chiefs expressed themselves in favour of retaining a form of Native Authority with the *oba* at its head, but wished to enlarge the Council by the addition of more of the *uzama* and *eghaebho*. They also demanded an increase in the number of Districts, with District Heads to be appointed for one year only; and they urged the abolition of direct taxation and a return to the old system of 'tribute and labour'. The Lieutenant-Governor eventually recommended a Council of up to sixteen chiefs; that the number of Districts should be increased to six; and that in each District four to six village chiefs should sit in turn as court presidents. These proposals were substantially put into effect and though modified from time to time remained the basis of administration for the rest of Eweka's reign.

Agho's death, the administration's recognition of the need to make more use of the *oba*'s authority, the creation of more council, judicial, and executive posts, and the growth of the Native Administration bureaucracy gave Eweka wider scope for exercising patronage, and greater freedom of political manoeuvre. From this point onwards the *oba*'s traditional prerogative of conferring titles was somewhat more congruent with his ability to reward their holders with worthwhile posts. Consequently there was rather more *de facto* correspondence between the traditional ranking structure and the distribution of government-recognized competences. The *oba*'s Council started to play a slightly more positive role. With the encouragement of administrative officers, it began to meet more regularly and to submit proposals for the revision of customary laws to meet modern requirements; and also to make demands for the improvement of public services. A summary of the recommendations (by no means all heeded) of a meeting of council chiefs and district and quarter heads in 1922 provides a fascinating glimpse of the intermingling of old and new values and objectives:

'Whoever commits adultery with the wife of a *uzama* or an *eghaebho* should be fined £30. The ancient penalty was death.[?]

In the old days a master could give a wife to his faithful servant and take her away again if he should prove unfaithful. The chiefs want to revive this practice without being accused of slave-dealing.

In the old days if anyone was accused of harming a town he was liable to make sacrifices. This has now been stopped and the chiefs want it to be allowed again.

In the old days witches were sent to live in [particular] villages. Nowadays they are allowed to remain in the town i.e. with unfortunate consequences. [The next *oba* was to build, on the outskirts of Benin City, what can only be described as a row of almshouses for destitute witches.]

The forestry laws are bringing great inconvenience to towns and villages.

More standpipes are required in Benin City.

The prices of foodstuffs should be fixed, e.g. yams at 10 for 1s; a she-goat 10s etc.

More European firms should be encouraged to trade at Benin.

Benin should recover all its old villages now in other Divisions.

Any person who assaults a titled chief should be imprisoned.

The *oba* recommends that the sale of liquor should be checked by the introduction of licences; and that all-night meetings should be made illegal'.

The reorganization of 1920 did not, of course, eliminate strife between the *oba* and the District Heads, with the palace staff and the villagers playing their customary roles. However, though the District Heads still dealt directly with the administrative officers and retained almost feudal power over their districts, none of them was able to acquire anything like the monopoly of British trust that had been Agho's; and the *oba* was better equipped to defend himself. The reorganization had by no means removed all the grievances of the ex-paramount chiefs, but as Eweka's reign progresses, the pattern of conflict takes on what I would regard as a more normal aspect. There are numerous violently expressed disputes between the *oba* and particular chiefs, especially District Heads, but they do not add up to a crisis of dichotomous, breakdown proportions. More than at any other time during the period with which we are concerned, the administrative officers of the 1920s managed to avoid identification with a narrow ruling faction.

Conscious of the threat which any *iyase* potentially constituted, yet bound by custom to appoint one, the independent *obas* of Benin had hit upon the idea of conferring this title on men of independent wealth and influence who were not previously deeply involved in the politics of the capital. Some, for example, were wealthy traders operating on the fringes of the Benin sphere of influence. By appointing an 'outsider' *iyase* the *oba* hoped to enjoy at least a 'honeymoon' period of good relations with him and perhaps also use him as an ally against the restricting power of the senior palace chiefs. Eweka followed this precedent by giving the *iyase* title to Okoro-Otun, a man who, though of part-Edo descent, had been brought up by his mother's people who were Ekiti Yoruba; and who, having become a successful freelance warrior and trader, eventually settled in Benin, some say at Eweka's invitation. To the end of his life Okoro-Otun is said not to have been able to speak Edo without mixing it up with Yoruba, but as *iyase* he served Eweka loyally. However, there was no guarantee that the loyalty of an *iyase* towards the *oba* who appointed· him would be extended to his heir – as tradition shows, and as Eweka's son was to discover by experience.

Akenzua II (1933-) and the Benin road to party politics

Eweka II died in 1933 and was succeeded by his son *Okoro* Edokporhogbunyunmwun, who adopted the style Akenzua II. Akenzua, who was in his early thirties, was widely hailed as a new type •of natural ruler, carefully trained for the task of leading his people along the path of enlightenment. After attending local schools he had been sent to King's College Lagos, where he achieved both academic and sporting success. On leaving school in 1918 he was appointed a transport clerk in the Benin Native Administration and later on served as his father's secretary. In 1928, after spending two years at Abeokuta, where he was sent to study the working of a native administration at that time regarded as one of the most advanced in southern Nigeria, he was given a District Headship. In the meantime his father, with government encouragement, had invested him with the title of *edaiken* and he took up his residence in the heir-apparent's court at Uselu. Akenzua's accession was accomplished without overt dispute — a fact which must be accounted for partly by government acceptance of the rule of primogeniture at its face value (which permitted formal training of the successor); and partly in terms of the restraints placed on intra-dynastic rivalry by the British conquest, which had put the kingship itself in jeopardy. Unlike their nineteenth-century analogues, Akenzua and his father had remained on terms of intimacy and mutual trust and the political environment in which they lived served to identify rather than oppose their interests.

Akenzua immediately substantiated his progressive image by disbanding his father's harem and freeing girls betrothed to his father from their obligation to marry himself. He dispensed with many of the palace attendants, urging them to go out and earn their living, and devised a form of clothing for his formerly naked pages. At the same time he demonstrated his devotion to the dignity of his office, and his accession promoted a new bout of cultural reconstruction. His succession rites — his father's funeral and his own installation — were performed with a splendour and attention to customary detail not seen in Benin since the 1897 débâcle.[31] A little later he had his mother posthumously installed as Queen Mother and built a mausoleum for her remains. He also reconstituted the order of Body Titles *(Egie-Egbe)*, whose members represented physical and metaphysical components of his person and took it upon themselves to share his spiritual burden.

His familiarity with his father's and his more remote predecessors' predicament in the early years of their reigns made Akenzua well aware that he would have to work hard to establish his authority; and he had the additional burden of promoting the acceptance of new government policies and regulations which were rarely universally popular. Although he had not been engaged in a contest for the throne, his

31.*Nigerian Daily Times*, 15-4-33.

accession brought forward a new generation of young ambitious men, his friends and associates, many of whom, like himself, had had a considerable amount of formal education. According to precedent he created new titles for some of these followers, while others were appointed to vacant titles; and he began to recommend them for positions on the council and courts and in the native administration. The older chiefs inevitably saw these new developments as a threat to their own security and it was not long before they began to show signs of reaction. By 1935 this clash of interests was manifesting itself in the familiar guise of a quarrel between the *oba* and the *iyase*, which took the overt form of a dispute about traditional prerogatives.[32] The *oba* objected to *iyase* Okoro-Otun's appearing in the streets wearing a beaded head-dress and preceded by a ceremonial scimitar (*ada*). According to precedent the *eghaebho* were permitted to display these marks of rank only on particular ceremonial occasions. Under pressure from administrative officers, Okoro-Otun surrendered his beaded crown and undertook not to use the sword illegally again. This was by no means the end of his differences with the *oba*, but at this point it is necessary to signal the emergence of a new interest group.

As a result of the introduction of schools and new economic opportunities over the previous thirty years, there was by this time a growing intelligentsia of teachers, clerks, and civil servants whose literacy gave them access to Western political ideologies; and – overlapping with it in interests and personnel – a new commercial elite of transport owners, rubber and timber producers, middlemen, traders, and the like. Many of these were sons of the original paramount chiefs – in this sense the economic policies of the early administrators had paid off. The *oba* himself belonged to the intelligentsia and so did some of his closest associates, but there were others who saw the growing power of the palace clique as an obstacle to their own interests. Soon after Akenzua's succession an organization calling itself the Benin Community presented a petition to the government which was uncompromisingly anti-traditional in tone. It demanded that the *oba*'s Council should be opened to Muslims and Christians (who had been excluded because they refused to undergo title-taking rituals) and the abolition of customary rules limiting, according to rank, the height of houses and the use of *iroko* wood in their construction. More startlingly, it demanded the introduction of individual ownership of land and the election of Quarter chiefs by ballot.

32. BP.1103, 15-8-35.

At this point, then, it is useful to distinguish three fairly clearly defined sectors within the Benin political class:

1. The 'old guard' of titled chiefs (especially the District and Quarter Heads) who had come to power in Eweka's reign.
2. The *oba*, his retainers and functionaries, and his 'new men'.
3. What we may call the radical modernist element. Over the years an independent-minded ascetic named H. O. Uwaifo was to prove the most uncompromising exponent of this point of view.

Despite the fundamental divergence of their interests, the older chiefs and the anti-traditionalists were to find a surprising amount of common ground during the later part of the 1930s in opposition to the power of the palace, and to government-inspired measures and regulations which the *oba*, as Sole Native Authority, was required to support and implement.

By the 1930s the District Head system had outlived its administrative usefulness. Wage labour had replaced levies of labourers and carriers. Direct taxation on the basis of nominal rolls was well established and tax clerks rather than quasi-feudal lords were required for its collection. Similarly, the increasingly complex regulations concerning such matters as sanitation, the felling of trees, the planting of permanent crops, etc., could be enforced more efficiently by officials of the appropriate Government and Native Administration departments. The abolition of the system was also consonant with the new phase of indirect rule ideology which insisted that native administrations and judiciaries should be based on authentic indigenous institutions. Throughout southern Nigeria district officers were being instructed to conduct enquiries into these institutions and to make recommendations for administrative reorganization based on their findings. By 1936 Macrae-Simpson, in his Benin Division Intelligence Report, duly recommended that the District Headships should be abolished. He proposed the constitution of village and village group councils which would be responsible to the *oba* for local affairs and which at a later date might be represented on a central state council. The Quarter Headships of the capital would be replaced by a form of administration based on the traditional wards. Macrae-Simpson also made proposals for the reform of the Native Authority. When he made his report the Council consisted of the *oba*, nine District Heads, ten Quarter Heads, and seven other chiefs who, together with the *oba*, also constituted a court of appeal. Claims to places on the Council had long been presented in terms of placement in traditional hierarchies and though the criteria of membership had never been clearly defined, only three members were below *eghaebho* rank. With more information at its disposal than ever before, the administration began to draw with increasing explicitness on its own model of the nineteenth-century polity. Macrae-Simpson proposed the enlargement of the Council to include all the *uzama* and *eghaebho* — a total of about fifty-four chiefs.

Not all these proposals were put into effect. Indeed, the process of reorganization took several years to complete and it was achieved only after prolonged political turmoil. The District and Quarter Headships were, however, immediately abolished and their incumbents experienced the same kind of deflation that had been the lot of the ex-paramount chiefs twenty years before. They remained on the Council, with increased salaries, but this was no compensation for their lost prestige and perquisites. The *oba*, to whom the village chiefs and headmen were now directly responsible, and who had a big say in the running of the administrative bureaucracy, stood to gain from this reorganization. For this reason, and because he was the sole recognized instrument of British policy, he was bound to become the object of the grievances of the dispossessed chiefs.

It will have been noted that Macrae-Simpson's recommendations took no account of the views of the anti-traditionalists. The increased power of the *oba* and the entrenchment of the principle by which access to office was by way of preferment to traditional titles were clearly against their interests.

The dispossessed chiefs and the modernists were drawn closer together by their common opposition to a series of administrative measures effecting the interests of both groups. The first of these was an attempt, in 1937, to control the indiscriminate planting of permanent crops, which partly originated in complaints by villages close to the capital of an alleged shortage of farming land due to the reservation of large areas of forest, and to the setting-up of extensive rubber, cocoa, and palm-oil plantations by residents in the capital. In the past there had been no shortage of land and the citizen of the capital had a recognized right to establish farms anywhere, either in the forest or, by arrangement with the elders, on land belonging to villages. The curtailment of these rights by a regulation which stated that permanent crops could be planted only with the *oba*'s permission, was construed as an attack on this right. The new regulation might have been expected to bring the *oba* the consolation of support from the villages. However, the villagers, who had developed the habit of planting up every food farm with permanent crops after the completion of the yam and cassava harvests, were equally opposed to them. A more serious issue, which threatened a general insurrection in the capital, arose out of the government's decision that it would be more equitable, and more profitable to revenue, if the water rate in Benin City were to be calculated on an assessment of the size of houses; hitherto a flat rate had been levied. The furore that ensued has since become, under the name 'The Great Water Rate Agitation', one of the legendary landmarks of Benin political history. The details of the dispute are less relevant here than the fact that it served to cement the two groups opposed to the *oba* into an effective coalition; and to polarize the residents of the capital into pro- and anti-palace factions.

The members of the Benin Community had quickly learned to pursue their quest for participation in the administration in the guise of appeals to traditionalist sentiments. Thus, when the *ezomo* alleged that the *oba* was transgressing the prerogatives of the *uzama* by awarding titles to his subjects, the modernists were vociferous in their support. The strategy of their attack on the *oba's* position is illustrated by the following quotations from a Benin Community address of welcome to the Lieutenant-Governor in February 1938:

'There is a set of puppet chiefs of no substantial means who have gained appointments by their close relationships and domestic services to the *oba* . . .

'The people of Benin City are at the mercy of the villages for their farming rights . . .

'The *iyase* is the Prime Minister, the mouthpiece of the natives and without plebiscite he moves the great majority of the war chiefs and the whole community.'

The *iyase*, himself returned to the fray, complaining among other things that the *oba* had refused to admit his sons to the palace associations, and demanding the return of his confiscated headdress. However, Okoro-Otun, though a useful symbol of opposition, was no Agho, and on this occasion the government gave the *oba* firm backing. He also retained a solid basis of support within the political elite. In reply to the Benin Community's allegations, thirty-five council chiefs and ten others petitioned the government,[33] defending Akenzua and

33. BP.1472, 12-2-38.

pointing out that all his troubles were due to his being made the tool of government policy. Allegations were also made around this time about the subversive activities of his opponents, who were said to be inciting villagers against tax-collectors, enrolling them as members of the Benin Community, and collecting suscriptions. This is the first sign we have from Benin of the emergence of anything resembling modern party politicking.

The struggle between the palace clique and the opposition coalition, which gained increasing popular support, grew to alarming proportions. A sensation was created by the discovery of paraphernalia of sorcery in the Residency garden. As was the custom in times of serious crisis, the the *oba* sent chalk and kola nuts to many important priests 'for the purpose of appeasing the gods in the interests of all the people generally'. He also expressed his determination to uphold his authority by creating a number of new titles, each one reaffirming the supremacy of the kingship. Eventually, however, the administrative officers found themselves forced to listen to the representations of the Benin Community, which requested permission to produce its own Intelligence Report. This request was granted and the proposals made in the Benin Community Intelligence Report formed a basis for discussion in the preparation, by H. F. (later Sir Hugo) Marshall of an Intelligence Report on Benin City.

Out of all these activities there emerged, in 1940, a new organizational model which sought to take account both of the hierarchies of the traditional polity and of the desire of the new elites to participate in the government. Benin City was divided into 24 wards, each with its own (somewhat informal) council responsible for preparing nominal rolls and collecting tax. There was also to be a Benin City Council of forty-eight members, composed entirely of two representatives from each ward (to be chosen by consensus rather than direct suffrage). The City Council was empowered to make rules for the government of the capital and had control of its own funds, subject to the overriding authority of the *oba* in Divisional Council. The Divisional Council was to consist of seventeen senior chiefs (three *uzama,* six *eghaebho n'ore,* three *eghaebo n'ogbe* from each of three palace associations, and the *ihaza,* head of another order), twenty-four ward representatives, and representatives of village groups throughout the Division. The Native Authority was now to be not the *oba* alone but the *oba*-in-Council.

This new pattern of government persisted, with modifications of detail, through the war years. The *oba* remained in a strong position, still able to exercise considerable patronage and retaining his right to make all land allocations in Benin City. The basis on which title-holders were selected for the Divisional Council still remained a source of grievance and of petitions, and served to create both solidarities in excluded orders and dissension within those represented. For the next major crisis, however, we have to move on to the post-war period.

By 1947 the modernists were again in revolt against what they described as the *oba's* autocratic behaviour. The measures of popular representation which they had achieved in 1940 had, in fact, given them very little control over either policy-making (which, in effect, remained with the British) or the bureaucratic machinery of the Native Administration. Once again, as in 1920 and the 1930s, the polarizing issues were supplied by the government, this time in the form of increases in taxes, licences, and summons fees. The approach of a new crisis was signalled in a predictable manner. *Iyase* Okoro-Otun had died in 1943 and the *oba* had been in no hurry to name a successor. Now, in 1947, the Benin Community Taxpayers Association (a successor to the Benin Community) began a vociferous campaign for the appointment of an *iyase* who would voice the popular will and curb palace autocracy. The TPA had, as its core, many of the men who had led the campaign for popular representation in the late 1930s and it also obtained the support of titleholders who had failed to secure official positions, dismissed former employees of the Native Administration, and others who, for personal reasons, were antipathetic to the *oba*. The modernists proceeded to mobilize popular support by appealing to traditional values and precedents. The argument that only an *iyase* could defend the Edo against the combined power of the white men and the palace clique had wide popular appeal and the outcry against the *oba's* failure to fill the title was soon almost universal.

The *oba*, with his father's and his own earlier experiences in mind — and with all Benin tradition confirming the inevitability of such experiences — was determined not to be forced to appoint an *iyase* against his will. In an attempt to put an end to the *oba/iyase* polarization factor, once and for all, he not only refused to confer the title but announced his decision to abolish it. 'It is my prerogative to abolish any title; this prerogative is inalienable', he asserted in the *Nigerian Spokesman*, 11 November 1947; and he went on to give reasons for his action. Everyone believed, he said, that whoever was made *iyase* must become the *oba's* enemy. 'The accursed name of *iyase*, not the character of the holder of the title, was the cause of the *iyase* becoming the arch-enemy of the *oba*.' In the old days, he continued, the *oba* could send a troublesome *iyase* to war − from which he was not expected to return − but this was now impossible. The *oba* went further. In place of *iyase* he proposed to create a new title, with the same privileges and rank (but without power or authority), which would be conferred automatically on whoever proved worthy enough to marry the *oba*'s eldest daughter. The new title was to be *obadeyanedo*, which can be approximately translated: 'the *oba* overshadows the Edo'.

It is widely conceded in Benin that the *oba* had always enjoyed considerable freedom in awarding titles, creating new titles, and even, within limits, in altering the order of precedence between them. Nevertheless, it appears to be the case that all the *uzama* titles and the uppermost titles in each *eghaebho* order have remained unchanged for centuries; and that their inviolability was one of the cardinal rules of the Benin political game. The widespread passionate reaction to Akenzua's attempt to abolish the *iyase* title helps to confirm this interpretation. Within the next few weeks he was subjected from all sides to a barrage of attack and abuse. Some went so far as to demand his deposition and rumour had it that his immediately junior brother was preparing to replace him. Mass demonstrations took place in Benin City. Petitions poured in from organizations of expatriate Edo in virtually every major Nigerian town. With a mass insurrection threatening, the government no longer found it possible to give the *oba* its support. Virtually isolated, and under pressure from chiefs and administrative officers. Akenzua was forced to retreat. On 17 February 1948, he announced that, in order to comply with the wishes of his chiefs, he had decided to confer the *iyase* title on a man who at that time was *esogban*. The *esogban* was a very old man, illiterate and nearly blind. He had been a warrant chief, a member of the Judicial Council and Native Authority Treasurer. Acceptable to many of the chiefs, he was hardly likely to appeal to the modernists. Faced with a renewed outburst, the *oba* had once more to retract and, under great pressure from the government, he eventually consented to give the title to the nominee of the Taxpayers' Association.

The new *iyase* was the epitome of the new elite. A rich farmer and timber-producer, he had for many years served as the Resident's Clerk. His name was Gaius Obaseki and he was a son of Agho, who had been made *iyase* thirty-four years before. The new *iyase* was a man of great enterprise, charm, and ability, and, like his father, he quickly gained the confidence of the British administrators. With his appointment came a complete reorganization of the Native Authority, which was henceforth to be defined not as 'oba-in-Council' but as 'oba and Council'. The oba was to be the President of the Divisional Council with the iyase as Chairman. There were to be two other ex-officio titled members, the esogban and eson (both eghaebho n'ore), and seventeen other chiefs to be elected by the palace associations. A further sixteen chiefs, who had been members of the old Council, were allowed to remain as ordinary members. In addition there were to be sixty-four members elected to represent wards of the capital and administrative areas of Benin Division. The most significant new development, however, was the creation of a number of Committees (Administrative, Staff Discipline, Finance, Income Tax Appeals) to oversee the Native Administration bureaucracy, members of which were to be elected by the Council. Finally the iyase was also to be Chairman of the Benin City Council.

It immediately became evident that, in practice, the Native Authority was going to be not the oba and Council but the iyase and Council. Immediate steps were taken to lower the oba's dignity and curtail his prerogatives. The Council voted to reduce his salary from £1,800 to £800 p.a. and passed a rule forbidding him to confer any title without the Council's consent. The oba was not a member of the crucial Administrative Committee and henceforth he was to have no control over appointments to the courts or administrative services. All the Committees were, in fact, dominated by the modernists. Some of these men brought great energy and ability into the running of the Native Administration and the administrative officers frequently expressed delight at their efficiency. The oba seemed almost as impotent as his father had been after the 1914 restoration. However, as events soon showed, the pendulum of power had swumg too far for the new regime to maintain its legitimacy for very long.

Signs of a reaction began to appear as early as October 1948, with the formation of a new organization called the Reformed Benin Community, which the oba himself described as consisting of 'dynamic youths and progressive aristocrats'. At a meeting of this group he read out a letter from a youth, calling his attention to 'what is a great menace to the Binis, particularly the youths. This is Ogboniism which dominates the Council. Remember, this is not Yorubaland'. The oba agreed with the writer that the ogboni had no place in the Benin Constitution and could not be allowed (as he put it) to pollute the political system.

The *ogboni* referred to here is not the indigenous Yoruba earth cult of that name (Morton-Williams, 1960) but the Reformed Ogboni Fraternity of the Christians, which had had its origin about the time of the First World War among a group of prominent Yoruba Christians in Lagos and Abeokuta. It is probable that the R.O.F. was partly modelled on freemasonry (certainly Masonic signs are used in the paraphernalia of the Benin Lodge) and intended to perform a similar function, though it also incorporated features of the indigenous *ogboni* that were felt not to be inconsistent with Christianity. It shared with both the old *ogboni* cult and freemasonry a great stress on secrecy. An R.O.F. Lodge had existed in Benin at least since the early 1930s, recruiting most of its members from the educated and commercial elites, though some of the older chiefs were induced to join by their educated sons. Before 1948,. however, it had never been considered to have any direct political significance. That it now began to be perceived as a menacing and sinister cabal was due to the fact that its head, the *oluwo*, was none other than the new *iyase* while other members of the new ruling elite (including the *oba's* two immediately junior brothers) were also office-holders in it.

In order to make the nature of this organization clear, it is worth summarizing several clauses from its printed constitution:

8. No political topics shall be discussed in the Lodge nor can the Lodge concern itself in politics.

9. All members or initiates shall regard themselves as 'children of one another' and shall act towards one another as such wherever they meet.

10. Members of the Fraternity are in duty bound to help one another in distress, to succour in adversity, warn against danger, and be charitable under all circumstances.

16. Implicit obedience is required by all members to the laws, regulations, obligations and orders given in Council by the *oluwo*.

23. Admission into membership shall be payment of a free initiation.

I have no means of knowing whether Clause 8, barring political discussion, was adhered to in the Benin Lodge before the reorganization of the Native Authority in 1948. However, the high degree of overlap between the *ogboni* elite and the new ruling clique made it inevitable that the R.O.F. should, from this point onwards, become an important, and more or less overt, factor in Benin politics. Given the control now exercised by prominent *ogboni* over the administrative bureaucracy, the other clauses which I have quoted clearly take on a political significance. Within a year of Gaius Obaseki's appointment as *iyase* and Chairman of the Councils, the Taxpayers' Association had become firmly identified among the general population as a front organization for the Ogboni Lodge, though some of the more active members of the Association were not, in fact, *ogboni*. The feeling grew, not only among the ordinary villagers, but also among the educated men in the capital and other towns, that they had been betrayed. Having joined the general outcry for an *iyase* to defend them against a palace clique, it now appeared that they had only succeeded in placing even greater power in the hands of a more dangerous oligarchy operating from the secrecy of the Ogboni Lodge. The R.O.F., which had gone unnoticed for many years, took on sinister and fearful implications. It was a secret cult, with mysterious initiation rites, and in the old days such cults had never been allowed to operate in Benin City. Moreover, it was an alien cult, associated with the Yoruba, and had no place in Benin culture.

By 1950 the great majority of the Benin people, both in the capital and the villages, believed themselves to be at the mercy of an oppressive oligarchy. It was widely believed that all Council members and most court judges, police, and native administration officials of all kinds — sanitary inspectors, forest guards, and the like — had all been initiated into the R.O.F., and were, therefore, able to use their positions to exploit and oppress without fear of retribution. Those who had refused to join, it was believed, had all been ousted from their posts. Some of the British administrative officers, too, were alleged to be *ogboni* (European membership was in fact not unknown). Whatever the exact degree of truth in these beliefs and allegations (I cannot go into the evidence here) it is possible to say that they were by no means entirely unfounded.

Up to about 1951 most administrative officers were unwilling to believe that the anti-*ogboni* outcry was in any way spontaneously generated. They preferred to see it as a deliberate plot by the *oba* and reactionary chiefs, and by disgruntled ex-employees of the native administration, to recover their positions. In the course of time they were forced to revise this view. Nevertheless, such motivations were bound to be present, and the impetus towards organized opposition to the Ogboni T.P.A. group naturally came first from those most closely affected. Two distinct organizations emerged:

1. *Aruosa*

This was an attempt by the *oba* to found a national church of Benin. Its doctrines and beliefs were drawn entirely from Benin religion – the *oba* himself wrote a creed, scriptures, and 'hymns' – but its forms of worship owed much to the example of Christian church services. *Aruosa* – which had been founded at the end of 1945 – was developed as a focus of Edo values in opposition to the alien *ogboni* cult. It gained some success, mainly among older people, and played a part in the mobilization of anti-*ogboni* sentiments.

2. *Otu-Edo*

This organization, which grew out of the Reformed Benin Community had, in 1950, been transformed into something like a modern political party. Its early meetings had been convened and attended by a heterogeneous collection of chiefs, priests of royal cults, and other traditionalists, and of young ambitious men who were opposed to the ruling clique for various reasons. Although the *Otu-Edo* expressed their opposition to the *ogboni* in terms of their loyalty to the *oba*, Akenzua himself circumspectly avoided overt participation in their activities. The leadership of the *Otu-Edo* was taken over by a former civil servant, H. Omo-Osagio, who had spent many years in Lagos. He had long been a close associate of the *oba*, who had conferred two successive titles on him, and also appointed him a priest of *aruosa*.

By 1951 the population of Benin Division was divided into two clear-cut factions. All quarrels and disputes, all clashes of interest, tended to be interpreted in terms of the opposition of *Otu-Edo* and *ogboni oba* and *iyase*. Families were divided. European administrators were assigned by the Edo to one side or the other, according to which way their sympathies lay, or appeared to lie. Edo expatriate organizations also split into factions, though the majority of Edo 'abroad' were now as vociferous in their loyalty to the *oba* as they had been in condemning him three years before; and at home many of those who had vilified him three years before gave him their unstinting praise.

In the Benin villages war songs were sung and the exploits of the great warrior *obas* of the past were recounted. Purveyors of medicines purporting to give protection from gunshot and matchet toured the villages and did a roaring trade.

Into this highly charged situation we have to introduce a new factor. Although there were already Benin members of Dr. Azikiwe's N.C.N.C.

(National Council of Nigeria and the Cameroons), the rapid growth of nationalist politics in post-war Nigeria had had relatively little effect on Benin internal affairs – except in so far as it helped to spread ideas about democracy and party organization. In the summer of 1951, however, the first elections were to be held to the Western Nigerian House of Assembly. In the region as a whole, the contest lay between the N.C.N.C. and Awolowo's newly formed, Yoruba-based Action Group. The clear-cut division of Benin into two political camps, and the obvious numerical superiority of the anti-*ogboni* sympathizers, provided a rich opportunity for a few men who aspired to enter national politics. Although several of them already had affiliations with the nationalist parties, they directed their attentions to turning the *Otu-Edo* itself into a modern political party and the three men who were chosen as its candidates campaigned almost wholly on the local issues of destroying the power of the *ogboni* and restoring the *oba* to his rightful position.

Shortly before the regional elections, elections were held for a new Benin Divisional Council, and, in these, *Otuo-Edo* candidates were universally successful. The end of *ogboni* domination unleashed a wave of violence throughout Benin Division. By this time there were a few *ogboni*s in most villages. Many of these were now driven out and some of their homes burnt down. The *iyase*'s compound in Benin City became a temporary refugee camp for fleeting *ogboni*s. In a few places there were serious riots and the Resident was obliged to call on the *oba*'s · assistance to restore order. The Divisional Council and its powerful Committees passed entirely into *Otu-Edo* hands and immediate steps were taken to restore the *oba*'s dignity, by raising his salary and reaffirming his prerogative of conferring titles. The *iyase*'s downfall was as abrupt as that of his father, thirty-one years before. Though still ex-officio Chairman he was no longer to be seen at Council meetings.

The introduction of direct suffrage and regional self-government and the developments of named political parties, were to have far-reaching effects on the pattern of political conflict at Benin, and this is therefore a convenient point at which to draw a halt. It is worth noting, however, that this latest confrontation between *oba* and *iyase* was to have implications for Western Regional and National politics in the 1950s. In the course of the 1951 local and regional campaigns at Benin, the *Otu-Edo* had become associated with the N.C.N.C. and the Taxpayers' Association/*ogboni* with the Action Group. Its association, in the minds

of Edo electors, with the *ogboni* helped to put the Action Group at a
permanent disadvantage in Benin. This, indeed, was one of the reasons
why Omo-Osagie, who proved himself a brilliant political campaigner,
was able to deliver the *Otu-Edo* majority vote to the N.C.N.C. with
predictable regularity.

CONCLUSIONS

The outstanding landmarks of Benin political history in the period with
which we have been concerned are the periodic 'reorganizations' — i.e.
the redistributions and redefinitions of the competences allocated by
their colonial rulers to members of the Benin political class; and the
confrontations between ruling cliques and opposition coalitions that
alternate with them. Reorganizations are motivated (*a*) by the
government's searching for more effective administrative machinery for
the implementation of its policies and (*b*) by the necessity of
containing internal political conflict and of coming to terms with
demands on the government which can no longer be safely ignored. A
proper treatment of the first set of motivations would have involved us
in the task of relating the government's actions at Benin to its general
policies for southern Nigeria as a whole — a task which the present
writer is not qualified to undertake. In so far as we had assumed rather
than analysed British objectives, the interpretation of Benin political
history offered in this paper is necessarily incomplete and distorted.
However, the aim was not to write a comprehensive political history
but only to throw some light on the way in which political concepts,
norms, and habits evolved in the traditional polity come through into
the colonial period and, by interacting with new objectives,
opportunities, and administrative structures, help to shape the course of
political change.

The continuities to which I have sought to draw attention reside not
in the formal framework of government, which was subject to a
sequence of disjunctive, non-repetitive changes, but in the style and
structure of political competition and conflict. I refer not merely to the
enduring appetite of the Benin political class for factional intrigue but,
more specifically, to the persisting relevance, in a changing
environment, of a model of political conflict which is expressed in
terms of such binary oppositions as: *oba/iyase, oba/edo,*
Palace/anti-Palace, capital/villages, territorial chiefs/palace emissaries,
and 'old guard'/'new men'.

In analysing the political events of the immediate post-restoration period (p. 109 above) I drew attention to the coexistence of contradictory organizational models in terms of which various sectors of the political class formulated their divergent interests and objectives. The administrative structure arrived at in 1920 (which appears to have afforded a reasonably viable balance between palace and anti-palace groups) was followed by the imposed 'centralized bureaucratic' model of the mid-1930s and the 'representational' model formulated by the modernists and essentially given approval by the government. These, in their turn, served as the basis for the crystallization of new interest groups. My purpose here is to point out that the tactics used to forge alliances between divergent interest groups, and to amass support for demands made upon the government and upon the ruling clique who were its agents, draw to a considerable degree upon the pre-colonial conscious model of political conflict. By espousing the traditionalist causes of the *ezomo* and the *iyase* as well as defending the interests of the population of the capital (in regard to the permanent crops and water-rate ordinances) the modernists mobilized the support of both the former District Heads and the general population for their assault on the combined power of the government and the palace oligarchy. In their second major campaign after the war they again rallied widespread support by demanding that the *oba* fulfil his obligation to appoint an *iyase*.

In these and other examples, the enduring potency of the implicit rules of the pre-colonial political game as rallying points for concerted political action is manifest. By presenting the *oba*'s alleged disregard for the *ezomo*'s prerogatives, his failure to appoint an *iyase* and his attempt to abolish the *iyase* title as transgressions of immutable rules, the anti-traditionalists were enabled to advance their own interests and thus to push forward the process of political development. Similarly, the attack of the ruling *ogboni* clique on the king's prerogatives and its own lack of, and contempt for, traditional legitimacy were the main targets of the successful campaign of the *Otu-Edo* in 1951, which, on the one hand, restored the *oba*'s authority and, on the other hand, launched its leaders' careers in national politics.

Finally, I draw attention to the structure of the political process that unfolds between one reorganization and the next. With the possible exception of that of 1920, each major reorganization generates a powerful ruling clique and a scatter of divergent interest groups. While the particular nature of the interests involved varies from one cycle to the next, these groups can regularly be categorized as 'dispossessed' (former paramount chiefs, former District Heads, former N.A. employees), 'deprived' (titled chiefs who had failed to secure competences, unrepresented commercial and educated elites), and 'exploited' (the 'ordinary' people of Benin City and the villages). Groups of the first two categories are similarly motivated by their desire for competences and employment but may be divided in their espousal of different organizational models. Sooner or later, however, they unite and secure the support of the exploited groups in terms of shared opposition to specific administrative measures (especially fiscal innovations and increased taxes) introduced by the government and implemented by the ruling elite. This opposition, we have suggested, gains effectiveness in so far as it is capable of being expressed in terms of traditional norms of conflict. The noisy confrontation that ensues between the opposition coalition and the government-backed ruling clique is resolved when the govenment is forced to adopt a more neutral stance from which it can negotiate and regulate a fresh distribution of competences. At this point the cycle recommences.

If this 'unconscious model' of a competitive process is accepted as valid, the question must be asked: What are its historical limits? Certainly one might expect to have to discard it for the period after 1951 when the political struggle lay between named, enduring local parties affiliated to nationalist parties contesting for power at the regional and federal levels. But the problem I find more absorbing is whether a study of the processes leading to confrontation crises during the colonial period can help us to ask the right questions about the precolonial confrontations to which the Edo themselves conceptually assimilated them. Further consideration of this problem must await another opportunity.

Patrimonialism and Gerontocracy in Benin Political Culture

ELDERHOOD AND KINGSHIP

In the late fifteenth century, when the first Portuguese explorers reached the area of the Niger Delta, Benin City *(Edo)* was already the capital of a powerful kingdom and an expanding military empire. If tradition be relied upon, a dozen or more kings of the Oranmiyan dynasty which is said to have continued unbroken up to the present day, had by that time succeeded each other. According to its mythical charter, this dynasty had originated in a request by the elders *(edion)* of the Edo to the *Oghene n'Uhe* (Oni of Ife) that he should send them a king. The Oghene sent his son Oranmiyan, but the latter found the language and manners of the Edo uncongenial to him. He therefore contented himself with begetting a son by the daughter of an Edo village chief and departed for home. Trained for the kingship by some of his father's followers who had been left behind for the purpose, Oranmiyan's son, Eweka, was accepted by the Edo as their first Oba (king).

There is little reason to doubt that this dynastic myth incorporates a folk memory of the advent of alien rulers, but, I have suggested elsewhere (Bradbury 1967: 1-3), that the particular form which it took served to epitomize the relationship between the Oba and the Edo on which the social order of the kingdom was founded. As a scion of a stock which provided the rulers of other kingdoms, the Oba was a being set apart from his subjects and had an intrinsic right to be obeyed. Yet, as the myth asserts, the kingship came into being by the will of the elders of the Edo community. The first Oba was himself born into that community and he and his successors were therefore bound to respect its norms and institutions.

Thus interpreted, the myth gives expression to two opposed yet complementary conceptions of authority which pervade Benin political culture: the authority of kings and the authority of elders. These two conceptions of authority conform, in many respects, to Weber's ideal

types 'patrimonialism' and 'gerontocracy' (Weber 1947: 346 ff.), and I
shall therefore make use of these terms. The crucial point of difference
between patrimonialism and gerontocracy lies, as Weber observed, in
the basis of the relationship between the holders of authority and those
who are bound to obey it. Where gerontocracy obtains, governors and
governed share equal membership rights, in the corporate group whose
boundaries define the area over which authority is exercised. Their
reciprocal role-expectations are defined first in terms of common
membership rights, and secondly in terms of relative seniority. The
elder's authority is in no sense a private possession but is exercised,
transmitted, and devolved according to gerontocratic rules. We may add
that – presuming male authority and excluding women – the governed
are the potential successors to the governors.

By contrast, patrimonialist conceptions place primary emphasis on
qualitative differences between the governors and the governed. The
ruler's uniqueness, which may be justified in various ways, allows him
to 'own' his subjects in a sense in which elders do not own their juniors.
Since it belongs to him as a private possession, the patrimonial ruler can
devolve his authority as he wishes. In the extreme case he alone has the
right to choose his successor.

In the nineteenth-century Benin kingdom, gerontocratic principles
were most explicitly manifested in the structures and processes of
village government. Ideally, the whole male population of the village
was ranked according to order of birth, and it was in this order that
men passed through the youth (*iroghae*), adult (*ighele*), and elder
(*edion*) age-grades. The *edion* (literally 'those who (are) senior') were the
repository of the land laws, rights, and reputation of the village, which
they held in trust back through the generations of their predecessors to
the first nameless elders who had founded the community. The shrine
of the dead *edion* was the village council hall. Here the living elders
assembled to judge disputes and conduct village business. They were
presided over by the oldest man (*odionwere*) who, by virtue of his
closeness to them, was the priest of the dead *edion* as well as of the
village earth (*oto*) in which they were buried. Except in a minority of
villages which had hereditary chiefs (*enigie*), the *odionwere* was the
village head. In most villages the next four elders (*edion nene*), but in
some the next seven (*edion nihiron*), were accorded special respect.

It would be wrong to say that the elders had no legislative functions.
From time to time they purposefully modified the rules which
governed intra-village relationships. Nevertheless the emphasis, in their

authority, was on the conservation of that code as it had been handed down to them from the original elders. In consultation with his fellow-elders, the *odionwere* regulated the performance by the two lower age-grades of their customary community roles. The *ighele* had policing functions and carried out the more skilled communal tasks. It was from their ranks that troops were recruited into the Oba's army, on the basis of a nationally organized seven-point cycle of age-companies. The *ighele* were explicitly regarded as the collective heirs to the collective authority of the elders, and relations between the two grades displayed the characteristic ambiguities of the holder-heir relationship (cf. Bradbury1966: 144-52). To the *iroghae* (youths) fell the more menial community tasks and it was they who carried the village's annual tribute to the Oba in the capital.

Strict age-ranking was subject to various qualifications. In some villages the *odionwere* was the oldest man of the oldest ward. In villages that had hereditary chiefs, the position was sometimes reserved for the oldest man of the chief's ward. There were also various kinds of adjustment between the authority structure of the family and that of the village community (see Bradbury 1957: 31-34), but, though it was regarded as desirable that each family should be represented among the *edion*, they were not primarily conceived of as a body of lineage representatives. Order of birth into the village community *per se* was the dominant criterion for the ascription of authority. The norms and structures of village government served as a model for the government of territorial and associational groups of all kinds, including, as I shall suggest, the kingdom as a whole and its central administrative organs.

Patrimonial authority inhered (by definition) in the kingship, though certain hereditary chiefs also possessed patrimonial rights within their own limited domains and subject to the Oba's overriding jurisdiction. Conceptually, each Oba conferred the right to rule on his successor when he designated him as his legitimate senior son. Ultimately, as we have suggested, this right derived from outside the Edo community. It was justified by the unique capacity, transmitted from king to king, to prosper and revitalize the community. The fertility, health, and longevity of the Edo depended on the Oba's capacity to use his own person to transform natural vitality into social value. Annually, in the complex *Igue* rite, his body was brought into contact with the life-giving products of the forest. His vitalizing energy was thereby regenerated. Then, under conditions of ritual control, the Edo people were exposed to its creative force.

Dynamism was the essence of the kingship in its political as well as in its mystical dimensions. Whereas the gerontocratic social order of the village was a cyclical ahistorical order, the political order of the kingdom was in constant flux. At his death, the individuality of the elder was assimilated to the undifferentiated collectivity of his predecessors in that status (Bradbury 1966: 132). The past kings, as depicted in legend and anecdote, were lively individual personalities, each of whom had left his imprint on the political culture. Every change in the fortunes of the state and the configuration of its institutions was attributed to their creative genius and political strivings. As they strove to impose their will on 'the Edo', order was repeatedly reduced to chaos and a transformed order re-emerged. In the annual cycles of festivals in honour of the past kings, the multi-dimensional structural-historical relationship between the Oba and the Edo was continuously re-created. Ritual enactments of 'events' in the reigns of past kings, and the myths and legends which interpreted them, provided the rationale for the structural position of each state office and institution. They also furnished the ideological idiom of political dispute. According to patrimonialist representations, rank, competences, and prerogatives were shown to be privileges granted by one king and therefore liable to be redefined or withdrawn by another. Opposition to these claims took the form of denying the Oba the right to alter the dispensations that were demonstrated to have been made by his predecessors. Rank was equated with antiquity. Administrative segments and individual office-holders laid claim to their various capacities as age-sanctified rights. In these and other ceremonials both the political tensions between the Oba and the various segments of the political elite and the institutionalized compromises that regulated them were ritually objectified. The refusal of individuals or groups to perform their customary roles was a sign of disaffection.

According to Weber, in a gerontocracy 'administrative functions are performed "on behalf" of the corporate group', whereas appropriation by the chief personally is a phenomenon of patrimonialism. It may vary enormously in degree to the extreme cases of a claim to full proprietorship of the land and to the status of master over subjects treated as slaves' (Weber 1947: 349). These criteria of extreme patrimonialism were fully realized in the Benin ideology of kingship, but each was countered by an opposite principle. 'The Oba owns the land'(*Oba nya oto*) was no shibboleth; he appointed an official to regulate its distribution and also a band of 'surveyors' to show people their boundaries. Yet the land belonged to ward and village communities and was administered by their elders (Bradbury *1957:* 76). As Dapper rightly reported in 1668 'all the Benin people, high and low, are bound to acknowledge themselves to be the slaves of the king' (cited in Ling Roth 1903: 91); but Nyendael was no less accurate when in 1701, he wrote: 'All male slaves here are foreigners; for the natives cannot be sold for slaves, but all are free, and alone bear the name of the king's slaves' (Bosman 1967: 402); In fact only freeborn Edo had the right to be branded with the facial and body markings which distinguished 'the Oba's slaves' (*evien-Oba*) from 'real slaves', that is the slaves of (ordinary) 'people' (*evien-onbhan*) and the private slaves of the reigning incumbent (*evien-Omo*). Finally, all administrative titles and capacities were held to be privileges conferred by the king; but, as I hope to show, those who held and exercised them did so as 'elders' either of the côporate political associations to which they belonged, or of the Edo community as a whole.

THE KINGDOM AS AN EXTENSION OF
THE OBA'S HOUSEHOLD

A primary characteristic of patrimonialism is that 'governmental offices originate in the household administration of the ruler' (Bendix 1960: 334). In this respect the pre-colonial Benin régime had a markedly patrimonialist flavour. The Oba's palace retainers were divided into three major segments among which were distributed the menial, craft, administrative, and ceremonial functions necessary to maintain his household and his royal dignity. Briefly, the *Iwebo* had charge of royal regalia, the *Iweguae* supplied the king's servants and attendants, and the *Ibiwe-Eruerie* were responsible for the discipline and welfare of his wives and children. These retainer associations were also the main instrument for the recruitment and training of governmental personnel and for the execution of the Oba's civil and ritual authority throughout his domains. Their senior titled officials, the *Eghaebho n'Ogbe* or Palace Chiefs, were great officers of state whose range of governmental functions excluded only that of military command. As a corporate group the *Eghaebho n'Ogbe* were formally ranked below two other groups of chiefs: the *Uzama*, whose titles were hereditary, and the *Eghaebho n'Ore* or Town Chiefs who, like the Palace Chiefs, were appointed by the king; but in terms of power and prestige they were by no means their inferior.

Iwebo, Iweguae, and *Ibiwe* were constituted as corporate associations. Each was made up of a number of grades of untitled retainers and two tiers of titled offices, *Ekhaenbhen* and *Eghaebho n'Ogbe*, within each of which titles were ranked in lineal sequence. To each association as a corporate group and to their component subdivisions and individual offices specific administrative competences were assigned.

Recruitment into retainer service was open to all male freeborn commoners. Indeed, in principle, every *ovien-Oba* was by paternal filiation a member of one of the retainer divisions. However, unless he was formally initiated into his association ('entered the palace') his membership of it remained purely nominal, affording him no access to its apartments in the palace or to its revenue or deliberations. Since Benin villages were made up of a number of patrilineal groupings of disparate origins, each village contained members of all the palace associations. There is, however, no evidence that members of the same associations constituted structural units at the local level. Nominal palace affiliation was mainly significant as a mechanism of political socialization. Symbolically, it afforded the individual a sense of direct participation in the central institutions of the patrimonial régime. As he grew up every young Edo became aware of a direct bond between himself and the king, bypassing the distance-maintaining chains of official communication whose links were village headmen, chiefs, and the agents of territorial administrators based in the capital. These symbolic functions were the more effective in that they were linked to practical opportunities for advancement. For the ambitious young villager initiation into the lowest grade of a retainer association was the first step on a ladder whose highest rungs were the great Town and Palace titles. His prospects of reaching the top were slight, for he had to compete for promotion against the sons and grandsons of chiefs who in terms of family wealth, influence and opportunities for acquiring political and administrative expertise, enjoyed great initial advantages. Nevertheless, there was no formal status barrier to upward mobility and it was by no means unknown for talented men of humble origins to achieve high office.

It seems probable that the systematic recruitment of retainers on a universalistic basis dates back to a period at which the Benin kings were seeking to create a centralized régime and to mobilize popular support for it among the freeborn Edo population. Indeed it is possible that in the sixteenth and seventeenth centuries, when the Benin state was at its apogee, periods of service in the palace were obligatory. In the nineteenth century the bulk of initiated retainers were drawn from patrician families resident in the capital, that is families with an established tradition of court and government service. Even so, the proportion of villagers who entered the palace was considerable. A new initiate into the lowest grade of his association spent a week or two in the palace, during which time he paid fees to existing members, took oaths of loyalty and received instructions in his duties and obligations. Villagers who secured the patronage of the Oba or Palace Chiefs remained at the capital to compete for administrative assignments and promotion. However, a court career, though it was prestigious and could be materially rewarding, was also precarious. Many retainers of village origin returned sooner or later to a life of subsistence farming. Thus in any village there were men who had some direct experience of retainer service and who, on their visits to the capital, had entry into the palace. This was one of the more important ways in which direct communication between the court and the villages took place. Thus retainerdom, apart from its overt administrative functions, was an important mechanism for maintaining a high level of commitment among the general population to the ideology and values of the patrimonial régime. The presence of erstwhile retainers in the villages also helped to temper relations with active retainers who visited them on a variety of extractive missions.

It was not only at the individual level that the political community was conceived of as the king's household writ large. The population of each of the numerous wards into which the capital was divided was constituted as a corporate group of craftsmen or ritual or ceremonial functionaries. Each of these groups, whose internal affairs were regulated through a system of appointive or hereditary offices combined with graded structures derived from the village age-grades, claimed to have been founded by one of the past kings to perform some special service for himself and his successors. For purposes of administrative coordination, each group of special functionaries was affiliated to one of the palace associations. However, the more important groups, such as the *Ewaise* (the king's doctors and diviners) and the *Ihogbe* (the priests of the king's divinity), whose functions were continuous, claimed equality of status with the palace associations and conducted their business with the Oba in person.

Many villages were similarly incorporated as bodies of special functionaries charged with specific duties relating to the upkeep of the royal household, the administration of the king's estate, and the fulfilment of his ritual and secular functions. These, too, carried out their tasks under the surveillance of Palace Chiefs. Villages lacking specific retainer functions had no corporate association with the palace. They were assigned for purposes of tribute collection, military recruitment, and their own support to individual title-holders of all the chieftaincy orders. Tribute was rendered collectively in the forms of yams and other foodstuffs. For the village youths, the annual tribute-carrying expeditions to the capital were the event of the year. When they had delivered their loads to the Oba they could test their strength in wrestling contests with the Oba's pages. The most popular rags-to-riches stories are those which recount how a youth's wrestling prowess caught the eye of the king, who took him into his service and set him on the road to high office. The founders of some of the most patrician families are said to have started their careers in this way.

HEREDITARY ELDERHOOD AND
PATRIMONIAL PREFERMENT

The dominant positions in the government of the nineteenth-century Benin kingdom were occupied by the Oba and his appointed officials of the *Eghaebho n'Ore* and *Eghaebho n'Ogbe* orders. It was the kingship and the Town and Palace titles, together with their associated competences and prerogatives, that constituted the main arena of political competition and conflict. According to dynastic traditions this had not always been the case. Many legends recount the struggles of the early kings to escape from the domination of the *Uzama*, a group of hereditary nobles whose first five members are identified as the descendants of the elders who had invited the *Oghene n'Uhe* to send them a king. The fourth Oba, Ewedo, is said to have moved the palace from its original site, which was surrounded by the settlements of the *Uzama*, to its present location a mile or two away; and to have begun to confer titles on Edo commoners in order to enlist their support against the nobles. But it is the fifteenth Oba, Esigie, who is credited with finally disposing of the threat which the *Uzama* presented to the king's personal authority. Esigie is attributed to the early sixteenth century and tradition has it that European visitors, armed with guns, assisted him in quelling the powerful nobles. When the *Uzama* showed their disaffection by refusing to play their part in the king's rituals, Esigie is said to have nominated a new set of *Uzama* to replace them.

Eventually, however, the real *Uzama* submitted to the king's superior power. Their rank and ritual competences were restored, but from Esigie's time onwards traditions no longer portray them as a serious threat to the Oba's authority.

These myths and the rites which enacted them provided the charter for the ambiguous, but important, position which the *Uzama* occupied in the nineteenth-century Benin régime. In so far as their relationship with the king perpetuated that between the first elders and the first king, the *Uzama* were conceptually located outside the boundaries of patrimonial authority. Unlike the Town and Palace Chiefs, they held their offices by hereditary right. Spatially, too, they were set apart. Whereas the appointed officials were bound to reside within the wall and ditch which surrounded the capital, the villages of the *Uzama* lay beyond it, and the fact that they had to cross the ditch to reach the Oba's palace was a potent symbol of their detachment. Within their own villages the individual *Uzama* were virtually autonomous rulers. While accepting that they could not inflict the death penalty without the Oba's consent, they otherwise claimed complete jurisdiction over their own subjects, who were *evien-Uzama* rather than *evien-Oba*. Although on a much smaller scale, their households were organized along the same lines as the royal court and staffed by retainers on whom they conferred titles. By a curious twist of the gerontocratic/patrimonial dichotomy, these hereditary palatine privileges reinforced the role of the *Uzama* as the elders who 'owned' the kingship. Being semi-independent rulers and having themselves some of the attributes of kingship, they were able, at least in symbolic terms, to treat with the Oba on a basis of near equality, and thus to act as the guarantors of the compact between the Oba and the Edo which gave the patrimonial régime its legitimacy. This compact was ritually renewed each year at the Festival of the Oba's Father, when the Oba stepped down from his throne to sacrifice a goat to the earth in which the dead elders of the nation were buried; the *Uzama*, as *edion*, made reciprocal contributions to the offerings to the king's predecessors. But the most important of the system-maintaining functions performed by the *Uzama* as elders related to their role as 'kingmakers'. To these I shall return later.

These gerontocratic conceptions of the status of the *Uzama* were countered by other representations which placed them within the purview of the king's patrimonial prerogatives. The latter position was justified by the legends and rites which recounted Esigie's victory over their ancestors, but also by myths which indicated that their individual titles had been conferred on the primeval elders by the first Oba. On this basis the Oba claimed ultimate jurisdiction over succession to these titles; hereditary succession could be held to be a privilege that might be withdrawn rather than a perpetual right. In the absence of an independent judiciary and formal law, where such a conflict of principles coincided with a conflict of interests, the issue could only be settled by political action. Where no conflict of interest was at stake, the conflict of principles was dealt with by a series of symbolic compromises. The Oba normally respected the principle of hereditary succession and, in return, the *Uzama* acknowledged themselves, though not their subjects, to be *evien-Oba*. As such, they were eligible as individuals to receive patrimonial preferment to administrative competences. The benefices and prerogatives assigned to them tended to be appropriated as hereditary rights, though from the king's point of view they were only privileges that had to be renewed when each title-holder was succeeded by his son. The succession procedures are of particular interest. In principle the holder of a *Uzama* title, like the king, designated his senior son as his heir. Before the latter could be inducted into office, however, he had to pay accession fees both to the king and to his fellow-*Uzama*. Furthermore he had to be initiated into one of the Oba's palace associations, a procedure which involved not only swearing oaths of loyalty but also the implication that he had served, however nominally, as a retainer in the king's household. Finally, he received his title from the Oba through the medium of the latter's senior appointed official, the *Iyase*. There was one exception to this procedure: *Oliha*, the senior member of the order, was inducted by the Oba himself. The significance of these succession procedures will, I think, become clear as this essay proceeds.

THE KING AND HIS PATRIMONIAL STAFF

The subversion of the power of the hereditary *Uzama* is linked in tradition with the growing power of officials directly appointed by the king. The establishment of the *Eghaebho n'Ore* and *Eghaebho n'Ogbe* as contraposed rank orders is attributed to the twelfth Oba, Ewuare, though some of the titles he incorporated in them are said to have been created by earlier kings, Ewuare was the grandfather of Esigie, the Oba who is credited with having got the upper hand over the *Uzama*. Tradition-derived chronologies locate him in the fifteenth century, just

beyond the range of the earliest Portuguese descriptions of Benin, so there
is no contemporary documentation of his existence or his achievements.
Nevertheless, so many of the characteristic features of the pre-colonial
polity are attributed to his creative genius that it is difficult to avoid
associating the name Ewuare with an important phase in its evolution.

The innovations ascribed to Ewuare hang together with remarkable
consistency. As well as founding the *Eghaebho n'Ore* and *Eghaebho
n'Ogbe* orders, he is said to have been the first Oba to persuade his
freeborn subjects to let their sons take up retainer service in the palace.
It was he, too, who first decreed that all his freeborn Edo subjects
should be marked with the common pattern of scarifications which
distinguished *evien-Oba* from royals, slaves, and foreigners, all of whom
were excluded from the palace. Another of his accomplishments was to
organize the population of the capital into corporate wards, each
characterized by the particular craft or ritual service which it owed to
the king. The majority of these groups, together with similar ones
located outside the capital, trace their foundation to Ewuare and his
immediate successors, Ozolua and Esigie. Ewuare is also said to have
been the first Oba to confer the heir-apparent's title, *Edaiken*, on his
senior son. This attribution coincides with an apparent shift in the
pattern of succession to the throne indicated in oral king-lists. Before
Ewuare's time the kingship was transmitted collaterally. From the reign
of his son, Ozolua, it passed lineally, except for a period in the
seventeenth century following a failure in the direct line. Ewuare,
Ozolua, and Esigie are also credited with the creation of the extensive
empire whose existence is confirmed in the earliest Portuguese accounts
of Benin.

With the later and better-documented examples of Buganda
(Southwold 1961) and Ashanti (Wilks 1967) in mind, it is at least a
useful heuristic hypothesis that these traditions represent a phase of
political centralization and administrative differentiation in which the
kings were able to subvert descent-group-based claims to authority, and
appropriate to themselves a large measure of control over the means of
administration. Wilks has convincingly related what he calls the
'Kwadwoan revolution' of late eighteenth- and early nineteenth-century
Ashanti to the demand for a more differentiated and professional
administrative organization posed by military expansion over extensive
and culturally heterogeneous territories (Wilks 1967: 211 ff.). This
paper proceeds on the hypothesis that the main structural outlines of
the nineteenth-century Benin polity were established as the result of

broadly similar developments taking place in broadly similar circumstances as far back as the fifteenth and early sixteenth centuries. The detailed structural and procedural configurations of the nineteenth-century régime I take to be the product of conflicts and compromises between subsequent generations of kings and officials pursuing their individual and group interests in an environment of historical contingencies.

ELDERHOOD AND THE PATRIMONIAL RÉGIME

The tiered hierarchies of offices in each retainer association were founded on a series of 'untitled' grades which the Edo themselves saw as being analogous to the village age-grades. The *edion* grade of *Ibiwe-Eruerie* and the *edafen* grades of *Iwebo* and *Iweguae* were equated with the *edion* grade of the village to the extent that a man who achieved *odion (odafen)* status in the palace was automatically recognized as an *odion* of his village. His rank in the village order of birth might not be materially affected: he could not become *odionwere* before those who were born before him; but he was exempted from the prestations to existing elders and the rites of passage which marked promotion to village elderhood, and he was no longer obliged to participate in the activities of the *ighele*. Palace elders were easily distinguishable in the village by their hair style, which was like that of state chiefs and a simpler version of the Oba's own coiffure. Their appearance alone served to remind villagers of their allegiance to the Oba and the fact that they had the right of entry into the palace afforded their opinions special respect in village councils. Thus the concept of equivalence between palace and village elderhood was of some importance as mediating between the political cultures of the village and the state.

The fact that the Edo established continuities between village and palace grades should not be allowed to obscure the differences that existed between these institutions. Progress through the palace grades was a function not of age but of achievement. Advancement depended on wealth and on ability to secure the patronage of the king and palace chiefs. Furthermore, the grades within each palace association were internally differentiated, as the village grades were not, into groups of specialized functionaries, trained in particular skills and charged with specific duties relating to the fulfilment of the Oba's ritual and governmental functions both in the palace and in his wider domains.

Nevertheless promotional procedures and role-relationships within and between the grades of the associations were informed by gerontocratic norms. As in the village, promotion involved prestations to existing members. It is true that, in the village, the cost of promotion was so low as to exclude only the most wretched individuals, whereas wealth was an important differential in competition for promotion through the palace hierarchies; but underlying this difference was the common principle that status within the group was conferred by the group as a corporate body. Preferment by the Oba had to be matched by acceptance by the elders. Seniority within the untitled grades was reckoned, if not by age, then by the analogous principle of date of entry. Tasks and perquisites were apportioned to individuals and groups by the Oba or his titled agents, but benefits also accrued to the grades as collectivities and these were shared according to seniority. At a palace feast, as at a village feast, the grades received and ate their portions separately.

Within each association the elders, like the village elders, were the repository and defenders of the group's rights, traditions, and rules of behaviour, which they held in trust from the dead *edion*. Each association had its shrine to the spirits of past elders, and service at this shrine was led, as in the village, by the living elder nearest to them in seniority (cf. Bradbury 1966: 139 ff). When a palace elder died his senior son was obliged to perform the rite of *izakhwe*, whereby the deceased was assimilated to the company of palace elders in the spirit world, precisely in the same way as he was bound to assimilate his father to the dead elders of his village, kin group, and any other association in which he had achieved elderhood. In the palace, as in all these other groups, completion of *izakhwe* was a prerequisite for the recognition of the senior son himself as an elder (Bradbury 1964: 108-9; 1966: 140).

Having established the presence of gerontocratic norms in the infrastructure of the patrimonial régime, we may follow them upwards into its superstructure. This consisted, as has been indicated, of the Palace and Town hierarchies of chieftaincy, which together made up a single promotional field. A system of individual titles conferred arbitrarily by a king who had the right to alter their rank order and to redistribute competences between them, smacks of that extreme form of patrimonialism which Weber (1947: 347) called 'sultanism'. This view of the title system existed (and still exists) at the level of a conscious model, and argument and action predicated upon it are readily

distinguishable ingredients of political conflict in both the colonial and
pre-colonial periods (Bradbury 1968). But it coexisted with equally
explicit and quite contrary principles. One of these was the notion that
once a man had 'completed' his title, it was his for life. The only
'constitutional' means whereby the Oba could render it vacant was by
making out a charge of treason against the holder, that is, a charge
meriting the death penalty.

A clear distinction must be made between the conferment of a title
and its 'completion' (*orefo*), which could take place soon after
conferment, or much later, or never. Conferment was the king's private
prerogative, exercised by the despatch, by night, of a personal emissary
(*ukonyenbhen*, the messenger of joy) to the successful applicant's
home, to tell him of the honour bestowed upon him. In making his
choice, the Oba could seek advice and he himself might be subjected to
much political pressure, but there was no constitutional impediment to
the exercise of his free will. However, before the new title-holder could
take up his office he had to be approved by his fellow chiefs. This
meant that he not only had to pay fees to the Town and Palace orders
as corporate bodies; and to the king himself, but also that he had to
visit each chief who had completed his own title, pay him a fee, and
kneel down before him to seek his blessing. Only when he had done this
could be complete his title, that is, undergo a public ceremony of
induction performed, in the Oba's presence, by the senior Town Chief
(*Iyase*) acting explicitly in his role as the Oba's chief spokesman but
also, by implication, in his role as the leader of the people (*okao evien
Oba*). Any chief who had not received his fees could attend this
ceremony and halt the proceedings, at least until an apology and
reparations had been made. It was at the completion ceremony that the
Oba informed the new chief, through the *Iyase*, what benefices and
prerogatives he was conferring upon him. Finally, the chief took oaths
of loyalty to the king and to his order or sub-order.

It will be apparent that the conferment and completion ceremonies
demarcated an arena in which bargaining and conflict over the
distribution of offices and competences took place between the Oba
and his chiefs. Indeed the title-making procedures as a whole (which are
far more complex than can be indicated here) represent a compromise
between 'sultanic' arbitrariness and the rights which the chiefly orders
were able to appropriate as corporate groups. Before completion there
was nothing to stop the Oba revoking the title. Once the chiefs had
sanctioned the completion rites, he was no longer free to do so.

There was, of course, an immense gap between the ascriptive context of promotion to village elderhood and the highly competitive context of recruitment to state titles, but parallels between village elders and state chiefs were quite overt. The manner in which the chiefs sanctioned the induction of a designated title-holder was regarded as homologous to the procedure whereby a villager, seeking promotion to the *edion* grade, had to kneel before each elder in his house to present him with yams and seek his blessing. Thus, according to contrary but equally explicit principles, the chiefs' authority derived from both the Oba and from the community. It was as elders of the Edo that the Town and Palace chiefs accepted the Oba's appointees into their ranks.

The interplay of patrimonial and gerontocratic ideas is particularly explicit in a final phase of the title-taking procedure, of which two phases have already been distinguished. When a man accepted an *eghaebho* title from the Oba he thereby mortgaged to him his whole personal estate. In order to redeem it he had to perform a most elaborate and costly rite known as *inyahien*, which by no means all chiefs succeeded in accomplishing before they died. *Inyahien* involved the chief in a further round of prestations to the king and his fellow-chiefs. At the culmination of this rite the chief wore on his head a block of white chalk, over which was sprinkled the blood of a cow sacrificed to his head by the Oba's own priests. This chalk was known as *ede,* meaning, literally, 'grey hair'. The late *Osuma*, who was one of the few chiefs to have performed *inyahien* in the twentieth century, explained that the *ede* signified the Edo belief that no man was worthy of a voice in public affairs until he had the experience and wisdom that comes with age. The central meaning of *inyahien* is, I think, plain. It effected a symbolic resolution of the contradiction between the patrimonial and gerontocratic components of chiefly authority. By empowering his own priests to bless the head of the chief and thereby relinquishing his claim to death dues, the Oba recognized the complementarity of the kingship and the community as sources of authority.

It was more particularly the Town Chiefs who assumed the mantle of elders of the Edo community. The paradox noted elsewhere (Bradbury 1967: 25-28) that, although they were appointed by the king, they were yet regarded as the proper defenders of the Edo against Palace tyranny, becomes intelligible in these terms; as do the contradictory elements in the role expectations of their leader, the *Iyase,* who was both the Oba's first subject (*okao-evien-Oba*) and his most likely worst enemy. According to the Edo model of political conflict, the *Oba* and *Iyase* occupied polar positions around which opposing factions were always likely to crystallize (Bradbury 1968).

The first four Town Chiefs, *Iyase, Esogban, Eson,* and *Osuma* were known as The Four *Eghaebho (Eghaebho n'Ene)* or The Four Pillars of Edo *(Ikadel 'Ene Edo)*, the latter term — which refers to the four poles supporting the roof of a farm shelter or market stall — being also applied to the *Edion n'Ene* — that is, the four oldest men of a village. Moreover, the *Esogban* was — figuratively but functionally — the 'oldest man' of the Edo community, the *Odionwere-Edo*. In his offical house he kept the altar of the *Edion-Edo* on which was placed the *Ukhurhe-Edo*, the carved staff which symbolized the authority of the dead elders of the nation. Across the broad avenue which divided the palace from the rest of the capital, the shrine of the *Edion-Edo* confronted the row of walled quadrangles which housed the altars of the past kings. This symbolic confrontation had great political significance. In times of political crisis, when there was serious dissension between the king and his chiefs, a request by the Oba to the *Odionwere-Edo* that he should sacrifice to the *Edion-Edo* was a clear indication of the king's desire to restore peace. By renewing the compact between himself and his predecessors and the people and their dead, he indicated his willingness to negotiate a settlement of the issues at stake.

The Oba's inability to dismiss officials who had completed their titles — whether in his own reign or his predecessor's — was an important restraint upon his personal power. Another such restraint was afforded by the popular conviction that the rank order of the uppermost titles in each hierarchy was unalterable. Opposition to the king's claim to the right to promote, demote, and abolish titles at will was expressed in the gerontocratic formula that titles should rank in order of their antiquity; that is, by reference to the position in the king-list of the Oba who had created them. The king's ability to put his 'sultanic' claims into effect depended upon the efficacy of the political support that chiefs adversely affected could secure from other chiefs and from the public. As far as lesser titles were concerned, the cross-cutting of interests that I have described elsewhere (1968: 198-9) gave him considerable manipulative scope. But the senior titles in each group appear, from both tradition and such contemporary documents as bear upon this matter, to have remained undisturbed over a period of centuries. Indeed, the senior titles in each order or sub-order are said to be those which were given to the founding members when it was first established − in may cases by Oba Ewuare.

The sacrosanct quality of these senior titles rested, in part, on the fact that they were associated with ritual functions indispensable to the fulfilment of the Oba's mystical obligations to the Edo. The king's mystical powers were ineffective unless they were complemented by mystical powers inherent in the community itself. At the level of the kingdom these powers were concentrated in the senior chiefs − especially the Town Chiefs − just as at the village level they were concentrated in the elders. The precise order of rank among the village *edion* was not of crucial importance until it became necessary to fill a vacancy among the *Edion n'Ene*. The first four positions had the character of offices, and seniority resided in the office rather than in the age of the incumbent − though ideally the two should coincide. This latter requirement was absent with respect to state titles but, in Edo eyes, the titles *Iyase, Esogban, Eson* and *Osuma* were the oldest in their order and therefore equivalent to the *Edion n'Ene*. Their rank order was as immutable as that of the four days of the Edo week with which they were ritually associated (cf. Bradbury 1967).

CONCLUSION − THE PRINCIPLES DRAMATIZED IN THE CEREMONIAL OF SUCCESSION

Nowhere are patrimonial and gerontocratic principles more intricately opposed than in the formal and ceremonial procedures by which the kingship was transmitted. In order to become an elder of the nation, an Edo commoner had first to receive a patrimonial appointment. Again, as we have noted, before the successor to the *Uzama* title could be inducted into office he had to be initiated into one of the palace associations. This involved not only taking an oath of loyalty to the king but also serving, if only nominally, as a retainer in the royal household. With one exception, the *Uzama* were inducted into office by the *Iyase*, the senior title-holder of the Town order. The exception was the most senior of the *Uzama*, the *Oliha*. A new *Oliha* had to be invested by the Oba personally. This was not a device to avoid questions of seniority between *Oliha* and *Iyase*: the Edo were asserting the complementary relationship between the king and the elders of the kingdom, just as they did in the creation of a new king.

According to the patrimonial ideology, the king himself chose his successor. He made his will known by causing the child whom he regarded as his senior son to undergo a series of rites of passage which culminated in the bestowal upon him of the title of *Edaiken*. Like all other patrimonial appointees, the heir-apparent, however, had to make prestations to the chiefs and be inducted into office by the *Iyase*, acting in his dual role as spokesman for the Oba and for the Edo. Thereupon he took his place as the most junior member of the *Uzama* order.

When these nobles ate together, the *Edaiken's* task, as the most junior of them, was to share out the food, just as the most junior *odion* in the village served food to the village elders. When the senior *Uzama, Oliha*, broke kola nuts the *Edaiken* was the last to receive his portion. It will be recalled that the *Uzama* were identified as the elders whose request to the Oni of Ife led to the founding of the dynasty. In the rituals of kingship they, rather than the Town Chiefs, were explicitly cast in the role of *edion* (elders). Thus it was by admission to the *Uzama* order that the future Oba achieved elderhood. Through the elderhood of the *Uzama*, the Edo asserted their claim that, in the final reckoning, the Oba ruled by the will of the community. In their capacity as *edion* they owned the kingship. They received the fees that the heir paid on his accession, and a new reign began when the *Edaiken* knelt before them to be pronounced Oba by the *Oliha*.

The Edo say '*Oba* makes *Oliha* and *Oliha* makes *Oba*!' The ceremonies thus characterized show dramatically the dialectic of patrimonialism and gerontocracy in the Benin polity.

2
Benin Village Life

The Benin Village

(Edited sections of University of London Ph.D. Thesis)
1956

THE SOCIAL STRUCTURE OF BENIN : THE VILLAGE COMMUNITY

Introduction

The main characteristic features of the social organization of the Edo-speaking peoples as a whole can be briefly itemized: the compact, discrete village settlement as the basic unit of the wider political organization; the three-tier age-grade organization; the agnatic descent system with its marked emphasis on primogeniture. A few preliminary points may be made at this stage.

It may be assumed that within the area most effectively controlled by the Benin state authorities (an area which, it has been suggested, corresponds more or less to the present Benin Division) there was, in the past more freedom of movement for the ordinary individual than in neighbouring areas where hostility between neighbouring villages, tribes and chiefdoms was endemic and relatively uncontrolled. Again the military activities of the Benin state ensured a more or less regular flow of war captives into the area, who were sent out into the villages to cultivate the land on behalf of their masters. To these must be added the overflow from the wards of Benin City of that part of the population which could not be supported by the specialist activities of the ward guilds, while in the opposite direction moved villagers seeking advancement in the capital by attaching themselves to title-holders and other influential men there. As has already been noted there was also probably a considerable amount of migration out of the Benin kingdom into neighbouring areas. All these factors must have contributed to a high rate of population interchange as between village and village, village and capital, and the Benin kingdom and the area outside the most effective control of the state. This in itself would be unfavourable to the development of large-scale localized kinship groups but it must be combined, as will be shown, with a descent system and a pattern of inheritance and succession which leads to the continual proliferation of such groups rather than their solidarity.

Apart from its effect on population movements the centralizing authority impinges on the local community in other ways. In the past it took the organization of warfare and raiding out of the hands of the village and chiefdom rulers and this will be seen apparently to have had an effect on the complexity of age-group organization. Opportunities for advancement in the palace associations and other state institutions may have been an important factor inhibiting the development of title-associations with political functions in the local community. Finally, proximity to the capital appears to affect the scale of local political organization in that the size of chiefdoms and the degree of power delegated to their rulers by the *Oba* tends to increase towards the boundaries of the kingdom.

All these factors, then, must be borne in mind in seeking to explain the pattern of village social organization.

An analysis will be made of the relation between certain types of cult and the authority structure of groups up to the level of the village. No more can be said about these cults until the structure of the groups to which they are relevant has been analysed.

I DOMESTIC AND FAMILY GROUPINGS

a. *Households, farming groups, and families*

These three groups are the units of residence and of the domestic economy and need to be carefully defined. The senses in which the terms are employed are as follows:

1. The household is the aggregate of persons living together in a single building, which is generally owned by one of them. Every house has a single owner, belonging first to the man for whom it is built and passing on his death to his senior son, or failing sons to his immediately junior full – or half – brother. If the heir already has his own house, however, he may allow the inherited house to be occupied by some of his kin. The occupants of a house do not necessarily constitute a single house-keeping unit and may, indeed, be divided into several such units.

2. The farming unit is a group of persons who habitually co-operate in working the same land and share in the produce (i.e. co-operation is regular and obligatory). It is characteristically small and generally

corresponds to the nuclear or the compound family, together with any additional dependents of the head of the family. It may, however, take various other forms all involving at least an active male and a female dependent.

3. The family is a group based on a nexus of conjugal and kinship bonds. Since the scale of family organization may, for a given body of persons, vary considerably in different contexts of child-rearing, economy, jural authority and ritual action it is necessary to distinguish several types or levels of family organization

The nuclear or polygamous compound family, consisting of a man and his wife or wives and children, constitutes a basic unit of economic co-operation and social solidarity. It is generally linked by close jural and ritual ties to other similar units through Kinship between the respective family heads. But the larger families thus formed need neither form a single household nor be joint controllers, workers and consumers of resources.

A jurally and ritually bound group of nuclear or compound families of kinsmen will be called a 'joint family' if co-resident and an 'extended family' if it occupies two or more houses. A joint family occupying a single household may form part of a wider extended family.

While all types of families distinguished here are corporate groups jurally and ritually, the elementary family (nuclear or compound) is also a co-residential and a housekeeping unit, the joint family is rarely a housekeeping unit and the extended family is neither a co-residential nor a housekeeping group. A farming group may correspond to a household, form part of a household, or embrace persons living in different houses. It may approximate to a nuclear, compound or joint family, or section of a family, or even include persons of different families. The manner in which households, farming groups and families interlock will now be explored more fully.

b. *The size and structure of households*

The Edo village consists of a compact collection of essentially rectangular houses facing on to one or more village streets or cleared, sandy spaces. Houses vary in size from three to about twenty reception rooms, bedrooms, stores and kitchens, the largest houses being those of some important hereditary village chiefs (*enigie*). The larger houses usually enclose a rectangular space (*Eghodin*), into which the roof slopes all round, where the women of the household spend most of their time when at home. The *Eghodin* is situated towards the back of the house, being surrounded on three sides by a single row of alternating kitchens and women's bedrooms. The forepart of the house consists of a series of interconnecting rooms of which the one giving on the street and sometimes one or two more, are reception rooms. The household head has his own bedroom and, apart from storerooms, the remaining rooms are used as sleeping quarters by other men and boys.

Instances are found of houses – belonging usually to a father and his sons or brothers – which share a common wall. Often there is an interconnecting door, but each house is nevertheless a self-contained unit.

In the typical Edo village the number of persons occupying a single house varies from one to twenty or more. When a person lives alone it can usually be accounted for in terms of some physical disability.

The following summary, based on a census and genealogical study in the village of Ɛkhɔ n'Idunbhonlu, 14 miles east of Benin City, may be taken as representative of the composition of villages in the kingdom.

Number of persons	Number of households
1	3
2–5	8
5–9	29
10–14	8
15–20	2

Total persons 360	Total households 50

The post-marital residence pattern among the Edo is strongly virilocal. It is normal for a man to bring his first wife to live in his father's house, or to the house of his senior full or half-brother if his father is dead. An only son is likely to remain with his father until the latter dies, when the house will pass to him; but if he has junior brothers he is almost certain to move out and build his own house as they become old enough to give their father adequate assistance on his farm or as the first of them approaches marriageable age. The latter in turn will move out as he becomes replaceable by a junior brother.

In Ekho village, the three persons living alone were physically disabled. All the other 47 houses contained at least one married man and his wife or wives, and any children. In 34 of those houses the core of the household was a single elementary family. Of the other 13 households, 11 comprised more than one elementary family and the other two an elementary family together with the male remnants of other such families. These 13 households fall into three sets:

i   In six, the married men were father and son or sons.
ii In five, the component families were headed by other categories of kinsmen: in one, a pair of full brothers; in another, a pair of paternal half-brothers; in two, pairs of maternal half-brothers; and in the fifth, a man who had living with him a junior brother of his deceased father, only recently returned to the village.
iii In two, the family heads were non-kin.

The core of the household in by far the majority of cases is a single nuclear or compound family. The other arrangements are unlikely to persist over a long period of time and there are in most cases special circumstances to explain the cohabitation of the men at the head of each constituent group.

Many households have attached to them kin and affines who are not members of the core elementary families. Surviving members of the conjugal family of a householder father cluster round his sons in their households after his death. In addition to his own conjugal family and his mother and siblings a man may have with him, at any time, widowed or divorced sisters, daughters, or, more rarely, mother's sisters, who may have children with them. A woman may, with her father's permission, send a child to be brought up by her father or brother. It can be a gesture of respect and gratitude on the part of the husband of a very fruitful wife. In some circumstances a child may live in the household of his divorced or widowed mother's new husband, though normally he lives with his patrikin. Finally, a householder may have with him, for a shorter or longer period of time, his wife's mother or sister. It would be shameful for him to live in his father-in-law's house, though he might choose to reside in the village of a wife from another village.

c. *The farming group*
All Edo villagers are cultivators and the yam farm is the focus of productive activities and the indispensable basis of subsistence. The farming group is the body of persons who work one or more yam plots and share in the benefits deriving from them, either directly or by exchange.

Any member of a village may select any piece of village land provided it is not already in use or chosen by somebody else. New plots are selected in January, in forest or bush-fallow land, cleared in January or February, and planted in March at the beginning of the rains. Plots are first used for the cultivation of yams, though maize is usually interplanted in rows, and women plant other vegetables round tree stumps in the farm clearings. In the following year, yams are succeeded by maize and cassava. Tree crops are also harvested, men laying claim to oil-palms and coconut palms, and land may be cleared for plantations of kola and rubber trees, all individually owned.

The division of labour in respect of yam cultivation is fairly straightforward. Men and boys choose the sites, clear and burn the bush, hoe the ground, do most of the planting, insert the vine poles and train the vines. Women and girls do the weeding, and the two sexes co-operate in gathering the harvest, sorting it out and storing it. But the yam crop is not complete without the subsidiary crops that are grown on it and these are the preserve of the women. A man who has to tend his own subsidiary crops feels very ashamed and, indeed, very few men do so. On the other hand women rarely own yams while they are in the ground, only after the harvest.

The farming group, then, should contain at least one member of each sex old enough to play a full part in productive activities and, from the Edo point of view, the ideal farming partnership is that between spouses. A polygamist divides each of his yam plots into as many portions as he has wives (though a very young wife may share the plot of an older woman for a few years) and each woman raises her subsidiary crops on her plot. Generally speaking the elementary family forms the most stable farming group; but more ephemeral groups may be formed of a man with his married sons and their wives while the sons are still young men, or they may be headed by the eldest group of brothers. Of such groups, which correspond to the joint family, the most stable is that of a man and his only son, and their wives and unmarried children. When the harvested yams have been sorted out, the owner of the farm indicates to each woman member of the group her share of the harvest.

d. *The elementary family*

The elementary family takes two forms. It may be a nuclear family consisting of a man, one wife, and their children or a compound family, consisting of a man and two or more wives and their children. To these may be attached the man's mother and unmarried, widowed or divorced patrikin[1], other children of his wife and, more rarely, affines.

The elementary family is a co-residential group, occupying a separate house or a separate apartment in a composite household; and it is a farming group, though some of its members may belong to other farming groups as well. It is also a housekeeping unit but if it contains a number of women with children, it may, for this purpose be split up into a number of sub-units. Out of her stores each of the wives must feed herself and her children and, in her turn, prepare the meals for her husband. Normally each wife cooks for her husband on a separate day though they often make arrangements between themselves to allow one to go to the market or the farm on particular days.

Within the family, at all levels, personal relations are conceived of in master-servant terms. In the elementary family a man's wives and children are his servants. *Obhoxan-bhɛn* means, in the first instance, 'my wife' but it can also mean 'my boy' or 'my servant'. Its effective plural *ibiɛka-bhɛn* 'my people', also implies the subservience of the speaker's dependents – as in the conventional greeting *d'ibiɛka-a ma*, 'are your people well?' Superordination – subordination within the family is organized on a sex and age basis. Thus even a mother is the servant of her son so long as she lives in his household though this aspect of their relationship is usually overshadowed by his affection and respect for her. She in turn has moral authority over her daughters-in-law who are expected to fetch and carry for her.

In return for their services to him the head of an elementary family and the household group built around it has the moral obligation to care for their material and spiritual welfare. He should make regular offerings at his paternal ancestor shrine, either directly, if the shrine is under his control, or through his father or senior brother. He should seek wives for each of his sons, and provide the marriage payment in the case of the first wife of each. Conversely he receives the marriage payment on his daughters and the services of his son-in-law, and his obligation towards them does not cease when they move to their husbands' households. It is incumbent upon him to see that they are fairly treated and to approach his paternal ancestors on their behalf and on behalf of their children after marriage.

1. Since most of these attached kin are members of the conjugal family of the man's father it would be possible to speak of the group as a whole as a 'joint family'. However, in this patrilineal and virilocal society, it is more convenient to reserve this term for groups in which two or more *living* married, male patrikin are co-resident, particularly since, on the death of a polygamist his children tend to split up into groups of full siblings.

The joint family[2]

The term 'joint family' is applied to a composite grouping in which two or more elementary families live together in the same household under the jural authority of the head of one of these families. The most common type of joint family is that in which a man has living with him one or more married sons with their wives and children. Alternatively it may consist of the elementary families of full or half-brothers or other patrikin or quasi-patrikin of different generations; or, more rarely, the relationship between the family heads may be that of stepfather-stepson or mother's father or brother — daughter's or sister's son. To this sort may be attached other persons as for the elementary family.

Except when an only son continues to live with his father, and in the first years of the subordinate family's existence, the joint family rarely constitutes a single farming group or housekeeping unit, though there may be a great deal of informal co-operation between its members. It emerges as a corporate group mainly in the contexts of jural and ritual authority and ritual action and *vis-à-vis* the local community as a whole.

The head of the joint family is responsible for the behaviour and welfare of all its members. Although his son has immediate authority over his own wives and children, it is to him that his daughter-in-law's kinsmen will protest if they consider that she has been misused. Then again, the village council can hold him to account for any anti-community behaviour on the part of members of the family. The chief backing for his authority lies in the fact that his relationship to his paternal ancestors is closer than that of any others in the family group; and the ancestor cult provides the strongest sanctions against misbehaviour within the joint and extended families.

f. *The extended family*

The extended family is constructed along similar lines to the joint family but differs from it in a number of ways. It occupies more than one house; it is never a single farming group or housekeeping group; with separate residence goes an attenuation of authority; and it sometimes embraces a wider range of collateral patrikin.

The characteristic extended family is made up of a man and his married brothers and sons with their wives and children, and possibly the sons and unmarried daughters of his deceased brothers or father's brothers with their wives and children, the whole group occupying several, usually neighbouring houses, within a village community. It

2. See also Bradbury, 1957 : 28-30

may form part of a ward or a whole ward.

• The most senior man has a theoretical moral authority over its other members. This springs partly from the values associated with age and patrilineal kinship and partly from his closeness to the ancestors of the patrilineage. But heads of constituent joint or elementary families may have ancestor shrines of their own, weakening the solidarity of extended families of wide range. As a politically significant section of the local community, too, the degree of solidarity of the extended family varies inversely with its size and the range of collateral kin it embraces. Its full role in Edo social life will become clearer later.

g. *Summary*

In order to describe the range of domestic and family groupings found in Edo villages it has been necessary to consider the residential and economic basis of such groupings and the several contexts in which they become corporate groups.

Finally it should be emphasized that not every elementary family and joint family constitutes a part of a wider extended family, for the heads of these groups may have no close patrikin in the same village community. Thus this community is an aggregate of extended, joint and elementary families each of which may have the same formal status *vis-à-vis* other such groups and the community as a whole.

II THE SIGNIFICANCE OF UNILINEAL DESCENT IN THE LOCAL COMMUNITY

Evidently there are certain agnatic and virilocal tendencies in the Edo kinship system, yet the patrilineages are very small. The widest effective patrilineage (except for some politically important ones) is that constituting the nucleus of the extended family together with any patrilineal descendants of the family head, or his father, living elsewhere. Beyond these limits, patrilineal bonds of obligations and sympathies unite persons only as individuals and not as co-members of corporate groups.

This limited range of lineage organization will now be examined with regard both to the internal characteristics of the descent system itself and also to external factors associated with it.

a. *Primogeniture and 'mother-groups'*

It is characteristic of the Edo kinship system that more emphasis is placed on lines of descent than on corporate lineage groups, and one of the keys to this situation lies in the Edo rule of primogeniture. From the sociological point of view the most important kinship relation in Edo society is that between a man and his senior son *(ɔmɔdiɔn nokpia)* the oldest legitimate son borne to him by any of his wives. This son is recognized from birth to be his father's chief heir and successor[3]

A further differentiation between sons of the same father arises from the fact that the Edo practise polygamy and that the children of different wives of the same man constitute sub-units within the sibling group. The Edo kinship terminology distinguishes between *obhi-erha-bhɛn,* my father's child, and *obh'iye-bhɛn'* my mother's child', the latter term normally being taken to imply full siblingship, though the more extended form *'obhi-erha-obh'iye bhɛn'* my father's child, my mother's child' may be employed where it is desired to emphasize this.

In a polygamous family the children of one mother are expected to show more solidarity than half-siblings. This is expressed in the frequently repeated saying:

"*Ɔbh'iye wɛ: 'Ɔ-ke nɔ sɛ irɛn gha lel' ɛe   sɛ'* "
("The mother's child says: 'Wherever he goes I will follow him'.")

"*Obhierha wɛ: 'Giɛ'dɛgbe'.*"
("The father's child says: 'Wait till tomorrow'.")[4]

This solidarity of the 'mother group'[5] is reflected not only in the greater affection, loyalty and mutual assistance that normally characterises full-sibling as compared with half-sibling relationships, but also in the pattern of inheritance. Within the full-sibling group the senior brother has the same kind of status as the senior male member of the sibling group as a whole.

b. *Inheritance of property and wives*

When speaking of inheritance in general terms the Edo will say that the senior son is his father's sole heir, and that on his father's death all the latter's property passes to him. In some lines of descent — and particularly those in which hereditary titles or offices pass down — this indeed appears to be so, in the sense that the senior son has no legal

---

3 See Bradbury, 1965

4 That is to say, a man will rush to do something for his mother's child immediately, but he will be in no such hurry to assist his paternal half-brother.

5 'Mother-group' is here used in the sense of a set of siblings who have the same mother and the same father.

obligation to share the inheritance with any of his siblings, though he is morally expected to make gifts out of it to them. The social identification between an hereditary office-holder (such as the *onogie* of a village or sub-chiefdom) and his senior son is even closer than in other lines and the inheritance passes *en bloc* with the title.

In most other lines, however, other sons have a legitimate, though never an equal, right to inherit from their father. If the deceased leaves only one wife with surviving children all her sons may claim a share. In a polygamous family the sons of each mother form a distinct unit for this purpose, and only the eldest of them receives a formal share, though, again, out of this he is expected to show generosity towards his junior full brothers.

The house in which the deceased lived is one of the most important considerations and in all cases this should pass to his senior son. In order to ensure that it will pass, on his own death, to his own son, the heir must, however, perform his father's mortuary rites. The senior son should not prevent any of his father's descendants from living in the house so long as there is room for them. Nor, on the other hand, need he occupy it himself, if he has already built a house of his own.

Widows with surviving children are free to choose whether they will marry one of their husband's heirs or go elsewhere. A woman who has young children may prefer to marry the brother or son of her husband who then becomes the guardian of her children but she is under no obligation to do so. If she marries another man she may take her infant children with her for the first few years, but when they become old enough to do without her their father's heir may claim them, though, as indicated in the last chapter, they themselves may later choose to return to their mother. Old widows, past the age of child-bearing, generally stay with one of their sons or, if they have none, return to their own patrilineal relatives, while young childless widows and girls who had been betrothed to the dead man pass to his heirs.

Three main points emerge from study of the Edo pattern of inheritance. In the first place the group of patrikin principally concerned with the disposal of a dead man's property comprises his junior brothers and his children and thus represents a depth of only two descending generations from the apical ancestor. Beyond thse limits the rules of inheritance become uncertain and there is no wider patrilineage whose headman can apply sanctions to ensure that the property is correctly distributed. The possible heirs may apply for a ruling from a more remote senior patrikinsman, particularly if he lives in the same community and is looked upon, by them, with respect: but in practise they are equally likely to seek a settlement from the non-related head of the ward or village in which the dead man resided. Secondly, 'mother-groups' emerge as distinct sub-units within the sibling group in matters of inheritance. And finally the oldest son of all has much stronger claims than any of his brothers.

Yet the importance of primogeniture as one factor limiting the scale of lineage organization lies not so much in inheritance of property as in the succession of the senior son to his father's statuses.

c. *Succession to statuses*

A senior son is unlikely to succeed as head of his father's farm group, especially if he has married brothers or half brothers, who will prefer to assert their economic independence. He does succeed to his father's jural status, with jural authority over all his siblings and responsibility to the community for their conduct. His brothers and their children still come to him to settle their disputes with each other or with their wives. He remains, too, the ultimate protector of his married sisters *vis-à-vis* their husbands' families, and it is his duty to see both that they are not ill-treated and that they act as reasonable wives. Should one of his sisters leave her husband and refuse to return he theoretically becomes responsible for refunding the marriage payment that was made upon her. In fact, however, at the present day a man has, in general, so little effective control over his married sister that he is rarely held accountable for her desertion.

It is as his father's ritual successor that the senior son fulfils the role that validates his authority in other matters. Having 'buried' his father and 'planted' his spirit (see 'Father and senior son in Edo mortuary ritual') above the senior son becomes the intermediary between the spirit and the rest of his agnatic descendants; they cannot approach 'the father' except through him. All of a man's descendants must join in his worship. Neglect to 'feed' him with offerings and sacrifices, or lapses in family and kinship morality, incur his anger and he may punish the offender or his or her close kin with barrenness, illness, accidents, death or some other catastrophe. On the other hand a piece of good fortune affords an opportunity for self-congratulation on the scrupulous regard one has shown for 'serving' one's father and for practising 'the things he taught us'. Knowing the hopes, fears and weaknesses of his fellow-worshippers this enables the senior brother to manipulate ritual sanctions.

Succession to a man's ritual statuses is often divided, for a time at least, some passing down a generation to his senior son, but some going to a successor of his own generation, the senior of his surviving brothers.

Firstly, let it be assumed that the dead man was his father's senior son. In virtue of his age, and of being the priest of his father's spirit, he will have been the head of the lineage and extended family stemming from his own father. On his death, his authority over his own siblings passes to his next surviving brother but, as has been indicated, immediate authority over his descendants passes to his senior son. This son is, however, in accordance with Edo ideas about seniority between generations, morally subject to the authority of his father's brother. The latter thus becomes the head of the extended family and lineage and is known as *oka'ɛgbɛe*, 'the leader of the family (lineage)'[6]. Yet his authority over it is not so complete as that of the man he replaces for the latter was senior son (*ɔm'ɔdiɔn*) as well as *ɔka'ɛgbɛe*, and, therefore, the guardian of his father's altar which on his death passes into the keeping of his own son. The dead man's siblings must continue to be represented at this altar, for it is still their only approach to their dead father and, therefore, the senior brother takes his place there as a second priest[7].

At a certain stage in its development, then, the extended family has a dual headmanship and a dual priesthood. Both the *ɔm'ɔdiɔn's* and the *ɔka'ɛgbɛe's* presence are required at all important rites; they offer prayers and sacrifices together, one sitting on each side of the *aru-erha*, though the *ɔm'ɔdiɔn* takes the lead. Each of these two men has authority over his own sibling group and their patrilineal descendants and wives, but in imposing ritual sanctions on any member of either group, they must act together. The younger man is expected to defer to his senior kinsman and to seek his advice in settling disputes between, or punishing, those under his authority. Again, if he himself has a dispute with a younger brother it is to their father's brother that he will go for a settlement. The *ɔm'ɔdiɔn* may, however, be a hereditary village chief, in which case his personal authority may overshadow that of the

6 *ɛgbɛe* means, in the first instance, a group of patrikin but the *ɔka'ɛgbɛe* is the head of the extended family and the lineage that is co-terminous with it.

7 It should be stated that after his senior brother's death this man may be permitted to set up an altar to his father in his own house. He does this by taking an *uxurhɛ* from the *aru-erha* which has now been re-dedicated to his senior brother. However, he must still officiate in rites at the senior altar, and, indeed it is to his advantage to do so if he wishes to retain his authority over the extended family as a whole.

older man. In practice the two must achieve some kind of mutual adjustment and much depends on their respective ages and personalities. As opposed to his junior brothers, the ɔm'ɔdiɔn is not only more closely identified with his father but also, after the latter's death, with his father's next senior brother.

It now remains to consider the proliferation of lines of descent and of the extended families and ancestor-worshipping groups associated with them. This process is represented schematically in Fig. 4, in which, for ease of exposition, it is assumed (a) that pairs of brothers are born throughout the generations, (b) that the members of senior generations die before the members of junior ones, and (c) that brothers die in order of seniority.

Fig. 4a represents the type of extended family which has just been described, in which the roles of ɔm'ɔdiɔn and ɔka'ɛgbɛe are vested in separate persons. B having died, his senior son D has re-dedicated the ancestor altar to him. D and his father's brother C are, respectively, the ɔm'ɔdiɔn and the ɔka'ɛgbɛe, the priests of their respective ancestors B and A, and the intermediaries between those and the rest of their descendants.

In Fig. 4b C has died and his own son P has set up an altar to him. P, and through him Q, R and the rest of his father's descendants now have direct access to their immediate ancestor C (and through C to A and more remote lineal ancestors), without attending the altar of which D is the guardian. Indeed C is not among the ancestors worshipped at that altar. C's 'children' may continue to attend important rites conducted by D, for his *aru-erha* is the one at which C was himself a priest, but in seeking direct benefits from the ancestors it is to their own dead father that they will make supplication, at the altar dedicated to his name. Again, P is in no way dependant upon his patrilateral first cousin D in exercising ritual sanctions over his siblings and his own and his brothers' children. If he does continue to pay respect to D and to regard him as ɔka'ɛgbɛe it is only because the latter's line is senior to his own, and this is likely to be of little significance unless it is a line in which a hereditary office passes. Thus, in the situation represented in 4b, D and P are, in effect, both ɔm'ɔdiɔn and ɔka'ɛgbɛe in their respective extended families and lineages. Each will be assisted at his *aru-erha* by his own brother (E and Q respectively) for the Edo hold that 'the father' should always be 'served' by two priests.

If, on the other hand, B and C have another brother who survives them, and who is significantly older than D and P, he will succeed C as

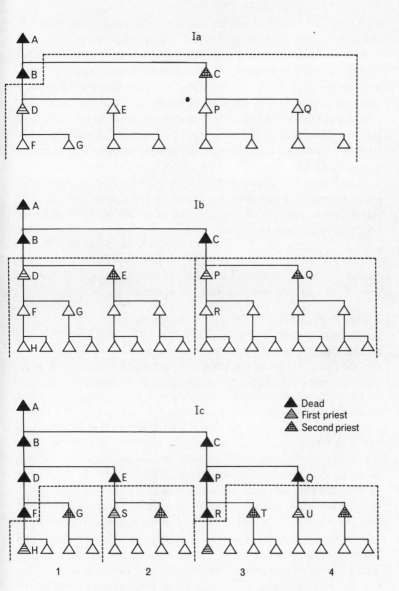

Fig 4. *Proliferation of ancestor-worshipping groups.*

ɔka'ɛgbɛe and as second priest at the altar to B. He may also assist P in serving his father, particularly if he and C were full brothers.

Fig. 4c represents a later stage when D, F, E, P, R and Q are dead. There are now four separate *aru-erha*. The *ɔm'ɔdiɔn* are H, S, V, and U and the *ɔka'ɛgbɛe* G, S, T and U. The members of extended family 2 may still attend rites at the altar dedicated to F and the members of family 4 at the altar dedicated to R, but the fission between 1 and 2, on the one hand, and 3 and 4 on the other will, in all probability, be complete, although their common apical ancestor is only three or four generations back.

It will be clear, then, that the potentialities for fission are present in every generation for, while, in a set of brothers, only one can be his father's senior son, yet each of the others can himself have a senior son and thereby become the founder of a new line. So long as one of their fathers' brothers (or their fathers' father's brothers) is still alive patrilateral cousins remain, in some degree members of the same extended family, lineage and ancestor worshipping group but otherwise there is little to hold them together in a corporate group.

d. *Hereditary offices and the scale of lineage organization*
It has been hinted in several places above that the scale of lineage organisation is affected by the fact that certain offices are hereditary in the patriline. As far as the village community is concerned it is the office of *onogie* (pl. *enigie*) that is significant in this respect.

The very presence of this office creates for the *onogie's* patrikin, a focus of common interest that is lacking for other groups of patrikin. The title and office of *onogie* should pass down a single patriline from father to senior son. Certain factors may intervene, however, to upset this mode of succession. Principally an *onogie* may die without surviving sons or when his senior son is still a child. In the former instance the next successor in most lines is his senior surviving brother, while in the latter case this man will become the regent or *edayi* (from *dayi*, to support, hold up) until his brother's son is old enough to become *onogie* himself. However, it may happen that an *onogie* dies leaving neither brothers nor sons. Now if a commoner dies without such close kinsmen there is no question of a successor having to be found for him. His patriline simply dies out. But, for political reasons, the line of *enigie* must be perpetuated. In some villages it is the custom for an *onogie* who dies without close patrikinsmen to be succeeded by a daughter's son, if such be available, but more often the office passes to a more remote agnatic collateral. This in itself is sufficient to extend the effective range of the *onogie's* lineage group.

There are, however, further contributory factors. The Oba may confirm a favoured *edayi*, and subsequently his son, in office; or he may choose among a number of claimants all descended from *enigie*. Another is the mutual support an *onogie* and his patrikinsmen can give one another in the community.

All these factors, then, contribute to the extension of the *onogie's* lineage both laterally and in depth. Fig. 5 illustrates the line of *enigie* and *edayi* at Ekho village over the last five generations. On the death of *Asa* the office passed in regular fashion to his senior son *Emuze* who, after his succession, was killed fighting for the *Oba* in Ishan. At this time his son *Ɔbɛgiɛe* was still a child, and *Ɔbhɛbhɛn* became his *edayi*. *Emuze's* early children are all said to have died young and thus *Ɔbhɛbhɛn* who was himself only a few years junior to *Emuze* had four sons who were considerably older than *Ɔbɛgiɛe*[8]. Each of these in turn succeeded his father as *edayi* though none of them reigned for very long and *Okundiawa* and *Ɔsɛnbhota* are said to have died after one and three years, respectively, in office. *Ɔbɛgiɛe* was then confirmed by the late *Ɔba Ɛwɛka* as *onogie* but he did not complete his father's mortuary rites and was thus not regarded as having validated his succession. On his death *Aiminyɛnbhɔmɔ* was appointed as *edayi*. When the latter died the lineage and the village community were disturbed that the succession seemed no longer to be passing, in the orthodox fashion, from father to senior son. *Ɔba Ɛwɛ*ka then produced a candidate of his own, *Igiehɔn*. While still a child *Igiehɔn* had been presented by his father, *Ɛrhumusɛe*, to *Ɔba Obhoranbhɛn*, as a servant, and had accompanied the latter in his exile to Calabar. Later he returned and became a courtier to *Ɛwɛka*, *Obhoranbhɛn's* son. After *Aiminyɛnbhɔmɔ* died when the succession had become doubtful, *Ɛwɛka* stepped in and made *Igiehɔn* the substantive *onogie*. *Igiehɔn* in turn, died while his heir, *Egiebɔɛe*, was still a child and his collateral kinsman, *Uwadiae*, was chosen as the most suitable person to act as *edayi Egiebɔɛe* performed his father's mortuary rites while still under age and in 1953 he took over from *Uwadiae* and was confirmed as *onogie* by *Ɔba Akɛnzuwa*.

The line of *enigie-Ɛkhɔ* thus illustrates the vagaries of succession to hereditary titles and the way in which the office, as such, provides a

8 It is just possible that *Ɔbhɛbhɛ* belonged, in fact, to the same generation as *Asa*. Some informants suggested that this was so but the members of the *onogie's* lineage asserted that the relationships were as shown in Fig. 5.

common focus of interest for a lineage of considerable depth and range. The present *Ɔka'ɛgbɛe* of the lineage is *Irɛnbhifo*, the oldest living descendant of *Asa* and he was preceded by *Uwagbɔe*. It is to be observed that all living members of this group are the descendants, within two generations, of former *enigie* or *edayi* and thus have a potential personal interest in the office.

All living members of the lineage shown in Fig. 5 (with the exception of *Ɛgbɔgie*, the representative of the deprived senior line) regularly attend rites at the ancestor altar dedicated to *Igieho*, though most of them have separate *aru-erha* in their own fathers' names.

The kinship structure of the village community

It is now possible to summarize the kinship structure of the village community. The village consists of a number of wards each of which comprises one or more extended, joint and elementary families, all of which may constitute separate units *vis-à-vis* the rest of the community.

Figs. 6 and 7 illustrate the structure of three separate wards at Ekho and are for the most part self-explanatory. However, the following points may be noted:

(1) Fig. 6 represents the *onogie's* own ward. It contains two main groups of patrikin, that of the *onogie*, and the one in which *Ɔmɛgui* is the senior man.[9] They are linked only by the marriage between *Egiebɔ* and *Iyayi* but the solidary effect of the *onogie*ship is such that *Ɔmɛgui* and his kinsmen frequently attend rites at the altar of the past *enigie*. In this respect it is also significant that *Iyayi* is an ancestress of *Uwadiae* and is thus one of the 'mothers of *enigie*' who are represented by an *uxurhe* placed on the altar dedicated to the past *enigie*.

At the time for which Fig. 6 was operative the heir to the late *onogie* had not yet been installed in his father's office and his kinsman Uwadiae was acting as his *edayi*. The young *onogie* himself was living with his mother in the household of his senior maternal half-brother in *Idunbh'Ogo*, the ward illustrated in Fig. 7. They had settled there so as to keep a certain distance between the young *onogie* and his patrikin, out of a fear that those who regarded themselves as having a right to the office might attempt to harm him by sorcery or some other means.

(2) Fig. 7 represents a ward in which there is one dominating extended family, that of the *ɔdiɔnwere, Iyawe*. The latter, his two sons, and an attached uterine kinsman live in four houses which form a single block under one roof, in the manner described in the last chapter.

9 This group of patrikin, too, tends to show solidarity over a wider range than is normal. This is probably due to the fact that a hereditary priesthood is vested in it.

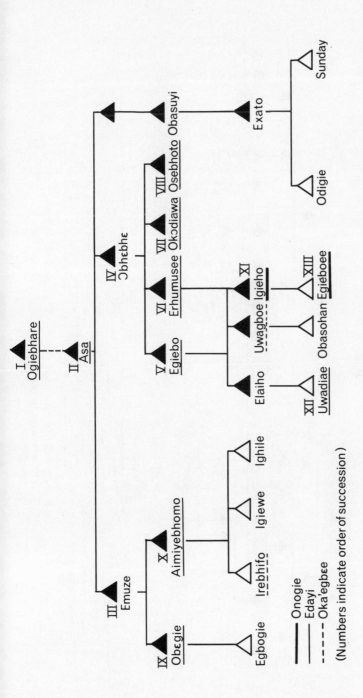

Fig 5.   *Line of Enigie and Edayi at Ekho village*

Onogie
Edayi
Oka'egbee
(Numbers indicate order of succession)

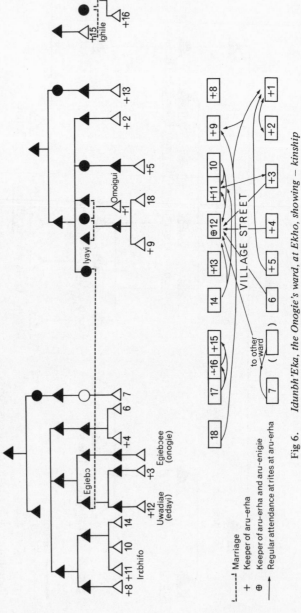

Fig 6. *Idunbh'Eka, the Onogie's ward, at Ekho, showing — kinship links between household heads*

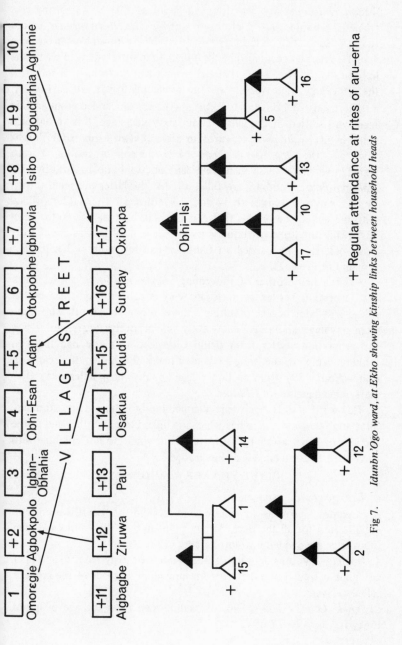

Fig 7. · Idunbn'Ogo ward, at Ekho showing kinship links between household heads

(3) Fig. 7 *Idunbh'Ogo* was founded about seventy years ago by one *Obhi-Isi*, a hunter and 'doctor' sent out by *Ɔba Obhoranbhɛn*, before the latter succeeded his father *Adolo*, to establish a hunting camp on Ekho land. He was later persuaded by the *onogie* to join the village. Five household heads (5, 10, 13, 16, 17) claim descent from *Obhi-Isi* as shown in the genealogy. The origins of the remaining heads are as follows:

The heads of households 2, 11 and 12 are descended from an Edo man who settled in the village about sixty years ago. 8 is an old man who, in his youth, was captured in a war between his natal Yoruba town and the *Ɔba's* armies, and 14 is the son of another Yoruba war-captive. Both these men were sent out to Ekho to farm by *Ɔba Obhoranbhɛn*. 1 and 15 are full brothers, the latter the senior. Their mother was a full sister to 14 and she returned to her father's village with her son, 1, before his first marriage. His brother, 15, on the other hand, did not leave his father's natal village until he was about forty years old. He had married an Ekho woman but none of her patrikin remain in the village.

3 is the half-brother of the young *onogie* mentioned above. 4 is a first-generation settler from Ishan who bought rubber trees in the village and later began to cultivate there. 6 is a blacksmith who came from a village about ten miles away ten or twelve years ago. 7 is a first-generation settler from Benin City who formerly had his own farming camp on the *onogie's* land. Finally the father of 8 came to Ekho about 1897 from an Edo village about twenty miles away after marrying a daughter of *Obhi-Isi*.

This ward is thus a very mixed collection of independent, extended, joint and elementary families which are linked to each other and to the families of other wards by affinal ties but which do not combine with each other to form large-scale kin groups.

III THE VILLAGE COMMUNITY

a. *The age-grade organization*

Age grades provide a village-wide system of stratification and organization for all the men. At any point in time the youths and men of a village are divided into three grades or *otu*:

1. *Iroghae* — youths and young men from their early teens to an upper age limit of round about thirty. An individual member of the grade is called *ɛroghae*.

2. *Ighele* (sing. *ɛghele*) — mature, adult men from the age of about thirty to forty-five or fifty.

3. *Ediɔn* (sing. *ɔdiɔn*), the elders.

To each grade are ascribed specific rights and duties *vis-à-vis* the community. The characteristic tasks of the *iroghae* are the sweeping and cleaning of village streets and open spaces; the care of community shrines which must be swept out every fifth or ninth day, the clearing of paths leading to farms, streams and other villages; and the more menial tasks associated with house-building, such as carrying mud, water and other materials to the builders. Formerly it was they who carried tribute to the *Ɔba* and the village's sponsor in Benin City.

To the *ighele* fall the more difficult communal duties, the felling of large trees and the heavier and more skilful tasks involved in house-building and the building and repair of shrines and, nowadays, schools; most of the actual construction of walls and roofs is done by them. They may also be instructed by the elders to assist the *iroghae* in any work which proves too onerous for the latter; otherwise they supervise them in whatever they are doing.

Before the coming of British administration the *ighele* were the fighting force of the village and the executive arm of the elders and the village headman. In the past the control exercised from Benin City appears to have been sufficient to make serious inter-village or inter-chiefdom warfare rare, over most of the Benin kingdom. This is reflected in the lack of specifically warrior elements in the age-grade organization as compared, for example, with the Ishan and Ivbiosakon areas. Any village in the kingdom might be called upon to provide men for the *Ɔba's* wars, and when such a call was made it was the *ighele* who would go to fight, but they did so as part of a larger force, not as a village unit. Nowadays the most important functions of the *ighele* have been superseded by the military, police and judicial activities of the central government and in many villages they no longer exist as a formal grade, individuals now passing directly from *ɛroghae* to *ɔdiɔn* status. A more extreme centralization of political activities has thus brought about a simplification of the age-grade structure.

The *ediɔn* are exempt from the communal manual tasks incumbent upon the other two grades, though they may lend voluntary assistance in, and are expected to supervise and direct, such operations as house-building. In the villages where the middle grade has disappeared the younger *ediɔn*, corresponding more or less to those who would, in former times, have been *ighele*, must assist in building and their failure to do so results in enquiries by the senior elders and the possible infliction of fines. In the traditional system the *ediɔn* are the repository

of the law, customs and traditions of the community. Led by their
senior member, the ɔdiɔnwere and together with the hereditary chief
(onogie) in those wards and villages which have such chiefs, they
constitute an administrative and judicial council for the ward or village.

The answers that were given to initial enquiries among the Edo
suggested that the order in which individuals are admitted to the
iroghae grade determines their relative status vis-à-vis other men in the
village for the rest of their lives. Ɛroghae, ɛghele and ɔdiɔn represent,
for the Edo, the three natural stages of life through which every man, as
a useful member of the community, should pass.

As an ɛroghae he is the servant of his elders, a street-sweeper, strong
and sensible enough to use a machete or to act as a labourer in
house-building, but still neither robust nor cunning enough to make a
good warrior, nor sufficiently skilful to perform the more difficult
communal tasks such as building a straight wall or constructing the
framework of a roof. The ɛghele is the adult man in the prime of his
life, whose mental capacities and technical skills have matured and
whose physical vigour has not yet begun to desert him. The ɔdiɔn is
past his physical prime but in the course of time he has acquired a
wisdom befitting him to guide and rule the succeeding generations. Age
lends respect and obedience to its possessors. The word ɔdiɔn means,
literally, 'he who is senior'; diɔn is used as an active verb signifying 'to
be senior to' as in ɔtɛn-bhɛn n' ɔdiɔn-bhɛn, my brother who seniors
me', 'my older brother', a description which carries overtones of a
master-servant relationship. Further deference is owed to the ediɔn on
account of their closeness to the ancestor spirits and, in particular, to
the collective dead (ediɔn) of the community with whom they are
identified in name.

These are the Edo stereotypes of the three natural stages in the life
of the adolescent and adult man. The extent to which any individual
fulfils the ideal pattern at a particular time depends both upon his
personal qualities and upon his status in other institutions.

An elderly man's promotion to full standing in the ediɔn grade may
be delayed until long after that of most of his contemporaries, while
another may be promoted when still a young man. Limitations are set
upon the representation of each household and family. In promoting a
man from ighele to ɔdiɔn status the elders take account of whether his
father is still alive. In some villages it is held that a man cannot become
a full ɔdiɔn while his father is living, but this does not imply that he
must continue to take his place indefinitely with the ighele. When his

age-mates whose fathers are dead are promoted from *ighele* to *ediɔn* he too becomes exempt from the tasks appropriate to the *ighele*, but whereas they, in theory, immediately become full members of the village council, he, in theory, does not. For, in Edo eyes, he is still under the authority of his father who continues to represent him and his dependants. Men who have passed out of the *ighele* grade, but whose fathers are still alive, thus stand in an intermediate position between the *ighele* and *ediɔn*. In some villages they are called *ediɔn nikotɔn* (the lower *ediɔn*). In practise, the extent to which an elderly man whose father is alive can be excluded from a voice in village affairs depends, to a large extent, on the interplay of personalities. As will be explained in the next chapter, the character of village council meetings is such that any person has the opportunity to make himself heard. In any case a son who has reached late middle-age is expected to advise and support his father, sitting with him at village meetings and even deputising for him on occasions when he is not present, or if he is too old to take an active part in village affairs. As will be seen, in many villages the sole village headman is the oldest man (*ɔdiɔnwere*). He is often very infirm and a number of examples were found of villages where the *ɔdiɔnwere's* senior son was the *de facto* village head.

It is significant, however, that at least in principle the group consisting of a father and his sons and their dependents should have a single representative among the full *ediɔn* in whom authority in the village is vested. No similar restriction is placed on two or more brothers having full *ɔdiɔn* status at the same time. If two brothers are both *ediɔn* it is expected that the junior one will defer to the senior but it is not usual to find brothers taking different points of view in village meetings, and a number of instances were observed where men willingly acquiesced in the censure of an older brother. It is both rarer and, in Edo eyes, more reprehensible for a man to disagree with his father in public. It was seen in the preceding chapter that the solidarity of the father/son type of extended family is noticeably greater than that of the fraternal type. This is clearly reflected in the different ways in which they are represented among the full *ediɔn*

A second modification of the principle of promotion strictly according to seniority must be noted. As has been seen in the previous chapter when an elderly man dies his statuses pass in part ot his senior son and in part to his next surviving brother. The former replaces his father in virtue of the principles of lineal descent and primogeniture and the latter his senior brother in virtue of his age. This, too, is reflected in the arrangements for promotion to the senior age-grade, for, when an ɔdiɔn dies, his heir, having completed the mortuary rites and established his father's shrine, may be permitted to become ɔdiɔn before other men in the village who are older than he is but whose fathers are still alive. That is, he can apply to the existing ediɔn to be co-opted by them. They are not bound to accept him, however, and are unlikely to do so unless he is of such an age as already to have given some service among the ighele.

Any man who wishes to become ɔdiɔn must seek the approval of the senior ediɔn, the ɔdiɔnwere and the hereditary village headman (onogie), if the village has one, by presenting them with certain gifts. If they agree to his promotion he then undergoes the simple rite de passage described in 'Fathers, elders, and ghosts in Edo religion', where the relations between the living ediɔn and the spirits of the collective dead are discussed.

The head of the whole age-grade organization is the senior ediɔn, known as the ɔdiɔnwere. In a majority of villages he is also the village headman in respect both of internal and external relations. When speaking in general terms the Edo state that the ɔdiɔnwere should be the oldest free-born man in the village, and in many villages this is indeed found to be the case, but this statement must be qualified in several senses. In selecting an ɔdiɔnwere factors taken into account may include whether the man's father was born in the village; whether the office in that particular village is confined to candidates from one ward, or from the different wards in rotation; or whether his seniority is judged less on actual age than his being longest a member of the ediɔn grade. The ediɔn, together with the onogie in villages which have such hereditary chiefs, make the final decision as to who should be ɔdiɔnwere.

In general it may be said that the Edo consider that actual age is the best qualification for becoming ɔdiɔnwere, given that the man is a native of the village and belongs to the right ward. In nearly all the villages where a check was made it was claimed that the ɔdiɔnwere was in fact, the oldest among the otherwise qualified men. It seems likely, however, that once a man becomes ɔdiɔnwere his seniority by age is taken for granted.

Within the ediɔn grade, as within the lower grades, the relative order of seniority between all members is more or less known. It comes out particularly on occasions, as at a feast, when there is something to be shared between them. There are always, however, doubts and differences of opinion as to the relative seniority between certain more junior members of the grade and it is only at the older end that it becomes fixed in everyone's minds.

In each village the four (*ediɔn nene*) or seven (*ediɔn nihirɔn*) senior *ediɔn*, including the *ɔdiɔnwere* are set apart from the rest in status and respect. Again, these are nearly always claimed to be ranged in order of actual age, though it is possible to show, in some instances, that this is not, in fact, so. For example, a man who has a high rank in one of the palace associations may, on that account, be included among the four or seven senior *ediɔn* of his village while others older than he remain ordinary *ediɔn* : and non-natives, impotents and otherwise incapacitated individuals may be excluded permanently.

Any of the *ediɔn nene* or *ediɔn nihirɔn* may act in the *ɔdiɔnwere's* place in his absence. They occupy the most important positions in village meetings and at rites in the shrine of the collective dead, and at feasts their share is set aside from that of the rest of the *ediɔn*. It is to them that a prospective candidate for promotion to the grade makes gifts, and when a house is about to be built they join together in making certain offerings on the site. Otherwise they do not emerge conspicuously as a distinct group, though their status gives extra weight to their opinions in respect of decisions made at the village level.

Relative seniority between those at the highest level in the age-grade organisation is thus, at any particular time, rigidly defined. It does not, however, necessarily determine the order of succession to the office of *ɔdiɔnwere* for the four or seven senior *ediɔn* may come from any ward in the village and they may include non-natives.

b. *The village and the ward*

Each village is a spatially discrete entity apparent to the eye. It is divided into wards, which may be either separated from each other by small patches of bush, or closely grouped so that ward boundaries are not immediately visible. There are two kinds of village plan. In the first each ward consists of a cluster of houses arranged around a central open space, while, in the other, all the houses in the village are arranged along one or both sides of one or two long streets. Both types seem to be of long standing but the second has been encouraged by the coming of motor-roads.

The extent to which a ward emerges as an important corporate group within the village community depends to a large extent on the size of the ward itself and of the village as a whole and, to a lesser extent, on the distance between wards, which, however, is not usually more than a few hundred yards. In large villages, with populations of say 800 or more, separate wards may have some of the features which were stated above to be characteristic of whole villages and they, themselves, may be divided up into sub-wards. Wards are rarely land-holding units or tribute units and only infrequently do different wards of the same village have hereditary chiefs but they are quite often the units for age-grade organization, though the corresponding age-grades of different wards co-operate together in tasks undertaken on behalf of the village as a whole.

All wards have their own ɔdiɔnwere. In large wards, and particularly in those which function as separate age-grade units, he may have considerable administrative and jural powers, and if the ward worships its own collective dead as distinct from the collective dead of the village as a whole, he is their priest. In villages of average size (say 300-500 persons), however, the corporate life of the ward community tends to be submerged in that of the village as a whole. Disputes even between members of the same ward are taken to the ɔdiɔnwere or onogie of the village, rather than the ɔdiɔnwere of the ward in question. The chief significance of the ward in such villages lies in the more intense informal co-operation which exists between ward members, in certain ritual contexts, and in the formation of dancing and play groups.

A full analysis of the division of functions in all contexts, as between villages and their component wards, in relation to population size and spatial distribution, would require a more extended treatment than it is possible to give here. The description of the village community which follows must, then, be taken to refer to villages of medium size, while bearing in mind that some of the functions here ascribed to village office-holders are, in larger villages, often carried out within the ward.

c. *Types of village headmanship*

It will be apparent from what has already been said that there are two kinds of village headmanship. Every village has an ɔdiɔnwere, chosen on the basis of qualifications described in the last chapter and some have, in addition, an *onogie* or hereditary chief. The former office is not hereditary in any sense while the latter, in the normal course of events, passes from father to eldest surviving son.

In villages which do not have an *onogie* the ɔdiɔnwere is the sole village headman in respect both of intra-village affairs and of the external relations of the community either *vis-à-vis* the other communities of the village-group or chiefdom of which it forms a part;

or if it stands independently, as many villages do, *vis-à-vis* the central authority of the Benin kingdom. In villages which have *enigie* there is, in effect, a dual village headmanship, somewhat analogous to the dual headmanship of the *ɔm'ɔdiɔn* and *ɔka'ɛgbɛe* in the fully-developed extended family. The *ɔdiɔnwere* like the *ka'egbee*, owes his status mainly to the fact that he is the oldest member of the group in which he has authority, while the *onogie*, like the *ɔm'ɔdiɔn* is, in normal circumstances, the senior son of his father.

Some *enigie* claim to be descended from chiefs who reigned before the founding of the present dynasty at Benin or before the villages or chiefdoms over which they rule became incorporated in the Benin state. Others are, or are said to be, descended from non-royal favourites of past *Ɔba* or, more often from the latters' junior sons. When the late *Ɔba's* heir succeeds, it is the custom for him to make one or more of his immediately junior brothers the chief of a village or a group of villages which have not previously had an *onogie* or in which the line of hereditary chiefs has failed or been discontinued.

An *onogie's* chiefdom may consist of a single village (or even, in exceptional circumstances, a single ward) but more often he rules over a number of villages for which he has general responsibility to the *Ɔba*. Here, however, we are primarily concerned with the village in which the *onogie* lives, and the relation within that village between his role and that of the *ɔdiɔnwere*. Insofar as the Edo see an ideal division of functions between these two headmen the *ɔdiɔnwere* is primarily concerned with the age-grade organization and with the internal affairs of the village. His age invests him with wisdom, and knowledge of what has been handed down from the past *ediɔn* and he is the repository of the traditional laws and customs of the community. The *onogie* on the other hand represents the community in its external affairs. In practice however, the locus of authority within the village as between these two, depends on their respective personalities and followings and, though not so much at the present day, on the extent to which the *onogie* can count on support from outside.

All *enigie* traditionally have the right to tribute in kind and services, in the form of labour for building and cultivating, from their subjects, though at the present day few receive either. They differ within wide limits in the degree of their wealth and following. The wealthier and more powerful *enigie* live in large houses, built in the same style as those of high-ranking title-holders in Benin City, have many wives, keep courts modelled on the *Ɔba's* court, and can give titles to their subjects.

Others are hardly distinguishable in their mode of life from the commoners who are their subjects.[10]

The extent to which an *onogie* dominates the village in which he lives depends on his wealth, his following in the village and in other villages of his chiefdom and in the degree of support which he receives from above — which at the present day is very little. In some villages which have both kinds of headman the *onogie* completely overshadows the *odionwere*, taking most of the decisions in respect of intra-village affairs, settling most of the disputes and even directing the activities of the age-grades.

On the other hand an *onogie* should respect the opinions and advice of the *odionwere*. While the hereditary chief is, in some sense, the representative of a power which lies outside the community, the *odionwere's* authority derives mainly from the community itself. The succession of an *onogie* to his father is dependent upon the approval of the *Oba* but the appointment of an *odionwere* is the village's own affair; he is the king-pin of the main unifying institution in the community, the age grade organization. Then again, the *odionwere* is an old man while the *onogie* may be, in the eyes of his subjects, a mere boy to be respected on account of his descent, but still lacking the wisdom that comes only with age. When kola nuts are being shared at any gathering an *onogie* should give them to the *odionwere* to divide and pray over. Finally the *odionwere* is the priest of the collective dead of the village, whose shrine (the *ogw-edion*) is, for the community, what the *aru-erha* is for the family and lineage. The well-being of the existing villagers depends on good relations with their predecessors and the *odionwere* is the only channel through which such such relations can be maintained.

The Edo do not see the relations between the *onogie* and *odionwere* in terms of potential conflict (though such conflicts do occur) but rather in terms of mutual adjustment and co-operation in 'watching over the community'[11]. The one's authority is legitimized by his descent, the other's by his age. The presence of both is required at village meetings where important decisions are to be taken. Either, or both, can be approached to settle disputes, and in the villages where it was possible to make a close observation, there appeared to be no division of judicial functions between them, in the sense that one dealt

10 In general the size of chiefdoms, and the power of the *enigie*, increase with increasing distance from Benin City.

11 In this respect it is, perhaps, significant that in many villages the *onogie* and the *odionwere* should be members of the same ward.

with one kind of case and the other with another.

The relation between the roles of the *ɔdiɔnwere* and the *onogie*, within the village is thus a complex one and no general rule can be stated either as to where the main locus of power lies or as to the fields within which the authority of one or the other holds sway. A 'strong' *onogie* may keep all the power to himself while one with less influence within and outside the community may share his power more or less equally with the *ɔdiɔnwere*. The balance of power at the present day, when there is no longer strong support from Benin, lies mainly in the hands of the village community itself. It was noticeable that at Ekho, the village where it was possible to observe the relations between the *ɔdiɔnwere* and *onogie* most closely over a long period, there was a very delicate adjustment between the two headmen, to the extent that each submitted to the other disputes in which he or one of his dependants was involved. Other villagers sued' each other before either *'diɔnwere* or *onogie* indiscriminately, though each would generally call in the other, and other *ediɔn*, to assist him in making his decision.

d. *The village council*

The *onogie* — in those villages which have a hereditary chief[12] — the *ɔdiɔnwere* and the other *ediɔn* constitute a village council which meets at frequent, though irregular, intervals to discuss any matters of interest to the whole community, and to settle disputes. In large villages internal affairs within the ward may be discussed at separate ward meetings, the ward councils joining together to discuss matters affecting all of them.

The power to summon meetings (*iko*) is vested in the *ɔdiɔnwere* and the *onogie*. Any other villager who wishes to bring some topic to the notice of the community must arrange with one of these headmen to summon the *ediɔn* and any other persons concerned. The *onogie* holds meetings at his own house while in villages which have no hereditary chief they may take place either at the *ɔdiɔnwere*'s house or at the *ɔgw-ediɔn* the shrine of the collective dead.

All meetings are held publicly so that any man may attend, whatever his age-grade status. The *onogie*, and *ɔdiɔnwere* control the procedure but any *ediɔn* can initiate discussion concerning a matter which he wants to bring to the notice of the rest. Nor will a younger man be prevented from taking a full part in the proceedings if his opinions are respected and if he, in turn, defers to his seniors.

12 It will be assumed unless otherwise stated that we are dealing with villages which have an *onogie*.

The procedure at such meetings has a certain amount of formality. The *onogie* or *ɔdiɔnwere* begins by greeting the *ediɔn* and explains why he has called them together. When he has presented the problem to be discussed to them they, or those who are interested, give their opinions, each formally taking the floor by standing and saluting the others. The headman listens to what they say and after giving his opinion suggests what action should be taken. If there is still disagreement the matter is thrashed out again and, in most cases, agreement is reached, at least between the senior men.

Apart from their judicial functions village councils have been heard to discuss at length such varied topics as the organization of collective tasks such as road-clearing and the building of shrines or schools; age-grade recruitment and promotion contributions to funds for various purposes; the organization of aid for members of the village who are in difficulties[13]; the upkeep of village schools and the payment of teachers; the organization of community cult festivals; the need to perform sacrifices for the good of the village as a whole; the delegation of persons to go to other villages to consult a diviner on behalf of the community; and the carrying out of instructions from the central authority.

e. *Land rights and the assimilation of strangers*
According to an Edo dogma all the land of the Benin kingdom belongs to the *ɔba* – *ɔba nya otɔ-Ɛdohia*. It means on the other hand, that any one who lives in the Benin kingdom is subject to the *ɔba*'s authority and must give a proportion of each year's harvest to him, and, on the other, that all land which is not divided up between local communities is at his disposal. Both the *ɔba* himself and, with his permission, wealthy men of Benin City in former times settled war-captives and other dependants in unclaimed forest to found settlements. In time such farming camps developed into regular village communities, acquiring an age-grade organization, being assigned as a tribute-unit to a title-holder in Benin City (not necessarily the man who founded the village), and becoming liable to regular tribute to Benin.

13 This is of particular interest in view of what has been said about the solidarity of the village community. In one village where field-work was carried out one man became embroiled with almost the whole community. He joined a political faction to which the rest of the village was opposed, began to bring charges against his neighbours and relatives, and informed on those who had failed to pay tax, with the result that a number of people had to pay fairly heavy fines. It was generally accepted that these persons were suffering on behalf of the community as a whole. The *onogie* then called a meeting of the village and it was agreed that every *ɔdiɔn* should contribute to a fund to pay the fines.

Many villages were founded in the same way by the Ɔba themselves who sent out war-captives to cultivate the bush under the supervision of a trusted courtier. The status of these villages would, within a generation or two, be very little different from that of long-established settlements for, in principle, every man and a woman in the Benin kingdom is the Ɔba's slave. The word Ɔviɛn-Ɔba means both 'Ɔba's subject' and 'Ɔba's slave'; and it is significant that no stigma whatsoever attached to descendants of persons who were known to be war-captives sent out by the Ɔba to hunt or farm in the bush. The parents of the mother of the recent Ɛdayi of Ekho were both Yoruba who were captured by the Ɔba's armies, allowed to marry and then sent to Ekho where the then Ɛdayi married his son to their senior daughter, and a number of other persons in the same village admit to a similar origin without any sign of embarrassment.

As an alternative to setting up independent farming or hunting camps the Ɔba and other titled and prominent men in the capital used to, and to a certain extent still do, send out their dependants into existing villages where they are placed under the general authority of the *onogie* or *ɔdiɔnwere* and in a short time become completely assimilated to the village communtiy.

The *enigie* of chiefdoms are said to 'own' (*nya*) the land over which they rule. This again implies the right to receive tribute and services and, in addition, to be informed of the settlement of any new persons in the area of the chiefdom. Actual control over the land in both independent villages and in those which form part of a chiefdom (except for the village of the *onogie* himself) rests, however, in the hands of the *ɔdiɔnwere* and senior *ediɔn*.

As has already been indicated very little control of any kind is exercised over the use of village land by long-established residents. Control over the land, then, emerges mainly in relation to the admission of strangers14 who wish either to cultivate it or exploit oil-palms on a temporary basis; or to settle in the village or in an adjoining camp and become fully fledged members of the community.

Persons who wish to use the land belonging to a village, without settling on it, must seek the permission of the *ɔdiɔnwere* to do so. To him they present gifts of kola-nuts, palm-wine, and nowadays small sums of money, which he should share with the other *ediɔn*. These gifts are very small, amounting only to a few shillings normally, for land is

14 Here we are dealing with persons who wish to make use of village land on their own account rather than on behalf of a master.

not a scarce commodity. Each year the stranger land-user should make
further gifts to the ɔ *diɔnwere* and *ediɔn* out of what he produces, and
he is expected to contribute to the annual offerings made to spirits and
deities worshipped by the whole community, and, formerly, to the
tribute which the village used to pay to the *Ɔba*, and, if applicable, the
onogie.

On the other hand an Edo stranger wishing to become a member of
the community is exempted from all such contributions for the first
two or three years until he has established himself as a farmer, though
he is expected to make an initial small gift to the elders on taking up
residence. At first he will live in a temporary hut which he builds
himself or in the house of a kinsman, affine or friend. When the elders
see that he intends to settle down they will organize the building of a
house for him. He then becomes subject to the obligations incumbent
upon all villagers.

In the Benin kingdom, then, where land is plentiful, the land tenure
system is very simple and such control as is exercised over the land is
designed to add to the numbers of the village community rather than to
secure exclusive rights over its resources.

f. *Women in the village community*
If little has been said concerning the statuses and roles of the women
in Edo village life it is because, overtly at least, this is a male dominated
society. The women have no age-grade organization of their own, they
take no part in village meetings unless specifically called upon to do so,
and they are not eligible for political offices in the village. Insofar as
they participate in the political life of the community they do so
through their fathers, brothers and husbands. This is not to say that
they are not taken into account as a separate category in the
community with a legitimate voice in its affairs. Again and again one
hears at village meetings: 'This is what the women think' or 'This is
what the women want us to do'. The mother of an *onogie* or the
priestess of a community cult may, in fact, have considerable influence,
but it is expressed through her kinsmen rather than directly.

In each ward the senior woman is often spoken of as *ɔdiɔn-ixuo* –
'*ɔdiɔn* of the women' but this is not a political office in the same sense
as that of a ward of village *ɔdiɔnwere*. Her leadership of the women is
more informal. She does not call them to formal meetings but deals
with them separately by casual contact. She communicates their
opinion to the *ɔdiɔnwere* (whose wife she often is) and other *ediɔn* of

the ward, and she and other senior women are, from time to time, called before the village council to give their opinions on a particular matter or to receive certain instructions to be communicated to the other women. It is these *ediɔn* of the women who organize and collect the women's contributions to village funds, organize their activities in village ceremonials and in collective tasks such as the clearing and decorating of village shrines. Outside their own households and families they have no judicial role.

g. *Mutual assistance in the village*

The solidarity of the village community in non-political contexts is evident both in organized co-operative activities and also in the spontaneous help expected and given irrespective of kinship and affinal ties. There is, for example, a well-established organization of labour and activities for the building of houses, community shrines, and, nowadays, schools. When a house is to be built, the site is usually cleared and mud for the walls dug by the prospective owner aided by young kinsmen, affines, and age-mates. The actual building is an affair of the whole community. The work occupies five separate days, spaced at about weekly intervals. The different building and roofing tasks are carried out by the men of the *iroghae* and *ighele* age grades, supervised by the *ediɔn*, who also make certain small sacrificial offerings at the threshold of the building, and pray to *otɔ* (the ground, which is strongly associated with the collective dead who are buried in the village land) for the prosperity of the household and the safety of its members. The owner of the house must feast the workers during the days when they assist him, and the food is always divided into three portions, for the *ediɔn*, *ighele* and *iroghae* respectively.

Unorganized mutual assistance is noticeable particularly in situations of crisis, such as sickness or after a death. Besides sympathizers, those who can divine or others who wish to help go to participate without invitation or expectation of reward.

The common interest and sympathy expected of all members of the community in respect of the misfortune of one of its members finds its fullest expression in their attitude to the *onogie*. Early in 1953 the newly-confirmed *onogie* of Ekho contracted pneumonia. Its causes came mainly from within the household – he himself was said to have had sexual relations with a girl in the wrong part of the house, and his mother had had intercourse with one of her deceased husband's subjects – both serious offences whose remedy consisted mainly in sacrifices to the sick man's father. The sickness, however, brought all other activities in the village almost to a standstill. The house was continually filled with persons from every extended family and household in the village, bringing medicines, divining and suggesting possible courses of action.

h. *Conflicts in the village*

These examples are not intended to imply that the Edo village is a model of harmonious social relations, but only that, ideally, for the Edo, it should be a single moral community and that, to a considerable extent, there is conformity to this ideal. Open conflicts are, however, frequent and they tend to occur along particular lines of social cleavage.

Extended families and the lineages associated with them emerge as corporate groups in some situations of conflict; when, for instance, it is alleged that a betrothed girl has been given to another man, or a woman's agnates are accused of conniving at desertion of her husband. Such disputes call for the intervention of the *onogie* or *ɔdiɔnwere*. They rarely lead to a disruption of the village community.

Other lines of cleavage are between component wards of the village, and, in villages which have hereditary chiefs between the *onogie*'s lineage and other sections of the community. As between wards the main sources of conflict are relative ward seniority and the associated right to appoint the *ɔdiɔnwere* and the leaders of the lower age-grades. Some evidence was gained of such disputes leading to the splitting off of wards to form separate village communities. It has been stated that in large villages the wards fulfill functions which in smaller communities are operative at the village level. It seems probable that such wards represent a stage in the proliferation of villages, many independent villages have the prefix *idunbhun* (ward) in their names. The declining importance of age-grades and the replacement of the *ɔdiɔnwere*'s judicial powers by official courts reduces the potentiality for inter-ward disputes at the present day. The same is true of disputes between the *onogie*'s lineage and the rest of the community for his opportunities for exploiting his subjects are much fewer than they were.

Finally conflicts occur along age-group lines. There is potential hostility between the *ediɔn* and the *ighele* and *iroghae* who resent not only their subservience, but also the greater advantages that the old men have for acquiring wealth. There are two main sources of such wealth — fines levied upon offenders within the village community, and gifts from strangers who settle on village land or who seek permission to exploit its resources. Certain proportions of these gifts should be passed on to the lower grades but, in fact, they rarely are.

Such conflicts between age-groups, however, rarely lead to a disruption of the community, and no instances came to light of groups of younger men breaking away. Most young men are under the authority of an *odiɔn* in their own household or extended family and moreover the *ediɔn* as a group have at their disposal certain ritual sanctions which are denied to their juniors.

In this section an attempt has been made to illustrate the solidarity of the village community as a corporate group in comparison to the lack of solidarity in wide-scale kin groups. The intervention of representatives of the village in purely domestic disputes serves to emphasize this state of affairs.

VILLAGE COMMUNITY CULTS – UGIE– ƆVIA

a. *Introduction*

Editor's Note: The ritual life of the village has two main centres of interest, the cults of various sets of the dead, which are significant at every level of organization; and the cults of various divinities. The cults of the dead have been summarized and analyzed elsewhere: especially in Bradbury, 1957, *The Benin Kingdom*, and in 'Fathers, elders, and ghosts in *Edo* religion'. The rest of this study of the village community will therefore be devoted to a rather full account of the important cult of ƆVia in Ekho village. It is interesting particularly because no other extensive description of such cults among the Edo-speaking peoples has been published [PMW].

In most villages of the Benin Kingdom there is one cult which overshadows all others in the degree to which it is the concern of the community as a whole: indeed, one of the distinctive features of a village community is the possession of such a cult, though in large villages similar cults may be organized on a ward basis. There are many of these cults, differing in the object of worship, in the organization of the cult group and in details of ritual but, on the other hand, all have certain features in common.

In the first place the deity to which each cult is addressed has a dual aspect. It is conceived of as being, at one and the same time, a famous or heroic figure of the past and a natural feature of the environment which may be a valley, hillock, or small lake, but which is generally a river or stream into which the hero or heroine is supposed to have been transformed at death. Most, though not all, of these figures feature in legends connected with the 'history' of the Benin kingdom, and their activities in human form are assigned to the reigns of particular kings.

Associated with each hero-deity is a shrine housed in a special building, which may be within the built-up area of a village, or in a clearing in the bush some distance away. Control of the cult is in the hands of one or two priests whose offices may be hereditary or elective or assigned on the basis of some criteria which are held to indicate selection by the deity itself. Most of these priests are male but in some cases the priest, or one of the two priests, must be a woman or, alternatively, the office may be held by a member of either sex.

While worship of these deities, by the priests, acting on behalf of individuals who make application to them, goes on continually, there are annually, or at greater intervals, festivals of worship (*ugie*) in which the whole community takes part. On these occasions particular roles are assigned to major sections of the community. Principally, the men and the women have their own duties and, within the male group there are a number of sub-divisions organised mainly on an age basis.

In this chapter it is proposed to consider one of these festivals in some detail with a view to establishing its meaning and purpose both from a subjective, pragmatic point of view – that is from the point of view of the Edo participants and observers – and from a wider, objective, sociological viewpoint.

The *ugie* which will be described was performed in the first quarter of 1953 by the village of Ekho, about fourteen miles east of Benin City, in honour of Ɔvia, the main tutelary deity of the village. The Edo themselves think of an *ugie* as a festival of worship in honour of the deity concerned, and as a period in which relations between the worshippers and the object of worship are intensified. Thus by 'serving' the deity in this way they bring themselves into closer contact with it; in some cults, the deity itself is at one stage of the rites believed to possess the priest, while in others, including *ugie- via*, he or she is represented in the world by past worshippers who come back to visit their descendants. These spirits, as will be seen, are impersonated by their male descendants in the patriline. During the *ugie*, then, the real world and the spirit world are brought into closer proximity, and requests made to the deity are believed to be more effective at this time than at any other.

Most cults of this kind are found in more than one village and they are transferable from one village to another. Between neighbouring villages which have the same cult there are often special bonds on that account, but it must be emphasized that in all cases each village (or ward, where the ward is the unit of cult organization) constitutes a separate congregation.

b. *The Ɔvia myth*

The origin of the Ɔvia cult is accounted for in a myth, the following version of which was collected from the elders at Ekho:

Ɔvia was a very beautiful girl who lived at Uhen a long time ago. Many men sought to marry her but when she was still very young she told her parents that she would marry only a king. When she had grown to marriageable age the king of Oyo visited Benin where he heard of Ɔvia's beauty. So he went to beg her father for her hand and her father agreed.

When the time for her to go to join her husband approached, her father, foreseeing how this marriage would end, took a pot, a dog and a parrot and treated them with medicine so that Ɔvia might take them with her. He told her that if ever her husband should treat her badly she should pass through the pot and come home.

From her childhood Ɔvia had always worn a single white cloth, trimmed with the scarlet material called *ododo*. When she reached Oyo the king, noting her beauty and her fine clothes, made her his favourite wife, and arranged to have a door between his room and hers so that he could visit her at any time.

Soon the other wives became jealous of Ɔvia and the senior one plotted to make trouble between her and the king. She summoned all the other wives together to go to the bush with her to collect snails. Cunningly, she told all except Ɔvia to take bags with them in which to carry the snails home. When they were ready to return home they put the snails in their bags but Ɔvia had to tie hers in the cloth she was wearing. The slime from the snails soiled her cloth.

When they reached the palace the senior wife rushed to her husband and told him that Ɔvia had a disease, *ite*, which was causing her to menstruate continually, and warned him that if he continued to be intimate with her he would become ill too. So the king sent for Ɔvia and made her take off her clothes. Then he saw that the cloth was stained and was convinced that the senior wife had told him the truth. The other women laughed and jeered at her so she ran away and locked herself in her room.

In the evening, at the time when he usually visited Ɔvia, the king began to feel sorry for her so he went to look for her. When she refused to open the door for him he broke in and found that Ɔvia was melting away with her tears. So Ɔvia fell down into the pot that her father had given her, and became a river which ran out from the harem and along to her father at Uhan. When she reached her father she told him that no woman should ever be allowed to know her secrets for it was women who caused her to leave her husband's house.

The dog which she took to Oyo is the dog which to-day is used as a sacrifice to her. The parrot is the parrot whose feathers are used in the headdresses of her worshippers. The snail is the snail which is found in the Ovia river.

The significance of these allusions and the meaning of the myth as a whole will become clearer in the light of the following description of the *ugie*. Here it need only be said that the main purpose of the myth appears to be to explain the exclusion of women from many of the Ɔvia rites and the reservation to the men of the secret lore and language of the cult.

c. *The structure of the Ɔvia congregation*

For all practical purposes, the Ɔvia congregation is coterminous with the village community, including natives of the village now living elsewhere, though outsiders may request the priests to make offerings to Ɔvia on their behalf.

Within this congregation there is, as might be expected from the myth, a major cleavage along the line separating the sexes. The women, while they have a well-defined role in the *ugie* are debarred from active worship of Ɔvia. They are not allowed to visit her shrine − except on two special occasions − or to enter the sacred groves. There are certain ritual objects which they must see only under certain circumstances, or not at all, and a secret language and sacred lore, which are the preserve of the men. This should not be taken to imply, however, that the women do not take part in the benefits believed to ensue from Ɔvia worship; on the contrary, they are, in a sense, the major beneficiaries.

The male association of worshippers is sub-divided roughly on the basis of age into three grades − *ɔyɔ*, *igbe* and *ediɔn* − which correspond more or less to the secular age-grades of the village. Initiation into the first grade and subsequent promotions are at the discretion of the *ediɔn* and are marked by the payment of small fees. Additional charges are made for the revealing of sacred knowledge, mainly in the form of new names for common objects and answers to riddles, appropriate to the various grades. No particular time is set aside for initiation or promotion though there is a tendency for these to take place at the beginning and end of the *ugie*. It should be emphasized, however, that the *ugie* is not an initiation period as such though it has certain features in common with such *rites de passage* in other parts of Africa.

The rite of initiation into the ɔyɔ grade is a simple one. The candidate is seized, blindfolded and thrown on his back. One of the priests takes the *uxurhɛ*, the ritual staff which is the symbol of Ɔvia, and lays it along the initiate's body. The latter is then told that he must not reveal anything he might see to a woman or to a male outsider. He must swear never to practise sorcery or witchcraft, never to thieve or assist thieves and nowadays, never to bring the police to the village. The priest bangs the staff on the ground under each armpit, above his head and below his feet. Then he is allowed to get up and is shown the bull-roarer and instructed in its use. There are no rites of initiation into the higher grades.

The grades function as groups only on special occasions, namely during the *ugie* itself, at periodic rehearsals for it, and at certain mortuary rites for past *igbe* or *ediɔn*. It is the duty of children of deceased members of the two upper grades to provide a goat, a fowl and other offerings for sacrifice to Ɔvia, and failure to do so entails a curse in the name of the deity. In return for these offerings the male worshippers perform a dance outside the house of the dead man.

The Ɔvia cult in each village is headed and controlled by two priests (who will be referred to here as the senior and junior priests), elected by the male worshippers on the basis of their knowledge of the sacred lore and ritual. At Ekho the priests were, in fact the two oldest men, but this is unusual and, indeed, both of them were appointed while their seniors were still alive. The senior priest is called 'priest of the dry land', the junior 'priest of the water'. The latter is also known as *odede- ɛrinbhin* or *iye-ɛrinbhin*, that is, the 'grandmother' or 'mother' of the *ɛrinbhin*. The word *ɛrinbhin*, as has been indicated, is the plural form of *oribhi*, 'a corpse', and in its strict sense applies to the spirits of persons once incarnated in this world. In connection with the Ɔvia cult, however, *ɛrinbhin*, has a special significance. At the time of the *ugie* the men of the village, or a large proportion of them, retire into seclusion in the groves sacred to Ɔvia, whence they emerge masked, every other day. These masqueraders are known as *ɛrinbhin-Ɔvia* and each impersonates his immediately deceased patrilineal ancestor, that is, usually, his dead father or grandfather. The junior priest as the leader of these masqueraders, then, is their 'mother' or 'grandmother'. The significance of this will become clear later. The senior priest is never masked.

At all times other than the *ugie* one or other of the priests, or both, make offerings at the Ɔ*via* shrine every five days, accompanying them with prayers for themselves and their families, the village community and the Ɔ*ba* of Benin. Individuals from the village or outside, may approach the priests to make particular prayers or curses, in Ɔ*via's* name, in respect of sickness or other catastrophes, in seeking to beget or bear healthy children, etc.

In return for their services the priests receive the sacrificial offerings and small gifts. For the more important sacrifices they take with them the *uxurhɛ* which is usually kept in a small room which forms part of the senior priest's house. Women are not allowed to see this staff except at the *ugie* in the presence of the masqueraders: at all other times they must lock themselves in their houses when it is brought out.

Formerly, the property of anyone who was adjudged to have been killed by an Ɔ*via* curse became forfeit to the Ɔ*yia* priests. This is now forbidden but it is still common for the children of such victims to make gifts to the priests to avoid the possibility of a curse falling upon them.

d. *The shrine, groves and ritual apparatus*

The Ɔ*via* shrine, at Ekho, is situated in a clearing in the bush about half a mile away from the village and adjacent to a path leading to a neighbouring settlement. The shrine (*ogwa*) is a sun-dried mud building, with two doors in the front wall, situated at the centre of two clearings, in the form of a figure eight, which will be referred to as 'the Ovia groves'.

Inside the shrine on the back wall is an altar in the form of a mud platform on which are placed various pots, sculptured pieces of chalk, cowrie shells and a brass bell which is rung during prayers to attract the attention of the deity. The *uxurhɛ* which are the real symbols of Ɔ*via*, are placed on this altar when a sacrifice is being made. They are massive staffs about four and a half feet high, carved with representations of the Ɔ*via* masqueraders. They, more than anything else, are identified with Ɔ*via* herself who is sometimes said to enter them when she is called upon by the priests. On either side of the altar are two circular seats of dried mud on which the priests, and no-one else, sit.

During the *ugie* the men who go into seclusion build shelters in which to sleep at one side of the grove in front of the shrine. The uses of the other grove will be described later. Leading out of the second grove, and screened off from it, however, is a third small clearing which only the elders of the cult are allowed to enter. This is known as *Amɛ* − water − and is identified with the source of the Ovia river. There the priests and elders go to make special sacrifices and to hold conferences during the *ugie* when they do not wish to be interrupted.

In a very real sense the groves represent, to the Edo, the sacred world (*εrinbhĩn*) as opposed to the profane world of the village (*agbɔn*). The men, who are in seclusion there, are identified with their ancestors and thus they stand, as the Edo put it, on the threshold of *agbɔn* and *εrinbhin*.

The women were debarred from entering the groves or even from passing along the path from which they were entered, and a special diversion had to be cut through the bush so that they could go to the next village. At the village end of this diversion a barrier (*adixuo*) was erected beyond which the women were not to go and at which it was their duty to come and sing from time to time.

e. *The men go into seclusion*
On an appointed day in mid-January, 1953, the priests of Ɔ*via* at Ekho retired to the Ɔ*via* groves where they were to sleep for about two months. Each morning and evening their wives sent them food some of which they offered to Ɔ*via* with prayers for the safety of themselves and the villagers during the *ugie*. They asked that the women of the village would bear good healthy children who would grow up to survive them and cursed, in Ɔ*via's* name, anyone who would seek to 'spoil' the village by sorcery or witchcraft, or by bringing thieves or the police there. The emphasis on safety during the *ugie*, which came out continually in prayers and songs, was due to the fact that this was regarded as a ritually dangerous period. The masqueraders, impersonating their ancestors, were, as they put it, on the threshold of *agbɔn* and *εrinbhin* and it would be easy to slip over the brink.

Ten days after the priests retired the rest of the men began to go into seclusion. At first it had been thought that all the men who were fit would masquerade, but the elders decided that some should be left behind to look after the village and report what was happening there to them. Not all the men who were to masquerade went into seclusion at the same time. Some were delayed on account of their own sickness or that of a relative or for some other reason, and they joined in as they became available.

Once they reached the groves none were allowed to visit the village unmasked except with the special permission of the priests which was given only when their presence there was absolutely essential. Apart from these visits they were to go there only on two types of occasion, firstly, every other day to perform the *εrinbhin-*Ɔ*via* dances and secondly, when the priests sent them out to investigate certain matters or to carry instructions to those in the village.

f. *The regalia*

The first day at the groves was spent in constructing sleeping shelters and assembling regalia. Each man was to wear a suit of cotton 'pyjamas' with very long sleeves which came down to cover his hands. Over this would be draped two single circlets of fresh young palm leaves suspended from the waist and the shoulders. These palm-fronds had to be gathered afresh on each day intervening between two dancing-days and for this and other purposes, such as the collection of palm-wine, one of the ɔyɔ was assigned to each *igbe* and *ɔdiɔn* as his servant.

Round his ankles each dancer was to wear rattles made from seeds wrapped up tightly in thick stiff leaves. The most impressive part of the regalia, however, was the headdress. This was constructed on a skull-cap of bark-cloth into which a framework of soft sticks was pegged. Into these sticks were inserted a vast number of feathers — red parrot feathers, tied in small bunches, representing the parrot which, in the myth, ɔvia took with her to Oyo, and larger black and white feathers. In the centre of the headdress, at the front, a mirror was tied, from the front edge of which hung a string network veil which effectively concealed the face of the wearer. From the back hung a long, wide strip of the scarlet cloth known as *ododo*, again recalling the myth, and this was decorated with strips of brass in various forms, mirrors, coins and cowrie shells. From a loop of cord at the front hung the two small sticks, shaped like flattened baseball bats, with which they would beat out the rhythm of their dances, all other forms of musical instrument being forbidden during the ɔvia festival.

Thus with the exception of the feet, the whole body of the masquerader was concealed and it was regarded as a serious offence if anything but the feet should be revealed to any woman. This did not imply, however, that the women were unaware of whom each mask concealed. They had seen and, in some cases, helped in the preparation of the garments and, in any case, could recognize men they knew from their build and movements or, in the last resort it was said, by their feet.

When they were not being worn all the components of this regalia, except the cloth garments, were kept in the clearing behind the ɔvia shrine, the *ugbobodo*. Admission to *ugbobodo* was one of the secrets of ɔvia for which a small payment had to be paid. There each masquerader, after paying another small fee to the priests, fixed a small tree stump about two feet high, over which he placed his ankle rattles and headdress. The palm-fronds which were discarded after each dance were piled up behind the posts to be kept for a future occasion.

The stumps were arranged in rows and grouped according to the grades of their owners. The one belonging to the junior priest – the senior priest never masqueraded – was immediately in front of the entrance to the small secret grove (amɛ) and it was followed, in order of seniority, by those of the other elders of the cult. The stumps belonging to members of the other two grades were similarly arranged.

g, *The secret language and names*
The male worshippers have a secret language, of the same structure as everyday Edo, but with coined and borrowed words substituted for the normal vocabulary. At Ekho its use was restricted to greetings, the naming of certain common and ritual objects, and a few conventional phrases.

Each of the men in seclusion also adopted a title or pseudonym; some of these were Benin state titles, some the names of birds and animals, and others referred to the prowess of their owners in the Ɔvia dances. These names were not supposed to be known by the women, who, however, were not permitted to use the ordinary names of the men. Instead they referred to each one by the name of his immediate ancestor – his father, grandfather, or, occasionally, great-grandfather.

h. The dance of ɛrinbhin-Ɔvia
Every second day throughout the *ugie* the ɛrinbhin came out to dance in the village, or in some other village that had invited them and was prepared to feast them. The first dance of the series was said to be 'for' the *ediɔn* – the collective dead – and was performed in front of their shrine. The second dance was for the senior priest, the third for the second priest and the fourth for the women as a whole; and thereafter all dances were regarded as being for the community at large, unless an individual or group invited the ɛrinbhin to dance specially for them. Those who were honoured by dances were expected to give generous rewards in money.

For each dance the ɛrinbhin wore their regalia and fresh palm-fronds (omɛ). They had to leave the groves backwards by a special entrance, through which no unmasked person was allowed to pass without incurring penalties. On each occasion the senior priest 'opened the way' for them by removing the sticks placed across this entrance and praying to ꞅvia that they would not be harmed in the dance, that ꞅvia would open the path to money and children for them, etc.

The ɛrinbhin entered the village in a particular order. The ꞅyꞅ arrived first, followed by the igbe and finally by the ediꞅn accompanied by a junior ꞅyꞅ carrying the uxurhɛ. The senior priest was the last to arrive. He took his place on the verandah of the house before which the dance was to take place and other elders who were not in seclusion ranged themselves on each side of him. The three grades of ɛrinbhin lined up in front of him with the junior priest in the centre, holding the uxurhɛ.

The priests saluted each other and the senior one then made an offering of kola nuts and water at the foot of the uxurhɛ. This rite is known as imiamɛ ('I see water') and its purpose is said to be to make the ground and the village cool so that the dancers will not fall down. The priest prayed for the dancers:

'Nothing will happen to you. You will not die. You will not be lost at ꞅgwa, like a snake that runs into the bush and is not seen again.'

After some of the water had been poured on the ground the priest and his companions drank the rest. The junior priest then moved the staff about over the wet patch, then stamped on the ground with his feet. Representatives from each of the three grades in turn danced a few steps in the wet sand until it was completely covered. The junior priest then raised the uxurhɛ and touched the top of it on the backs of the hands of the seated priest and elders, saying: ' a gha ru a re ' – what you sow you will reap (literally, 'what you do you will eat'). Then placing the bottom of the staff in their palms he prayed: 'May all the things that you ask reach your hands'.

'Do not let the war of thieves come, do not let the war of witches come. Do not let us meet with any dangers'.

After imiamɛ the uxurhɛ was laid against the wall of the house and the ɛrinbhin arranged themselves in a circle to begin the formal dancing. The dances were highly organised, intricate and for the most part vigorous. They were accompanied by the beating of the sticks which each masquerader carried and by songs from a solo voice and chorus. There would be no point in describing the movements of the dance here. Its final stages are, however, of some interest, for they consisted of the so-called obodo in which individually, and in reversed order of seniority, members of the ꞅyꞅ and igbe grades performed a kind of acrobatics, twirling in the air with both feet off the ground, turning over violently with hands and feet resting on the ground and, in some cases, walking on the hands. The *obodo* always aroused great interest and enthusiasm. Women cheered on their own fathers, brothers, sons and husbands and particularly good performances were accorded much applause.

After a rest a second cycle of dancing followed and, towards the end of the *ugie*, a third; but *imiamɛ* was performed only before the first cycle. Between the groups of dances the women of the village formed themselves into a body and sang their own special songs appropriate to the occasion.

At the end of all the dancing, in the early afternoon, the *ɛrinbhin* dispersed and wandered round the village stopping in front of some of the houses or in front of residents of the village or visitors to demand gifts of money. In return for these gifts they granted requests for blessings and curses. The blessings were stereotyped:

'You will live long. You will not die on your husband. Your husband will not die on you. You will bear good children. You will not meet with bad things. You will not be lost like a snake that runs into the bush' etc.

The curses, on the other hand were directed against those whom individuals believed were seeking to harm them by physical means, or by sorcery and witchcraft, and in each case *Ɔvia* was asked to kill the evil-doer or to let him suffer the harm which he intended others to suffer. One man sought a curse upon the 'killer' of his wife who had died recently. He produced a number of offerings and prayed over them:

'If it was a natural death that killed her do not let bad things happen to anyone. But if she was killed by someone you should kill that person and let his or her property be scattered. You should kill the one on whose behalf I have been making sacrifices'[15]

Others cursed those who they believed had stolen from them, set fire to their houses or brought them into trouble with the police. The majority of curses, however, were directed against sorcerers and witches who were believed to be harming the applicant or her children, who were 'spoiling' her pregnancies etc. No names were mentioned, though, in fact, the applicant often had a particular person in mind.

Curses and blessings secured from *Ɔvia* at the time of the *ugie* are held to be more effective than at any other time and, indeed, it is said

15 The last sentence refers to the fact that if a sorcerer or witch is revealed he or she will be forced to make sacrifices to save the victim.

to be impossible to revoke a curse laid at this time until the next *ugie* is being performed. Thus one woman sought the revocation of a curse which she said had been placed on her in a previous incarnation, the last time the *ugie* was performed at *Ekho*.

i. *Other activities of the ɛrinbhin outside the ogwa*

Apart from their visits to Ekho and other villages to dance, some of the *ɛrinbhin* were, from time to time, sent out by the priests to perform special duties. During the *ugie* there were two disputes which aroused considerable feeling. In one a woman was accused of bewitching a sick woman who eventually died. One night, when she was forced to go outside to make sacrifices the alleged witch was said to have seen the bull-roarer. This was regarded as putting the whole community in danger and the priest sent out about four of the *ɛrinbhin* to order her to produce a number of objects for sacrifice. The other case was one of sorcery. A woman was alleged to be attacking another woman, and causing her to be sick. This led to violent public quarrels and the *ɛrinbhin* were sent out to warn the accused to make amends by performing the requisite sacrifices to amend the wrong she was supposed to have done. She was warned that if she failed to do so ɔ*via* would undoubtedly kill her.

Another group of *ɛrinbhin* were sent out to investigate an alleged breach of the regulations concerning the cutting of palm-fruit and others went to a neighbouring village to settle a misunderstanding which had arisen over the arrangements for the *ɛrinbhin* to dance there.

j. *Activities at the ɔgwa*

Much of the free time at ɔgwa was spent in gossiping – the main themes of the gossip will be described below – and recounting the wonderful deeds of ɔ*via* in the past. The priests had many stories of how people who had served ɔ*via* had had their requests fulfilled, though for years they had been seeking the same things from other deities. There were, however, many things to do there, besides making conversation. On the free days the ɔyɔ would go out into the bush to tap palm-wine and to collect the palm-fronds which they and their *igbe* or *ediɔn* masters would wear on the following day. The priests made prayers to ɔ*via* each morning and evening, and they were continually being approached by men from Ekho and other villages with requests, on their own behalf or on behalf of women, for laying or revoking curses. From time to time they performed sacrifices in respect of the breach of some taboo by a member of the village whom they had called upon to make amends. The opportunity was taken to call in outstanding burial dues for any senior son who had failed, by this time, to make offerings to Ɔvia in respect of his deceased *igbe* or *ediɔn* father and thus subjected himself to a curse. Money was usually accepted in place of the sacrificial offerings and the curse thereby removed.

k. *Ritual prohibitions*
For the period of the *ugie* certain taboos were enjoined upon the whole community or upon particular sections of it. For the most part these were strictly adhered to and where lapses did come out into the open sacrificial offerings were exacted from the offenders.

Of those prohibitions applying to the whole community the most important was the ban on sexual relations for all residents (permanent and temporary), from the day the priests went into seclusion until the seventh day after the men returned home. It was said that failure to expiate, by sacrifice, a breach of this taboo, would undoubtedly result in the death of the offenders or their children within the year.

A second universal prohibition forbade quarrelling at this time. Actual fighting was worse than quarrelling and quarrels between the men in seclusion were regarded as more serious than those in the village. On several occasions, however, *ɛrinbhin* were sent to the village to investigate quarrels, to warn the offenders, and, sometimes, to exact penalties from them.

The cutting of palm fruit during the *ugie* was another offence, the explanation of this being that the palm tree provides an important part of the *ɛrinbhin* regalia.

Of the regulations which applied solely to the men in seclusion the most important was undoubtedly the ban on washing and shaving. A breach of this taboo was regarded as so serious as to be unthinkable and, to my knowledge, no breach occurred, though this was regarded by some of the young men as the most irksome of all the regulations.

Most of the taboos, however, fell upon the women. They were, on no account, to touch the masqueraders or any part of their regalia; or join in their dances or their songs, nor should they sing, hum or whistle any tune other than the one it was their duty to sing during the festival. When going to the bush or along the paths in the region of the groves the women were required to shout continually – *gh'ogboe, gh'ogboe* – 'behold an ignorant person!' – so that any of the men from *ogwa* who were going to collect palm fronds or palm wine might hide themselves until they had passed by. Most important perhaps were the prohibitions which forbade them to see any of the men's activities at night when the 'voices' of *Ɔvia* – bullroarers, speaking tubes, rattles etc. – sounded in the village. The sounding of these instruments was spoken of as 'closing the road' and when they heard them the women were forced to lock themselves in their houses. One woman who was alleged to have seen a man using the bullroarer was fined heavily and forced to provide many objects for sacrifice.

1. *The women's songs*

It might appear from what has been said above that the women play only a negative role in the *ugie-Ɔvia* that their only duty, albeit an essential one, is to scrupulously observe the ritual prohibitions enjoined upon them. Such an impression would be completely mistaken, however, for they have, in addition, a number of positive responsibilities which are equally indispensable to the success of the rituals. Chief among these is the obligation to sing certain songs at specified times and places. At Ekho there were three main kinds of occasions for these singing-sessions. Each morning and evening small groups of women and girls from neighbouring households gathered outside the door of one of them and sang for a more or less prolonged period.

Then again parties were formed regularly, on a household, extended family and ward basis, to go and sing at the *adixuo*, the barrier on the path to the groves beyond which the women were not allowed to pass.

The third occasion on which the women were expected to sing was when the *ɛrinbhin* came out to dance in the village. At such times they all put on their best clothes and formed a single group to sing, both before the men began to dance and during the interval between the dances. Whenever the dance was held in another village, as many of the women as were able would go there, by a different route from the men, and sing in the same fashion. Women from Ekho who were married into the host-village would join the Ekho women on such occasions while the rest formed a separate group to sing in competition.

It should be emphasised that these singing sessions were not merely addenda to the men's activities, indulged in by the women for their own enjoyment. On the contrary any slackness on the part of the women was immediately seized upon and condemned by the priests and elders. As will be shown below, many of the songs have both the character and the force of prayers and as such they are an important part of the rituals.

From the sociological point of view the content of the songs is of considerable significance for not only do they provide clues to the pragmatic meaning of the *ugie* but they illustrate very clearly the underlying social values which it expresses. All the songs are closely concerned with the *ugie* itself. Moreover they must all be sung to a single tune whose use is forbidden on any other occasion while, conversely, no other tune may be sung by the women during the period of the *ugie*.

A large number of the songs refer to the exploits and appearance of the men in their role as *εrinbhin*. Their regalia and dancing are praised and boasted about and the women express anxiety that their menfolk should dance well, that they should not fall down, or make any mistake which will bring criticism upon them. Each is anxious that her own relatives will dance particularly well so that strangers who come to watch will go away and spread their fame abroad.

'The spectators will not criticize my father in the dance to-day
Dance and swagger my prince of this world'.

'He into whose mouth God has put truth
Come and look at my *εrinbhin*
Tell you children, tell your grandchildren
Tell your great-grandchild the king of children'.

Though the women sing as a group each directs her song especially to her own husband, father or brothers (all of whom, according to the conventions of the *ugie* are referred to as *erha* 'father') whom she wishes to outshine the rest.

'You do not praise the duiker as you praise the antelope'.

'My father you should take a good name
And with it build a fence about yourself'.

The relatives of the senior priest at Ekho sang a special song referring to his exalted position and his role as chief intermediary with the deity.

'Favourite servant of the king
Salute the king for me
My great *Odede*[16]
To salute a person for someone is not a heavy load'.

Another set of songs expresses very clearly the ritual dangers attending those who go to serve Ɔvia at the ɔgwa and the anxiety of the women that they should come through them safely.

'A-man-cannot-be-punished-for-what-he-does-not-do
That is my father's praise-name
The red cloth (i.e. part of each man's regalia) will return home safely'.

The frequently repeated line 'Rain beats the junction of heaven and earth' expresses the peculiar position of the men in seclusion, on the threshold of this world and the spirit-world. The most potent source of danger is recognised explicitly in 'No woman shall kill my father at the ɔgwa'. Another line which is frequently shouted at the end of songs combines the sentiments of pride and fear — 'Safe journey, leopard; safe journey, elephant'.

Other songs express the dependence of the women upon the men who, it must be remembered, are at this time identified with their ancestors who are believed to have supernatural powers on their own account, and as the servants of Ɔvia. So the women pray to them in song, for the things they want most in the world.

Finally, and perhaps most significantly, one may single out the songs which express, in a more or less direct fashion, the importance of co-operation between the sexes for the successful prosecution of the ugie.

A woman's songs then, as might be expected, are, for the most part, expressly concerned with the expected role of the women both during the ugie'and in social life in general. They stress the position of women as daughters, wives and mothers and especially as the producers of children without which they can be of little significance in the community. Their dependence upon the men and the ancestors is recognized and their obligations as servants of their menfolk are accepted. Moreover, it is through their husbands, fathers, sons and brothers that they themselves gain status and it is in their exploits and achievements that they should have pride. Some of the songs, too, admit and regret the faults which the society usually lays at the door of women and they pray that they themselves will not submit to evil impulses which will

16 The 'favourite servant' is the priest himself; Ɔvia is the king. In this sense odede is used as a praise-name for an old person, implying great wisdom and respect.

cause them to become embroiled with their menfolk, their co-wives etc.
In a few songs, too, the hardships which fall to the lot of women are
mentioned but in a mood of resigned self-pity rather than rebellion. In
the last resort, however, it is the unity of, rather than the gulf between,
the sexes which is stressed, and their indispensability to each other.

m. *The women 'kill' the ɛrinbhin*
The day eventually arrived when the ɛrinbhin had to 'die' so that
their impersonators could return home and take up again their statuses
as ordinary men. As one might expect it was the women who were
designed to kill them.

The masqueraders came out in the same way as on all previous
occasions but the senior priest was this time absent, for, it was said, he
should not see the ɛrinbhin die. The dancing, which on this last
occasion, as on the first, was held outside the shrine of the collective
dead of the village, was perfunctory, but this time everyone was to
perform the acrobatic *obodo*. As each dancer twirled round in the
centre of the circle his senior wife or, if he was unmarried, his mother
or sister, stepped into the circle and tossed a cloth over his head. Then
he began to stagger around weakly, crying '*ekagha kpa bhɛn*' — 'a
woman has killed me' — while the woman embraced him face to face,
and back to back, thus touching him for the first time since he went
into seclusion.

As each ɛrinbhin was despatched he was led out of the circle of
dancers and took his position in a single file on the path to the *gwa*.
Finally only the junior priest was left and he, too, was dealt with in the
same way. Then he took the *uxurhɛ* in his hands and turned to face the
women. He told them the ɛrinbhin were now going to die and the men
to return home. He ordered the women not to sing their Ɔvia songs
again. He warned them that if, after the death of the ɛrinbhin, anyone
in the village should do a bad thing Ɔvia would kill that person. Then
he went on to pronounce certain curses — against those who might try
to harm their co-wives, against women who would seek to spoil another
woman's pregnancy etc. To each curse the women gave their assent and
this was ratified by banging the *uxurhɛ* on the ground. Finally the
women were told to go home.

The ɛrinbhin then marched back to the Ɔgwa to be greeted by the
senior priest — 'you have done well'. They lined up in front of the
secret retreat of the elders where the priest took a small bunch of
feathers from each man's headdress as a token of his success in bringing

them safely through the *ugie*. Then the *ɛrinbhin* began to dismantle their headdresses.

n. *Ohuhu*

The 'dying' of the *ɛrinbhin* was not yet fully acted out, however. The following day they came out once more into the village to 'die' in front of and 'for', as they put it, the women. Now, however, they presented a marked contrast to all their previous appearances. Before, · their aim had been to make themselves as beautiful, exotic and unearthly as possible. They had presented in the eyes of the villagers a spectacle of almost unrivalled splendour. Now they were dark, drab and dusty and of enormous bulk. They still wore the bark-cloth skull-caps which had been the foundation of their feather headdresses but even these were covered with several layers of dried-up brown palm fronds. Around his shoulders each man had further layers of old palm leaves and a third set was suspended from his waist. These were the *omɛ* that had been cut afresh for each dance in the cycle, then saved up for this occasion.

Their attitudes matched their apparel. Whereas before they had been sprightly and virile in all their movements they now drooped and staggered about, still crying 'A woman has killed me'. Their former élan had completely disappeared. All this had its meaning for the watchers. Were they not dying? An old woman pointed out, and did people usually look beautiful when they were dying? Their ungainly size had its significance, too, for when a person dies of a disease which makes his body swell, it is assumed that he has been killed by *Ɔvia* or some other deity who kills in this way, as a result of a curse.

Each *ɛrinbhin* visited his own house and lay down on his bed, kicking his legs in the air, rolling about, and groaning to simulate the dying of his ancestor. Then they made a tour of the village, embracing the women face to face and back to back, taking babies in their arms to bless them, and rolling in the dust to 'die' for the woman. Each person they met was obliged to give them presents of money or cowrie shells, in return for which they listened once more to the requests he or she had to make to *Ɔvia*.

The junior priest was the last to arrive and he made a systematic tour, carrying the *uxurhɛ* and going from house to house. Many of the women had saved their last petitions to present to him. To each he gave a blessing and a promise that their prayers and curses would be granted.

On this day, for the first time since they went into seclusion the men ate in their own houses, though the women were not allowed to see them. The food and wine had to be of the best. By this time inter-sexual relations had relaxed somewhat and some of the old women even ordered one of the elders back to ɔgwa half-jokingly, but with serious intent, too, for he had drunk much wine and they were afraid that he might commit some ritual indiscretion for which he and they would suffer later. By mid-afternoon all had returned to ɔgwa and they were not to appear masked in the village again.

o. *The women go to ɔgwa*

The same evening the women were to pay their only visit to the groves during the *ugie*. For this purpose they divided themselves into ward-groups and each group provided a dog and subsidiary offerings — pieces of chalk, cowries, firewood, yams, coco-yams, kola-nuts, snails, empty snail-shells, peppers, eggs etc. The snails and snail shells were intended as a payment to ɔvia for the right to hunt snails in the bush surrounding the shrine, and the firewood was to give them a similar right to collect firewood there.

There subsidiary offerings were carried, for each ward, in an enamel bowl, by a recently married girl, for, according to the old women, any woman who had not yet conceived would undoubtedly become pregnant within a month after performing this service.

About six o'clock the various groups of women made their way to the groves. There the men were waiting for them, lined up in a tight horseshoe formation, with the two priests, one masked and the other unmasked, immediately in front of the shrine. With the priests was a titled chief from Benin City who had come to represent the ɔba and to see that this, perhaps the most important of all the rites, was carried out properly. This chief, ɔbɔbaifo, had agreed to conduct the proceedings on the priest's behalf for the latter was afraid that he might make some mistake and thereby endanger himself and the rest of the congregation. For the main purpose of this rite was to pronounce formal curses upon all those who would seek to 'spoil' the village by physical or mystical means and it was thus essential that no slip should be made in the wording of the curses, which might then react to the detriment of those they were designed to protect.

The women advanced to the centre of the horseshoe and on the instructions of ɔbɔbaifo they grasped the rope tied to one or other of the dogs. Then, individually, but simultaneously, they began to confess and pray forgiveness for any breach of the ritual regulations which they might have committed with the aid of two assistants listening in, and

from subsequent checking it was possible to form the following
impression of what each woman might have said:

'Ɔvio behold the dog that I bring to sacrifice to you because of the
forbidden things I have done. I saw your face, I saw your back, I saw
your whole body. I saw you in the daytime, I saw you at night, I saw
your lamp. I saw you going to the bush to collect palm fronds, I saw
you in the bush collecting palmwine. I have joined in your songs, I have
danced with you, I have touched your body, I have embraced you. The
things that a woman is forbidden to do, I have done them all. Ɔvia, I
beg you, do not kill me, do not kill my husband, do not kill my
children. Let us all be well. May all the forbidden things I have done be
on the head of this dog'.

Thus these dogs were offered as a substitute to Ɔvia for the women
who were alleged to have broken the taboos. It was not suggested that
they had actually done so, and, indeed, those who were questioned
afterwards strongly denied that they had. They might however have
done so unconsciously so it was safer to confess everything. The dogs
were then handed over to the priests to be sacrificed later on.

Ɔbɔbaifo, the Benin chief, now took the uxurhɛ, banged it on the
ground and prayed for the long life of the Ɔba of Benin. Then he began
to address the women, asking them what they thought would be good
for the village. No-one presumed to answer and he was asked by the
older women to tell them what to say. Then he began to recite a long
series of curses, to each of which they were to give their assent. Taken
together they expressed very clearly the main pragmatic purpose of the
ugie. Curses were directed against anyone who would seek to commit
any form of anti-social behaviour in the village, those who would make
false accusations against their neighbours, those who would seek to
harm, by physical or mystical means, the men who were at ɔgwa,
whether by making them ill, or by spoiling their farms; against women
who sought to make their husbands impotent so that they would have
an excuse for going to find a richer husband and women who would
spoil another's pregnancy, or seek to harm their co-wives out of
jealousy; against those who would try to kill their own or their
co-wives' children.

Ɔvia was asked to punish all these evil-doers either by killing them
or by turning the harm they sought to do back on themselves in an
exaggerated form. To each curse the woman responded by repeating the
last phrase while Ɔbɔbaifo banged the staff on the ground. At the end
he encircled them with it, banging it on the ground behind their backs

at the entrance to the grove.

The women were now told to go back home and wait for their menfolk to return to them. Some of the men who were not masquerading, however, still had some last requests to make to ꓛvia and the senior priest himself cursed the sorcerer whom he believed had killed his son's wife 'even if it is my son or my daughter or anyone from my family, ꓛvia should kill that person'.

While all this was going on the ɛrinbhin stood motionless grunting rhythmically in low voices while from behind the shrine came the sound of the bull-roarer and the other voices of via. Now they lined up in front of the shrine in order of seniority and as the priest called out their names, they retired, one by one, behind the shrine to take off their regalias.

p. *The parrot goes to the river*

The following morning soon after dawn the rite known as 'the parrot goes to the river' (ꓛxwɛ ri ɛzɛ) was performed. All the men who had been in seclusion lined up, in order of seniority and marched in single file through the village down to the nearby river. No-one, male or female, was supposed to see them on the way there or on the way back.

Reaching the river they entered the water still in the same order and washed themselves and their clothes for the first time since they went into seclusion. Thus one of the most stringent taboos of the period was ended and they were taking on again the status of ordinary men. Finally they marched, naked, back to ꓛgwa where they shaved off their beards.

The rest of the day was spent in preparing to return home. Chairs, mats and clothing which had been used at ꓛgwa were purified by the priest so that they could be taken back and used in the village again. Then some last prayers and curses were spoken and special blessings were sought upon those who had played a big part in making the *ugie* a success, ꓛbꓛbaifo solemnly cursed:

'The things that were done in this secret place, it is here they will be lost. The man that takes home the quarrel he began here, ꓛvia you should kill him' and again, one of the curses most dear to the men:

'The woman who uses her sex in collecting your money and then leaves you and does not return your money, ꓛvia will kill her '.

q. *The coming home*

By about eight o'clock that evening the women in the village had retired to their rooms. The men came home and retired immediately to their own rooms for there was to be no contact between the sexes till the following morning. Then at dawn shouts of joy broke out all over the village as the women discovered their husbands, fathers and brothers safely returned from 'the junction of heaven and earth'.

They embraced the men in their own houses and then, in small groups, went from house to house, publicly embracing all the returned men − a most surprising sight amont the Edo. To each they shouted 'We shall do it all again together' while the men replied 'We shall do it again. You will not serve Ɔvia for nothing.'

Many of the restraints between men and women which operated at all other times disappeared for a few hours. They embraced each other indiscriminately, if decorously, and it was even stated that the men might visit the women's latrines, which would be a most serious offence at any other time.

The ugie was not quite over. The ban on full sexual relations remained for a further week and there were still one or two small rites to be performed, but there is no need to describe these here.

r. *Conclusions*

For the participants the main purpose of the ugie was a cathartic one. Again and again they assured each other: 'Wait till the ugie is finished; then you will see that the village will be cool'. Coolness implies a state of ritual purity in which the worshippers of Ɔvia need not fear the malevolence of others seeking to harm them by either physical or mystical means.

From the sociological point of view the festival is to be seen in terms of three sets of social relations. Its most insistent theme is undoubtedly the separation of the sexes which finds its most characteristic expression in the prohibition of sexual relations. But segregation goes much further than this. The men who go into seclusion represent the whole male community and those who remain at home do so only on account of special circumstances; none would admit that he never intended to go to ɔgwa. The men, then, are at the junction of agbɔn and ɛrinbhin; they are identified with their dead fathers and grandfathers, the past worshippers of Ɔvia[17] who come to speak for her, as they say, because she herself is too fearful to be seen.

The women, on the other hand, remain securely in the profane world, and are cut off from the ɛrinbhin by their ignorance of the

17 It is in accordance with the pattern of ancestor-worship that only the most recently deceased ancestors are impersonated and that all their descendants taking part use their names.

secret law and language of the cult and by the manifold taboos which forbid them to see or come into contact with certain ritual paraphernalia, or to join the activities of the *ɛrinbhin*. Infant boys could go with their fathers to the groves but their grandmothers were forbidden to do so. The *Ɔvia* myth, as has been seen, seems primarily designed to explain the reservation of the main ritual activities to the men.

The second important set of social relations reflected in the cult-festival concerns the men alone. They are divided into grades which roughly correspond to the secular age-grades. Each grade keeps its regalia in a separate part of *ugbobodo*. The grades enter the village in a particular order, perform their parts of the dancing in a particular order and so on.

Thirdly, and perhaps most importantly, the *ugie* sets off the village community from all other local groups by uniting it in a common purpose as it is united at no other time. Every major section of the community has its own duties to perform which are indispensable for the common purpose. Time after time it was pointed out that the *ugie* would make Ekho's name famous. Spectators were attracted from far afield to watch the dancing and to seek to share in the benefits which are believed to derive from the *ugie*, and the villagers were continually exhorting each other not, as it were, to let the side down.

The key to the social effectiveness of the *ugie* lies in the atmosphere of mystical danger which it brings to the village, through the fact that the men place themselves in closer contact with the supernatural world than at any other time. In the everyday world the women are largely dependent upon the men for their physical and mystical well-being. Their role in village affairs is a subsidiary one. They must cook for and generally look after the menfolk and support them by adhering to certain taboos. In the mystically dangerous atmosphere of the *ugie* the number of these taboos is increased and so is their importance, for their breach at this time is more dangerous than at any other. They must, therefore, be more circumspect in their behaviour than at other times. At the same time their dependence upon the men is increased; they must trust them to do, at *ɔgwa*, what they believe will be good for them. Thus the role of the women in everyday village life is given a clearer, symbolic expression in the performance of the *ugie*.

The same argument applies to the sub-divisions of the body of men in the village. The authority of the elder over the younger men is more complete at *gwa* than at any other time. The seniority-juniority set is always conceived in terms of a master-servant relationship but this is exaggerated at the groves where each man is explicitly made the servant of an older man. The authority of the elders is more irksome at this time than at any other. It is they who receive the fees and the greater part of the gifts that are given to the men. The younger men feel more strongly the deprivations of not being able to wash or to have sexual relations. A good deal of the gossip at ɔgwa consisted of the complaints of the younger men that the elders were taking more than their fair share of the benefits and that they were browbeating them in one way or another. The attempt of the elders to extend the period of seclusion caused a good deal of ill-feeling between the elders and the two lower grades.

Yet, at this time, these conflicts could not safely be expressed in open revolt. Just as the men were in closer contact with the sources of supernatural power than the women, so the older men were in closer contact than the younger. And, moreover, there was the fear of the consequences of open quarrelling at this time. On the day that the men went home from seclusion there was an interesting sidelight on this state of affairs. The young men of the ɔyɔ grade drank a lot of palm-wine, then began to perform dances appropriate to preparations for warfare and for wrestling competitions. They hoisted on their shoulders their champions — those who had been most brave in standing up to the elders and refusing to be browbeaten by them while at ɔgwa — and visited the houses of all the elders, who gave them small gifts.

The *ugie* then gives symbolic expression to the authority structure of the village community by throwing the main cleavages into greater relief in a situation where observance of the expected roles of the various sections of the community is of paramount importance. It does this in the interests of order and common well-being. The irksomeness of conforming to the greatly augmented code of behaviour is more than compensated for by the consequences which are believed to ensue. The *ugie* is, of course, greatly valued for its recreational aspects. Its songs and dances are enjoyed to the full by those who take part in them and they afford an opportunity to individuals to show off their prowess. But the important benefits are of a more serious kind. The community is split up into its component parts only so that each can play its proper role more effectively to the advantage of the community as a whole. If, from the objective point of view, the *ugie* has any lasting value it must lie in the greater awareness that it gives to different sections of the community of their own roles, and in the fact that it expresses the self-conscious solidarity of the whole community.

To test this hypothesis it would be necessary to compare the *ugie-Ɔvia* with the *ugie* of other similar cults and this is impossible here. But it may be stated that while no other cult demands the segregation of the sexes to the same extent, in all of them distinct roles are set aside for men and women, and among the former for different age-groups. The Ɔvia cult is, in any case, by far the most widespread cult of its kind and there is evidence that it was spreading rapidly and displacing other community cults in recent times.

3
Religion and Art

Father and Senior Son in Edo
Mortuary Ritual

ATTITUDES TO DEATH

Edo mortuary ritual varies according to the social statuses and circumstances of the deceased. In this paper I shall deal only with the rites performed for a man who is survived by one or more sons. Even within this category there is abundant variability on such grounds as rank, office, wealth, and clan affiliation, but it is with the common elements, not the variability that I am here concerned.

Edo attitudes to death depend on the degree to which the deceased has fulfilled his social destiny. The older a man is, the more descendants he has, the higher his rank and prestige, the more acceptable does his death become. The peaceful demise of an old chief with numerous progeny is as much an occasion for rejoicing in his life's achievement as for sorrow. To die childless, or sonless, is the most dreaded fate, and when one asks:

'Why do you want many children?' the reply is often: 'So that they may bury me well'. The Edo believe that one who is not properly 'buried' cannot enter the society of his dead kin and associates. For his survival as a social being he is dependent on the performance of the mortuary ritual by his children. Again and again, at the climaxes of these rites, one hears the song: 'This is what we bear children for'. In a sense, the funerary ritual is the most potent symbol of the parent – children relationship as it is ideally conceived in Edo culture.

1. The material for this paper has been collected during periods of field-work made possible by grants from the Royal Anthropological Institute (Horniman Fund) and the International African Institute, and during my present appointment (1960) as a Research Fellow of the Benin Scheme, University College, Ibadan.

THE SENIOR SON AND THE *EGBEE*

In the mortuary rites two main groups of participants are to be distinguished.[2] First, there are the *ibhi-orinbhin* or 'children-of-the-deceased', headed by the oldest surviving son *(ɔm 'ɔdiɔn)* who is identified as *obhi-orinbhin*, 'child-of-the-corpse'. So long as the latter is alive no one else can take it on himself to 'bury the father'. On the other hand, failure to perform the funeral rites invalidates his claim to be the principal heir and successor and, although, within limits set by the lineage elders, he may make use of his father's property, when he dies his brother may step in, perform the rites and take away the succession from his son. Inheritance rules vary but, at the least, the senior son takes his father's house, a majority of his inheritable wives, and the bulk of his movable property, his siblings sharing the remainder. By virtue of his position as principal successor to and ritual intermediary with, his dead father he assumes authority over, and responsibility for, his siblings (and his sons' wives and children) in varying degree according to his age and their sex, age, marital status, residence, and other personal circumstances. The father's hereditary offices pass to him and he is recognized as the immediate or potential successor to his statuses in other, non-kin, groups.

The ambivalence described for other patrilineal societies[3] in relations between fathers and sons, where the obligation to love and respect conflicts with the knowledge that one must replace the other, is intensified among the Edo by the unusually close identification of the father and *one* of his sons. The difficulties inherent in this relationship – and they are explicitly recognized by the Edo – tend to grow as the two men grow older and can be finally resolved only by the father's death and the redefinition of their respective statuses which it entails. The change in the relationship between father and senior son is a dominant theme running through the mortuary ritual.

The second main group of participants consists of the senior men of the bereaved lineage, whose point of fission may be only one and is seldom more than three generations back from the deceased. This group of lineage elders is, in the present context, identified as the *ɛgbɛe*, though this word also applies to the lineage as a whole and to the dispersed clan of which it forms a part. Primogeniture tends to the formation of new segments at each generation, for each of a set of

2 There are other categories of participants, such as widows and affines, but their roles are less important for the purposes of this paper.
3 Most notably by Fortes for the Tallensi.

brothers will, ideally, have a senior son who, after his death, sets up a shrine to him, where his descendants worship him (and his lineal ancestors) separately. The solidarity that lineages maintain over a limited number of generations is not based on rights in a common estate — such residuary rights as there are being rarely more than nominal — but on the need for the exercise of jural authority and mutual support over a wider range than that represented by the descendants of a recently deceased man. Lineage cohesion is as much a factor of the demands made on groups of kin by the wider political society as of the internal logic of the descent system itself. Thus, for example, when he succeeds his father a senior son is often too young to take his full place among the elders on the village council. He and his father's descendants must therefore be represented by their patrikin who are already *ediɔn*.

Within the lineage, then, the authority of senior sons as heads of segments is counterbalanced by that of the oldest man of the lineage (the *ɔkaɛgbɛe*) and the other elders. It is they who settle the more serious disputes and represent the lineage in external dealings. The *ɔkaɛgbɛe* is also the senior priest of the *ediɔn-ɛgbɛe*, the collective dead of the lineage. While the 'children' carry out the mortuary rites the *ɛgbɛe*, as the guardians of lineage and clan custom, control and direct them, and supervise the subsequent division of the dead man's property. At the beginning of the 'second burial' or 'funeral' they appoint two representatives (*adan*), a man and a woman, to keep vigil with the substitute corpse, and to advise and direct the senior son. The *adan* must be younger than the deceased (for no one older than him can take an active part) and they must have 'buried' their own fathers.

THE LIVING AND THE DEAD

The Edo make a clear distinction between two spheres of existence: *agbɔn*, the visible, tangible world of the living; and *ɛrinbhin*, the normally invisible sphere occupied by a supreme God, other deities, spirits, and supernatural powers. That *ɛrinbhin* has the same root as *orinbhin*, a 'corpse' or 'dead person' is an indication of the pervasive role of the dead in Benin religion and in many contexts, though not in all, *agbɔn kebh' ɛrinbhin* can best be translated 'the living and the dead'.

Relations between the living and the dead take many forms, for the latter are scarcely less differentiated than the former. First they are categorized according to their age, sex, parental status and office at death, and to whether and what kind of mortuary rites have been performed for them. Then, one effect of the mortuary rites themselves is to factor out the former statuses of the deceased, which are thereupon treated as if they were separate entities and assimilated to different social groups; so that, in effect, the same man is worshipped after his death in a number of guises. The supreme obligation of a senior son is to 'bury' (re) his father and to 'plant' (kɔ) him, that is to instal or rededicate a shrine at which to 'serve' him as an ancestor. But he must also ensure his father's assimilation to the collective dead of the various kin, territorial, and associational groups to which he belonged. For the deceased is believed to travel a hazardous route to the spirit-world to seek acceptance among the ancestors of his lineage and the dead of other groups of which he was a member on earth. His journey and acceptance are a constant theme of the mortuary rites which are, indeed, indispensable for their accomplishment. It will be seen from the description that follows that, explicitly and implicitly, Edo mortuary rites draw a parallel between the progress of the deceased towards acceptance by his dead kinsmen, neighbours, and associates, and the progress of his senior son towards recognition as his heir and successor in the world.

While one purpose of these rites is to transform the dead man into an ancestor who will reside indefinitely in the spirit world, watching over his descendants and demanding their attentions, yet, in song and prayer, he is constantly urged to return in a new incarnation among his descendants. Informants, when pressed, can explain away this paradox but they rarely think it necessary to do so. It is, in fact, a very meaningful paradox. The ancestor, by establishing the roots of the descent group in the past, has the function, among others, of legitimizing the authority of family and lineage heads and of providing sanctions for the maintenance of proper relations between kin and spouses. The belief in and desire for reincarnation refer to the dependence of the descent group for its continuity on the renewal of personnel. The consequences of bad relations between kin and between man and wife are sickness, death, and failure to produce and keep children. That the dead should be conceived both as ancestors — that is as the perpetual guardians and judges of kin morality — and as the reservoir from which the group renews itself is hardly illogical, given the dogma that vitality is a function of harmony and justice in human relations.[4] Much of the ritual and symbolism of Edo mortuary rites

4 Compare the close identification by the Nyakyusa and other Bantu peoples of the 'shades' and the semen. 'The shades', says Professor Monica Wilson, 'are identical with the procreative principle'. (Wilson, 1959, pp. 5—6).

derives from the recognition that the continuity of the descent group involves the redistribution and redefinition of statuses and the orderly transmission of jural authority through the generations.

THE MORTUARY RITES

As in many societies Edo mortuary rites fall into two parts which I shall call the 'interment' and the 'funeral'.[5] Interment of the corpse generally takes place on the day following death or the next day. The funeral rites may begin immediately afterwards, but it is usual to leave an interval of from a week to more than twenty years, according to the age, wealth, and other circumstances of the senior son.

THE INTERMENT RITES

Immediately his father dies the senior son is asked by the *gbee* to produce a new white cloth, a mat, a 'sponge' (that is a bundle of fibre), soap, and a small earthenware bowl. He, and any of his siblings who are present, are instructed to sprinkle the corpse with water from the sponge, that is to 'wash' their father's body. Some of the *ɛgbɛe* younger than the deceased then wash the body all over, shave off a band of hair round the forehead and pare the finger-nails. The hair and nail-parings are inserted into a lump of white 'chalk' which, together in some lineages with the bowl and sponge, is kept by the senior son until the funeral rites, when this assemblage serves as a substitute corpse (*akpa*).[6] When the body has been wrapped in the white cloth provided by the senior son (to which may be added another contributed by the second son — that is the next oldest by a different wife) it is laid out on the deceased's couch which has been covered with the new mat and another piece of white cloth.

Next the *ɛgbɛe* kill a goat, provided by the senior son, over the sponge and dish used to wash the corpse. This goat is 'for the *ɛkun*' (the loins and buttocks) of the dead man for 'it is the *ɛkun* that is used in begetting (bearing) a child'. The immediate reference is to the movements of the *ɛkun* in coitus but *ɛkun* here stands for the reproductive organs and processes in general. Thus, as the senior son's

---

5 The Edo term *irorinbhin*, 'burial of the dead', covers both sets of rites but is more generally taken to refer to what I call the 'funeral'.

6 There is a ready explanation for the use of hair and nail-parings. 'The nails do not rot, the hair does not rot', say the Edo. Further inquiry makes it clear, however, that it is not only their relative imperishability that is significant, but also their capacity for continuous growth and renewal, which persists for a short time even after death. *Akpa* can also mean foetus.

prayer indicates, the goat is killed to honour the deceased as a begetter of progeny:

> My father, behold the goat I come to kill for your *Ɛkun*, the *Ɛkun* you used to beget us all. Protect me, protect all my relatives, protect my children, so that we may be able to 'bury' you; so that we may meet with no hindrance while we are doing it.

But this sacrifice also has the purpose of 'settling the father down' (*si-erha-kotɔ*), that is, in the immediate context, of preventing him wandering about and causing trouble and, in the context of the rites as a whole, of establishing him as an ancestor.[7]

A soup is made by the female patrikin and daughters-in-law of the deceased from the heart, head, and intestines of the goat and this is offered, with yam, to the spirit of the dead man. He is informed that the senior son is now prepared to bury him and implored to be patient and to accept what is done for him. There is a constant need to placate him, for it is feared that in his loneliness he will try to 'draw' his wives and children after him. The food is consumed by the children and other patrikin of the deceased, and the remaining meat is divided, a shoulder and some other portions going to the senior son (to be shared with the other children) and the rest to the *ƐgbƐe*.

After this sacrifice the *ibhi-orinbhin* are called, in order of seniority, to 'salute' their father and those who have not already done so should present a cloth and a small sum of money. The money and such cloths as are not used in the rites are shared out at the end between the *Ɛgbɛe*. Three strands of ideas seem to underlie these offerings of cloth. First they are understood as a mark of affection and a token repayment for the father's care for his children while he was alive. Then, in many contexts (e.g. following sexual misdemeanours) to take a new cloth denotes a return to normality after a moral relationship has been disrupted. That it is a white cloth is significant for white symbolises ritual purity and peace, summed up in the word 'coolness' *(ɔfure)*. Here, I believe, the offering of a white cloth indicates a fresh start in relations between the father and his children, a wiping-out of past conflicts, and a reassertion of the ideal parent-child relationship.[8] Thirdly, the tying-on of a new cloth is a common feature of rites

---

[7] *Ɛ* kun here has reference to 'sitting down'. 'To sit down in one place' is associated with freedom from anxiety, the opposite notion being 'running here and there', i.e. looking for remedies for one's difficulties.

[8] When an *onogie* or state title-holder dies he cannot be interred until the Oba has sent a piece of cloth (*ukpɔ- guae*, 'the palace cloth') to his heir. The Oba's refusal to do this brands the deceased 'an enemy of the Oba', and his children may be forced to dispose of the corpse secretly in the bush.

marking passage from one stage of life to another, the 'dressing' of the person undergoing the transition being the responsibility of the parent or master. To give a cloth in the dead man's honour, then, refers not only to his own changing status but also to his role in bringing up his children, and to their reciprocal obligation to care for him in old age, and to 'serve' him after his death in a new and intensified spirit of respect and obedience.

When the site of the grave has been chosen an elder of the lineage marks its long axis with 'chalk' and the senior son takes a hoe and strikes the ground along this line seven times. Thus he 'clears a road for his father to pass' on his way to *ɛrinbhin*. In Benin City the grave is excavated by young in-laws and friends of the dead man's children; in the villages by members of the *ighele* age-grade.[9] The corpse is laid in the grave with the feet pointing to the west, that is towards Ughoton, the old port of Benin, where the dead are believed to embark in canoes and cross the sea to the spirit world which lies beyond the dome of the sky.[10] Prayers are said at the graveside by a senior man and woman of the lineage (younger than the deceased) who express the paradoxical hopes of the survivors. They pray for his survival as an ancestor:

> Your children whom you have left here, you should order money for them. You should send them children. You should send them everything that is used for living in the world. . . . As they have lived to do this for you, let their children live to do it for them. . . . As you looked after your children when you were in the world, so you should look after them unceasingly.

and they exhort him to predestine himself (*hi*) well for his next incarnation:

> You came to the world and you lived to old age. . . . When you come back may you once again bring a good body with you. Money, health, all the things

9 The grave-diggers act in an aggressive fashion, demanding gifts from the heir before they will remove imaginary roots blocking their progress. There is a symbolic connexion between them and the aggressive spirits, *ighele-ɛrinbhin*, who are believed to hinder the deceased's progress on his journey to *ɛrinbhin*. This is a projection of the relationship between the elders *(ediɔn)* and *ighele* in the village. While the *ighele* are the executive arm of the elders they often appear as a body in opposition to them, resenting their authority and what they consider to be their rapacity. As the *isotɔn* procession (see below) moves through the town, the *ighele* of each ward demand gifts before allowing it to pass, and the *ighele-ɛrinbhin* are said to behave similarly towards the dead man. They are the spirits of men who died in their prime and have not received proper burial.

10 It would be a mistake to expect too explicit a correspondence between the stages of the rites and the hypothetical stages of the dead man's journey. When I tried to do so an informant pulled me up sharply: 'A journey to *ɛrinbhin* cannot be compared to a journey in the world. It is like a journey one dreams of. We may dream we are in Lagos, without knowing how we got there. So it is for the dead. He will find himself in *ɛrinbhin* without knowing how he got there'.

that are used in living, you must bring them with you. . . . When you come again may sickness not send you back. May you not suffer the diseases of this world in your next incarnation. Great man you will come back.

Led by the senior son, the children throw chalk and cowries into the grave, praying for and to the deceased. Then the mood changes to one of shattering violence as the children hurl in clods of earth and the grave-diggers seize their spades and begin feverishly to fill up the grave. For the younger sons, daughters, and grandchildren this is always a moment of spontaneous and uncontrollable grief and older sons may be deeply and demonstrably moved. But if the latter, and, in particular, the oldest son, shows no sorrow, no one is surprised or shocked. Often he takes up an arrogant, boasting attitude: 'Look, look what I am doing for my father! May my children do the same for me!' He may seize a spade and begin to hurl earth into the grave or stamp down the filling in what seems to the observer very like glee. And informants will explain, 'He is proud that he is burying his father. He is glad that he has survived to inherit his father's wives and property. . . . The child who eats the inheritance does not weep for the dead'. The difficulties inherent in the father and senior son relationship are beginning to be resolved, for in burying his father the son is at once carrying out his greatest filial obligation and, in large measure, supplanting him. 'You should weep no longer' I have recorded a senior son admonishing his younger kin, 'The weeping is to fulfil our custom. You should be happy now because our father died in old age and none of us went before him'. But looked at in terms of personal gains and losses the father's death means different things for the senior son and his siblings. For him the father, who, however much he was revered, formerly stood in the way of his social fulfilment, is in process of becoming the main sanction for his own status and authority, which the funeral rites, as we shall see, are designed to enhance; while his siblings, in increasing measure according to their youth, are exchanging the authority of a reasonably indulgent father for that of a brother who may be less well-disposed towards them.[11]

---

11 I do not wish to imply that senior sons are not genuinely grieved or that intensity of grief is merely a function of personal calculations, but only that, on the one side grief is mitigated, and on the other exacerbated, by knowledge of what the father's death means for the individual. Today, when many sons outstrip their fathers in wealth and social standing while the latter are still alive, there may be little or no ambiguity in the son's attitude at his father's death.

THE FUNERAL RITES

In most cases the funeral occupies a period of seven days and consists of five main stages.

Iwaorinbhin

Iwaorinbhin, 'laying out the corpse', takes place at night in the presence of only the lineage elders and the senior son. The chalk, containing the hair and nail parings, is placed on the dead man's couch and covered with a white cloth. Another lump of chalk is buried in a small hole near the grave and here a goat is killed 'for the feet' of the deceased. The two *adan* chosen to keep vigil with the 'corpse' kneel (on the right knee only) on opposite sides of the hole. Between them, at right angles, kneels the senior son, who prays over the goat:

> My father, behold the goat, behold the kola that I bring to clear a road for you to pass. Protect me, protect all my siblings, protect the *ɛgbɛe*, protect my children for me. . . .

The goat is to induce the 'father's' feet to carry him swiftly to his home in *ɛrinbhin*, for until he is accepted there he is, in his insecurity, a danger to his survivors. One informant likens this act to the old custom of slaughtering a goat at the threshold to welcome an important visitor: 'As we kill a goat for the feet, so the *ɛgbɛe* in *ɛrinbhin* kill one to welcome our father'. Another thinks of it as welcoming the father into the house to watch the rites being performed for him.[12]

A 'salutation' follows, the children coming to kneel at the foot of the couch, presenting small sums of money and, if they have not previously done so, white cloths. The goat is cooked and some of the soup made from it and yam are placed in the hole, for the father's feet; the rest is consumed by the *ibhi-orinbhin* and the *ɛgbɛe* younger than the deceased. Morning and evening, until the substitute corpse is buried, the *adan* and others who are present dance round the hole, moving to the right — that is, in the 'father's' direction for 'it is through the father's *ɛgbɛe* one goes home' — and singing seven songs expressing filial

12 The Edo have cults addressed to the Head and Hand which symbolize components of the worshipper's individuality, but none to the feet. Asked why, informants will say, 'It is when we are dead they serve our feet.' In their association with death the feet stand opposed to (*a*) the head as a symbol of live-in-this-world, survival and personal achievement, and (*b*) the buttocks (at opposite poles of a security-insecurity continuum — see note 7). But they have also a particular connexion with dead parents, in that offerings to the father may be made over the right foot, and to the mother over the left foot, in the absence of a proper altar.

obligations, sorrow, and fear for the safety of the survivors. At the end of each song they raise their right hands towards the hole and say '*Odede a-rhetɔn*', which is said to mean 'Old one, use this song to be going!' Through this dancing (*ilɛga*) the deceased is urged and escorted on his way: 'If a chief is going to the Oba we dance with him to the palace and stretch our hands to the Oba. So it is when we *lɛga* for the dead.'

The 'father' is 'fed', night and morning, by the *adan*, who put offerings into the hole. They do this with the left hand, for some of the food offered is normally avoided by the *ɛgbɛe*; that is, the ingredients or the methods of preparation and cooking are proscribed (*wua*) except on this occasion. In some *ɛgbɛe* the participants eat the awua themselves and there are other breaches of clan avoidances. Thus the survivors identify themselves with the transitional state of the dead father. His condition, and that of the group which his death has disrupted, can be repaired only through the redefinition of statuses which the mortuary rites are designed to effect.[13]

Izakhwɛ

On the third afternoon a goat (or cow in the case of a titled man) is slaughtered at the threshold of the dead man's compound and the senior son has his right arm (*oberha*, the 'father's' arm) and shoulder smeared with its blood by the male *adan*; while the latter's counterpart anoints the threshold and the door frames. These represent the *ediɔn ɛgbɛe*, the collective dead of the lineage, and it is for them and the living elders that the goat is intended. It is 'the goat used to *zakhwɛ* for the *ɛgbɛe*'. *Zakhwɛ* means something like 'to take out of the bath' and *izakhwɛ* marks the end of the first phase of the rites in which the dead man is being prepared for presentation to his kin and fellows in *ɛrinbhin*. 'Just as a baby must be washed before it can be accepted into the family, so, unless the dead man is bathed, his *ɛgbɛe* will not receive him in *ɛrinbhin* .... Just as the son kills a goat for the *ɛgbɛe* here, so does his father kill one for the *ɛgbɛe* in *ɛrinbhin*. We can say it is the same goat.' Thus *izakhwɛ* gives ritual expression to two changes of status: the incorporation of the deceased into the collectivity of dead lineage elders and the recognition of his son as head of a lineage segment in the world.[14] A public demonstration of the second follows

13 These breaches of *awua* are a very important feature of the mortuary rites and deserve fuller treatment than can be accorded here.
14 The son is said to 'enter into his father's status' – *la ukpo erha-e*. *Ukpo* means a built-up seat or couch of pounded earth and also 'status', 'position', 'rank', or 'office'.

as the senior son, his arms supported as if he were a chief, leads a procession through the town.

There are, however, other forms of *izakhwɛ*. When a village elder dies his son must perform *izakhwɛ- bho* (*ɛbho*, 'local community', 'town'), directed to the village *ediɔn*, living and dead. The goat, kola, palm-wine, meat, and yams that are passed to the elders are explained as a repayment to the community for the benefits the deceased enjoyed as an elder. By *izakhwɛ-ɛbho*, the 'father' is assimilated to the collective dead of the village (*ediɔn- ɛbho*) while his son is recognized as the new head of his family. The same principle holds in respect of the deceased's status in other groups. A hereditary village chief's heir must *zakhwɛ* for each of the villages in his chiefdom which, by accepting the goats and other gifts, recognize him as their new *Onogie*. Again, if the deceased has attained the *ediɔn* (or equivalent) grade in one of the associations (*otu*) that conduct affairs at the Oba's palace his heir must provide a goat for sacrifice to the *ediɔn-otu*. He thereby becomes *ediɔn* himself and 'when his father reaches *ɛrinbhin*, the dead members of his *otu* will rush up to him crying "Welcome"!'

Isotɔn

Isotɔn takes place two days after *izakhwɛ* and begins with another procession round the town which, this time, is divided into distinct groups, each headed by a son or son-in-law of the dead man. Not all children need lead a separate party, but at least the senior son (or son-in-law) of each wife should do so, and in some *ɛgbɛe* the first grandchild has his or her own group. The groups march round in order of seniority of their leaders, with the general provisos that sons take precedence over daughters (or sons-in-law) and that children of the same mother do not lead consecutive groups.[15] Each party consists of the wives, children, junior siblings, matrikin, affines, and friends of its leader, and a band of drummers. Much prestige attaches to the size of each following and there is a great deal of competition expressed in songs that are as much in praise of each leader as of the dead man. But the opportunity for individual display takes place within the context of the procession as a whole, which gives visible expression to the structure of the entire unit of which the senior son is now the head.

Each group has carried before it the offerings (*ot ɔn*) which its

---

15 The detailed order is in fact settled by the *ɛgb ɛe* who take into account not only formal rules of precedence but the relative age, wealth, and prestige of the children concerned.

leader is to present to the *ɛgbɛe*[16] − a goat or cow, a mat, a piece of cloth, bundles of yams, legs of duiker, a calabash of palm-oil, coconuts and kolanuts, pepper, salt, cowries, and sticks of chalk − all objects of high social value in the domestic context. In Benin City a young boy carries the *okun*, a box with its lid propped half-open, covered with white and scarlet cloth and decorated with mirrors, beads, coloured scarves, and figures of men, gods, and animals cut out of brass sheet. *Isotɔn* is said to mark the dead man's crossing of the sea to the spirit world and the *okun* is believed to go with him, as a symbol of his wealth and social achievement. 'It is through the (number of) *okun* one knows a person who lives long, dies well, and had many children. It is just like someone going abroad to trade and making a big profit. When he returns he will have people carrying his profit on their heads. It is to show he has done big things in his lifetime and praised his hand.'[17]

The senior son arrives back to find the elders of the lineage sitting in a row in front of the house. He presents his *ot n* for their approval and if nothing is missing (it is, in fact, bad form to find fault with the senior son's *otɔn*) a petard is fired and his followers express their jubilation. The *otɔn* are carried into the house and the heir takes his seat beside the elders of the lineage. When the leaders of the other parties arrive they find their senior brother is no longer leading them, with his back towards them, but ensconced among the elders of the *ɛgbɛe* who sit facing them; their *otɔn* are presented to him as much as to the *ɛgbɛe*. Later, when the *otɔn* are divided, the senior son keeps his own, while those of his siblings are shared between him and the elders of the *ɛgbɛe* in varying proportions.

Isot ɔn, then, does honour to the dead man as one who has fulfilled his social destiny, and conducts him to his rightful place among the ancestors. But it also expresses the structure of the lineage segment and family group stemming from him; and their position in relation to the wider descent group. Most significantly, it marks the point at which the senior son is split off from his brothers and raised to his proper place among the living elders of the lineage.

16 Children who do not make public offerings of *otɔn*, perform '*otɔn*, inside the house' by making a monetary payment to their senior brother. The kind of *otɔn* performed is taken into consideration when the property is shared out.

17 The symbolism is here very complex for *okun* is also the word for the sea, and brass figures of *Olokun*, the sea-god, appear on the box. *Olokun* is the god of wealth and is also an important fertility cult for both wealth and children come across the sea. When the Oba dies there is only one set of *otɔn*, and one *okun*, a very large one which 'walks by itself'. The Oba's property is not divided, everything going to the son who succeeds him.

The substitute corpse is buried at dawn in a miniature grave close to the actual one, with rites similar to those at the original interment. The following day is 'the day we beat the dead with hunger' for he is no longer fed by the *adan*; nor is *ilɛga* danced again.

Arha and isuerhanfua

On the evening of the sixth day a wake begins which lasts till the following dawn. The senior son bears the burden of entertaining the various groups of drummers and the kin, affines, and friends who have assembled to pay their final respects to the dead. A brother, sister, or child (but not the senior son) of the dead man is chosen to be *enɔdiarhaya*, that is, to represent the dead man himself. Arrayed in fine clothes and adorned with beads the 'father', who must neither talk nor sleep before dawn, sits on his couch while his children and grandchildren come, one by one, to kneel before him, greet him with the clan salutation and offer him a few pennies. In return they receive pieces of kola nut and coconut, and sometimes, through a spokesman, a blessing or a warning. I have heard the 'father' explaining that though he is now going to *ɛrinbhin*, he will not cease to look after his children nor to punish them if they do wrong. After the salutations the 'father' goes outside to dance with his children for the last time. They sing:

> My father, you will come back soon.
> You will go and you will come back.

and, as the dance reaches its climax, we hear the song:

> This is what I wanted
> When I wandered about looking for a child.
>
> This is what I wanted
> When I suffered for the sake of a child.
> This is what I wanted
> When I spent my money looking for a child.
> This is what I wanted
> When I sold my clothes looking for a child.
> This is what I wanted when I said:
> 'My Destiny, let it reach my hand.'

All this represents not only a final leave-taking but the father's reception by his kin in *ɛrinbhin*. Towards dawn the senior men of the lineage perform a secret test to make sure that the dead man has accepted what has been done for him.

At dawn a procession, led by the *enɔdiarhaya* and the senior son, each with his arms supported, moves to the bush on the edge of the town where two forked sticks have been planted, with a third balanced across the top. When they reach there the 'father' touches the sticks with his buttocks and the senior and other children do likewise until the framework collapses. Others take strands of black thread from their necks and throw them over the sticks, which are then gathered and thrown away. A gun is fired. This 'casting away of the sticks' (*isuerhanfua*) represents the final disposal of the earthly remains and the release of the participants from the dangers of contact with the dead. It is, however, only the unwanted aspects that are dismissed. A piece of chalk dragged on a string behind the procession, as it moves with all possible speed (no one looking back) towards the house, represents that aspect of the deceased which must be retained and enshrined as an ancestor. By touching the sticks the *enɔdiarhaya* has ceased to 'be' the dead man. Having led his 'living' father away, the son now brings him back to the house as an ancestor. Someone runs ahead of the procession making a chalk line on the ground and through the doorway into the house, guiding the father home. As they enter the house a gun is fired to welcome the father. Then the piece of chalk is placed on the altar where the ancestor will be 'served'.

Ukɔnbhen

The father has now been 'buried'. It remains to 'plant' (*kɔ*) him. This may take place the same day or be delayed for a little time. If the deceased was himself a senior son the altar at which he served his own father will be used again (otherwise a new one must be constructed). The carved staves (*ukhurhɛ*) on it, which at the beginning of the rites were laid flat, are now raised up again, and new ones added, and, for the first time, the senior son takes up his position to the right of the altar; the *ɔka ɛgbɛe* sits on the left. The son begins to pray (I give a recorded example):

My father, Idehen, who has slept, I have buried you. Behold the goat, the palm-wine, behold the four kola nuts that I have brought to introduce you into the house. This is the place where you will come and eat now. Let me not die. Let my children not die before me. . . .

When he has finished praying for his brothers and sisters and their dependants, the *ɔka ɛgbɛe* begins:

As your son has raised you to a high position so you should raise him to a high position. Gather his house around him. . . .etc.

Other sons and daughters come to kneel and offer prayers for themselves and their wives and children. All are anointed with the blood of the sacrificed goat and the kola and palm-wine are shared out, while the wives of the senior son and the other women sing:

Let us praise him.
If a child does not know something he should be taught.
Iserihenhen (the senior son) whose lamp the whole town has seen, this is how your child will do it for you.

Iserihenhen has knelt down.
He has made an altar for his father.
His father told him to use his property.
That one's child is greater than oneself is no curse.

From this time on the senior son will be the main intermediary between his father and the latter's other descendants, though for important matters he will act with the ɔka ɛgbɛe or another elder of the lineage who represent collaterals whose ancestors can be approached at the altar. Apart from regular offerings, and contingent ones occasioned by births, marriages, sickness, and quarrels, the same congregation will meet annually for a festival of collective worship (ehɔ) which, in all essentials, takes the same form as ukɔnbhen itself.

CONCLUSIONS

In this paper, I have attempted neither a full description nor a complete analysis of Edo mortuary rites but have tried only to isolate one broad band of meaning running through a ritual and symbolic pattern of infinite complexity. My starting-point has been the conventional theory of *rites de passage*, in that I have been concerned to understand ritual and symbolic behaviour in terms of the redefinition of statuses demanded by the death of individuals and the on-going processes of group life.

In 'burying' their father the children seek to convert him into an ancestor and a 'spirit-elder' in the various groups of collective dead (*ediɔn*). As the latter he at once loses his individuality but as a 'father' he retains it for as long as it remains significant for the ordering of relations between his descendants. Yet it is fervently hoped that he will soon be reincarnated in one of these descendants. This paradox, it has been suggested, makes sense in terms of that set of values which links together the vitality of the kin-group, morality and harmony in relations between kin, the orderly exercise of jural authority, and the dogma that the dead retain an interest in their living descendants. It is with this set of values that Edo mortuary ritual is mainly concerned, and at its heart lies the relationship of parent and child.

But this relationship has its place within a wider scheme of social patterning for which one of its forms, that between father and son, is selected as a key principle of organization. Nor is this the only principle. Another is that of age which is significant both within the sibling group and within the wider descent group. The peculiar quality of the senior son lies in the fact that he combines within him the principle of father – son succession and that of age-seniority among siblings. In Edo society there is an unusual stress on primogeniture; that is to say, an unusually large portion of the dead father's jural status falls immediately to his senior son. The knowledge that this is so can lead to difficult relations while both are alive, and I have suggested that the mortuary rites constitute a symbolic resolution of the conflict between the roles of son and successor. At each stage changes for the better in the dead father's social condition are linked with the son's progress towards recognition as his heir and successor. By constantly elevating the senior son above his brothers the rites help to give him the standing and prestige which he will need to handle his new access of authority successfully.

Yet, strong as the emphasis on primogeniture is, the father's death does not, of course, imply the simple transfer of his jural status in its entirety to his senior son. To complete the analysis it would be necessary to consider the mortuary rites and symbols in much more detail – in terms, for example, of the relations between the senior son and his brothers; and between himself and his brothers, on the one hand, and the wider lineage on the other. Enough may have been said, however, to indicate that mortuary rites play a crucial role in the on-going processes of lineage and family development.

Fathers, Elders, and Ghosts in Edo Religion

In recent years, our understanding of the nature and significance of African ancestor worship has been greatly advanced by the work of a number of British and American anthropologists. Among them, Fortes, Middleton, and Goody have all emphasized the connection between the identity and behavioural characteristics of those dead that are chosen as objects of worship, and the distribution and character of authority in both the domestic and political domains of the society. Fortes has stressed the importance of early childhood experiences in generating attitudes of dependence and filial piety which can be generalized through a lineage system in which, as Goody (1962, p. 413) puts it, 'the distribution of authority ... is linked with the computation of the genealogy and with officiation at sacrifices'. It is the authority aspect of the relationship between successive generations of close kin that is projected onto the mystical plane, in such a way that the basic norms governing the behaviour of members of kin groups appear to the actors to be handed down from above, and therefore unchallengeable. Incontrovertibly just, yet arbitrary and aggressive in their dealings with the living, Tallensi ancestors reflect, not only the sentiments of piety and dependence, but also the underlying resentment that sons feel towards their fathers. The threat and experience of ancestral retribution for failures in submissiveness serve both to uphold the authority of the lineage heads, who control access to the ancestors, and to constrain them to act justly in their dealings with subordinates.

Goody (1962), accepting Fortes's basic propositions, has demonstrated that variability in the incidence of, and in the characteristic attitudes involved in, ancestor worship, as between the LoDagaba and the Lo Wiili, can be related to variability in the recurrent experiences of members of these societies in specific aspects of the relations between close kin of adjacent generations. Thus a difference in the personnel of the holder-heir relationship, with regard to the transmission of wealth through the generations, is associated with differences in the incidence of sacrifice; and it is also correlated with the degree of hostility projected onto agnatic and uterine ancestors, which varies with the extent to which it is necessary for individuals to suppress resentment against living fathers (who are both household heads and property-holders). (Goody, 1962, p. 410).

Comparing the findings of the writers I have mentioned, and others such as Colson (1954) and Gough (1958), it becomes clear that the distinguishing features of ancestor worship in different societies are related directly to rules of succession and inheritance, and to the distribution of authority in all the relevant sectors and levels of the social organization. These are factors which the individual experiences not so much in infancy as in later stages of life.

Goody (1962, p. 18) has expressed the view that 'in the morphological rather than the "evolutionary" sense, ancestor worship has been partially re-established as the elementary form of the religious life'. I take him to mean that in ancestor worship there is a readily discernible congruence between the form and organization of the cult (including relations with the ancestral beings) and the form of a social group, namely a kin group, membership of which is based on something other than mere common religious interests. It is a primitive religion in the sense that relations with the objects of worship derive very directly from the typical experiences of individuals in their relations with certain categories of living persons. When 'gods' are made, by men, out of men who have died and been re-incorporated into society by virtue of the status positions they occupied before death (and not by virtue of any supposed unique personal qualities), severe limits are set, I suggest, upon the imaginative capacities of the religious thinker. Similarly, in interpreting manistic cults of this kind, the social anthropologist is constrained to explain religious behaviour in terms of observed patterns of social interaction between persons occupying particular status positions. He cannot treat religious actions and belief as something apart from other kinds of social behaviour as he may, to a greater extent, be able to do in dealing with some kinds of theistic cult.

Manistic cults, in the sense in which I use this term, are not, however, invariably associated with a genealogical ordering of the 'gods' and their congregation. One of the objects of this paper is to examine how far it may be possible to apply the Fortes/Goody type of interpretation to cults of the dead which cannot, strictly speaking, be labelled 'ancestral'. Most recent research into ancestor cults has been concerned with societies in which kinship plays a dominant role over a wide field of social and political relations. I propose to examine some of the cults of the dead that are found in a society of a very different kind, that of the *Edo* of the Benin kingdom of Southern Nigeria who, for several centuries, have formed the nuclear population of a large and powerful centralized state. I shall not, however, be concerned with the way relations with the dead relate to the centralizing institutions of the state, but with the role of the dead in the village community, which is the basic unit of the political system.

CATEGORIES OF THE DEAD

Edo religious life is very complex (Bradbury, 1957, p. 52f.). It involves not only the dead but a supreme deity, other deities associated with the natural environment or with human skills, 'hero' figures that provide the focus of village and village-group cults, reifications of the components of human personality, and so on. Communication with the dead, however, accounts for a high proportion of all ritual activities and every kind of social group forms a congregation for the worship of its dead in some form or other. There are, in fact, many kinds of dead, each kind, as we shall see, corresponding to a status category among the living.

A primary division must first be made between what I may call the 'unincorporated' dead ('ghosts' of several varieties) and those dead who have been assigned a 'constitutional' position *vis-à-vis* the living, by a deliberate act of reincorporation. Both kinds interact with the living but they are distinguished from each other by the attitudes and behaviour of the living towards them. In general it may be asserted that, while relations between the living and the incorporated dead have a strong, positive, moral component, ghosts are dealt with almost entirely in terms of expediency. The incorporated dead are accepted as acting justly in their demands upon the living, who are morally obliged to submit to their authority and to sustain them; they are also believed capable of conferring positive benefits, in the form of vitality and prosperity, on their worshippers. Ghosts, on the other hand, while they may have just grievances against the living — for the very reason, perhaps, that their heirs have neglected to perform the rites that would convert them into ancestors and elders in the land of the dead — act out of anger and resentment, untempered with any capacity for exercising benevolence. The incorporated dead are the recipients not only of expiatory offerings but also of acts of thanksgiving and commemoration. Ghosts can only be bought off.

Of the incorporated dead we need mention here only three varieties, each associated with a separate field of authority. These fields of authority are distinguished from each other not only by their operational contexts (family and lineage; territorial communities and associations; the state) but also by different configurations of the principles — such as age, descent, citizenship, etc. — on which the right to command obedience and services is based. For all three types the act of incorporation is part of a complex series of mortuary and succession rites. From the actor's standpoint these rites do three main things:

1. They ensure the deceased his rightful place in ɛrinbhin (the world of the dead) in respect of the various authoritive statuses hè occupied at the point of death.

2. They reformulate and regulate his relationships with those among the living for whom he has relevance by virtue of the same statuses.

3. They effect, or prefigure, or symbolize, the transmission of these statuses to one or more successors.

I shall refer to the three types of dead in the following manner (using capitals where the status is that of deceased persons):

A. FATHERS (erha father) are named, individual, patrilineal ancestors, arranged genealogically in relation to each other and to their living descendants.

B. ELDERS (ediɔn, elders; sing. ɔdiɔn) are the undifferentiated deceased elders of kinship, territorial, and associational groups.

C. CHIEFS (enigie and ɔba) are the named predecessors of the living incumbents of hereditary political offices. Though the predecessors of a chief may be identical with his FATHERS, they are conceptually distinguished from them and may be worshipped at a separate shrine.

Only type A, FATHERS, can properly be called 'ancestors' if we restrict this term, as I think we should, to situations where relations between worshippers and worshipped are genealogically determined. The ELDERS of a kin group are, it is true, the collective ancestors of its living members but they are not identified as individuals and precise genealogical reckoning is, in this context, irrelevant. Kinship does not enter into the cults of ELDERS of territorial groups or associations; and, while CHIEFS are linked agnatically to their successors, in the cults of CHIEFS the congregation is neither confined to, nor necessarily structured round, a genealogically defined group. In this paper, then, the word 'ancestors' is used synonymously with FATHERS. It would also apply to MOTHERS *(iye)* but this category of dead does not concern us here.

Space precludes a detailed consideration of the role of dead CHIEFS in Benin religion, for this would involve us in the complexities of sacred kingship. I shall concentrate, therefore, on FATHERS and ELDERS, and examine how they relate to each other and to the distribution of authority in the lineage and the village community. In those villages which have an hereditary *onogie* the cult of *enigie* may be important, but its effect is to add a new dimension to the ritual life of the village without seriously altering the relationship between the cults of the ancestors and the ELDERS.

'FATHERS' AND 'ELDERS' IN THE LINEAGE CONTEXT

When a man who has no children dies, he is usually accorded only a perfunctory burial and no attempt is made to incorporate him as a FATHER. When a man leaves only daughters, the senior daughter's son, or her husband, acting on her behalf may undertake to 'bury' him. But, in the normal course of events, it is the senior surviving son, and he alone, who should take responsibility for 'burying' *(re)* and 'planting' *(kɔ)* his father, that is for converting him into an ancestor and dedicating an altar at which to serve him. Those who are not 'buried' and 'planted' are implicitly assigned to the category of childless dead of the lineage who, whenever sacrifices are made to the lineage FATHERS and ELDERS, are thrown scraps of food, to appease them and discourage them from snatching what is intended for the incorporated dead.

Even those who do leave sons go through a period of discorporation between death (and interment which usually follows death very closely) and the completion of the funeral rites, or 'second burial', a period which may vary, according to the age and wealth of the senior son, from a few days to upwards of twenty years. Lonely, and resentful, and jealous of those who have been translated to a higher status, the father's ghost may, in the meantime; commit acts of aggression against his former dependants, making them sick, causing them to have accidents or to lose their money, attempting, even, to 'draw them after him'. He must, therefore, be pacified by offerings made, in the absence of an altar dedicated to him, over the right foot of his heir. On the strength of promises of an early funeral the son may, it is true, ask his father to show benevolence, but his willingness, and indeed his ability, to confer benefits are in constant doubt. For children, health and prosperity come not simply from one's own FATHER but, through him, from his father and father's fathers back along the patriline. For effective contact with his ancestors, then, he must go to another altar in the lineage, presided over by a close kinsman who has already 'planted' his FATHER. At this stage, then, the heir's authority over his father's other descendants and their wives lacks effective mystical backing. Nor, until he has accorded his father ancestorhood, has he validated his claim to be the heir to his father's property, in the form of a house, permanent crops, inheritable wives, and movable wealth. It is true that the lineage elders may permit him to make use of this property, or parts of it, but he cannot have full control over it nor, should he die before planting his father, can he transmit his rights over it to his own son. His next surviving brother might then step in, perform the funeral, and divert the seniority of descent to his own line.

Once he has made his father into an ancestor, the first son assumes rightful authority over his father's other children, and their access to the FATHER is through him. In the division of his father's property, supervised by the lineage elders, he receives much the biggest share and if his father held an hereditary office he succeeds to that.

One result of the rule of primogeniture is that much of the ambivalence, described for other patrilineal societies, in the relationship of fathers and sons, is concentrated, among the *Edo* on the relationship between a man and his first son, for it brings about an exceptionally close identity and conflict of interests between these two. I have described in another paper (Bradbury, 1965) how the funeral rites serve to resolve this ambivalence, by drawing a dramatic parallel between the progress of the dead man's death journey towards ancestorhood, and the son's gradual assumption of his father's authoritative role in the domestic domain. The typical attitudes of a senior son during the funerary rites are discernibly different, in degree, if not in quality, from those of his brothers. Boastful, self-assertive, he is expected to show pride rather than sorrow. 'The child who eats the inheritance', say the *Edo*, 'does not weep for the dead'.

The rites themselves serve constantly to separate the first son off from his father's other children. On the final night of the funeral a wake is held in which the father himself, impersonated by one of his close kin, shares kola nuts and dances with his children for the last time. At the same time, it is believed, his kin in ɛrinbhin (the spirit world) welcome him with similar festivities. Towards dawn the elders of the lineage perform a test to determine whether he has indeed been accepted as FATHER and ELDER, and whether he is himself satisfied with the rites that have been performed for him. When this is affirmed the father's impersonator is led by his son to a nearby patch of bush where the unwanted, ghostly aspects of the father are finally dismissed. Then a piece of chalk, representing his ancestoral spirit, is dragged, on a piece of string, back into the house, where it is placed on the altar built to receive it. The son is now free to dedicate the altar, in the rite of *ukɔbhɛn* ('planting'), and to officiate there as his FATHER'S priest.

But before this climax is reached other rites have to be performed which reformulate the position of the dead man and his son, in regard to the former's status of elder of the lineage. Throughout the funeral rites the children-of-the-deceased (*ibhi-ɛrinbhin*), led by the senior son, are set apart from, and opposed to, the elders of the lineage (*ediɔn-ɛgbɛe*), led by its oldest man, the *ɔkaɛgbɛe*. Only those who have 'planted' their fathers are recognized as true elders of the lineage but they rank among themselves according to age. Between the elders and the sons, especially the first son, there is constant tension and friction, as the former try to exert their authority and the son seeks to free himself, as far as possible, from it. He can never do so completely, however, for not only do they know how to perform details of the ritual that are hidden from him – and which they may contrive to keep hidden from him, even when the funeral is completed – but their cooperation is necessary for the translation of the dead man into an ELDER. One of the heir's first acts, when he begins the funeral, is to present a goat, through the *ɔkaɛgbɛe*, to the *Ediɔn* of the lineage, requesting their help in achieving this aim.

Two other episodes in these rites require mention here. In the rite of *izaxwɛ ɛgbɛe* the senior son presents to the elders a cow or goat (according to his father's rank and prestige) which is sacrificed to the *Ediɔn-Ɛgbɛe* the dead elders of the lineage, on the threshold of the deceased's house. This serves to assimilate the deceased to the *Ediɔn* and, at the same time, it affords recognition, by the elders, of the son's right to assume his father's domestic authority. Two days later, in the *isot.ɔn* rite, the elders sit in a row on the verandah of the deceased's house to inspect and receive a collection of offerings (the *otɔn*) from each of the bereaved children. The *otɔn* which, together with decorated boxes, represent the wealth and prestige the dead man accumulated during his life, are first carried round the town or village in a procession led by the senior son. When he arrives back at the house he presents his *otɔn* for the elders' inspection. But before this takes place a curious dialogue is usually carried on between the son and the elders, through a 'messenger'. The son inquires why the elders have sent for him.

In this exchange it is clearly implied that hitherto the elders – those who have already 'buried' their fathers – have stood in the way of the son's direct access to their common ancestors. Now they are prepared to allow him access through his own FATHER, and to give recognition to his assumption of the latter's fatherly roles. But more than this, they are also prepared to accept him as an elder, as one of them. For after his *otɔn* have been perfunctorily inspected and carried into the house (to be retained by the son himself) he takes his seat alongside them. So that, when his brothers and sisters come to present their *otɔn*, their senior brother is no longer one of them, but one of the elders who receive their gifts. The *otɔn* will, in fact, be shared by the senior son and the elders in two more or less equal parts. The other sons do not necessarily become elders immediately but will gradually and informally be accepted as such as they grow older. What I want to emphasize here, however, is that while the first son succeeds to his father's elderhood he does so only in a general sense, for his position *among* the elders will not be that which his father held. Thus, to take the extreme case, if his father had been the oldest man in the lineage, *ɔka ɛgbɛe* and priest of the *Ediɔn-Ɛgbɛe* this office would pass not to the son, but to the next oldest man. The son, that is, does not succeed to his father's *specific* status as elder, even in the necessarily qualified sense in which he succeeds to his fatherly roles.

From this brief and simplified account it will, I hope, begin to be clear that, among its other functions, *Edo* mortuary ritual serves as an exegesis, for the actors, of the distinctiveness and the interconnectedness of the specific, individual authority of fathers and the more general, collective authority of elders in the family and lineage contexts. The death of a father and elder, who needs to be replaced in respect of both these statuses and who, in order to preserve the continuity of fatherly and elderly authority, must himself be made a FATHER and an ELDER, provides the obvious occasion for such an exegesis. In the day-to-day affairs of kin groups the interplay of these two types of authority is apparent. The relative autonomy of senior sons as intermediaries with their FATHERS, on behalf of the latters' children, is balanced against and limited by the overall authority of the elders as intermediaries with the *Ediɔn*, on behalf of the lineage at large. It is not possible, within the space allowed for this paper, to examine, in detail, how these types of authority are exercised. It can be said, however, that the elders exercise a supervisory control over the dealings of household heads with their subordinates, restraining or supporting them according to their assessment of the justice of their actions and decisions. Men often succeed to their fathers' positions as family heads at an early age, and they need both encouraging and restraining if they are to perform this role successfully. Family heads rarely adjudicate between their subordinates without calling in other elders of the lineage, nor are they expected to be judges in their own disputes with their younger siblings. Moreover, while they are still young they have no effective voice in the councils of the village elders and it is through the lineage elders who, by virtue of their age, are also village elders, that the community exerts its pressures on the younger members of its component kin groups. These external pressures are, to my mind, a potent factor in holding together a lineage group when the rule of primogeniture, and the lack of a lineage estate, are working in the opposite direction. For the lineage, as a group, holds no property in common, not even land. Its elders do, however, control property collectively during the interval between the death of a holder and the completion of his mortuary rites, and it is they who, once the FATHER is 'planted', supervise its division, in unequal proportions, between the first son and the children of his father's other wives. It is no accident that the solidarity of the lineage, and the authority of its elders, are more apparent during the mortuary rites of one of its members than at any other time.

Both the FATHERS' altar (*aru-erha*) and the lineage ELDERS' altar (*aru-ediɔn-ɛgbɛe*) are the scene of periodic commemorative rites, of confirmatory rites, and of expiatory sacrifices and offerings arising out of sickness and other disasters, which are divined to be the result of quarrels and other sins of omission and commission involving lineage members and their wives. But by far the greater number of these expiations are directed towards FATHERS rather than ELDERS. It would be possible to produce evidence to suggest that this preponderance is in accordance with a greater amount of suppressed resentment and hostility in relations between fathers and sons, and sons of the same father — relationships in which the control, transmission, division, and use of property are a constant potential source of conflicting interests — than in relations between the lineage elders and their subordinates. The direct, demanding aggressiveness of FATHERS, and their equally positive capacity for exercising benevolence, stand out

in contrast against the more shadowy, vaguer mystical powers of the
Ediɔn. The latter, it is true, are fairly often divined to be the cause of
troubles, particularly those that fall upon the kin group as a whole or
indiscriminately on a series of its members, but also of individual
disasters, generally as a result of a younger person ignoring or flouting
the elders' authority or following the breach of clan taboos. Very
frequently, however, they are seen as a secondary cause, as lending their
authority and their support to the demands of the individual ancestors
most directly concerned.

To bear out these assertions would take up the rest of this paper and
this is not my main intention. I have drawn attention to the expression,
in ritual, of two types of authority in the lineage context, principally in
order to pave the way for an exploration of the part played in *Edo*
religion by another kind of elderhood, namely elderhood in the village
community. The elders of the lineage and the forerunners they serve on
the lineage's behalf share common descent and, though precise
genealogical reckoning is not directly expressed in the ritual that joins
them, it still may be thought permissible to speak of them as 'collective
ancestors'. In the secular and religious notions of elderhood to which
we now turn, the ideology of descent has only a peripheral part to play.

'ELDERS' OF THE VILLAGE

Whenever the *Edo* speak of the *ediɔn* of any group they have in mind
those members of it who stand at the upper levels of a formal or
informal hierarchy, graduated according to age or length of
membership. The root *diɔn* means 'to be older than'. Not only descent
groups but groups formed on territorial or associational principles all
set their senior members apart as *ediɔn*, and the same men (and women
in their own organizations) can be *ediɔn* in a number of different
groups at the same time. In each group the *ediɔn* make policy, settle
disputes, and serve as the repository and defenders of the group's
traditions and regulations. They accept responsibility for its well-being
and good name, represent it in its relations with other groups and
individuals, and except the deference and obedience of its members
who are not yet elders. If the group holds any property in common it is
the *ediɔn* who control its use. Among themselves the elders are
generally arranged in recognized order of precedence, according to age
or length of membership, and the oldest man, or the one who has been
an elder longest, is usually designated *ɔdiɔnwere*.

Corresponding to every set of *ediɔn* there are the *Ediɔn* their forerunners, who demand that the living elders should uphold the customs and rules they have transmitted to them, and afford them mystical sanctions to assist them in dealing with infractions. The *Ediɔn* not only demand regular proof, in the form of offerings, of the group's continued respect for them but they also punish breaches of the rules they have laid down by bringing sickness and other disasters upon the group as a whole or its individual members. The *Ediɔn* are thought of in two slightly different senses, as: (*a*) the original founders of the group who laid down its customs and taboos; and (*b*) those members of the group who have, since its foundation, achieved elderhood, upheld its rules and conventions, modified them in accordance with changing circumstances, and passed them on to their successors. One by one, as the generations pass, elders die and are assimilated to the collectivity of their predecessors through the rites performed by their descendants and successors.

Descent groups, territorial communities at all levels up to that of the nation, occupational guilds, associations of retainers in the *Oba's* palace, cult groups worshipping particular deities – all these have their 'altars of the *Ediɔn*' (*aru-ediɔn*) where the living elders communicate with and give sustenance to the collectivity of their forerunners.

Forde (1962) has described how, among the Yakö, each of the associations of which a dead man was a member intervenes in his mortuary rites, demanding from his heirs that they should feast its members and take steps to fill the gap he has left in its membership. In Benin each of the groups in which a dead man was *edion* makes similar demands. I have already referred to the rite of *izaxwɛ-ɛgbɛe* which assimilates the deceased to the *Ediɔn* of the lineage; but the sons must also perform *izaxwɛ* for each of the other groups in which their father had achieved elderhood, by presenting the living elders of the group with a cow or goat (according to rank and prestige), yams, cooked meats, kola nuts, palm wine, etc. These are sometimes explained by informants as repayments to the group for the benefits the dead man himself received as an elder, that is for his share of whatever accrued to the elders as a group. But they have a religious as well as a secular purpose, for they are directed not only to the living elders but also to the *Ediɔn*, who receive them as offerings and sacrifices. The demand that the heir should fulfill these obligations comes from the dead man's survivors but also from his forerunners and, moreover, from the dead man himself. For, without the support of both the community he has left and the community he is seeking to join, he cannot accomplish the hazardous death-journey between the two. Thus the *izaxwɛ* offerings are both repayments for what he has received as an elder in this world and, as it were, entrance fees into the society of the various groups of *Ediɔn* in the land of the dead.

We have seen that, in the mortuary ritual, the deceased's progress to ancestorhood is paralleled by the son's assumption of the 'father' roles he has vacated in this world. Also he replaces his father as an elder of the lineage, though in a much more general sense, for although he is accorded nominal elderhood his ability to exercise it will depend on his age relative to that of the other lineage elders. I now wish to examine the manner in which the mortuary ritual serves to effect, or rather symbolize, succession to village elderhood. I limit myself to the village variety, because to consider the *ediɔn* of other groups would introduce too many complications, and also because I believe this to be the context in which many of the basic notions concerning the activities and interests of dead elders are generated. First it is necessary to give a little more detailed information about the age-grade organization (Bradbury, 1957, p.32).

Youths around sixteen years of age become *iroghae*, usually in small batches and at irregular intervals, at the discretion of the *ediɔn* and *ɔdiɔnwere*. Their passage into this grade is marked by a usually simple confirmatory rite, involving offerings of kola nuts and coconut at the shrine of the village *Ediɔn* (ɔgwediɔn), which is normally the meeting-house of the village elders. Henceforth they are liable to be called out, along with the other *iroghae*, by their leaders, the *ikairoghae*, who, acting under the instructions of the *ɔdiɔnwere* direct them in such menial 'public works' as road-clearing, trampling mud and carrying water for building operations, and, in the past, carrying tribute to the capital. After ten to fifteen years of this, by which time they are the oldest *iroghae*, they are promoted, in another simple ceremony, into the *ighele* grade where, under the *ikaighele*, they take part in those communal tasks demanding more skill and experience, perform 'police' duties as agents of the elders, and supervise the activities of the lower grade. In pre-colonial days it was from the *ighele* that detachments were generally chosen for service in the military campaigns of the state. We shall return to the *ighele* later for, as we shall see, they are the living counterparts of one of the varieties of unincorporated dead, namely the *ighele-ɛrinbhin*. What I wish to emphasize here, however, is that, in the normal course of events, promotion from *ighele* to *ediɔn*, as from *iroghae* to *ighele*, takes place right outside the context of mortuary rites.

When an elder dies, each of the elders junior to him moves up one step in the order of precedence, but as the body of elders becomes generally depleted the oldest *ighele* begin to pressure the *ediɔn* to promote them. When an understanding is reached, each of the candidates visits either all the *ediɔn*, or the most senior *ediɔn*, in turn, and presents him with a small bundle of yams, seeking his approval. Then, after a number of mimetic rites symbolizing the completions as *ighele*, they present offerings at the *aru-ediɔn* and each of them is lowered seven times over the altar. They are pronounced *ediɔn* of the village (and of other villages in the same chiefdom or village group) by the *ɔdiɔnwere*. Henceforth they have a rightful voice in the village council of elders, a right to share in such payments as are made to the elders, to share the elders' portion of feasts provided by individuals for the whole community, and so on. As they become older still, and reach the top ranks of elderhood, they will be recognized as eligible to deputize for the *ɔdiɔnwere* in making offerings to the *Ediɔn*.

This is the normal process by which *ediɔn* are 'made'. Yet in some villages in which I have lived elderhood is also conferred during mortuary rites. In the village of Ekho *izaxwɛ-ɛgbɛe* (for the lineage elders), and *izaxwɛ-ɛvbo* (for the village elders), used to be performed on the same day. The senior son of the deceased would produce two goats and the village elders would choose the bigger one, leaving the other for the lineage elders – an interesting token of the predominance of village interests. When the *izaxwɛ* offerings have been handed over to the village elders, the latter call upon the dead man's heir to nominate two persons, from among his patrikin, to be made *ɔdiɔn*. If he is not already a village *ɔdiɔn* himself, which he may well be, he will come forward himself with his immediately junior brother. If he is *ɔdiɔn* already, then he can nominate other brothers or patrilineal cousins for the honour. Presenting plates of coconut and kola nuts to the *ediɔn*, assembled in the village street facing the deceased's house, the candidates kneel before the *ɔdiɔnwere* and are pronounced *ediɔn* of the village. Generally speaking, the candidates put forward turn out to be young men, youths, even boys and it soon becomes clear that the elderhood conferred on them is of a largely 'honorary' or 'nominal' nature. It in no way cancels their obligations to continue to work with the *iroghae* or *ighele* until such time as, being among the oldest *ighele*, they are eventually promoted to substantive elderhood. it is true that when that time comes they will be absolved from making gifts of yams to the other elders but that is the only material effect of their 'promotion'.

Fortes (1962, p. 87), pointing out the office-like quality of all significant statuses, has recently described initiation ceremonies as 'the means of divesting a person of his status as a child in the domestic domain and of investing him with the status of actual or potential citizen in the politico-jural domain'. The relevance of this to the stage-by-stage process of making elders among the *Edo* is readily apparent, but it is the word 'potential' that catches my eye here, for it implies that such rites are not always designed to effect immediate transitions from one effective status to another, or to fill immediate gaps in the network of social relations. The conferment of honorary elderhood in the Benin village does not materially affect the recipients, nor does it do anything to restore the balance in the representation of kin groups in village affairs. Two honorary *ediɔn* do not compensate for one substantive *ediɔn*. This becomes abundantly clear when it is found that after the kin group has nominated its own 'replacements' for the dead man, both the *ediɔnwere* and, if the village has one, the hereditary *onogie* have the right to put forward new *'ediɔn'* from their own kin groups. Moreover, any other elder in the village may, by making a token gift to the dead man's heir, have one of his own sons made *'ɔdiɔn'* too. What is going on here, then, or so it seems to me, is not an act of succession to the specific *ɔdiɔn* status of a dead man. It is rather a symbolic recognition that the village community as a whole, its component kin groups, and its main authorities, are jointly responsible for seeing that, as the elders, who embody the community's values, die away, their authority is transmitted to a new generation of elders. It is succession to elderhood in its collective aspect, not in its individual manifestations, that is at stake. So the mortuary ritual not only affords an exegesis of the interplay of lineage and elderly authority in the lineage but links these two types of authority with a third, that of the village elders, in a more complex web of social relations. Village elderhood is essentially a community interest but, at the same time, it is symbolically recognized that, while the village can order its personnel, it remains dependent upon its component kin groups for their replacement.

It may seem pointless to view the collective authority of village elders, and its mystical coefficients, in the same theoretical terms that in the hands of Fortes and Goody, have proved so fruitful for the analysis of the relationship between the character and variability of ancestor worship, and the jural and property aspects of nuclear kin relations. Yet I think it is worth making the attempt, for it is of the nature of authority and property rights that, whether held by individuals or collectivities, they must be transmitted through the generations. I shall try to show, therefore, that there is a sense in which the holder/heir concept can illuminate not only the nature of ELDER-worship but also the relations of the living with one of the categories of the unincorporated dead, the *ighele- ɛrinbhin* (lit. *ighele*-dead), whose characteristics, as we shall see, are a negation of those of the *Ediɔn*.

The *ediɔn*, as a collectivity, hold jural authority over the rest of the community, men and women; authority which is passed on down the generations, individuals coming to share in it when they pass from the ranks of the *ighele* into the *ediɔn* age-grade. They do not hold tangible movable property of the kind that Goody finds so crucial in his analysis of LoDagaa ancestral and mortuary rites. They do, however, hold rights over land which, in the Benin kingdom, belongs to village communities as a whole and is not divided up between their component kin groups. They also own ritual paraphernalia and shrines, though these have no economic value. As land is generally abundant and any member of the community can farm wherever he likes, provided the tract he chooses is not already under cultivation, or earmarked for it, by someone else, the rights of the elders in land at first sight appear to carry no great benefits. They do, however, collect and share out dues from strangers who wish to work the land or its tree-crop resources, such as palm oil. They also collect court fines and fees and take to themselves a major part of anything else that accrues to the village community as a whole. It is rights of this kind, and the right to command non-elders, that are transmitted down the generations. Here the holder and the heir are both collectivities, namely the elders as a group and those who will succeed them as elders. And the act of succession does not take place at particular points of time – as it does among some related *Edo*-speaking peoples, where the senior age-grade retires, after a number of years, in favour of a succeeding age-group – but it is rather, a process continuing throughout time; a process which, I have suggested, is symbolized in the making of 'honorary' *ediɔn* during mortuary rites.

The alleged misuse of their rights and the arbitrary way in which they are seen, by their juniors, to use their authority to command, gives rise to constant resentment and accusations against the elders as a group. There is much in common between a father's authority over his sons and the authority of the elders over the other men in the village. The overt, expected behaviour of junior to senior villagers is much like that of sons towards their fathers, though necessarily lacking the same quality of affection and solicitude. Resentment of the elders' alleged selfishness can, on the other hand, be more easily admitted, and even openly expressed, for the collective nature of the elders' authority provides a general rather than a specific target. The younger men constantly meet in caucus to formulate their grievances and make plans for confronting the *ediɔn* with their misdeeds or demanding their share of the proceeds of some alleged secret agreement with strangers, involving village land or trees. They are rarely very successful, for the public solidarity of the *ediɔn*, combined with their mystical and magical superiority, and their individual authority in their respective domestic groups, give the old men considerable advantage. They are also usually adept at buying off some of their more vociferous juniors, either by quiet gifts or promises of promotion. The position of the official leaders of the *ighele*, who are expected to champion the cause of their fellows and at the same time to see that the will of the *ediɔn* is carried out, is a particularly anomalous one and this is recognized in the special protection that is sought for them, for the *Ediɔn*, on their installation.

Just as relations with the ancestors image father-son relations, so do relations between the village *Ediɔn* and their congregation reflect the corresponding aspects of the relationship between the living *ediɔn* and their apparent heirs. We have seen that, in the domestic context, the relationship of a senior son with his father is of special importance. Of somewhat analogous significance for the cult of village ELDERS is the relationship between the living elders and those who, as a group, are their obvious and immediate successors, namely the *ighele*. It is the *ighele*, the chief agents of the elders' authority, that are most resentful of that authority. Their hostility and opposition to the elders is coloured by their stereotype as the most virile and physically powerful section of the community, men in their prime of life and, moreover, warriors.

Linked closely, in *Edo* belief, with notions about the incorporated, collective *Ediɔn* are others concerning the unincorporated, collective *ighele-ɛrinbhin*. These are the men who have died in the prime of life, before passing out of the warrior phase into wise and experienced elderhood. Leaving no sons to 'plant' them, or sons who are as yet too young to do so, they have also been denied the opportunity of becoming *Ediɔn* in *ɛrinbhin*. Thus they are the collective, village expression of the ghostly fathers and childless dead of the lineage. They wander about in the bush, and it is they whom the foolhardy will see if they go to their farms on a rest-day. Removed from subordination to the living elders, the *ighele-ɛrinbhin* are free to express their resentment in whatever way they can. The obvious target for their anger and jealousy is provided by those men who have died as elders, and whose translation into FATHERS and *Ediɔn* has not yet been accomplished; those, that is, who are temporarily outside society but have the right and the promise of being taken back into it. Thus the *ighele-ɛrinbhin* are thought to constitute the chief obstacle to the dead father and elder as he makes his dream-like death-journey, through the forest and across the waters, to seek acceptance among his kin and associates who have gone before him. One of the overt aims of mortuary ritual is to protect the deceased against their activities.

Protection is afforded in various ways. Prayers are addressed to the Ediɔn, asking them to help the dead man on his way, and to accept him. Cowrie shells and other offerings are strewn along the route of funeral processions in a direct attempt to appease the *ighele-ɛrinbhin* themselves. But some of the mimetic acts of the participants in these rites are of particular interest, for they afford the living *ighele* a splendidly ambiguous role. While they are constrained by their position in the community to afford their assistance to a man who was recently their elder, and who will soon be assimilated to the *Ediɔn*, they are, nevertheless, given the opportunity to express their resentment against elders in general. Thus they play the part of dutiful village *ighele*, supporting one of their number in his obligations towards his dead father and, at the same time, they play the part of their dead counterparts who cannot be controlled, but must be bought off. Let us examine their role more closely.

It is the senior son who marks out the line of his father's grave and strikes the ground with a hoe along it, to 'cut a road' by which his father will travel. But it is the *ighele* of the village who actually dig the grave and in doing so they find numerous, usually imaginary, roots, which cannot be cut through until they have received a 'bribe' from the heir. Thus they join their counterparts among the dead in hindering the progress of the dead elder. Then again, as the funerary procession makes its way from ward to ward of the town or village, symbolically

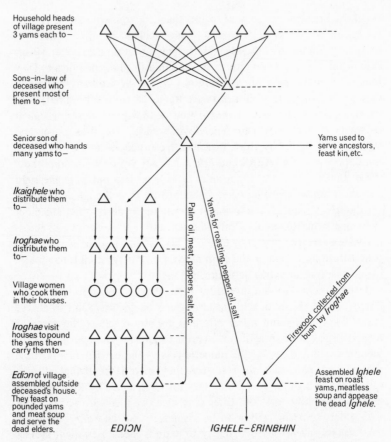

Fig. 8. Movement of Yams in the Igbizu Rite at Ugboko.

escorting the dead man on his journey, the *ighele* of each ward hold it up and demand a ransom before they will allow it to pass. The *ighele* and the *iroghae* also take part in these processions. First, they move on ahead, 'clearing a way' for it to pass. Then, turning about, they charge back towards it, in menacing fashion, stamping out the steps of a war dance as they confront the dead man's senior son. So, from moment to moment, their role changes as first they lead, then oppose, the dead man's progress.

In some villages of the Iyekorhiomwo district in the south-east of Benin Division, the *ighele* play an important part in a phase of the funerary ritual for dead elders known as *igbizu*. This corresponds, in part, to the *ilɛga* rite which is carried out, night and morning, for several days, in the deceased's house, by his children and lineage members. In *ilɛga* the participants first give food to the 'feet' of the dead man, represented by a piece of white 'chalk' placed in a small hole, to encourage them to carry him on his journey. Then they dance round the hole, singing seven songs, escorting him on his way. In the village of Ugboko a similar episode takes place, but with reference to the deceased's status as village elder. The chain of events involved with it is complicated, but it can be summarized thus:

First, the senior son, accompanied by his brothers, must carry kola nuts and coconuts to the *ɔgwediɔn* where the *Ediɔn* are enshrined. There, through the *ɔdiɔnwere*, he informs the *Ediɔn* that he is now ready to begin his father's funeral. The *Ediɔn* are asked to allow the deceased to 'find a road by which to pass to *ɛrinbhin*'. But the accomplishment of this journey depends not only upon the *Ediɔn*, but on the cooperation of all those members of the living community, kin and affines, men and women, elders, adults, and youths, with whom the deceased has associated and who have rights and obligations in respect of him. What happens is this (*see Figure 8*): All household heads present 3 yams each to each of the dead man's sons-in-law living in the village (those living elsewhere may get them from their own fellow-villagers if the latter follow this custom). Each son-in-law then ceremonially presents the bulk of the yams he receives (some say 200) to the dead man's heir, dancing along with them to his compound. At this stage the yams are a token of the esteem of the sons-in-law, of gratitude to the father for conferring his daughters upon them, of recognition that the child-bearing capacities of these women are still the concern of their own patrilineal ancestors. The heir sets some of the yams aside to feast his kin at various points in the rites, but a large number of them are handed over to the *ikaighele*, who give them to their *iroghae*, who, in turn, redistribute them to all households in the village, placing them on the thresholds. The women of these households cook them and the *iroghae* go round pounding them into 'fufu'. Then in the evening, they carry the 'fufu' to the front of the deceased elder's house, where the assembled elders junior to the deceased feast on them, with soup and meat provided by the heir. This feasting, which some interpret as symbolizing a meal prepared by the dead man for his fellow *Ediɔn*, may go on for from two to seven days. During the same period the *ighele* of the village also assemble, each night, outside the same house, where they remain, eating, singing, and sleeping till morning. Here, on a fire made by the *iroghae* from wood they have collected from the bush, the *ighele* roast yams and cook a simple soup of palm oil, pepper, and salt. The ingredients of this meal, roast yams and meatless soup, are appropriately enough, the kind of offering that is made to those nameless, amoral spirits — such as the *ighele-εrinbhin* themselves — who, because they have failed to achieve full social destiny, are placed outside the confines of human society. Night and morning the *ighele* dance *il ε ga*, 'Dance and meet the *Ediɔn*', as they escort the deceased on his journey. By keeping watch over him, and encouraging him, they fulfil their pious obligations to one of their seniors, in the same way that children do so for their father. Yet, in the character of the meal they prepare and eat, there is a reminder of the less harmonious relations that underlie the proper attitudes of elders and juniors towards each other.

I have chosen to emphasize the role of the *ighele-εrinbhin* not because they are in themselves a particularly important feature of Benin religion, but because, in their interaction with the living and with dead fathers and elders, they serve to throw into sharper relief the meaning, for the *Edo*, of the *Ediɔn*, of whom they are the negation. For the essential difference between the *Ediɔn*, who demand service and expiation for infractions of village norms and the flouting of the elders' authority, and the *ighele-εrinbhin* who can only be appeased, is that while the former achieved and passed on the authority-status of elder, the latter died while they were still only heirs to it. Here, therefore, not only do we have the legitimate authority of elders projected onto the *Ediɔn* whose actions are incontrovertibly just, but the resentment of their 'heirs', and the elders' fear of that resentment, are projected onto a separate category of dead, whose actions are neither just nor legitimate.

The *Ediɔn* are of the village, the ordered, controlled, social world. They are those who have, in achieving elderhood, triumphed over disorder and evil. The *ighele-εrinbhin* are those who have failed in this respect and, as a result, have found themselves outside the social order. They are of the bush, which is a constant threat to order and control — the source, it is true, of vitality and growth (food, 'medicines') but, at the same time, something that cannot be allowed to run wild, something that must be tamed, if possible; and, if it cannot be tamed, kept at bay. The shrine of the *Ediɔn* is the centre of community life and it is often at the geographical centre of the village. The *ighele-εrinbhin* have no shrine, nor can they be worshipped, but only appeased. The vigour and vitality that the word *ighele* connotes must be made to operate within the bounds of order. Once it gets outside them, into the bush, as a result of men dying before they have socially fulfilled themselves, then it becomes an unmitigated menace. So the *ighele- εrinbhin* must be fought back, or bought off, by individual and collective action because they represent failure, measured in terms of the society's evaluation of old age and fatherhood.

Outside the context of mortuary ritual, where it is simply assumed that the *ighele- εrinbhin* will take every opportunity to hinder the dead elder's progress, interaction with these spirits occurs only in limited contexts. It is when an elder persistently fails to conduct himself with appropriate wisdom and self-control, or when a living *ighele* behaves recurrently in a manner which the elders see as a threat to them (i.e. when he steps outside the bounds of legitimate *ighele*-hood) that divination is likely to reveal the actions of the *ighele- εrinbhin*. The remedy is to appease them by offerings and pleadings. But the offerings given to them are of the same nature, and made in the same spirit, as those given to witches and unknown living enemies. While offerings to FATHERS, ELDERS, and CHIEFS are partaken of by their worshippers, those given to the *ighele- εrinbhin* are simply cast away, secretly, usually at night, outside the village, very often at the junction of two bush paths that symbolizes the junction of this world and *εrinbhin (ad'agbɔn ad'εrinbhin)*. The *Ediɔn*, by contrast, are worshipped in the daytime, publicly, in their shrine or in the middle of the village street. They make their demands on the living when people fail to fulfil their moral obligations towards them, when they break the village taboos laid down by the *Ediɔn* themselves, when they flout the community rules that the elders hold in trust. But they are also worshipped regularly and willingly, and they are called upon to witness and sanctify various kinds of *rites de passage*.

It is, to my mind, clear that the ritual episodes I have described constitute, for the *Edo* themselves, explanatory models for their own society. These are simple models, at a low level of abstraction, constructed by drawing out from the totality of behaviour in certain fields the essential features of particular sets of social relations. These models can be, and are, extended to embrace other sets of social relations in other fields of authority – associations (with their ELDERS), state institutions (with their CHIEFS) – and to link them together in a meaningful synthesis. All this is done in terms of beliefs and actions concerned with the various categories of dead. Nor are they static models for it would be possible to produce evidence to show that they are deliberately altered, by what amounts to a legislative process, to meet circumstances which are recognized to have changed. To take a simple example, in discussing the *izaxwɛ* rites at Ekho village I have said that the deceased's heir produced two goats of which the village elders would choose the largest, leaving the inferior one for the lineage. During my stay there, however, the procedure was changed. It was recognized that under modern conditions the village community was no longer in a position to maintain its dominance over the interests of its component kin groups. The kin group was no longer willing to take second best and *izaxwɛ* often became the occasion for quarrelling. So it was decided that henceforth the two goats should be presented quite separately and that each group should be free to accept or reject what it was offered on its own merits.

In my last paragraphs, in discussing the contrasts between the character and behaviour of the *Ediɔn* and the *ighele-ɛrinbhin* I have hinted at the implicit existence, in *Edo* thought, of another kind of model, of a more abstract, ideal order. Its terms are no longer simple status-categories and social relationships but sets of opposed ideas such as 'day' and 'night', 'bush' and 'village', 'growth' and 'control', under which a wider range of human experience can be ordered. The opposition between day and night refers not only to the *Ediɔn/ighele-ɛrinbhin* opposition but also to the dichotomy between the elders and the 'elders of the night' – i.e. the witches. Bush/village and growth/order are conceptual dichotomies which enable the *Edo* to deal with some of the ideas we have already set out and some of the features of divine kingship and its ritual in terms of the same explanatory schema. But models and explanations of this type are not a substitute for the kind of conceptualization which, following Fortes and others, I have stressed in this paper. They are, rather, complementary to it. It is as necessary for the observer as it is for the actors to operate at both levels of abstraction.

I Ezomo's bronze *ikegobo* or Altar of the Hand
Height *c*. 16 inches. *Photograph: W. B. Fagg, 1958*

II The late Ezomo Omoruyi with his son, late Ezomo Asemwota (since deceased) and his collection of bronzes; in front, Ezomo Ehenua's iron war gong with a modern replica; at right on bench, a bronze plaque supposed to date from Ehenua's time.

IIIa Further views of Ezomo's *ikegobo*
Photographs: W. B. Fagg, 1958

IIIb Terracotta *ikegobo* of a smith, in the British Museum
Wellcome Collection. Height 9 inches
Photograph: W. B. Fagg, 1958

IVa Wooden *ikegobo* of type A
belonging to a carver
Height *c.* 4 inches
    Photograph: R. E. Bradbury

IVb Two wooden *ikegobo* of type B from the house of the Onogie of Obazagbon
    Photograph: R. E. Bradbury

Ezomo's Ikegobo and the Benin
Cult of the Hand

The bronze 'shrine of the Hand' (*ikegobo* or *ikega-obo, i.e. 'ikega* of the
hand') illustrated here[1] (Plates I & II), one of the most ambitious, if
not technically the most accomplished, castings known from Benin, is
still in the possession of the Ezomo of Uzebu. The Ezomo, one of the
seven hereditary nobles, *Uzama Nihinron*, who constitute the highest
order of chieftaincy in the Benin Kingdom, was, in the past, one of the
two supreme military commanders.

In this paper I shall not be concerned with the technical or aesthetic
qualities of the casting. I propose, rather, first to show its meaning for
its owner as a supposed 'historical record' and secondly to consider it
and other *ikegobo* as ritual objects in the context of the Benin Cult of
the Hand.

Benin Bronzes as Historical Records ·

While it is still not clear what proportion of the Benin plaques and
other bronzes were intended to record particular, rather than types of,
persons and events, a considerable number are either certainly or very
probably narrative in intention. By 'narrative' I mean simply that they
were intended to convey some information about specific events or
particular persons. Provided that they can be properly dated and
interpreted such bronzes are potential sources of certain kinds of
historical information, but dating and interpretation present many
difficulties.

1 The material for this paper has been collected at various times during periods
of fieldwork financed respectively by the Royal Anthropological Institute (Emslie
Horniman Anthropological Scholarship Fund), the International African Institute,
and the Benin Historical Research Scheme, University College, Ibadan (directd by
Dr. K. O. Dike). To each of these bodies and to the C.S.S.R.C., the Nigerian
Federal Government and the Carnegie Corporation, which jointly provided funds
for the Benin Scheme, my thanks are due. I have derived much benefit from

With few exceptions bronzes of this type belonged to the Oba of Benin. Most of them were removed from his palace during the Benin Expedition of 1897 and nearly all are now in museums or private collections in Nigeria, Europe and America. While it is possible to confront informants with a few objects, and show photographs of others, the interpretations evoked are, on the whole, disappointing. Even with the best informants (and the only person that I have met who had an intimate acquaintance with the palace bronzes before 1897 died in 1959) it is not always possible to distinguish between a remembered and a spontaneous interpretation. Faced with a bronze plaque a good informant, out of his own experience of Benin culture and traditions, can easily convince himself, if not always the enquirer, that he knows exactly what or whom it represents. This problem is, of course, being tackled 60 years too late, but it would be idle to suppose that anyone in Benin, even in 1897, would have been able, in the case of objects two or three centuries old, always to give an accurate account of the artist's original intentions. Such accounts must always have been subject to the same modifying influences as other kinds of oral tradition. Nevertheless it remains true that the bronzes contain much potentially valuable information about Benin society, culture and history over a very long period and no opportunity should be lost to find out what the Benin people themselves say about them.

In this respect Ezomo's *ikegobo* seems a good subject for enquiry. There is no doubt of continuous ownership in the same hereditary line since the object was made, though its antiquity is questionable on stylistic grounds. What the late Ezomo Omoruyi (who died, a very old man, in September, 1960) had to say about it is almost certainly not very different from what he was told by his father, Osarogiagbon, who died in old age in 1914. Through him, then, we can perhaps gain some idea of how such objects were regarded when they were still a living element in Benin culture. In order to do this it will be necessary to give a little of the social background.

discussions with Mr. William Fagg who has, in addition, kindly provided photographs of Ezomo's *ikegobo* to illustrate this article.

This article is intended as a tribute to Chief Omoruyi, the late Ezomo, whose house guest I was in 1953-54. A man of great dignity and kindness, and of an infinite gentleness which seemed to belie his warlike ancestry, he was yet filled with pride in the deeds of his forefathers. He was a great patron of the Benin bronze-casters and when the bronze figures of his ancestors were stolen in 1958 he commissioned a series of plaques depicting the seven Ezomo of his line who preceded him. These he added to a plaque showing himself, and another earlier one in memory of his mother.

The Ezomo

Only four certain examples of bronze *ikegobo* are known to me.[2] Apart from bells, hip masks, bird-headed staffs, ornaments and charms, cast bronzes were, in the past, the almost exclusive preserve of the Oba. That the Ezomo should have a casting of such size and complexity is in itself remarkable and this is recognized in the story that it was made secretly (see below). However, the Ezomo in certain respects, stands apart from all other Benin chiefs and, while not the highest in formal rank, he must in many ways be regarded as next to the Oba in prestige and status.

Third in formal order of precedence among the seven *Uzama* (Bradbury, 1957, pp. 35f., 43f.), the Ezomo had for long been the wealthiest and most influential of them when Benin City was captured in 1897. He lived in semi-independent state in his own town of Uzebu, just outside the inner wall of Benin City, where he kept a court which was a smaller and simpler version of that of the Oba. There he ruled his own subjects with little interference from above, creating titles and re-awarding them without reference to the Oba. Apart from the Oba, Iyoba (Oba's mother) and Edaiken (Oba's heir) the Ezomo alone is permitted to wear a coronet of red stone or coral beads. His wives, like the Oba's, are called *iloi* and they are subject to similar restrictions and rules of conduct. These and other attributes of kingship set him apart from other chiefs. On the most important ceremonial occasions the Ezomo and Edaiken used to support the Oba's arms, one on each side; this group is said to be illustrated on many bronzes.

The Ezomo owed his pre-eminence to the fact that he was a supreme war chief, conducting most of the more important military campaigns on the Oba's behalf. As a result of these campaigns, and of the fact that the title was hereditary .by primogeniture without any division of property, successive Ezomo were able to accumulate much wealth, especially in the form of slaves, who were put to work in farm camps. Their wealth and influence were further extended by the fact that they administered a large number of villages and vassal chiefdoms from which they derived tribute and services in addition to those that they organized and collected for the Oba.

2 See Read and Dalton, 1899, Plate IX, Nos. 1 and 2. These two examples undoubtedly belonged to the Iyoba (Oba's mother) and Oba respectively. On stylistic grounds they can be fairly confidently attributed to the nineteenth century; Read and Dalton remark that they appear to be 'of comparatively modern manufacture.' See also von Luschan, Plate XCII, and figs. 468, 469 (pp.322f.), f or a very unusual example.

In spite of his position and advantages the Ezomo is portrayed in tradition as being, for the most part, loyal to the Oba. A 'king' in his own right at Uzebu and when conducting his campaigns — for once outside Benin City his powers over his men were absolute — he is said nearly always to have remained faithful. In this respect he is sharply constrasted with the other great war chief, the Iyase. The Iyase was the non-hereditary head of the 'town chiefs' (*Eghaevbo n'Ore*) and in the nature of the political structure of Benin he seems almost inevitably to have come into conflict with the Oba and 'palace chiefs' *(Eghaevbo n'Ogbe)*.

While the *Eghaevbo n'Ogbe* were essentially courtiers, owing their status to their position in the palace organization, the leading *Eghaevbo n'Ore* tended to be men of wealth and influence who had made their way in life independently. The *Uzama*, as a group, stood somewhat aside from the day-to-day affairs of the state. Like the kingship, their titles pass from father to senior son, in contrast to the *Eghaevbo* titles which are open to any man with the right qualifications, whatever his descent. There is some difference of opinion as to whether succession by primogeniture was always followed for the other *Uzama* titles, but the Ezomo title is generally agreed to have been hereditary for only eight generations including Ezomo Omoruyi. The present line, at any rate, goes back only thus far and the way in which it came into being is important for the interpretation of the *ikegobo*, whose central figure is believed to represent Ehenua, the founder of the line.

Ezomo Ehenua and Oba Akensua 1

The following traditions concerning Ezomo Ehenua have been collected mainly from Chief Omoruyi, the late Ezomo, though they are widely known with but slight variation:

Ehenua is said to have been the illegitimate first son of Oba Ewuakpe and not, therefore eligible to succeed him.[3] Ewuakpe later had another son, who was to become Oba Akenzua. While the latter was still young his father told him about his brother, whose relationship to the Oba was kept secret, and asked him to treat him kindly if ever they should meet. Ehenua was brought up by Ode, the Iyase of the day.

---

3 Any children born to the future Oba before he had passed through a particular *rite de passage* were regarded as 'children the leopard has thrown away' and disposed of or disowned.

While Ehenua was still a boy Iyase n'Ode was warned by a diviner that he would die at Ehenua's hands. He therefore plotted to kill him, but Ehenua heard of this and fled to Ishan where he grew up into a strong and powerful man.

Meanwhile Akenzua became Oba after defeating his brother Ovbiozuere who, with the support of Iyase n'Ode, his maternal relative, had usurped the throne. The Iyase retired to a village 20 miles north of Benin and Ovbiozuere fled, both continuing to have hostile relations with the Oba.

One day Ehenua, who was now living in the Isi District, in the north-east corner of the Benin kingdom, came to Benin as the leader of a group bearing tribute to the Oba. Acting on a diviner's advice Akenzua kept him behind. Akenzua was at that time badly served by his people and Ehenua was ashamed to see him sending to the market to buy food for his wives. He asked the Oba for some strong men and proceeded to make war on the rebellious villages, sparing them only if they promised to send tribute.

In return for these services, and with his father's words in mind, Akenzua made him the Ezomo and eventually he agreed that the title should be hereditary in his line. According to one version Ehenua proceeded to defeat and kill Ovbiozuere who was still giving trouble. What is more generally accepted is that he finally defeated the powerful Iyase n'Ode who had been the main obstacle to the Oba's full control of his kingdom.

Ehenua went on reconquering and expanding the kingdom and it was largely through his efforts that Akenzua became one of the wealthiest and most powerful of Obas.

Ezomo Omoruyi was the eighth holder of the title in direct line of descent from Ehenua, and the names and some of the military successes of the intervening Ezomo are well remembered. The present Oba is the ninth since Akenzua I, who reigned in the early part of the eighteenth century.

Description of the Ikegobo

Ezomo Omoruyi explains the bronze *ikegobo* in terms of the story of Ehenua and Akenzua I. The figures on the vertical surface of the cylinder represent Ehenua himself surrounded by his warriors and attendants. On top sits Akenzua I making offerings to his ancestors for the success of the campaign, or giving thanks for victory. The heads of the sacrificial animals form the frieze round the pedestal.

The shrine is cast in four pieces. The pedestal, the figure of the Oba together with the dais on which he sits, and the leopard which stands in front of him were cast separately from the main cylinder and its surmounting group of figures attendant on the Oba. The leopard, a symbol of kingship, is free-standing and the holes in its feet have never been used to secure it to the top of the cylinder. There is no indication as to whether it formed part of the artist's original conception, but if so it is difficult to see why it was not cast in one piece with the cylinder itself.

The pedestal, cylinder and Oba-on-dais are made to fit together. Both cylinder and pedestal are hollow and open at the bottom. In the upper surface of the pedestal is a rectangular hole made after the casting was completed and situated below a cast hole in the top of the cylinder which is covered by the Oba's dais. Through these holes pieces of kola nut, palm wine and other offerings were dropped when the shrine was in use. The iron 'peg' projecting from the upper surface of the cylinder, which is used to support a carved tusk, appears to have been burnt in after the casting was complete.

I propose to divide the figures and objects shown into three main groups:

1. The figures on the vertical surface of the cylinder. These represent Ehenua and his followers and are numbered according to the diagram (fig.9).

(1) The large central figure is said to represent Ezomo Eheuna dressed for war. In his left hand he holds ropes attached to five severed human heads. Ezomo's explanation is that on only five occasions did the battle become so severe that Ehenua himself had to take part in the fighting. Each time he cut off a head. Four times he did it with a single stroke but the fifth time the first stroke slashed his enemy's face; this slash is shown on the middle head. Nearly all Ehenua's followers carry a single head and it is interesting to note that these heads vary considerably in such matters as tribal markings and hair styles, indicating that they represent people from different areas.

On his head Ehenua wears a helmet of cloth or leather to which are attached three tiny calabashes (*ukokogho*), of the kind which are filled with 'medicines' and worn by priests, magicians, warriors and others seeking magical protection. Such medicines were prepared for the Ezomo by a special group of 'doctors,' *Ewaise*, who occupied a separate ward in Uzebu, though the services of 'doctors' from outside would also be called upon. The *Ewaise* were responsible for the shrine of *Osun-okuo* (*Osun*, god of medicine, *okuo*, war) in Ezomo's compound. Some of the other figures also wear *ukokogho* on their caps or round their necks.

The symbol on the front of Ehenua's cap is called *onwe vb'uki*, 'the sun and the moon.' Ezomo explains that it was a charm with a protective purpose. Just as the sun and moon always reach their destinations in the evening and return the next day, so will the warrior return safely from his campaign. Another informant puts it thus: 'What you throw at the moon cannot strike the moon. What you throw at the sun cannot strike the sun. Death cannot kill the sun in the sky,' the emphasis here being on the warrior's immunity from his enemies' weapons. The armlets (*egba*) round Ehenua's arms have the same purpose. They are stewed in a medicine which gives them the power of diverting gunfire or protecting the warrior from wounds if struck by a sharp weapon. They are of the type known as *egba n'iri n'erinwi ri*–'armlet of the rope that the spirits tie' – a reference to the endless knot motif, a knot which cannot be untied by man.

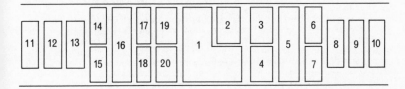

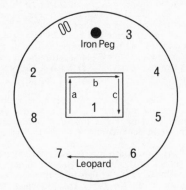

Fig. 9 Key to figures on vertical (above) and horizontal surfaces of Ezomo's Ikegobo

Not to scale. To the left of the peg are the feet of a missing figure.

To ropes tied round his neck are attached what appear to be small stone celts. These too are a symbol of power and strength. Celts are to be found as altar objects in many cults. They are believed to be thunderstones and they are particularly associated with *Ogiuwu* (King of Death) the deity who controls the thunder, though they are also important in connexion with the gods of iron (*Ogun*) and medicine (*Osun*). All these deities are, of course, concerned with war.

The weapon in Ehenua's right hand is a two-edged sword or *opia* (also the name for the all-purpose matchet) whose sheath, *aku-opia*, is tucked under his left arm. The circlets of beads round his neck (*ika* or *ikele*) and the beaded anklets (*iviawe* or *eguen*) denote his chiefly rank.

Flanking Ehenua's head are a pair of skulls, probably those of sacrificial rams or he-goats.

(2) & (19) The two figures to the right and left of Ehenua's head are ritual attendants, *ewaise*, holding charms. Chief Ezomo calls these charms *exwae*, i.e. consolidated lumps of pounded medicine, oval in form, which are kept in the *Osun* shrine and used to give power to curses or blessings. In this case they would

be licked and held out in the direction of the enemy, a curse would be pronounced and then the holder would blow along them. From their shape, however, the objects held are almost certainly another kind of charm, *ukokogho n' ogiode*, in the form of a curved calabash, filled with medicines and with the narrow neck open. *Ogiode* means 'guide'(*gie*, 'to point out,' *ode*, 'the road, way'). When the calabash is held with its open neck pointing towards the enemy it will guide the curse to its destination. Some informants say that it would guide the warriors themselves to the enemy.

(3) The object held by this figure looks like a clutch of sheathed spears. I am assured (but not completely convinced) that it represents a large pestle, of the type used for pounding yam, with a specially carved handle. It is called *ovbiodo ne-wi-y'okuo* (the pestle that is not lost in war) or *ovbiodo gha y'igbina to-y'owa* (the pestle that, when it has been used in a fight, goes home). That such pestles were taken on campaigns is widely known. The symbolism is as follows: when a quarrel breaks out between neighbours or members of the same household it is not unusual for one of the parties to pick up one of these heavy pestles and use it as a weapon. But when the fight is over it returns to its mortar and its task of pounding yam (this is, in fact not always so; pestles that have been used in fights are sometimes to be seen on shrines to *Ogun* or *Osun*). In the old days pieces of a pestle which had been used to fight were broken off, ground up and incorporated in a medicine which was rubbed on a ceremonial pestle of the type shown here. This was kept in the *Osun-ookuo* shrine and it would accompany the war chief on his campaigns. Warriors would touch it in the belief that as the domestic pestle returns to its mortar after a fight, so they would return home from the war.

(4) This short figure carries a shield (*asa*). Such shields were constructed of a strong light wood and covered with leather. It appears to have a protective calabash attached to it.

(5) & (16) Drummers. Their drums are probably the war drums, *izaduma*.

(6) & (14) Warriors carrying curved single-edged swords (*umozo*).

(7) & (15) Warriors carrying bows (*uhanbo*) and arrows (ifemwe). The crossbow, which was known in Benin from the sixteenth century, does not appear on this object.

(8) to (13) Six figures of warriors (*iyokuo* or *ibbiyokuo*) are arranged symmetrically round the back of the cylinder. They are almost identical and each, like Ehenua, is armed with an *opia*, though in every case but one it has been broken off. In distinction from the other figures, which represent Ehenua's personal and ceremonial staff, the warriors wear helmets with magical calabashes, and protective armlets. The objects hanging round their necks may be (as Ezomo says), bells used for identification in the fighting, or *ukokogho*, or leather amulets containing protective medicine.

(17) This figure is an *omada* or sword-bearer. The *ada* which he carries is a symbol of authority. In Benin City the Oba alone can have an *ada* carried in front of him in public. It is a mark of Ezomo's special status that he can do so at Uzebu and when he is away from Benin on his military campaigns. Generally speaking the Oba's gift of an *ada* to a subject chief indicates the delegation to the latter of powers of life and death over his own subjects

(18) This figure carries a long spear (*asoro*). Round his neck he wears a pouch of protective medicine.

(20) An attendant beating an iron gong (*egogo*).

II *Oba and attendants*.

(1)   The central figure on top of the shrine is Oba Akenzua I seated on a dais *(ogiukpo)*. His lack of ceremonial costume indicates that the sacrifices which he is making are contingent ones rather than part of an annual festival *(ugie)*. Ezomo's interpretation is that he is sacrificing to his ancestors for Ehenua's success in war. In his right hand he holds a kola nut — an indispensable part of any ritual offering — and in his left a ritual staff (*uxurhe*), which in most cults is the most direct symbol of the power of the god or spirit. It is banged on the ground to emphasize prayers, blessings and curses. Also in his left hand is the end of a rope to which are secured a cow *(a)*, he-goat *(b)* and ram *(c)* tied up ready for sacrifice and standing round three sides of the dais On the dais to the Oba's right is an

okpan — a big round wooden bowl with lid, containing kola nuts and other offerings — and to his left a calabash of palm wine for pouring libations. Between his feet is a cock's head with a disproportionately large piece of kola nut on each side of it.

(2) A trumpeter, blowing an elephant-tusk horn *(akohen)*.

(3) An attendant carrying an *ekpoki* or box-stool, made of wood, leather and bark and consisting of two cylinders, each on a circular base, one of which fits over the other. They are used to contain valuables, for carrying offerings and ceremonial gifts, and as 'thrones' over a wide area formerly subject to Benin influence.

(4) One of the *Ewaise* (Oba's doctors) carrying an iron staff, *osun-ematon*, which embodies the power of the god of medicine. These staffs have branch-like proliferations at the upper end, often worked in the form of bells, birds, chameleons and other animals. This one has a non-human skull attached to it and its purpose is to protect the Oba against evil intentions.

(5) to (8) Four bearded figures apparently representing European soldiers in tunics, trousers and helmets, and carrying guns. No special reason is given for their presence in this context, but they are clearly acting as the Oba's bodyguard.

III *The pedestal*. The frieze on the pedestal has heads of cows, rams, he-goats and cocks, interspersed with segments of kola nut, bottles or calabashes, and a bird. The bird apart, these are the usual sacrificial offerings to ancestors.

Ezomo's Ikegobo as a Historical Document

In considering Ezomo's *ikegobo* as a historical record we must take care to distinguish its significance for the owner from the value that it may have for the historian. Ezomo Omoruyi had no doubt that the two main figures represented Ehenua and Akenzua I and that some, at least, of the others were particular men whose names have now been forgotten; but, although it apparently portrays a triumphal return from a campaign, the Ezomo's interpretation of the five severed heads carried by Ehenua and the fact that the heads denote varying tribal origins suggest a generalized account rather than a particular incident. There is no indication that it refers directly to the struggle between the Oba and Iyase n'Ode. It represents a memorial to a great warrior who has conquered far and wide rather than the victorious outcome of a specific conflict. For Ezomo Omoruyi the bronze *ikegobo* was a tangible record of, and a focus for his pride in, the martial deeds and qualities of the founder of his line and I have little doubt that it played some part in keeping the story of Ehenua fresh in his mind.

For the historian and the ethnographer the *ikegobo* is a valuable concrete expression of certain features of Benin culture and society in the past. It dramatizes the ideal relationship between the Oba and his military commander. It indicates the elaboration of ritual and magical devices for procuring success in war and the remarkable degree of dependence upon 'medicines'. (Ezomo Omoruyi claimed that his

4 There is a firm tradition that the *akohen* was introduced by Oba Eresoyen, the son of Akenzua I. It is probable, however, that other kinds of tusk-horns were in use before that time.

ancestors were never defeated in war because they never fought until they were sure that their 'medicines' were strong enough to give them victory.) It emphasizes a head-getting element in Benin warfare which is hardly mentioned in oral tradition — except to say that the heads of conquered rulers were brought to the Oba[5] — and this is important for a proper understanding of the Hand cult in Benin, and for comparisons between it and the Ibo *ikenga* cult.

If the *ikegobo* were contemporary with Ehenua and Akenzua I it would provide information about the types of weapons, dress, ornament, ritual apparatus, etc., in use at the time, and the presence of European 'soldiers' would be directly significant. Unfortunately this is unlikely to be so. Its late owner firmly believed that Ehenua himself had it made and used it in worshipping his Hand, and the account of its casting is of some interest. The rule that large bronzes were not to be cast except on the Oba's orders was apparently nearly always rigidly adhered to. It was the practice, however, for warrior chiefs to take bronze-casters with them on their campaigns to repair guns, cannon and other equipment, and Ehenua is said to have had one of these cast his *ikega* secretly. On stylistic grounds it is virtually certain that at least the main casting and its surmounting figures, and the figures of the Oba and leopard, are of much more recent date than the early eighteenth century. Mr. William Fagg, who has examined the castings, suggests that the pedestal may be older than the rest and if so this may mean that the rest was a replacement for an earlier casting which had been destroyed. The evidence of informants — and persistent enquiries have been made both in Ezomo's family and among the bronze-casters — makes it very unlikely that the present casting was made during this century or indeed, from Ezomo's age, less than seventy years ago. If the main casting is a replacement then the question arises of how true a copy was attempted, and to what extent errors and anachronisms crept in. In dress, at least, all but the European figures have a distinctly nineteenth-century flavour. It is, of course, possible that the *ikegobo* was made by a nineteenth-century Ezomo for his own use and afterwards attributed to the founder of the line.

The European figures remain an interesting problem for there is a distinct possibility that Europeans took a hand in the internal conflicts of the Benin Kingdom in the later seventeenth and early eighteenth centuries. Nyendael (see Ling Roth, 1903, p. 14), who was in Benin in

5 It is possible that all the heads were meant to be those of rulers whom Ehenua conquered, but this does not seem very likely.

1699 and 1701, describes a situation remarkably similar to the conflict between Akenzua I and Iyase n'Ode of Benin tradition. The Oba of Nyendael's account had been at conflict with one of his 'street kings' for ten years and the latter was, at the time of Nyendael's visit, living two to three days' journey from Benin, an uneasy peace having been patched up 'by the mediation of the Portuguese'. Egharevba's approximate date for the death of Akenzua I, 1735, is probably very close, for Dutch sources[6] have recently revealed that an Oba died in 1734 or 1735. His accession, which Egharevba places in 1710, would, however, have to be put back to about 1690 in order to fit in with Nyendael's account and while this is not impossible there is no positive evidence one way or the other.[7] A relationship, however tenuous, between the Ezomo's *ikegobo* and an actual passage in Benin history recorded by a contemporary chronicler thus remains a tantalizing possibility.

The Cult of the Hand

The cult object known as *ikega* or *ikenga* is found, in various forms, over a wide area of the central part of southern Nigeria on both sides of the Niger. It is known by the same name, with slight variations, among at least the Benin, Ishan and Urhobo-Isoko sections of the Edo-speaking peoples, over a large part of Ibo country, among the Igala and among the Western Ijaw.[8] Everywhere it is associated with the hand or arm (the right arm is frequently specified), and with the prowess, strength and enterprise of the individual worshipper. A detailed comparative study is called for but is beyond the scope of this paper, which will be confined to *ikegobo* deriving from Benin City and the villages in its immediate neighbourhood. The wooden *ikegobo*, which I shall describe below, are all carved by, or in the style of, the *Igbesamwa*, a guild of

6 Personal communication from Dr. A.F.C. Ryder. It is virtually certain that Akenzua I's grandson, Akengbuda, was reigning when Landolphe visited Benin in the 1770s and 1780s. Landolphe (Vol. I, pp. 98-102) describes the Ezomo (*le capitaine-général des guerres*) in 1778 as living in considerable state: 'ce capitaine était le plus riche de toute la contree .... son pouvoir balançait celui du roi ... il possédait plus de deux mille esclaves ....marchànt aux combats il avait toujours cinquante à soixante mille hommes sous son commandement .... [il] n'avait guère plus de trente ans ....sa démarche aussi grave qu'imposante, son ton et ses manières pleines de noblesse, annonçaient la grandeur des fonctions dont il était revêtu.' This was almost certainly Ekenza, the grandson of Ehenua.

7 For a fuller discussion of this problem see Bradbury, 1959, pp. 273f.

8 I have to thank Mr. and Mrs. Philip Leis for calling my attention to the presence of *ikenga*, otherwise called *amabra*, among the Kabowei Ijo.

carvers who occupy a separate ward in Benin City, and whose primary function was to carve for the Oba and the rôyal court.

In Benin the word *ikega*, more frequently heard in the form *ikegobo*, has two connotations. First, it refers to that aspect of the worshipper's individuality which is associated with the hand or, rather, with the whole arm, for the word *obo* includes the hand and the arm. In this sense the words *ikega* and *obo* are synonymous. The right arm is not usually specified and some informants explain *ikega* as being 'the power of both hands together.' Melzian gives *ikega* as meaning 'wrist' but it is not in general use in this sense. It is true, however, that, when speaking of *ikega* informants invariably grip the right wrist with the fingers of the left hand to indicate firmness and power.[9] Secondly, *ikegobo* denotes the cult object itself.

The Hand is one of three Benin cults which have, as their object, some aspect of the worshipper's own individuality. To understand its place in the Edo view of human personality and of the individual's position in society, it is necessary to refer briefly to the two other cults, those of the Head and the *Ehi*.[10]

Every living person has an *Ehi* which is, in one sense, his or her Destiny, and, in another, a counterpart and guide in the spirit world. *Omwa* (the living person) and *Ehi* are the two halves of a single being, indissolubly linked through successive incarnations. Before birth each individual is believed to predestine himself *(hi)* by making a statement before *Osanobua*, the Creator, setting out a life programme and asking for all that will be needed to carry it out successfully. *Ehi* stands by to prompt and, after the individual is born on earth, remains in the spirit world to act as a guide and intermediary with *Osanobua*. Misfortune, and especially continued misfortune, can therefore, be explained in

9 Melzian gives, as a secondary meaning for *ikega*, 'anklet of cowries which is worshipped as *Obo* . . . women keep it on their (trays) for carrying merchandise in order to prevent things being stolen and for quick sale.' These circlets of cowries may be called *ikega* but only, I believe, when they represent an *ikegobo* on which they are normally kept. Other women use similar charms named after other deities. A case can be made out for deriving the word *ikega* from two roots, *ik-* and *ga* both implying circularity. *Ga* means 'to surround' and is found in *lega*, 'to move round.' *Ik-* appears in such words as *ika* or *ikele*, a circular bead necklace, *ikagha*, bridle, and *ikoro*, a broad brass or ivory armlet. There is, therefore, a faint possibility that *ikega* originally meant 'wristlet' (*ikegobo* would mean 'something that goes round the arm') and, by association, the wrist itself. Every *ikegobo* in use should have a cowry circlet round it and when the owner dies this may be buried with him instead of the whole object. I would not, however, press this etymology or an Edo origin for the word. One of Jeffreys's informants (1954, p.30) gives what appears to be a more satisfactory etymology from Ibo.

10 A long essay is in preparation dealing with these three cults in detail.

terms of a failure to '*hi* well' or to keep to the chosen life programme. The sufferer is said to have a 'bad *Ehi*' and prayers and offerings must be addressed to the *Ehi* asking it to intervene. At one level the *Ehi* represents the innate potentialities for social achievement with which each individual is believed to be endowed. Predestiny is seen as a limiting factor on the individual's capacity to achieve success through his own actions. Though one who has a stroke of good luck should, and often does, thank his *Ehi*, it is more often invoked in contexts of failure and misfortune. In operation the cult of the *Ehi* can be shown to have a particular association with the ability to beget, or bear, and keep, healthy children; that is, with the parent-child relationship. Here it is only necessary to say, in support of this statement, that in most lineages parents and children of the worshipper are not allowed to be present when he or she is addressing rites towards his or her *Ehi*. "

The Head (*Uhumwu*) symbolizes life and behaviour in this world, the capacity to organize one's actions in such a way as to survive and prosper. It is one's Head that 'leads one through life.' It is the seat of thinking (*iroro*), judgement (*enwae*) and will or character (*exoe*), of hearing, seeing and speaking; and on the successful co-ordination of these faculties individual fortunes depend. While *Ehi* implies a rejection of personal control over one's fortunes, *Uhunwu* admits a greater degree of responsibility for them. The characteristic rite is that of 'blessing' the Head, first thanking it for survival and prosperity, then asking it for further favours. On a man's Head depends not only his own well-being but that of his wives and children; and, since this dependence is reciprocal, he serves their Heads at the same time as his own. Thus the Head cult has a particular association with family headship. At the state level, the welfare of the people as a whole depends on the Oba's Head which is the object of worship at the main event of the state ritual year; and the Oba, in turn, sends out his own priests to bless the Heads of the chiefs through whom he rules.

While, in the past, the Head and *Ehi* were actively worshipped by the great majority of adults, the cult of the Hand was less universal. Today, a moderately successful man, asked if he has an *ikegobo*, will often reply: 'Why should I serve my Hand? What has it done for me?', indicating that it would be presumptuous of him to do so. General statements often imply that only people of wealth and high rank have *ikegobo* but this is not strictly so. A poor man, whose practical affairs

11 For my interpretation of the *Ehi* I lean heavily on Fortes's (1959) treatment of similar beliefs among the Tallensi.

are going badly, or who, more simply, injures his arm or hand, may be advised by a diviner to 'serve his Hand' (*ru Obo*). He will acquire an *ikegobo* from a carver, dedicate it, and begin to make offerings over it to his Hand. It is, however, unusual for a man to have an *ikega* until he is at least established as a householder with a wife and child; and women rarely have them unless they are of very high rank or are important traders. While a child's *Ehi* may be served 'through his Head' before a shrine is installed — the Head needs no shrine, though important chiefs have Head shrines — children do not serve their Hands.

The Hand, then, is regarded as a more positive symbol of wealth and social achievement than either the *Ehi* or the Head. While it is common to speak of an unfortunate person as having a 'bad *Ehi*' or a 'bad Head', 'bad Hand' is not used in this sense. Indeed, the characteristic attitude of Hand-worship is one of self-congratulation and self-glorification. The diviner may advise a man who is meeting with failure in some enterprise to serve his Hand, but in doing so, as the following diviner's verse clearly shows, he implies the consulter's personal responsibility for his fortunes, and counsels self-reliance:

> *Ogwega* says you should complain to your Hand
> If you do not want the weeds to spoil your farm.

'It is in your hands' translates directly from English to Edo. Again, the cult of the Hand is less concerned with the worshipper's roles in the kinship system than either the *Ehi* or the Head. It refers, rather, to his position *vis-à-vis* society and the world at large. While it is incumbent on a man to serve his Head for the good of his dependent kin, whether he makes a sacrifice to his Hand is entirely a matter of personal choice. The Edo themselves say: '*Igwe* is performed for our children, *Ihiexu* for our slaves.' At *Igwe* the annual rite of blessing the Head, the performer's chief co-participants are his wives and children; at *Ihiexu*, the annual rite for the Hand, it was slaves who fulfilled this role. Both domestic and farm slaves came, bringing gifts for their master, who feasted them in return. A sacrifice was made and the master rested his hand on the *ikegobo* while it was smeared with the blood. When the sacrificial animal had been cooked it was served with pounded yam, a large loaf of which was placed on the *ikegobo* (or on the master's hand which he rested on the *ikegobo*). It was the head slave who removed the yam and shared it with his fellows. *Ihiexu* was performed only by craftsmen and people of high rank and wealth, and it is generally described as having been an opportunity to show off wealth in slaves and property. Slaves, it is explained, represent *par excellence* 'the things man has got with his own hands,' things that belong to him alone, as an individual, rather than as, say, a father or a husband. Unlike the worship of the Oba's Head, which was the central public rite of divine kingship, the Oba's *Ihiexu* was not a public ceremony. The explanation given is that Oba Ewuare who, according to tradition, rose, by his own efforts, from inauspicious beginnings to be one of the greatest Obas, said that his Hand had done so much for him, that to do it justice in a public ceremony he would have to dissipate all he had gained.

In general, then, the Hand is associated with the success, judged in terms of wealth and prestige, of the individual in the context of human society and the world in general. It symbolizes his vigour, enterprise and industry in farming, trading or any other activity to which he turns his hand. It implies personal responsibility and self-reliance in a highly competitive and relatively individualistic society. All this is summed up rather well in the following Edo saying: 'If one's father does something for one, he makes one ashamed (*i.e.* by telling everyone how much one is beholden to him); if one's mother does something for one, she makes one ashamed; but if one's hand does something for one, it does not shame one'. [12]

The Hand, as one might expect, has a more specific meaning for those who are especially dependent upon manual skill or physical strength, that is for craftsmen, warriors and hunters. Smiths and carvers have *ikegobo* on which are depicted hammers, tongs, adzes and other tools of their trade. *Ihiexu* was particularly important for blacksmiths, who stopped work for seven days each year when they performed it, and both blacksmiths and warriors worshipped the Hand in conjunction with *Ogun*, the god of iron. In many houses the shrines of *Oba* and *Ogun* are adjacent to each other. According to some informants *Ihiexu* used to be performed in conjunction with *Isiokuo*, the great state war ceremony, and Ezomo Omoruyi confirmed that his father used to worship his Hand and *Ogun* just before *Isiokuo*, and prior to setting out on a campaign.

There are, indeed, some grounds for supposing that Hand-worship at Benin may once have had a more specific connexion with warfare. Many of the larger *ikegobo*, in both wood and bronze, whether or not they belonged to warriors, represent men dressed and armed for war. Here, it is worth recalling that, among the Ibo, *ikenga* have strong

12 Translated from Eguavon, p.37, No. 673

warrior connotations. Talbot (1926, Vol. II, pp. 142f.) writes; 'The Ika pray to the Ikengga for success in trade, war, hunting and farming. The heads of all leopards and of every enemy killed in war are offered up before the symbol,' and in Okigwi district the first sacrifice by a man who has killed an enemy in war is to the *ikenga*. Meek (1937, p.39) is more specific: 'But Ikenga is not a cult of much importance at the present time as it was formerly associated with the practice of head-hunting.... When a young man first obtained the head of an enemy in war he asked a lucky old head-getter to establish for him an Ikenga.' Some of Jeffreys's informants, too, confirm the warfare and head-getting themes in the *ikenga* cult. One of the commonest types of Ibo *ikenga* depicts a warrior holding a sword in one hand and a human head or skull in the other. That the head-getter theme was not absent from the Benin cult of the Hand is suggested not only by Ezomo's *ikegobo* but also by many of the wooden ones in which heads are shown impaled on spears. When a Benin warrior cut off his enemy's head his first act was to smear his arm and hand with the blood; and one of the songs at *Isiokuo* was:

> I have cut down a man for my Hand.
> A brave man that does not kill,
> That is a disgrace.

All this is consistent with the general interpretation of the Hand cult which I have given above. In a warrior society fighting skill and bravery, and particularly head-getting, are supreme tests of individual enterprise and prowess, a point of view clearly expressed in Ezomo's *ikegobo* and in the damaged one illustrated by von Luschan (1919, Plate XCII). But in pre-1897 Benin society large-scale farming (with slave labour), trade, 'medicine', craft specialization and especially political power and influence were, for most people, easier roads to prestige than skill in battle, though this last retained its glamour. Wealth, rank and political power, rather than personal daring, were the measures of social success and this fact must for long have modified any more exclusive connexion with martial virtues that the cult of the Hand might have once had.

Typology and Iconography

We are now in a position to review briefly the types of Benin *ikegobo*. In the neighbourhood of Benin City we can distinguish four main types:

A. Small, round, stool-like blocks of wood (up to about 6 inches high without the projecting peg) carved with representational and geometric designs, but not, normally, with human figures, on the vertical and, sometimes, upper surfaces.

B. Larger, wooden objects of the same general shape usually between 8 and 12 inches high (excluding peg), carved on the vertical and upper surfaces with figures, objects and other motifs.[13] *Ikegobo* of this type are usually provided with a carved stand, as shown in Plate IV(*a*).

C. Bronze *ikegobo* similar in design to type B but without a separate stand though the *ikegobo* itself may be cast in two or more pieces as is the case with Ezomo's.

D. Terra-cotta objects of similar design. I am grateful to Mr. William Fagg for calling my attention to the only known example, which is in the British Museum. Benin terra-cottas were produced almost exclusively in the bronze-casters' (*Iguneromwo*) ward and, from the tools depicted on it, it is certain that this example must have belonged to one of the titled smiths. Plate IV(*b*)

Ikegobo of type B and many of those of type A have, projecting from the upper surface, a 'peg' whose purpose is to support an ivory tusk. The bronze *ikegobo* of the Queen-Mother and of the Oba (Read and Dalton, 1899, Plate IX, Nos. 1 and 2) have, in place of a peg, a hole running down through the cylinder into which a stick could be inserted, the tusk being supported on the stick. It seems probable that such was the case, originally, with Ezomo's *ikegobo* and that its iron peg was burnt in at a later stage.[14]

13 Apart from the illustrations to this article see also Pitt-Rivers (1900). Plate CXXIII, for examples of *ikegobo* of type B.

14 A word must be said about the possible relationship between the tusk-supporting peg, and the pair of horns of the typical Ibo *ikenga*. Jeffreys's characterization of the Ibo *ikenga* as a 'ram-headed god' does not hold good for Benin, where I have been able to find no evidence of a specific association between *ikega* and the ram (or the sun). It is true that titled chiefs sacrifice rams to their Hands but this is a function of their rank rather than of the cult itself. Moreover, many people hold that the sacrificial victim *par excellence* is the crocodile, and fish is the commonest form of offering. The association here is with Olokun, the god of the sea and of riches.

It is true, nevertheless, that between Benin City and the Niger, among both the Ishan and the western Ibo *ikegobo* or *ikenga* can be found representing every intermediate stage between Benin types A and B on the one hand and the typical Ibo horned figure on the other. In some Ishan examples a pair of horns projects dirctly from the top of what is otherwise virtually a Benin type A *ikegobo*. Moreover, if we consider other Benin tusk-holding shrine furniture, such as bronze and wooden heads, we find that the 'hole-and-stick' method of supporting tusks is far more typical than the peg method. There are, therefore, some grounds for supposing that the peg on *ikegobo* may be derived from an original pair of horns.

As far as is known only the Oba, Iyoba (Oba's mother) and Ezomo ever had bronze *ikegobo*; the original ownership of the one illustrated by von Luschan (1919, Plate XCII) is unknown but it clearly belonged to a warrior. The distribution of the two wooden types is a function of rank and the circumstances in which they were acquired. Those of type B are usually to be found in the second public room of large, traditional, chiefs' houses on altars built of mud, polished and painted white, often beautifully moulded and with sculptured mud figures described as 'servants' or 'slaves' of the Hand. This type is acquired only by titled men and it is generally passed on from the original owner to his lineal heirs. In the house of the Onogie of Obazagbon, a hereditary village chief of the royal clan, there are remnants of about five *ikegobo* of type B. Ezomó Omoruyi recalls that, though Ehenua's was the only bronze one, there were, before 1897, a row of *ikega* belonging to past Ezomo. *Ikegobo* of type A are found in the houses of craftsmen and others who have been advised by diviners to serve their Hands, or who have wished to mark their own achievements. These small *ikegobo* do not, normally, have altars of their own, but are placed on or near, ancestral altars or, in the case of women, on altars to Olokun or some other deity. In the shrines of some deities are to be seen *ikegobo* representing the Hand of the deity itself.

Type A *ikegobo* are specific to their original owners and should be buried with them. 'You cannot leave your Hand behind,' it is said. Some say that, in the past, owners of large *ikega* would have smaller ones made to be buried with them; otherwise the circlet of cowries which is tied round the cylinder or slipped over the peg, is buried with the corpse. A son who inherits a type B *ikegobo* in no sense continues to worship his father's Hand. He should have a smaller one made for

On the other hand, as Mr. J. S. Boston pointed out to me, the stool-like character of Benin *ikega* is (though with considerable variation in the actual form) a more constant feature than the horns. The Ibo horned figure is often seated on a recognizable stool or stands on something clearly related to the form of the Benin *ikega*. Mr. Robin Horton writes to me, of Western *Ijo ikenga*: 'There are two cults in the Delta which seem related to your Benin *ikega*. One is called *ikenga* the other *amabra* . . *Ama bra* (right arm) is a personal cult connected with good fortune. So far as I can remember, cultivation of physical prowess is stressed. The cult object resembles a stylized form of the Ibo two-horned *ikenga*. *Ikenga* . . .is a personal cult of much the same significance. The object resembles a shallow stool, usually with stylized human eyes and nose carved in low relief on the top. Sometimes both types are loosely referred to as *ikenga*, and sometimes the labels are reversed; but the above is the most usual combination.'

Further study is clearly essential but it seems possible that we may be dealing with two, originally separate, cults which have impinged on each other; or with a single cult which, at an early stage, split up into Ibo and Benin varieties which, however, continued to exist side-by-side and influence each other.

himself, and this is kept on or near the inherited one.

The representational content of all types of *ikegobo* may be summarized as follows: the list is not exhaustive but it will serve to convey the range of symbolism involved:

(1) The hand itself is the most common motif. It is invariably carved including the wrist, in an upright position, showing the ventral side, but with the fist clenched and the thumb pointing upwards and outwards. The treatment ranges from near realism, in what are probably earlier examples of type B, to a more formalized, blocked-out form. Ezomo's *ikegobo* is very unusual in having no hand shown in this way.

(2) Figures in ceremonial costume, representing the original owner with attendants (who may be warriors), one or two of whom generally support his hands, a mark of high rank. The Oba's bronze *ikegobo* (Read and Dalton, Plate IX, fig. 2) also shows the Oba's mother and her attendants and two of his wives. The figures kneeling beside the Oba are probably Olukoton and Olukohi (*otun* and *osi* are the Yoruba words for right and left hand), two chiefs who have special duties at the Oba's *Ihiexu*.

(3) Figures of warriors with swords, spears, shields and ritual and ceremonial apparatus. They are often shown with heads impaled on spears and this motif also occurs by itself. The bronze *ikegobo* in von Luschan (Plate XCII) is unusual in that it depicts warriors actually engaged in fighting, others holding severed heads, a figure killing a leopard, and birds picking at beheaded corpses.

(4) Craftsmen's tools such as smith's hammers, anvils and tongs; and carvers' mallets and adzes.

(5) Marks of rank and wealth including (apart from the costumes and regalia of the figures) padlocked chests and boxes, casks of palm oil, beads, strings of cowries − the former currency − and female genitalia. The last were explained by the chief *Igbesamwa* carver as indicating that a man would not serve his Hand until he had wives and children. The commonest emblem of rank represented is a feather of the vulturine fish eagle (*oghohon*) called *igan-oghohon no-k'uhumw'ivie* 'the eagle's feather that tops the beads,' a reference to the fact that chiefs wear such a feather projecting above their bead headbands.[15] This motif is often latitudinally distorted but is usually to be found following the curve made by the wrist and thumb of the hand. The

15 The *oghohon* symbolizes longevity − from the fact that its feathers are all white. The wooden heads (*uhumwelao*) that decorate ancestral altars are furnished with *igan-oghohon*. See, e.g., Ling Roth, p.68, fig. 74.

leopard occurs as a symbol of kingship on Ezomo's *ikegobo*, on that of the Oba and on those belonging to village chiefs of the royal clan.

(6) Symbols of physical power, principally crocodiles which appear in pairs on the upper surface of stands of *ikegobo* of type B, encircling the main cylinder; and stylized elephant heads. In the latter the trunk ends in a hand holding a leaf or branch. The Edo think of the end of the elephant's trunk as having the form and function of a hand, and the leaf is said to refer to the elephant's habit of tearing off the leaves of young palm trees to get at the tender new leaves at the centre.

(7) Sacrificial offerings, including kola nuts, alligator pepper pods, pieces of coconut, fish, calabashes and bottles of palm wine, crocodiles and the heads of fowls, goats, rams and cows. A bowl of kola nuts is sometimes shown held by a servant or slave, usually female. Fish, kola nuts and alligator pepper are regarded as the most appropriate offerings on 'ordinary' occasions. The fish may be shown whole and coiled (*ikiehen*) or as a slab of fish with the head cut off. Human sacrifices are not shown (unless in von Luschan, fig. 469), though the Oba and Ezomo could, in the past, make human sacrifices to their Hands.[16]

Ikegobo, then, symbolize the whole range of notions underlying the cult of the Hand, and they do so with a directness that is unusual in African religious art. They illustrate rather well that quality of matter-of-factness that is characteristic of much Benin court art which, within the limits of its conventions, is more concerned with accuracy of representation, formal symmetry, and the satisfaction of the client's self-regard, than with the free play of the artist's imagination. While it has a more specific focus in the context of manual skill and physical prowess, Hand-worship can, in one sense, be regarded as the ritual expression of self esteem, and this point of view is stated uninhibitedly in the iconography of the cult object. Ezomo's *ikegobo*, though unusual in some features of its design, fits this general picture well. Apart from its associations its attractiveness lies in the unusual liveliness of the figures and a more fluid and imaginative design than one generally finds in Benin court art.

---

16 It is amusing to recall that Pitt-Rivers identified type B *ikegobo* as 'execution blocks.'

Ehi: Three Stories from Benin[1]

The three stories given below illustrate an idea about human life which can be roughly translated by the word 'Destiny'. Benin ideas about man's place in the cosmos and in human society are expressed symbolically in myths, legends and other forms of verbal art, and in a very complex system of religious beliefs and practices. Three cults stand out from the rest of Benin religion in that they are directly and explicitly concerned with the individual, as a unique person, making his or her way through life and being judged according to the values of the society.[2] The objects of worship in these cults are the Head, Hand and Ɛhi or spiritual counterpart) of the worshipper himself.

The Head is identified with personal 'luck' or 'fortune' and, according to whether he or she is successful or unsuccessful in life, a man or woman may be said to have a 'good' or 'bad' Head. The Benin people bless their Heads, and pray to them, annually and contingently. Sacrifices or offerings are made to the Head; it is thanked for the survival, well-being and successful achievements of the worshipper and his dependants, and implored to continue its favours. It would be mistaken, and indeed meaningless, however, to regard the Head as a symbol of 'luck' in the sense of mere chance. Fortuity plays little part in the Benin view of human fortunes. Behind almost every happening, good or bad, lies ultimately the actions of human beings — though the immediate cause is often some supernatural agency. The real significance of the Head is that it is regarded as the controller of all conscious individual behaviour. "It is his Head that leads a man through life." It is the seat of such faculties as will (*ekhɔe*), thinking (*iroro*) and judgement (*ɛnwa*). of seeing, hearing and speaking, and on the

1 Collected in 1953 with the help of Mr. Samuel Atalobor to whom my thanks are due.
2 In my interpretation of these cults I am heavily indebted to Professor Meyer Fortes' masterly account of Tallensi destiny concepts in *Oedipus and Job in West African Religion*.

purposeful co-ordination of these depends a man's success in whatever he undertakes. It is perhaps not too fanciful to make a comparison between the Benin conception of the Head and the Ego of the psycho-analysts. The Head represents the purposive, sentient aspect of the human personality.

When a man blesses his Head he also blesses the other parts of his body, including his Hand. The Hand, however, is itself the object of a separate cult and its symbolic reference is to manual skill, physical strength and general vigour and enterprise. For those who depend especially on manual skill, such as craftsmen, or on physical strength, such as warriors, the cult of the Hand has a particular significance. For the rest it is generally worshipped only by people who believe themselves to have got somewhere in life through their own efforts. The ritual of thanking the Hand is in one sense an expression of self esteem. Since, as we have said above, the notion Head subsumes all purposive human behaviour, why is a separate cult of the Hand necessary? This apparent duplication can fairly easily be explained in sociological terms. The Head has special reference to family headship and to the kingship. The head of a family worships his Head not merely for himself but for all his dependants; and he worships their Heads too, for their relationship is one of mutual interdependence. Similarly the blessing of the Oba's Head is of profound importance for the whole people and his priests also bless the Heads of the chiefs through whom he rules. While the Head is thus of special significance in relation to a man's status within a domestic or political group, his Hand symbolises his vigour and enterprise in competition with his fellows in the community at large.

There is no need to continue this analysis here. It is only necessary to point out that both the Head and the Hand are concerned with what a man can achieve in life through his own efforts. In praising or blaming one's Head or Hand one is, in effect, claiming or admitting a large degree of personal responsibility for success or failure. It is realised, however, that success or failure cannot be wholly explained in these terms. Differences in status, rank, wealth, health, fertility and achievement are not entirely explicable in terms of human endeavour. Some people are obviously born to be rich and others to be poor; some to be farmers and others craftsmen; some to have uncountable progeny and others to be childless. It is this notion of predestiny that is symbolically expressed in the beliefs, practices and stories connected with the *Ɛhi*.

It is believed that before a person is born he goes and kneels before his Creator, *Osanobua*, and tells him what he wishes to be in the world — whether a farmer or a trader, a warrior or a carver; whether 'a thief or a chief' as the Oba of Benin once put it to me. And he asks for all these things, material and spiritual, which will enable him to carry through his chosen role successfully. This whole process is summed up in the verb *hi* which we may translate 'to predestine oneself'. When the person about to be born has made his or her statement, *Osanobua* bangs his staff on the ground and so sets his seal on these prenatal wishes. So when a man remains, despite all his efforts, wretchedly poor, or if a woman is barren or her children die, one after the other, it is said that he or she did not '*hi* well,' or that they are not acting in accordance with their predestiny. To put this in a more sophisticated way, abject failure is explained in terms of the innate potentialities of the individual and the use made of them.

Ɛhi is the spiritual counterpart and guide of the living person (*ɔmwa*). When the latter is incarnated in the world his *ɛhi* stays behind in the land of the spirits. The living person and his or her *ɛhi* are thought of as two halves of a single personality. Many people believe that these two halves alternate in successive incarnations, *ɛhi* becoming *ɔmwa* and *ɔmwa* becoming *ɛhi*. When a person goes before *Osanobua* to *hi* it is *ɛhi*'s task to stand by and advise him and remind him to ask for everything he will need "Since *ɛhi* was last on earth" said one of my informants, "he knows best what to ask for." Once the person has been born *ɛhi*'s task is to guide him along his chosen path and to ensure his well-being. Of the person who is an irremediable social failure it can be said "His *ɛhi* is bad". Close as a man and his *ɛhi* are they are yet thought of as being independent agents and so there is a possibility of conflict between them. *ɛhi* must, therefore, be propitiated in much the same way as other supernatural entities and failure to do this results in trouble. It is, indeed, not unknown for a man to propitiate his enemy's *ɛhi* in the hope of sowing dissension between them.

The *ɛhi*, then, is a personification of predestiny. "*Ɛhi* is the way a man has to go' said one old man. Put another way it is the symbolic recognition that people are born with different endowments, with different potentialities for social achievement. Without getting into deep psychological waters it seems very likely that the conception of the *ɛhi* is, in part, a mechanism for shifting guilt arising from failure on to some object outside this world. The shame that follows from childlessness or abject poverty is made more bearable if one can blame one's condition on something outside oneself and outside human society. The fact that *hi* is in one sense, an independent entity allows this to be done and also leaves open the door to hope, for *ɛhi* can be approached to set things right. At the same time, the notion that *ɛhi* is really another aspect of oneself recognises that the failure is ultimately in one's own make-up. This 'semi-detached' character of the *ɛhi* is thus a very subtle piece of symbolism. In theory of course, the successful man is as much or more beholden to his *ɛhi* as the failure, and people do, indeed, thank their *ɛhi* with offerings from time to time; but in practice there is a strong tendency to blame one's *ɛhi* for failure and to attribute success to one's Head or Hand, that is to one's good sense and enterprise – a very natural human reaction!

This background and explanation are necessary for the understanding of the stories that follow. Notions such as the Head, the Hand and the *hi* are not merely whimsical attempts to explain the vicissitudes of life. They are subtle symbolic patterns of reference through which the interplay of innate potentialities, accidents of birth, individual character, skill and enterprise, cooperation and competition, can be recognised as governing the progress of the individual through life. By performing this function they help the individual to adjust himself emotionally and intellectually to the vicissitudes of life in human society and they probably assist him to direct his actions more purposefully. At the one extreme they help him to shed some of his guilt for failure and at the other they provide a vehicle for the expression of self-satisfaction. Underlying all these is the notion of personal responsibility, for, as we have seen, even one's predestiny is determined by oneself. In this respect *ɛhi* is far removed from the Fate of the Greeks.

The Benin people, like any other, vary tremendously in the degree to which they understand the implications of their own symbolism. The deeper thinkers understand very readily the explanations I have given which are, indeed, largely derived from them. Others give little thought to such matters. One of the functions of the stories that follow is to express the ideas implicit in the notion of *ɛhi* in a form readily understandable to all. Not to realise this would be to miss much of their value.

USƐ [3]

In those days, long ago, there was a man caled Usɛ[1] who lived in wretched poverty, having neither food to give his mouth nor clothes for

3 Usɛ means 'poverty'.

his body. Year after year he planted two farms and a field of maize but at the end of the year he found not one ear of corn, nor a single yam to harvest. He suffered for a long time until at last he said, 'I am going to die. Even death would be better than to go on toiling, year after year, in vain, for there is no misery greater than hunger'. But, after all, Usɛ began once more to clear a farm, thinking that all years are not alike and that perhaps this time he would see the profit from all his past work.

When he had planted his crops he watched them day by day to see if they would be once more blighted or eaten by the animals. Whenever he visited his farm he would pray: 'My father Osa, if it is because of my evil deeds that I never have crops to harvest, forgive me. Life cannot always be wretched, without hope of success'. For the first time his crops grew abundantly and the corn stood firm. He was very happy. When the harvest time came he took a basket and went to the farm to bring home his corn, but to his horror he found not a single stem standing. The bush-pigs had eaten them all, every one. He began to cry, saying 'I have the strength to work but I see no benefit from my labour'.[4] He decided to follow the trace of the bush-pigs and eventually they led him to a river. He jumped in and arrived at the palace of Osanobua.[5]

When Usɛ had told his story Osanobua locked him in a dark room[6] and told him to put his ear to the ground. He ordered him not to speak a single word in answer to anyone. Just then Usɛ's ɛhi came to see Osanobua who said to him, "Us was here just now. He came to tell me how wretched he is through his sufferings in the world." Ɛhi replied, "Yes, he is suffering. Let him suffer! He did not say he would be a farmer when he went to the world. He said he would grow prosperous through setting traps, but when he got there he abandoned his intention and took up something else."[7] And Usɛ's ɛhi went home.

Osanobua then unlocked Use's door and asked him whether he had heard what his ɛhi had said about his actions in the world. Us said he had heard. So Osanobua told him to go back to the world and do exactly as his ɛhi had said.

4 This, as so often, is the point at which the Ɛhi becomes important, when all other efforts have failed.

5 Osanobua is the supreme deity. In Benin cosmology the way to the spirit world is always through the waters.

6 Osanobua does not allow Usɛ to see his Ɛhi because it is believed that if a man sees his Ɛhi he must die.

7 Note the attitude of Ɛhi to Usɛ. He is disgusted with Usɛ because the latter has strayed from his predestined career.

When he got back to the world he took some wire and a matchet and went to the bush and began to set a row of traps. As he was inserting the first stick into the ground it struck something as hard as a stone. The tears welled up in his eyes. ' My *ɛhi,*", he said, "you told me that I must set traps if I want to be prosperous but the first stick I pick up will not even penetrate the *ground.*' He picked up an iron rod and began to dig with it and very soon he struck a pot of beads. Eagerly he picked it up and joyfully he took it home. The beads were of the most precious kind. Two of them alone would buy a man. Usɛ sold them all and became by far the richest of men.

From that day to this people have always said 'If you do not do what your *ɛhi* has told you, you cannot prosper".

This somewhat naive little tale illustrates in a straightforward manner the idea that if a man tries to do something he is not cut out for he will not succeed. Like most stories about the *ɛhi* it deals with the theme of otherwise inexplicable failure despite every human effort.

AI S'AGBƆN HI[8]

In a town in Iyekorhiɔmwɔ in those days, there were two sons of one mother. The older one lived in abject poverty. His cloth would not meet round his waist and his house was only three courses high[9]. He had neither servants nor slaves. When he went to his farm he himself had to carry both water and fire. His younger brother was so rich that he did not know all his slaves, for they were so many. He had more than forty wives and, when he wanted to eat, the one that brought his soup never needed to carry his yam as well. It was impossible to traverse the whole of his farm. He went there only once a year, when his slaves had finished tying the yams to the racks. Whatever he said all the people in the town accepted it. Any decision he made they abided by it. But when the older brother spoke no-one took any notice for he was a poor man.

There came a day when the senior brother went to the house of the master-diviner, Ogiɔbo, to ask him to make a medicine that he could use to kill his younger brother whose riches overshadowed him in everything. The diviner told him what ingredients he must look for so that he would be able to make the medicine. When he had found all the ingredients he brought them to Ogiɔbo. Ogiɔbo told him 'Before you

---

[8] The title means 'You cannot reach the world and then *hi*' — that is 'Your destiny is settled before you are born and you cannot change it'.

[9] Instead of the normal four courses for commoners.

make use of this medicine you must first rub this calabash, in which it is kept, on the body of a pregnant woman. If you do this it will show you an example of how quickly the medicine works'.[10] The man was very happy for he was eager to send his brother to the spirit world before his time.

The next day Ogiɔbo gave him the calabash of medicine and told him that towards evening he would hear of a woman in protracted labour. Everyone would be trying to help her but their efforts would be in vain. 'When you get there rub your own eyes and the woman's belly with the medicine. Then, indeed, you will see a wonderful thing. When you have finished there people will call you to another woman, and what happened the first time will happen again, but in a different way'.

Ogiɔbo gave him the medicine and he left for home. On his way he met some people who told him of a woman in difficult labour. All the doctors had done whatever they could but without success. He smiled. He did not even go home but made straight for the place where the woman was. The people gathered there were surprised to see him bring out a calabash of medicine for he had never been known to be a doctor before. He did exactly as he had been told by Ogiɔbo and at once he saw the child in the woman's womb. His mouth fell open in astonishment when he saw what the child held in his hands – a matchet, a calabash of water, wire for making traps, an axe and a fly-switch.[11] He uttered a sigh of amazement. 'What is it? What is it?' the people asked excitedly. 'Perhaps he has seen that the woman will not be able to deliver the child.' But at that moment the child appeared.

Some of the people immediately fell on their knees and begged him to come and deliver a child at their own house. He went with them and did exactly as he had done with the first woman. Then he saw the difference between the two babies, for this second one was wearing many beautiful clothes. He had people supporting his arms[12], attendants in front of him, and others at his back. He was in the middle of them and behind him stretched a long procession.

The man now began to think to himself. 'So it is not here that such things are decided' he said. 'It is in the land of the spirits that people are made rich'. He went back to Ogiɔbo, returned the calabash of medicine to him and told him what he had seen. Then he knelt down to

---

[10] Ogiɔ bo is deceiving him because he does not want to be a party to murder.

[11] Indicating that this child was predestined to be a farmer.

[12] As the arms of the Oba and other chiefs are supported on ceremonial occasions.

ask Ogiɔbo not to be angry with him. He said he would never again seek to use bad medicine against his brother for he now understood that it was in the land of spirits that people were made rich, and in the land of the spirits he himself had been made poor. Ogiɔbo advised him how he could win his brother's friendship.

At first light the next day, the older brother slung a hoe and a matchet across his shoulders and set off for his younger brother's farm. Before the sun rose he had hoed two rows. When his brother's servants came to the farm and saw him working there they were afraid because he had never been seen there before. They ran to tell their master what they had seen and immediately a great crowd of people set off for the farm with their master in the middle of them. When he got there he was struck with a great fear to see his senior brother working for him.

'What is this my brother?' he asked. 'Do you want to kill me?' 'I have no intention of killing you' the older brother replied. He started from the beginning and told his brother how he had gone to see Ogiɔbo and of the different things he had been shown. It was these, he said, that made him think deeply and decide that the only way of becoming his brother's friend was to plant his yams for him. His brother took his hoe from him and put it down. He took him home. He brought out a he-goat and many cases of gin and called many dancers and drummers. When darkness came the two of them blessed their heads with the goat. They danced different dances until dawn. The younger brother filled the whole place with food from the floor to the roof. He gave twelve wives, six slaves and many clothes and servants to his older brother. Then they took many things and presented them to Ogiɔbo who had made that calabash of medicine. From that day the two brothers were always happy together. Nobody was allowed to make the older man suffer and whenever people met together to discuss something, it was to the senior brother that they could first stretch out their hands.

The moral of this second story is clearly that one should accept one's destiny and make the best of it. Here destiny is treated as though it were immutable and this idea is given amusing expression in the description of the babies in the womb, already accoutred for their chosen careers. The title *Ai s'agbɔn hi* means literally, 'One cannot reach the world and then *hi*'.

The force of this story lies in the relationship between the two brothers, which runs quite counter to the ideal situation. Ideally, it is the senior brother who should be the wealthy one, the master, the taker of decisions; and his younger brothers should be subordinate to him.

But it is recognised that the norm is not always realised in these matters. Seniority and the ability to succeed do not necessarily go together and this story explains why. Incidentally, at the end the story prescribes the correct relationship between the rich younger brother and the poorer older one to whom he yet gives the care and respect which is his due.

ɛHI-WILL-EŃRICH-ME, [13]

There is a story that begins with Erhamwoisa and his wife. She bore him three children and he said that they themselves should choose their names. The first said 'You can call me Ogiso-will-enrich-me".[14] The second said he would like to be called "Other-people-will-enrich-me".[15] And the third said he would call himself ' ɛhi-will-enrich-me'.

Day after day Ogiso-will-enrich-me would collect things together and present them to Ogiso, the Oba. Other-people-will-enrich-me was continually doing favours for other people. 'When the time comes that I have nothing left' he said 'other people will provide for me'. But ɛhi-will-enrich-me simply prayed to his ɛhi every day.

One day ɛhi-will-enrich-me got ready and went to the bush where he found the messengers of the spirits wrestling together. They called to him and asked him his name and he told them he was called ɛhi-will-enrich-me. They asked him his father's name. He said it was Erhamwoisa. Then they wanted to know how many brothers he had. 'There are three of us' he said. 'What are the names of the others?' they asked. 'One is called Ogiso-will-enrich-me and the other, Other-people-will-enrich-me', he replied.

So they asked him to come and wrestle with them. They wrestled and wrestled and wrestled until they were all very tired. Then ɛhi-will-enrich-me said he was hungry. Ugbogiorimwi, their leader, gave him a yam. 'You will know what to do with that' he said.

When ɛhi-will-enrich-me arrived home he found that his mother and father were dead and his brothers Ogiso-will-enrich-me and Other-people-will-enrich-me were dancing to celebrate their funeral. He

---

[13] Ɛhi-gha-fe-mwɛ

[14] Ogiso-gha-fe-mwɛ . Ogiso is the title of the legendary first dynasty in Benin.

[15] Ɛrɛe gha-fe-mwɛ. Ɛrɛe means 'other people' but it is generally used to imply one's fellows who are ill-disposed to one. When the supernatural cause of an illness or other misfortune cannot be precisely identified sacrifices are made to the Ɛrɛe.

had no-one to dance with him so he walked slowly to the place where his father's house had been. There he cleared the bush and built a shelter. Then he collected some wood but found he had no means of making a fire. 'If only I could get fire from someone' he said. 'I would take my matchet and cut up this yam'. Then he heard a voice from inside the yam 'Gently!' it said, "The-slave-of-the-Oba-is-not-negligible is in here". So Ɛhi-will-enrich-me cut it open carefully. As soon as he had done so he saw many houses standing to his right and still more on the other side. On the very spot where he had gathered wood stood a house. People, goats, hens, sheep and everything in the world were inside the house.[16] Ɛhi-will-enrich-me felt a great joy in the bottom of his belly.

One day he got ready and went to find out why he could not beget any children. He went to the house of Ɔbiro, the master-diviner, and told him all this troubles. Ɔbiro died on the spot and decomposed. 'Am I really seeing this?' Ɛhi-will-enrich-me asked himself. He got up and set off for home but when he reached the end of the village street he met a man wearing a mortar for a cap and using a pestle as a walking stick. It was Ɔbiro. He asked Ɛhi-will-enrich-me to go back to the house with him, so he retraced his steps. When they got there Ɔbiro told him that he had been to the spirit-world to enquire from Ɛhi-will-enrich-me's Ɛhi about this matter of children. Ɔbiro said that soon he would see, at the foot of a plantain stem, a girl who would bear a child for him. Ɛhi-will-enrich-me thanked him and went on his way.

When he got home he sat down and thought about it but soon he got up again and walked to the end of the street. When he reached the base of the plantain stem a fruit fell from it and dropped between his legs. He picked it up and found that is was very light. 'There is nothing inside it' he said, but he kept it. He went on a little farther and found a basket. Someone had laid a cloth in the bottom of the basket and on this rested half a plantain, a yam and some hair.[17] He went on a little farther. Then he heard the spirits calling him, telling him to keep these things and take them home.

When he got home he picked up the plantain. He decided to peel it and roast it, but as soon as he began to do so it opened and a young woman stepped out. Then he thought he would cut up the yam and

16 All these are the gift of his Ɛhi, (that is of his destiny) who has sent them to him in the yam. For some, it is implied, the yam is the basic necessity for existence. For others it can be the source of great wealth.

17 The purpose of the hair does not appear in this version of this story. I think my informant may have left it out by mistake.

plantain in the basket. Immediately riches tumbled from them and covered everything. Finally he took the cloth from the basket and money poured out of it and filled the whole house. His house was now like the Oba's palace.

Ogiso-will-enrich-me looked at Ɛhi-will-enrich-me. He said he would take something to Ogiso and Ogiso would make him rich, too. But when he got there Ogiso told him never to enter his palace again and that if he did so his sword-bearers would put a gag between his teeth.[18] To Other-people-will-enrich-me came other people demanding more gifts and when he had nothing to give them they killed him.

Ogiso now began to ask who was this other man that he was always hearing about. They told him it was Ɛhi-will-enrich-me. Ogiso said they should inform him that in seven days time the two of them would count their riches in each other's presence. 'If your wealth surpasses my own' he said 'let my father's people and my mother's people be killed.[19] If my own riches are the greater then may the same happen to your relatives'.

When the day for counting their riches arrived, Ɛhi-will-enrich-me's people gathered and went to Ogiso's palace. Ogiso came out with his people and began to count his riches. When he had finished Ɛhi-will-enrich-me began to count his own. He counted and counted until darkness came. On the fourth day he flung a handful of earth into the air and said he would never be able to count all his wealth. And the whole world was astonished.

Ogiso told Ɛhi-will-enrich-me to go home. 'It is no curse to be surpassed by another' he said. But the earth and the sky did not agree. The earth rose up and the sky came down to meet it and everyone was afraid. The people implored the earth and the sky saying that a whole nation should not be killed for the sake of one man. Ogiso did as he had promised. Ɛhi-will-enrich-me became the Oba, and Ogiso became his sword-bearer.

This story is rather more subtle than the other two, though its message is much the same. It contrasts the success of the man who cultivates his own potentialities with the downfall of the one who relies upon currying favour with his fellows or with those in authority over him. Note how on three occasions Ɛhi-will-enrich-me's Ɛhi intervenes through his messengers or through Ɔbiro. Ɛhi is here depicted as the

---

[18] That is, in readiness for execution.

[19] Ogiso is frequently portrayed as cursing himself and his family recklessly. It was this, it is sometimes said, that brought the downfall of the dynasty.

guardian spirit directing his ward along his chosen path and so rescuing him from poverty and childlessness. As in the first story wealth is not achieved in any ordinary fashion but follows directly and mysteriously from the workings of pre-destiny, from the realisation of the innate potentialities of the individual. The symbolism is simple. Wealth springs from such basic everyday things as the yam, the plantain and cloth. Note however, the delicate treatment of that common African symbol of sexual virility, the plantain.

General Bibliography of Works
referred to in the Text

Adams, Capt. J. 1823. *Remarks on the Country Extending from Cape Palmas to the River Congo*. London.

Anon. 1823. An article in the *Royal Gold Coast Gazette* No. 21, Vol. I, Mar. 25th, 1823.

Armstrong, Robert G. 1964. 'The use of linguistic and ethnographic data in the study of Idoma and Yoruba history', *in* J. Vansina, R. Mauny and L. Thomas (eds.) *The Historian in Tropical Africa*. London: Oxford University Press for the International African Institute.

Baikie, W.B. 1856. *Narrative of an Exploring Voyage up the Rivers Kwora and Binue*. London.

Bendix, R. 1960. *Max Weber: An Intellectual Portrait*. London: Methuen.

Blake, J.W. (ed.) 1942. *Europeans in West Africa, 1450-1560*. Vol. I. London: Hakluyt Society.

Bosman, W. 1705. *A New and Accurate Description of the Coast of Guinea*. London edition, 1705. New edition, London: Cass, 1967. (For Nyendael's account.)

Bottomore, T.B. 1964. *Elites and Society*. London: Watts.

Bradbury, R.E. 1957. *The Benin Kingdom and the Edo-speaking Peoples of South-Western Nigeria*, with a section on the Itsekiri by P.C. Lloyd. Ethnographic Survey of Africa, Western Africa, Part XIII. London: International African Institute.

-- 1959. 'Chronological problems in the study of Benin history', *Journal of the Historical Society of Nigeria*, Vol.I, 4, pp. 263-87.

-- 1964. 'The historical uses of comparative ethnography with special reference to Benin and the Yoruba', *in* J. Vansina, R. Mauny and L.Thomas (eds.) *The Historian in Tropical Africa*. London: Oxford

University Press for the International African Institute.

-- 1965. 'Father and senior son in Edo mortuary ritual', *in* M. Fortes and G. Dieterlen (eds.) *African Systems of Thought*. London: Oxford University Press for the International African Institute.

-- 1966. 'Fathers, elders, and ghosts in Edo religion', *in* M. Banton (ed.) *Anthropological Approaches to the Study of Religion*. Association of Social Anthropologists Monographs, 3. London: Tavistock.

-- 1967. 'The kingdom of Benin', in D. Forde and P. Kaberry (eds.) *West African Kingdoms in the Nineteenth Century*. London: Oxford University Press for the International African Institute.

-- 1968. 'Continuities and discontinuities in pre-colonial and colonial Benin politics (1897-1951)', *in* I.M. Lewis (ed.) *History and Social Anthropology*. Association of Social Anthropologists Monographs, 7. London: Tavistock.

Burns, A.C. 1929. *History of Nigeria*. London: Allen and Unwin.

Burton, Sir Richard. 1863. 'My wanderings in West Africa', *Fraser's Magazine*, Vol. LXVIII, Feb., Mar., April, 1863.

Colson, E. 1954. 'Ancestral spirits and social structure among the Plateau Tonga', *International Archives of Ethnography*, 47, pp. 21-68.

Dapper, Dr. O. 1668. *Nauwkeurige Beschrijvinge der Afrikaansche Gewesten*. Amsterdam: (p.495 et seq.)

de Barros, João 1552. *Da Asia*. Lisbon. Dec 1. Bk. 3, Ch.3.

de Pina, Ruy. 1545. *Chronica que trato da vida do João II*, 1545.

Egharevba, J.U. 1947. *Concise Lives of the Famous Iyases of Benin*. Lagos: Temi-Asunwon Press.

-- 1952. *The City of Benin*. Benin: Aguebor Printers.

-- 1953. *A Short History of Benin*. (Second edition) Lagos.

-- 1960. *A Short History of Benin*. (Third edition) Ibadan University. Press.

Eguavon, S.I. n.d. *Itan Edo* (Edo Proverbs). Benin City.

Fagg, W.B. 1958. 'The Guinea Coast', *in* E. Elisofon and W.B. Fagg (eds.) *The Sculpture of Africa*. London: Thames and Hudson.

Fawckner, Capt. J. 1837. *Travels on the Coast of Benin*.

Forde, C.D. 1962. 'Death and succession: an analysis of Yakö mortuary ritual', *in* M. Gluckman (ed.) *Essays on the Ritual of Social Relations*. Manchester: Manchester University Press.

Fortes, M. 1959. *Oedipus and Job in West African Religion*. London: Cambridge University Press.

-- 1961. 'Pietas in ancestor worship', *Journal of the Royal Anthropological Institute*, XCI, 2, July-Dec., pp.166-91.

-- 1962. 'Ritual and office in tribal society', *in* M. Gluckman (ed.) *Essays on the Ritual of Social Relations*. Manchester: Manchester University Press.

Galvano, A. 1563. *Tratado*. Lisbon.

Goody, J. 1962. *Death, Property, and the Ancestors*. Standford, Calif: Standford University Press. London: Tavistock.

Gough, E.K. 1958. 'Cults of the dead among the Nayars', *Journal of American Folklore*, 71,pp. 446-78.

Jeffreys, M.D.W. 1954. 'Ikenga, the Ibo ram-headed god', *African Studies*, XIII, Part 1, pp. 25-40.

Johnson, Samuel. 1921. *The History of the Yorubas*. London: Routledge.

King, Lieut. J. 1823. In *Journal des Voyages*, Vol. XIII, Paris.

Landolphe, Capt. J.F. 1823. (Ed. J.S.Quesné) *Mémoires du Captaine Landolphe*. Paris.

Lawal-Osula, U.M. (ed.) 1949. Benin Native Authority: New Constitution 1948.

Lévi-Strauss, C. 1962. *La Pensée sauvage*. Paris: Plon.

Ling Roth, H. 1903. *Great Benin: its Customs, Art and Horrors*. Halifax: F. King and Sons.

Lloyd, P.C. 1954. 'The traditional political system of the Yoruba', *Southwestern Journal of Anthropology*, Vol.10, 4, pp. 366-84.

-- 1962. *Yoruba Land Law*. London: Oxford University Press for the Nigerian Institute of Social and Economic Research.

Macrae-Simpson, J. 1936. Intelligence Report on Benin Division. (Unpubl.)

Marshall, H.F. 1939. Intelligence Report on Benin City. (Unpubl.)

Mauny, R. 1956. *Esmeraldo de Situ Orbis par Duarte Pacheco Pereira*. Bissau.

Meek, C.K. 1937. *Law and Authority in a Nigerian Tribe*. London: Oxford University Press.

Melzian, H. 1937. *Bini Dictionary*. London: Kegan Paul.

Middleton, J. 1960. *Lugbara Religion*. London: Oxford University Press for the International African Institute.

Moffat and Smith. 1841. In *Journal of the Royal Geographical Society*, XI.

Morton-Williams, P. 1960. 'The Yoruba Ogboni cult in Oyo', *Africa*, XXX, 4, pp. 362-74.

Nadel, S.F. 1942. *A Black Byzantium*. London: Oxford University Press for the International African Institute.

Pitt-Rivers, A.H.L.F. 1900. *Antique Works of Art from Benin.* Privately Printed.

Read, Sir C.H. and Dalton, O.M. 1899. *Antiquities from the City of Benin . . . in the British Museum.*

Smith, M.G. 1960. *Government in Zazzau*. London: Oxford University Press for the International African Institute.

Southwold, M. 1961. *Bureaucracy and Chiefship in Buganda*. East African Studies, No.14. Kampala: East African Institute of Social Research.

Talbot, P.A. 1926. *The Peoples of Southern Nigeria*. London: Oxford University Press, 4 vols.

Uwaifo, H.O. 1959. *Benin Community Intelligence Report on Benin Division*. Oshogbo: F.M.S. Press.

von Luschan, F. 1919. *Die Altertümer von Benin*. 3 vols.

Weber, M. 1947. *The Theory of Social and Economic Organization*. London: Hodge.

Wilks, I. 1967. 'Ashanti government', in D. Forde and P. Kaberry (eds.) *West African Kingdoms in the Nineteenth Century*. London: Oxford University Press for the International African Institute.

Wilson, M. 1959. *Divine Kings and the 'Breath of Men'*. Cambridge University Press.

Bibliography of Works by R.E. Bradbury

1952. Some aspects of the political organisation of the Benin kingdom (summary), *in* West African Institute of Social and Economic Research. Annual Conference . . .1952.

1956. The social structure of Benin, with special reference to the politico-ritual organisation (the village community). Unpublished Ph.D. Thesis, University of London.

1957. *The Benin kingdom and the Edo-speaking peoples of South-Western Nigeria*, with a section on the Itsekiri by P.C. Lloyd. Ethnographic Survey of Africa, Western Africa, Part XIII. London: International African Institute.

1959. 'Chronological problems in the study of Benin history', *Journal of the Historical Society of Nigeria*, Vol. I, 4 pp. 263-87.

1959. 'Divine kingship in Benin', *Nigeria*, 62, pp.186-207.

1959. Review of Meyer Fortes, *Oedipus and Job in West African Religion, Man*, 59, 265, Sept., pp.166-7.

1960. 'Ehi: three Stories from Benin', *Odu*, 8, October, pp.40-48.

1961. 'Ezomo's *ikegobo* and the Benin cult of the hand', *Man,* 61, 165, August, pp.129-38.

1964. 'The historical uses of comparative ethnography with special reference to Benin and the Yoruba', *in* J. Vansina, R. Mauny and L. Thomas (eds.) *The historian in tropical Africa*. London: Oxford University Press for the International African Institute.

1965. 'Father and senior son in Edo mortuary ritual', *in* M. Fortes and G. Dieterlen (eds.) *African systems of thought*. London: Oxford University Press for the International African Institute.

1966. 'Fathers, elders and ghosts in Edo religion', *in* M. Banton (ed.) *Anthropological approaches to the study of religion.* Association of Social Anthropologists Monographs, 3. London: Tavistock.

1967. Notes (with J.D. Fage) to William Bosman, *A new and accurate description of the coast of Guinea*, with an Introduction by John Ralph Willis and notes by J.D. Fage and R.E. Bradbury. London: Cass (4th ed.), 1967. [1st. English ed. 1705.]

1967. 'The kingdom of Benin', *in* D. Forde and P. Kaberry (eds.) *West African kingdoms in the nineteenth century*. London: Oxford University Press for the International African Institute.

1968. 'Continuities and discontinuities in pre-colonial and colonial Benin politics (1897-1951)', *in* I.M. Lewis (ed.) *History and social anthropology*. Association of Social Anthropologists Monographs, 7. London: Tavistock.

1968. 'Comparative Edo word lists', *Research Notes* [University of Ibadan] , 4, June, pp.1-31.

1969. 'Patrimonialism and gerontocracy in Benin political culture', *in* M. Douglas and P.M. Kaberry (eds.) *Man in Africa*. London: Tavistock.

1969. (comp.) *Directory of African Studies in the United Kingdom Universities*. Birmingham: African Studies Association [UK] .

Index